WITHDRAWN

RUSSIA AND EUROPE
1825-1878

BY

A. LOBANOV-ROSTOVSKY

Professor of History
University of Michigan

PUBLISHED BY
THE GEORGE WAHR
PUBLISHING COMPANY
ANN ARBOR, MICH.
1954

Copyright
A. LOBANOV-ROSTOVSKY
1954

Composition and Lithoprinting by
BRAUN-BRUMFIELD, Inc.
Ann Arbor, Mich.

TABLE OF CONTENTS

		Page
Introduction		1

Chapter

I.	The Greek Revolution.	16
II.	Russo-Turkish War 1828-29.	28
III.	The Eastern Question after the War of 1828-29.	63
IV.	The Revolution of 1830 and the Alliance of the Three Northern Courts	86
V.	The Revolution of 1848.	116
VI.	Causes of the Crimean War	138
VII.	The Crimean War	163
VIII.	Congress of Paris.	193
IX.	Bismarck and Gorchakov	218
X.	The German Empire and the Rise of Panslavism	243
XI.	The War of 1877 and the Congress of Berlin.	272

INTRODUCTION

I

After the emergence of national states in Europe following the Renaissance, there were three great over-all settlements of European affairs at intervals of over a century. These were the Congress of Westphalia (1648), the Peace of Utrecht (1713) and the Congress of Vienna (1815). Each of these drew up a blueprint of the new map of Europe, each in turn lasting until the next settlement, and in the case of the Treaty of Vienna until the World War of 1914-1918 and the Congress of Versailles. They also give us an interesting yardstick for the measuring of the growth of the role of Russia in European affairs. In the Peace of Westphalia, following the Thirty Years War, Russia or Muscovy, had no part, being regarded as completely outside the pale of Europe even though she maintained active diplomatic and trading relations with most of the European countries. Neither did Russia participate in the settlement at Utrecht of the cycle of the wars of Louis XIV, but for a very different reason. Together with her allies Saxony, Poland, Denmark and Brandenburg-Prussia she was engaged in the Great Northern War against Sweden, which country had emerged, after the Treaty of Westphalia as one of the two leading military powers of Europe. By her victory over Sweden in this war Russia replaced her enemy as the main power in North Eastern Europe. A century later, at the Congress of Vienna, Russia had reached her climax as a great European power and practically dominated the European scene, not only during this Congress, which ended the cycle of French revolutionary and Napoleonic wars, but during the following decade as well.

A brief survey of Russia's rise to pre-eminence within the course of a century has to be given here. At the turn of the 18th century, owing to the weakness of the Muscovite state, Russia's position was still exceedingly unfavorable; she was hemmed in by a chain of powerful and inimical neighbouring states which had acquired control of much of her frontier territory. Sweden had cut her off from the coast of the Baltic and consequently from direct access to Western Europe; Poland was in control of the Western Ukraine and White Russia, lost by Russia to Poland-Lithuania in the XIV century, right up to the line of the Dnieper river; the Ottoman Empire, through her vassal, the Khanate of Crimea, controlled the coast of the Black Sea and the steppes of the Southern Ukraine and of the Don region. The reforms of Peter the Great, giving Russia a modern army, navy, industrial equipment and a modern school system, permitted her to break out of the semi-encirclement from the North, the West and the South and reach stable and permanent borders. Indeed Peter's victory over Sweden gave Russia the whole Baltic coast from the border of Finland to the mouth of the Dvina and the Gulf of Riga. Half a century later, Catherine the Great, by two victorious wars with Turkey and the Treaties of Kuchuk-Kainardji in 1774 and Jassy in 1792 evicted the Turks and acquired the whole Northern coast of the Black Sea and the Crimea. Poland, rapidly declining, became more and more of a puppet state of Russia and finally disappeared in the partitions of 1772, 1793 and 1795. This gave Russia the possession of the whole of the Western Ukraine, White Russia and Lithuania, and in the following year, of Kurland. A last wave of expansion took place during the Napoleonic wars, giving Russia Finland (1809), Bessarabia (1812) and Congress Poland (1815), after which Russia's European borders remain stabilized up to World War I. With the growth of Russia's power her influence was becoming increasingly felt in the affairs of Western and Central Europe and the milestones in this progressive assertion of Russian influence are clearly to be detected throughout the XVIII century.

These start with the occupation of Mecklenburg, Pomerania and Holstein by the Russian army in the later years of the Great Northern War after 1716, followed by an alliance with Austria in 1726, which lasts through the greater part of the century. This alliance was cemented by the consistent enmity of France toward both Austria, her traditional enemy, and Russia in whom she saw a menace to her whole diplomatic system based on close relations with Poland, Sweden and Turkey. As a result of the alliance of 1726, the Austrian and Russian armies fought side by side in the War of the Polish Succession (1733-35), in the war against Turkey (1736-39) and again in the Seven Years War against Prussia (1756-63). In the first of these wars, the Russians captured Warsaw and Danzig, and a Russian corps 20,000 strong appeared on the Rhine for the first time in history. In the Turkish war the Austrians were defeated, while fortune favoured Russian arms and Russia occupied Moldavia for the first time. It became apparent after the Treaty of Belgrade 1739, which ended this war so humiliatingly for the Holy Roman Empire, that Austria was ceding her place to Russia as the main enemy and the main menace to the crumbling Ottoman Empire.

INTRODUCTION

Following an easy defeat of Sweden in 1741-43, which gave Russia a portion of Finland, Russia faced a much more dangerous enemy in Frederick the Great of Prussia. The latter had at this time plunged Europe into the War of the Austrian Succession in which the Russian army came too late to be of use to Austria. But in the Seven Years War the role played by the Russian army, with the conquest of East Prussia, the crushing defeat of Frederick inflicted by the Russians at Kunersdorf, (1759) and the occupation of Berlin (1760), was so important, that even though the new Czar Peter III threw away the results of victory because of his admiration for Frederick the Great, Russia was acknowledged as a great power in Europe.

From now on the voice of Russia was heard loudly by all the cabinets of Europe and could no longer be disregarded.

Catherine the Great (1762-1796) further increased this prestige of Russia by her victories in the wars against Turkey, Poland and Sweden. In the first Turkish war (1769-1774) the Russians occupied the Roumanian principalities for four years, while the Russian fleet, sailing around Europe, appeared for the first time in the Mediterranean and destroyed the Turkish fleet at Tchesme (1770). The Treaty of Kuchuk-Kainardji ending this war opened the Straits of the Bosphorus and Dardanelles to Russian ships. Besides the cession of territory of the Southern Ukraine and the coast of the Black Sea to Russia, this Treaty was made the basis for a Russian claim to protect the Orthodox populations of European Turkey, thus leading to incalculable consequences to be discussed in detail in later chapters of this work. The thorny "Eastern Question" of European diplomacy was officially opened. Impressed by these victories, the Holy Roman Emperor Joseph II joined Catherine in the Second Turkish War; but here once more the Austrian Army fared badly, while the Russians under Suvorov won stunning victories at Fokshani, Rymnik and Ismail. Meanwhile, Empress Catherine was asked by the belligerent parties to mediate the bloodless war of the Bavarian Succession, which once more had brought Prussia and Austria face to face. This mediation resulted in the signing of the Treaty of Teschen (1779) which made Russia, together with France, the co-guarantor of the internal stability of the Holy Roman Empire. With the outbreak of the American Revolution Catherine organised the so-called League of Neutrals, composed of Baltic and Atlantic coastal powers, with the purpose of hindering British freebooting activities on the high seas. Thus the Russian tide was rising higher and higher in Europe when the French Revolution broke out in 1789 opening a new chapter in history.[1]

---

[1]Lobanov-Rostovsky, A., Russia and Europe 1789-1825. Duke University Press, 1947.

II

Russia was slow in joining the coalition of European Powers fighting the French Revolution. To the entreaties of Austria and Prussia, Catherine cynically replied that she was doing her share in fighting the revolutionary disease by eradicating "Jacobinism" in Poland. Her erratic son and successor Paul I at first announced his intention of remaining neutral, but changed his mind upon the occupation by Napoleon of the Island of Malta. The Knights of St. John, sought the Czar's protection from the French by electing him their Grand Master. It was as a result of this minor issue that in 1799 Russia joined the second coalition against France, thus entering a cycle of wars which was to carry the French to Moscow and the Russians to Paris.

The results of Russia's entry into the war in 1799 were immediate and far reaching. The Russian fleet sailed through the Dardanelles into the Mediterranean and conquered the Ionian islands from the French. Because of their location between the heel of the Italian peninsula and the West coast of Greece, these islands became a base for subsequent land operations against Naples. At the other end of Europe a Russian division jointly with the British landed in Holland; while a Russian corps under Rimsky-Korsakov was sent to Zurich, Switzerland. The main Russian army operating with the Austrians, with Suvorov as Commander-in-Chief of both armies, invaded Northern Italy. In a famous campaign Suvorov defeated three successive French armies and drove the French out of Italy. He was then ordered to cross the Alps and join with the Russian corps in Switzerland; but the Austrians, not keeping their bargain to await Suvorov's arrival, left Rimsky-Korsakov to be defeated at Zurich by a much larger French army under Massena. Suvorov was left in the Muotha valley without food or ammunition and trapped by very large French forces. He nevertheless defeated Massena, and working his way over high Alpine passes, brought his army out. Paul, incensed by the behavior of the Austrians and the defeat of the joint Anglo-Russian force in Holland, brought the war to an end by leaving the coalition, joining hands with Napoleon and menacing the British in India. His murder (1801), fortunately for Russia, brought a man of entirely different temperament and capacity to the throne--his son Alexander I.

Alexander, if a poor general, had real gifts of statesmanship and was a match for Napoleon in astute diplomacy. He combined an apparently vacillating foreign policy with an unswerving determination in pursuing his goal. This firmness he kept hidden under a gentle manner and much personal charm. Educated in the liberal tradition of the enlightenment of the late eighteenth century, he had been at heart a republican in his youth, and at the beginning of his reign he initiated a series of liberal reforms. These however were cut short by the flaring up of the second war with France, the war of the Third Coalition. For the next ten years the struggle with France determined his whole policy. In the first campaign of this long struggle the Russians under Kutuzov operated jointly with the Austrians in the valley of the Upper Danube and in Bohemia; while a British-Russian force invaded Naples; and a Swedish-Russian corps landed in Pomerania. The disastrous defeat of the main Austro-Russian army at Austerlitz (December 2, 1805) brought an end to the hostilities and knocked Austria out of the struggle. Alexander retreated with his army to Russia, but resolved to carry on the struggle against Napoleon, this time in alliance with Prussia. However, in a lightning campaign Napoleon destroyed the Prussian army at Jena (October 14, 1806) and conquered Prussia before the Russians had crossed the border.

Invading Poland next, Napoleon was forced into a hard winter campaign to overcome the stiff resistance put up by the Russians as they slowly retreated north toward East Prussia. There the two bloody battles of Eylau and Friedland were fought. It became apparent to Napoleon that Russia, as far as continental powers were concerned, was his most dangerous enemy. He then resolved upon a bold move to win Russia over. At the negociations for peace at Tilsit (July 1807) after his victory over the Russians at Friedland, Napoleon suggested an alliance between France and Russia based on a veritable partition of Europe into two zones - the West up to the river Niemen to be his domain and the territory east of the river that of Alexander. In return for this Alexander would join the Continental System of economic blockade against England and declare war against that country should a mediation for peace fail. France would undertake to mediate the war which Turkey had declared on Russia in 1806, and join Russia against the Turks should this mediation fail. Russia was also to induce Sweden to join the Continental System.

Alexander agreed to these conditions and the famous reversal of alliances occurred at Tilsit, which however did not bring peace to Russia. Indeed four minor wars followed the cessation of hostilities with France. Mediation having failed, Russia declared war on England. Since both sides avoided an encounter, this remained a bloodless war; Sweden refused to join the Continental System and Russia invaded Finland. After a hard and inconclusive campaign against Finnish guerrilas, the Russian army, in a spectacular march, crossed the Baltic Sea on ice. This brought about the surrender of Sweden and the ceding of Finland to Russia (1809).

The same year a re-invigorated Austria suddenly renewed hositilities with France in the so-called campaign of Wagram; and Alexander, since he was bound by his treaty of alliance with Napoleon, sent an army into Galicia; under secret instructions this army fought a strictly "phony war" against Austria to Napoleon's exasperation.

Lastly, the war with Turkey continued till 1812, when defeated Turkey ceded Bessarabia to Russia. Contrary to his pledge Napoleon did not join Alexander in this war. It was obvious that the alliance of Tilsit was insincere on both sides and this did not augure well for its durability; however, as long as it lasted, the situation was somewhat similar to the one existing today - Continental Europe was ruled by two superpowers, France and Russia. Friction and suspicion arose between the allies with reference to the problems created by these wars, and particularly with regard to Napoleon's policy of recreating and strengthening an independent Poland under the name of the Grand Duchy of Warsaw.

By 1811 the quarrel between Napoleon and Alexander came into the open, and Napoleon took the fatal resolution to invade Russia in order to bring Alexander under his control. Realizing the danger of this undertaking, Napoleon carefully and methodically prepared for the invasion during the ensuing year. He mobilized all the resources of his vast Empire and forced Austria and Prussia to side with him. The Grand Army of nearly 1,200,000 men, compared with the forces at the disposal of Alexander, represented a ratio of 6 to 1; of these, half or 600,000 men, participated in the invasion.

Napoleon crossed into Russia in June, 1812, hoping to crush the enemy in one decisive battle. The Russians however were elusive and drew him inland. After the bloody rearguard action at Smolensk, Napoleon was unable to pin down the enemy except at the last line of defense before Moscow. Here, on September 7, was fought the bloodiest and most stubborn battle to date of Napoleon's career - the battle of Borodino. As a result of the losses incurred the Russians abandoned Moscow. However, the fire which destroyed the city nullified the advantages of its capture by leaving the French without shelter or food. Alexander refused the offer of peace proffered by Napoleon, and while the French army was becoming increasingly disorganised in the destroyed city the Russians re-equipped and refitted their army. When, with the advent of late fall weather

INTRODUCTION 7

Napoleon decided to winter in the Southern Ukraine, he found his way barred by the re-invigorated Russian army which forced him back on to the very road he had taken during his advance.

With the Russians attacking him constantly and with guerrilla bands harassing him on all sides, Napoleon's retreat soon turned to disaster, and at the crossing of the river Berezina he lost half his men and nearly all his equipment. The remainder of the invading force either disintegrated or perished in the forests of White Russia. On December 5, 1812, Napoleon abandoned his army to its fate and fled in disguise to Paris. After some hesitation Alexander decided to carry the war into Germany. The Russians re-occupied Poland and entered East Prussia. Whereupon the Prussian army changed sides and joined the invading Russian army under Kutuzov, who was appointed Commander-in-Chief of the Allied Forces. By the Treaty of Kalisch (February, 1813) Alexander pledged the restoration of Prussia to its former size and called upon the German people to rise against French domination.

Napoleon, however, after re-organizing what remained of his forces was able to start a counter-offensive in the Spring of 1813 and inflict two heavy but not decisive defeats on the Russo-Prussian army at Lützen and Bautzen, forcing the Allies to retreat into Silesia. At the ensuing armistice of Pleisswitz both sides prepared for further struggle. As a result of diplomatic negotiations between Metternich and Alexander, Austria was persuaded to join the coalition, though at the heavy price of the appointment of the over-cautious Austrian General Prince Schwarzenberg as Commander-in-Chief of the Allied Armies. Austria alone maintained her army as a separate unit, while the divisions of the other armies were to be pooled.

A coalition involving Austria, Russia, Prussia and Sweden, with the backing of England (who had terminated her war with Russia by the peace of Örebro) came into existence. When the war was resumed in August, after some initial successes, Napoleon was forced back to Leipzig, where, in the three days "Battle of the Nations," October, 1813, his doom was sealed.

After this crushing defeat, Napoleon with only 60,000 men remaining, fell back to the Rhine. At the turn of the year the Allies started crossing the Rhine, preparing for the invasion of France. During this whole campaign the Russian Army, judging by its losses and the casualties inflicted upon the enemy, carried the heaviest brunt of fighting, with the Prussians coming next and the Austrians and Swedes far behind. The Russians occupied Berlin once more, installed a Russian governor in Saxony, liberated Westphalia from the French and pushed as far as Hamburg.

During the course of the invasion of France in the spring of 1814, the long smouldering jealousies and rivalries between the Allies came into the open, and particularly during the abortive Congress of Chatillon. Both Metternich and Castlereagh, fearing the ascendancy of Russia, wanted to proceed cautiously and to be lenient with Napoleon. Alexander on his side urged the advance on Paris. Being supported by Prussia, he threatened to break up the coalition and to march on Paris with the Prussians, irrespective of the policies of the other allies. Schwarzenberg purposely procrastinated. When Napoleon, in a last desperate move to save his capital, boldly marched toward St. Dizier, far in the rear of the Allies, Schwarzenberg terrified, ordered a general retreat. In a violent scene with Schwarzenberg Alexander insisted that the order be rescinded and that the advance on Paris be resumed - and won his point. Thus it was that the task of storming the defences of Paris fell to the Russians and that the city surrendered to Alexander. With the fall of Paris (March 30, 1814), the military contribution of Russia in the Napoleonic Wars came to an end except for the capture of some French border fortresses the following year during the short campaign of Waterloo.

III

The triumphant entry of Alexander into Paris at the head of the Allied Armies represents the high watermark of the Czar's career. Alexander rode between the King of Prussia on his left and Schwarzenberg, representing Emperor Francis of Austria, on his right. The latter had tactfully remained in Dijon. It also marks the beginning of a decade in which Russia becomes the dominant power on the Continent. Once in Paris, Alexander, single-handed, assumed the undisputed leadership of the allied coalition and took all the decisions; he presided over a council of Senators and French dignitaries, who decided upon the restoration of Louis XVIII to the throne; he forced the abdication of Napoleon, and decided that he would be exiled to the island of Elba; it was Alexander who insisted that the new King should grant a liberal constitution to France, and supervised closely the work of a joint Franco-Russian Commission which worked out its terms. This constitution known as the Charte Constitutionnelle became the Constitution of France which lasted until the revolution of 1848. This interest and interference in the internal affairs of France continued till beyond the settlements of peace both at Paris and at Vienna. Alexander was popular with the French who appreciated the stringent discipline he imposed upon his troops while they were in occupation of

Paris, as well as the forbearance shown to the Parisians by the Russian Military Governor of Paris, General Sacken. Louis XVIII realized that the best chance of support of French interests in this crisis came from Alexander, hence, after the second occupation of Paris and the signing by the Allies of the Peace of Paris (November 1815), he dismissed Talleyrand, whom he personally disliked, and appointed as Prime Minister the Duc de Richelieu. This Richelieu, a descendant of the great Cardinal, had entered the Russian Army as a French royalist emigré under Catherine II and had made a brilliant career in Russia. He was appointed by Alexander Governor General of Novorossia (the territory conquered from Turkey) and was responsible for the building up of Odessa. A friend of Alexander and personally devoted to the Czar, Richelieu, during his tenure of office in France, maintained a close correspondence with Alexander and kept him informed of the internal political developments in France, asking and taking advice with reference to the measures against the royalist extremists, the "Ultras", or against the increasingly unruly Chamber.

By the Second Treaty of Paris, France was obligated to maintain an allied army of occupation under the command of the Duke of Wellington. Part of the occupationary force consisted of a Russian Army 60,000 strong which occupied Champagne. France also had to pay an indemnity of 700,000,000 francs. It was Richelieu's ambition to get rid of these onerous terms; hence in 1818 he appealed to Alexander. As a result of this appeal Alexander called the Congress of Aix la Chapelle, which consolidated the French debt and ended the military occupation. France regained her status as a great power and joined the four power alliance which had been formed against her, but had been carried over into the peace years. Even after the resignation of Richelieu, Alexander remained closely in touch with French affairs through his ambassador in Paris, Pozzo di Borgo. The latter was a Corsican by birth and a former schoolmate of Napoleon. Out of hatred for his illustrious compatriot Pozzo had entered the Russian diplomatic service.

A second major question occupying the mind of Alexander was the fate of Poland. Owing to the influence of the friend of his youth, the Polish Prince Adam Czartoryski, who was for a while directing his foreign policy, Alexander had a friendly feeling toward Poland and deplored its partition. But the events after Tilsit had showed him how dangerous a united Poland could become if allied to his enemies. He therefore found a solution to the problem by unifying Poland and making her once more independent, but with himself as King of Poland;

thus Poland would be united to Russia only through having a common sovereign. He also pledged to give Poland a very liberal constitution. This policy was first put forward during his stay in Paris in 1814 and Poles welcomed it. The Polish Legion, which had fought under Napoleon passed into Russian service. Austria and England became seriously alarmed. The storm broke at the Congress of Vienna, which had been specifically called to decide the disposition of the territories outside of France which had been incorporated in the Napoleonic Empire. Since Poland could be unified only at the expense of Austria and Prussia, the co-partners of Russia in the parition of Poland in 1795, Alexander proposed that his two former allies should cede to him their Polish territories and compensate themselves elsewhere - Austria in Northern Italy and Prussia in Saxony. It was this Polish-Saxon question, as it was called, which nearly wrecked the Congress - it played directly into the hands of the wily Talleyrand, who as the representative of defeated France, was doing everything he could to sow discord among the victorious powers. He was so successful that on January 3, 1815, Metternich and Castlereagh met secretly with him and signed a military convention between France, England and Austria against Russia and Prussia.

What saved the Congress from collapse and possibly Europe from a war between former allies, was the flight of Napoleon from Elba and his re-assumption of power in Paris. All intrigues and discords were forgotten in the face of this danger, and the allied armies were set in motion for the coming campaign. A compromise settlement, which became the Treaty of Vienna, repartitioned Poland once more, Russia however receiving the major portion with the capital Warsaw. This territory was known henceforth as Congress Poland. Alexander kept his pledge - proclaimed it an independent Kingdom with its own administration and army, and was crowned King of Poland. In 1816 Poland was given a liberal constitution. Even Polish historians most hostile to Russia acknowledge that the years which followed were for Poland years of real prosperity and peace. Unfortunately, when Alexander in later years came more and more under the influence of Metternich, he lost interest in this constitution, convened the Polish Diet less frequently and appointed his brother Constantine as viceroy. Constantine was a military martinet and a boor and made himself disliked by the Poles - thus the seeds of a coming insurrection were sown.

However both the French and Polish issues appeared to Alexander as facets of a much greater idea which dominated and directed his thought throughout his whole political career the red thread of Alexander's policy. This idea is traceable from as early as 1804, reappears in a new guise in 1814, once more changes pattern in 1818, and finally modified, it reemerges in 1821-1822. This idea was that there should be a Federation of European Nations which would grant protection to the smaller states comparable to the protection granted to a citizen of a civilized community by the police. He proposed the integration of small countries into combined larger units, and obligatory arbitration to avoid war. He first suggested these ideas to Pitt during the negotiations for the formation of the Third Coalition in 1804-1805. After the fire of Moscow in 1812, the psychology of Alexander underwent a change - from the agnostic rationalist he had been, he turned to religion for consolation; two years later he came under the influence of an evangelist, Baroness Krüdener. Under her influence Alexander's idea of European Federation changed and took on religious and ethical overtones. At the signing of the Second Treaty of Paris (1815) Alexander officially proposed his plan of European Federation under the name of the Holy Alliance.

Addressed to all the signatories of the Treaty of Vienna, it was to be a pact in which the sovereigns, regarding themselves as brothers of one family and citizens of the Kingdom of our Lord Jesus Christ, were to apply Christian ethics both in their dealings among themselves and in their dealings with their subjects. This pact was signed by all the nations concerned with the exception of Great Britain; the Pope and Turkey were omitted. The pact, together with the extension of the four power alliance of Chaumont (March 1814), became the basis for the status of Europe in the so-called period of Congresses.

In 1818 at the Congress of Aix la Chapelle, Alexander returned to the idea of a Federation, and drew up a memorandum suggesting the creation of an international army and an international general staff. The idea was turned down by England and Austria, who, in the guise of compromise, accepted the inclusion of France into the Four Power Alliance. Hence Europe was to be governed and supervised by the "Pentarchy" or the alliance of the five great powers.

Meanwhile Alexander, as a result of his religious views, was undergoing a political conversion. Up to 1818 he remained a liberal. He supported the South German States of Baden and Württemberg in their constitutional reforms against the opposition of Austria. Metternich complained bitterly that revolutionary propaganda was emanating from the Russian embassies in Germany and Italy. However during the next two years Alexander's views changed completely and came to approximate those of Metternich, who exultantly spoke of the conversion of the "terrible Alexander." Contributing events which brought about this change of view were: the revolutionary agitation fostered by secret societies of the Carbonari type, which were spreading from country to country; the assassination in Germany of the writer Kotzebue (a Russian secret agent); and the short lived mutiny in the Semenovski Guard Regiment. At the Congress of Troppau-Laibach in 1820/21 which was called to face the revolution in Naples against King Ferdinand, Alexander wholeheartedly supported Austria's military intervention against the Neapolitan revolution, and proposed that the Powers should automatically send their armies to any country menaced by revolution. This brought about a break in the five power alliance. The decision of Austria, Russia and Prussia to send the Austrian Army under General Frimont to support King Ferdinand was taken in spite of the opposition of England and France. Thus at Troppau-Laibach the Holy Alliance evolved into its final form - a conservative alliance of the three autocratic powers against the liberal parliamentary powers of Western Europe. This marks a very important change in Russian diplomatic history. The tide of Russian influence which we have seen rising and spreading over the whole map of Europe had now ebbed and was being canalised into this alliance with the two Central European powers. This alliance will become the pattern of Russian diplomacy for the whole nineteenth century. The alternate pattern - an alliance with liberal France appears only in the first decade (The Tilsit alliance) and the last decade of the century (the Franco-Russian Alliance of 1894).

In 1822, when the Congress of Verona met to discuss the problem of the Spanish revolution, Alexander, in his crusading counter-revolutionary zeal, offered to send the Russian army into Spain. When the Congress objected to this scheme, he ardently supported French military intervention. After his return from Verona and during the three last years of his reign, Alexander lost interest in foreign affairs. Pressing problems of internal policy occupied him. Among these were the serious revolutionary agitation in the army leading up to the Decembrist revolution of 1825, and also the question of the succession to the throne. His brother Constantine, after his marriage with a Polish lady, had renounced his rights in favour of his younger brother Nicholas. Tired and more and more absorbed by religion Alexander spoke openly of abdicating and finishing his days in a monastery.[2]

---

[2] The question whether Alexander did die in 1825, or secretly went to Siberia and lived there until 1864 as a monk under the name of Fedor Kuzmich, has never been settled.

It is this state of mind which explains Alexander's passivity with reference to the very important events occurring at this time in the Balkans and which were to become the next major issue of Russian diplomacy.

IV

While earlier, in the reign of Catherine, and later, in the reign of Nicholas I, the Balkans loomed as the major issue of Russian foreign policy, during the reign of Alexander, absorbed as he was in vast European schemes, they occupied a subordinate place. However very important developments were taking place in the Balkans during his reign which were involving Russia more and more. The revolutionary spirit of nationalism, generated by the French Revolution, had spread to a Turkey weakened by defeats at the hand of Russia during the wars of Catherine. In 1804, inspired by this new spirit and badly oppressed by the tyranny of the Janissaries, the Serbs rose in rebellion under the leadership of Karageorg and joined their forces with the Russian army fighting the Turks in the war of 1806-1812. The Serbs thus won a degree of independence from Turkey, but during the Napoleonic invasion of Russia, the Turks, profitting by Russia's absorption in her struggle against Napoleon, reconquered Serbia. Karageorg fled, and Milosh Obrenovich, subservient to the Turks, was made by them puppet ruler of Servia. With the end of the Napoleonic wars, Russia came into the picture once more. Milosh, who had rebelled against Turkish domination in 1815, was finally acknowledged autonomous Prince of Serbia, though still as a vassal of Turkey. Serbia gained the right to have a Skuptchina (or national assembly) and a separate internal administration, though the Turks maintained their garrisons in the main Serbian fortresses.

This measure of autonomy gained by Serbia produced a chain reaction in the Balkans affecting both Roumania and Greece. In 1814 a secret revolutionary society for the liberation of Greece from Turkish domination was founded in Odessa. This society, called the Hetairia, established cells all over Greece. The society was headed by Prince Alexander Ypsilanti, whose family, of Greek extraction, had ruled Moldavia. He was a major-general in the Russian army and A.D.C. to the Czar. In March, 1821, acting without the knowledge or consent of the Czar, Ypsilanti crossed the Pruth river with armed bands and started an insurrection in Moldavia and Wallachia. The Czar was at the time at Laibach. He immediately assured Turkey of his neutrality and disavowed the movement. He also cancelled Ypsilanti's commission in the Russian army. Ypsilanti's insurrection backfired inasmuch as it set off a Roumanian national insurrection under Vladimirescu which was at odds with the Greek movement. After some initial successes Ypsilanti was easily crushed by the Turks; he fled to Hungary where he was interned by order of Metternich.

However in Greece proper the revolution broke out in April, led by Ypsilanti's younger brother Demetrios,[3] and became a major issue of European diplomacy for the next ten years. The Turks were caught unawares, the more so as their army was fighting the rebellious Ali Pasha of Jannina in Epirus, and Greece was easily liberated. The Sultan Mahmoud II retaliated by instigating the murder of the Patriarch of the Greek Orthodox Church in Constantinople and also of a number of prominent Greeks during Easter celebrations. Count Capo d'Istria,[4] at this time directing Russia's foreign policy, urged Alexander to declare war on Turkey. Alexander however was tired of wars and contented himself with sending an ultimatum and breaking diplomatic relations with Turkey. Capo d'Istria resigned and left for Switzerland; he was succeeded by Count Nesselrode who directed Russian foreign policy for the next 30 years.

Meanwhile the Greeks proclaimed their independence and promulgated a constitution at Epidaurus in 1822. However rival governments appeared which led to civil wars, while the Turkish army, having at long last quelled the insurrection of Ali Pasha, started a powerful counter-offensive through the Northern Mountains. Fierce fighting on land and sea followed, with civil strife weakening the Greeks' power of resistance. A turn for the worse occurred which endangered the very existence of Greece, when the Sultan appealed to his powerful vassal, Mehemet Ali for aid, and the latter dispatched his French trained modern army and navy under the command of his son, Ibrahim Pasha, to the assistance of the Turkish forces operating in Greece.

Even though Alexander had refused to go to war on behalf of Greece he kept a close watch on the situation and exerted considerable diplomatic pressure. In his mind the Greek question was to be integrated with the problem of general relations between Russia and Turkey. Having broken off relations with Turkey he could not deal directly with her. In the meantime Metternich and Canning, distrusting Russia's peaceful intentions,

---

[3] The city of Ypsilanti, Michigan was named in honour of Demetrios Ypsilanti.

[4] Capo d'Istria was a Greek lawyer from Corfu who had entered Russian diplomatic service.

were working for a reconciliation between Russia and Turkey. In 1824 Alexander invited the other powers to a conference in St. Petersburg to work out a plan for a settlement of the Greek question. Metternich, who regarded the Greeks merely as rebels against a legitimate government was lukewarm; France was more interested in Spain than in Greece, while England sent Stratford Canning as a mere observer. The conference thus achieved nothing except to reveal the divergence of views between Metternich and Alexander on the Greek issue, and thus it paved the way for a temporary re-orientation of Russian policy toward England and France. Turkey meanwhile, under pressure from Britain, took the first step toward reconciliation with Russia by partially accepting the ultimatum - namely the clauses concerning Moldavia and Wallachia but not Greece. As result of this concession Russia appointed a chargé d'Affaires to Constantinople.

"Matters stood at this point when three important developments ushered in a new phase in the situation. These were the death of Louis XVIII in 1824 and the advent of Charles X, which prepared the way for closer co-operation between Russia and France; the death of Alexander I in 1825, which brought the energetic and aggressive Nicholas I to power; and, finally, the appearance in Greece of the Egyptian army under Ibrahim Pasha."[5]

---

[5]Lobanov-Rostovsky op. cit. p. 426.

CHAPTER I

THE GREEK REVOLUTION

I

Ibrahim Pasha had landed in Greece in February 1825 and by the end of the year the situation had become so critical that something had to be done by the Powers if Greece was to be saved. Nicholas I, young, adventurous and ambitious was known to be contemplating action and uneasy reports of an impending Russian ultimatum to Turkey reached London. Canning's policy was to maintain the neutrality of England and achieve whatever results were possible for Greece through diplomatic action. On the other hand he did not want Russia to get the credit for saving Greece. Thus it was that under the pretence of congratulating the Czar upon his accession to the throne a diplomatic mission was sent to St. Petersburg to carry on the negotiations already started in London with the purpose of restraining Russia and keeping her in line with British policy. This work was assigned by Canning to the Duke of Wellington in the hope that the latter would have a special appeal for the young, military-minded Czar. At the same time Sir Stratford Canning, in Constantinople, set himself the task of working for the prevention of direct Russian intervention in Greece, so undesirable for the British. The massacres of Greek populations, however, had reached such proportions that Lieven in London brought these atrocities to the attention of the British Government which instructed Stratford-Canning to intercede with the Porte. The latter did so but merely obtained vague promises and no concrete results. Matters had reached this stage when the Duke of Wellington arrived in St. Petersburg on February 26, 1826. The Duke was to inform Russia of a Greek demand for British mediation and if possible obtain Russia's support in the matter; should Russia suggest a new conference on Greek affairs the Duke was to make British acceptance conditional on a promise by Russia neither to recur to force, nor to aim at any territorial aggrandizements commitments and to have the conference held in London rather than in St. Petersburg. Should the Porte turn down the Anglo-Russian mediation England was to co-operate with Russia in demanding the support of the other powers. Above all the Duke was to stress privately the disinterestedness of Great Britain in Greece and the absence of any feeling of jealousy toward Russia.[1]

In an audience with the Czar, Wellington was told bluntly that it was an error to think that because Russia had expressed sympathy for Greece she was prepared to go to war for that country. The Czar added that he himself considered the Greeks as rebel subjects of Turkey, but that he was opposed to the establishment of an Egyptian state in Morea and would act jointly with England to block such a scheme; he would feel justified in intervening only in such an event, particularly if it led to the wholesale deportation of Greeks from Morea. However, Nesselrode was much less specific and stated that although by principle the Czar was opposed to the idea of supporting rebels, nevertheless he was deeply interested in the fate of the Greeks. It was at this point, 15 days after the arrival of Wellington in the Russian capital, that the Russian ultimatum was sent to Turkey on March 17.

In deference to the Duke of Wellington and to British desires the ultimatum did not mention Greece. It dealt solely with the problems resulting from the non-application of the Treaty of Bucharest, namely, the conditions in Moldavia, Wallachia and Serbia and asked that plenipotentiaries should be sent to the Russian border to discuss these issues. It gave six weeks for an answer after which Minciaky, the Russian Chargé d'Affaires in Constantinople, was instructed to demand his passports. Still it remained an ultimatum to Turkey and, though the Greek issue was left out, the latter would inevitably be engulfed in the broader question of relations between Russia and Turkey should war result from the ultimatum. The sensation produced by this ultimatum in European capitals was very great indeed. "With one stroke Russia had torn asunder the "spider web" which the allied powers had been indefatigably spinning around her for 5 years"[2]..... Metternich was exultant, French diplomacy set to work actively to persuade Turkey to give in, and the Turks, frightened, accepted the terms by sending plenipotentiaries to the conference which opened at Akkerman. Wellington worked more feverishly than ever to avoid the danger of war, and the result was the signing by Nesselrode, Wellington and Lieven (the Russian ambassador in London who accompanied the Duke), of the so-called Protocol of St. Petersburg on April 4, 1826, the first diplomatic document dealing with the status of Greece.

---

[1] Driault, Edouard et L'héritier, Michel. Histoire Diplomatique de la Grèce de 1821 à nos Jours., Paris 1925-1926. Vol. I. p. 313-314.

[2] Driault et L'héritier, op. cit., Vol. I, p. 316.

Coming as a result of long negotiaions in which a compromise solution was sought between opposing views, the protocol embodied the following suggestions: Greece was to remain a dependency of Turkey and pay an annual tribute but would enjoy complete autonomy and self-government as well as liberty of conscience and trade; the Greeks would be obliged to purchase all evacuated properties belonging to Turks in Greece and in the islands. As for the actual limits of the new state these were left to future negotiations. This protocol was to serve as a basis for the settlement of the Greek issue even if Turkey turned down the offer of mediation, and would be communicated to the courts of Vienna, Paris and Berlin which would be requested to guarantee any treaty resulting from the protocol. Lastly, the two signatories pledged themselves not to take any personal advantages, commercial or territorial, of the Greek situation.

The sensation produced by the signing of the protocol was as great as the one produced by the ultimatum. LaFerronays (the French ambassador in St. Petersburg), in an audience with the Emperor, asked if the Holy Alliance was still in effect, and Nicholas assured him of his attachment to the system which had kept peace in Europe for a decade. Metternich was furious and comparing the ultimatum to the protocol he said, "Nicholas had a good idea, Wellington's was deplorable. The first will lead to everything, the second to nothing,"[3] and he asked his ambassador, Esterhazy, to find out in London just what was meant by Greece. In the meanwhile there occurred the tragic siege and capture of Missolonghi April 22, and this Greek disaster produced a profound impression in Europe. In Turkey the Sultan was exultant and in no mood to be conciliatory. Metternich believed that this event would kill the protocol and forthwith he dispatched an Austrian squadron into the Eastern Mediterranean to protect the Austrian ships from what he called "Greek pirates". In Paris consternation reigned. Public opinion, worked up by the tragedy of Missolonghi, was demanding action, but the government, afraid of being driven to espouse a lost cause, was leaning more and more toward Mehemet Ali. Stratford-Canning, British Ambassador to Turkey, wrote to the Greek Government counselling not only to moderate its demand but to renounce its claim of independence and accept a modified Turkish rule.

Alone, Russia maintained a determined and aggressive stand against Turkey and obtained by the convention of Akkerman the fulfilment of all the demands made in the ultimatum.[4] She did more. Lieven, having returned to London, started negotiations with

---

[3]Driault et L'héritier, op. cit., Vol. I, p. 320.

[4]The Turks under this convention confirmed all the privileges previously granted to the Roumanian Principalities at the insistance

Canning with regard to the application of the protocol of St. Petersburg. As Canning suggested a rupture of diplomatic relations with Turkey, should the latter refuse to accede to the protocol, Lieven replied in a confidential note stating that if Russia did not obtain from Turkey a final settlement of the Greek issue along the lines of the protocol, the Czar would consider the role played by his government to be humiliating and one to which he could not allow himself to be exposed. "The Emperor has raised the Greek question only with the firm determination to solve it and it is with the personal conviction that the British Cabinet shares his sentiments (partage ses sentiments) that he has authorized me to concert with your Excellency in regard to such ulterior measures as would become indispensable..... should Turkey fail to be impressed by the recall of ambassadors."[5] The hint of war was unmistakable. After much hesitation the French Government announced its adhesion to the Protocol on December 18, six months after it had been concluded, but with a reservation in regard to the recall of the ambassadors. However, Metternich, in the name of the principles of the Holy Alliance, suggested the re-establishment of the authority of the Sultan in Greece and the islands. With some slight technical advantages for the Greeks, he suggested a return to the status quo of 1821. Thus the Greek issue had rent asunder the Three Northern Courts, and in place of the Holy Alliance had created an Anglo-French-Russian alliance. This was the first time since the Napoleonic Wars that Russia switched to this alternate system of alliances which has served as a counterpart to the alliance of the Three Northern Courts throughout the nineteenth century whenever the latter system proved unworkable for Russia. Metternich was right in accusing Russia of having violated the spirit of the Holy Alliance which she had created, but he was wrong in thinking that Nicholas had become a tool of Canning. The policies of Russia and Great Britain remained independent though parallel.

(continued)

of Russia. The hospodars (princes) were to be elected by the councils (divans) and the nobility (boyars) for a period of seven years, with the consent of Russia in the choice of candidates and be dismissed only by joint permission of Russia and Turkey. In connection with Serbia, the Turks confirmed full autonomy under the Treaty of Bucharest 1812, and recognized Prince Milosh as hereditary prince under Ottoman suzerainty. Other clauses dealt with the question of the Straits and the tenure of certain Circassian border fortresses.

[5]Driault et L'héritier, op. cit., Vol. I, p. 339, 340.

Following the settlement of the Russian claims at Akkerman, Russia appointed Ribeaupierre ambassador to Constantinople, thus stressing the re-establishment of normal relations. Upon his arrival at the Turkish capital on February 11, Ribeaupierre raised the Greek issue with the Reiss Effendi (Turkish minister of Foreign Affairs) Saida Pasha, declaring that his mission had the double purpose of assuring the execution of the Treaty of Akkerman and the pacification of Greece. But the Turks once more evaded the issue. In April the three ambassadors jointly demanded from the new Reiss Effendi, Pertew Effendi, an official acknowledgement of the Protocol of St. Petersburg but once more the Turkish minister found reasons to delay his reply. It was only after the fall of Athens in June that the reply came. Flushed by this victory, Turkey declared its clauses inadmissible. Once more a deadlock had been reached. Something had to be done and the allied powers were, as always, anxious not to allow Russia to do it single-handed. Negotiations which had been going on for the conversion of the protocol into a formal treaty were speeded up and resulted in the London treaty of July 6, 1827. The Treaty of London declared (Art. 1) that the signatory powers offered their mediation in the Greco-Turkish war along the lines decided upon and incorporated in the protocol of April 4. However, it went one step further and stated specifically that if, after a period of one month, Turkey had not accepted the mediation of the powers, they would establish commercial relations with Greece and appoint consular agents there; if further, in the same period of one month, Turkey did not accept an armistice, the allies would take such naval measures, with their squadrons cruising in the Levant, as to obtain "the immediate purposes of the armistice, by preventing any clash between the contending parties, without however taking part in the hostilities."[6] Lastly, the ambassadors of the three powers in London were to keep on deliberating in common and to decide upon such ulterior measures as might become necessary. Thus a veiled threat of action was to be found in the treaty and out of it came the battle of Navarino and the Russo-Turkish war. The treaty was supposed to be secret, but it mysteriously found its way into the British press. Early in June, at the time the negotiations were proceeding for this treaty, the Russian Baltic fleet under the command of Admiral Seniavin was ordered to sail to Portsmouth. The Czar himself reviewed the departing fleet and Seniavin carried with him secret instructions to the effect that in Portsmouth he should detach a squadron under Admiral Count Heyden for action in Greek waters.

---

[6]Driault et L'heritier, op. cit., Vol. I, p. 366.

II

The delay set for the Turkish reply to the allied proposals had been reduced from a month to 15 days after the publication of the treaty in the British newspapers. Considering time for transmission to Constantinople the deadline was set for August 31. At the news of the treaty, Sultan Mahmoud II let himself go in a delirious rage. On August 1, the Egyptian fleet of Mehemet Ali, assembled at Alexandria, sailed for Greek waters to deal a death blow to the Greeks and operated its junction with the Turkish fleet at Navarino. In his rage the Sultan declared that if the allies interfered with it he would send in addition 50,000 men overland to conquer every inch of Greece. On August 31, the Turkish reply was conveyed to the three ambassadors--it was brief: "Our reply", said the Reiss Effendi, "is that the Sublime Porte can not and never could hear anything said in favour of the Greeks--this declaration is positive, absolute and final."

There was nothing to do but put the coercive clauses of the Treaty of London into effect. The British squadron under Admiral Codrington was at Corfu, the French under Admiral Rigny at Milos and the Russian squadron under Admiral Heyden was on its way from Portsmouth. By September 20, Codrington and Rigny had operated their junction before Corfu at Zante and the Russian squadron arrived at Zante on October 13. Thus the allied fleet was in full force and two days later, October 15, sailed for the bay of Navarino where the Turkish-Egyptian fleet was anchored.

There is no need here to go into a detailed account of the unsuccessful negotiations between the allied commanders and Ibrahim Pasha for the purpose of obtaining an armistice or to discuss the reasons for sailing the squadrons into the bay of Navarino; these developments preceded the arrival of the Russian squadron and Heyden had no part in them. Suffice it to say that the decision to anchor the allied squadrons in the same bay where the Turko-Egyptian fleet was stationed was inevitably fraught with the dangers of a serious clash, the more so that on receiving intelligence about the departure of a Turkish squadron from Navarino, Admiral Codrington informed the Turkish Capitan Pasha, Tahir Pasha, that he had orders to prevent any movements of the Turkish naval forces which might be directed against the Greeks. Early in mid-afternoon on October 20, the Allied Fleet under the supreme command of Codrington sailed into the harbour of Navarino in two columns, the first composed of the French squadron with 7 sails and the British squadron with 11 sails; the second column, slightly back, consisted of the Russian squadron of 8 sails, 4 battle-of-line ships of 74 guns each and 4 frigates totaling 452 guns. The Turko-Egyptian fleet was composed of 82 sails with about 2,000 guns lined up in a crescent under the protection of coast batteries. The allied fleets had to pass through a narrow entrance into the bay and this delayed the Russian squadron, coming in last. The breeze having died down, it took the Russian squadron more than an hour to reach its battle station. By this time the battle had already started. The French and British flagships sustained the fire of the Egyptian fleet, but "the victory was soon afterwards secured by the Russian division under Count Heyden engaging the Captain Pasha Tahir whose squadron formed the starboard division of the Turkish line."[7] By nightfall, out of 82 Turko-Egyptian ships only 29 remained afloat and the Turks were estimated to have lost between 4,000 and 6,000 men. The Russian flagships, the Azov and the Gangut, were badly damaged and the Russians lost 59 killed and 139 wounded, as compared to 75 killed and 197 wounded for the British and 43 and 183 respectively for the French. After the battle the Russians sailed with the British to Malta to have the damaged ships repaired. This battle together with the blockade of the Dardanelles which followed the Russo-Turkish war was to be the last Russian naval venture of the century in the Mediterranean.

Nicholas was exultant at the news of the victory and decorated Admiral Codrington with the Order of St. George of the 2nd class and Admiral Rigny with the Cross of St. Alexander Nevsky. He wrote a personal letter to Codrington congratulating him upon the "glorious victory". France was discretely pleased and England was nonplussed. Emperor Francis spoke of wanton murder and Metternich called it "a frightful catastrophe" and accused Nesselrode of speaking and acting like Danton and Carnot. Thus the Russian attitude was singled out by the Turks as being the most offensive. Though Russia played a relatively secondary role in the whole Navarino incident it was for Russia alone that the after effects of the battle proved serious.

On November 2, when the news of the battle of Navarino reached Constantinople, the three allied ambassadors sent their drogmans to the Reiss Effendi to express their regrets for the occurrence and at the same time expressing their hope that the future actions of Turkey would not render such a collision once more inevitable. As was to be expected the Sultan and the Porte gave vent to such an explosion of fury at the news of the destruction of the Turkish fleet that this move on the part of the ambassadors was futile and on the 9th a demand came from Turkey for indemnities, complete satisfaction and non-interference in Greece. To this the ambassadors

---

[7]Finlay, George. History of the Greek Revolution, London, 1861, Vol. II, p. 182.

replied the next day with a note which reiterated their resolution to work along the lines set down by the Treaty of London, accused the Turks of starting the battle and therefore refused an indemnity and in turn demanded categorically that Turkey declare its adherence to the earlier proposals made by the three governments. No reply was given to the note and it became known that a council was held at the Porte under the chairmanship of the Sultan himself which debated the issue of war with the allies. The Sultan favoured war, his ministers were against it, no final decision was taken. After waiting two weeks for a reply to their collective note the three ambassadors had another interview with the Reiss Effendi on November 24 in which they were told that Turkey could accept only the complete submission of the Greeks. Three days later, November 27, the ambassadors asked for their passports and left Constantinople; on December 12 the Conference of London once more officially confirmed the Treaty of London, adding that in any eventuality the three powers promised each other real and active cooperation. A week later the Sultan issued a manifesto to the Muslim world calling for a Holy War against the infidels.

Thus far events were leading to a war against the three allies. Russia, however, was in a peculiar position because the departure of Ribeaupierre from Constantinople had left no one to protect her numerous interests in Turkey, to see that the clauses of the Convention of Akkerman would be respected or to maintain the proper guarantees with regard to her vital commerce and navigation on the Black Sea. In short, her interests were vitally affected. Accordingly, and acting in the spirit of the Conference of London, Russia submitted the following plan of action to the allies: an ultimatum was to be delivered to the Porte, following which the Russian Army would occupy Moldavia and Wallachia and the allied squadrons would blockade Greece so as to cut the supplies of the Turkish Army; this could be followed up by a joint attack on Alexandria or a march on Constantinople according to circumstances. France was willing to adhere to a part of this plan, namely to support the Russian occupation of the Principalities and consider a blockade of the Dardanelles. But Great Britain balked and Lord Dudley, the British Foreign Secretary, replied to the Russian proposition declaring that England was working for peace and wanted to avoid hostilities with Turkey since the invasion of Ottoman territory would lead to unpredictable consequences. The main object being the liberation of Greece, he suggested the blockade of Alexandria which would result in the evacuation of Morea by Ibrahim Pasha. As for the rest he suggested the establishment of commercial relations with Greece as per the Treaty of London. Nesselrode replied sharply that England was overlooking the special interests that Russia had in Turkey which were apparently of little concern to England. Wellington, on his side, wrote to LaFerronays declaring that England was interested in the maintenance of the Ottoman Empire and not in its destruction.[8] To stress the pacific nature of British policy the King's speech delivered on January 29, 1828 stated: "Notwithstanding the valour displayed by the combined fleet, His Majesty deeply laments that this conflict should have occurred with the naval force of an ancient ally; but he still entertains a confident hope that this untoward event will not be followed by further hostilities and will not impede an amicable adjustment of the existing differences between the Porte and the Greeks."[9] Admiral Codrington was recalled. All this indicated that the conflict was not between Turkey and England but Russia and England and the Triple Alliance appeared to be doomed. Meanwhile the manifesto of the Sultan calling for a Holy War was received in St. Petersburg and construed as being directed essentially against Russia. Indeed, Russia was mentioned specifically as Turkey's main enemy in inciting the Greeks to rebellion. The refusal to fulfil the Convention of Akkerman, the closing of the Straits to Russian ships and the persecution of Russian merchants in Turkey followed in rapid succession. On February 26, Nesselrode sent to Lieven a circular note to be brought to the attention of the British as well as the other governments, outlining Russia's position. The hostile acts of Turkey specifically directed against Russia, it declared, forced Russia to have recourse to arms. In so doing, she did not wish any territorial conquests or the destruction of the Turkish Empire but merely the execution of the Protocol of April 4 and the Treaty of London. She would fight until she attained this aim but being left to herself in the coming war she would consult only her own interests as to the means of gaining her ends. War was declared on April 26. England decided that this was the end of the alliance and her Mediterranean squadron was reinforced. French diplomacy was busy trying to patch up the breach in the alliance and made a démarche in London pointing out that England could not oppose the advance of the Russians in time to save Turkey. England therefore decided that the best course was to maintain in existence the Treaty of London and thus have a restraining hold over Russia.

---

[8] Driault et L'heritier, op. cit., Vol. I, p. 404.

[9] Mowat, Robert Balmain, History of European Diplomacy 1815-1914, London 1927, p. 50.

III

However much Russian diplomacy may have been acting on behalf of the Balkan Christians, the concern which Russia showed over their fate was purely indirect because it did not affect her vital interests. Not so the question of the Straits. The importance of these "keys" to the back door of Russia was a growing issue as the Russian seaboard on the Black Sea was acquiring an increasing importance as the main outlet for Russia's agricultural and, later, industrial production. It has been rightly said that the question of the Bosphorus and Dardanelles was as far as Russia's direct interests were concerned, the whole Eastern question: "For Russia the whole famous Eastern Question may be summed up in these words: To which authority are the Straits of the Bosphorus and the Dardanelles subjected to? Who possesses this authority?"[10] But by its very nature, since Turkey and not Russia was in control of the Straits, the problem became one of Turkey's power as an independent nation. It was in Russia's interests that Turkey should not become too strong militarily and thus be a danger to Russia and not too weak and thus become the prey of some other powerful state.

With the treaty of alliance signed in December 1798 between Russia and Turkey against France, Russian warships were for the first time allowed to pass the Straits on their way from the Black Sea to the Ionian islands. Under the clauses of this alliance Russia was to co-operate with the Turkish fleet by sending a squadron of 12 warships through the Straits. Conversely under Article 9 of the treaty no vessels of other countries were to be allowed to pass the Straits. In 1804 the Russian Ambassador in Constantinople, Italinsky, was instructed to negotiate a renewal of the alliance along the following lines: Turkey was not to co-operate with France, but ally herself with England and Russia for the purpose of blocking Napoleon's ambitions in the Eastern Mediterranean and the Balkans. The Russian navy and supply ships proceeding toward the Ionian islands were to be given free passage of the Straits whereas any attempt by other powers (presumably France) to enter the Black Sea would be repulsed by the joint action of Russia and Turkey. This treaty was duly signed on September 23, 1805, valid for 9 years. But the impression produced by the victory of Napoleon at Austerlitz coupled with the pressure brought in Constantinople by French diplomacy resulted in a change of front and the Turks began preparing for war with Russia by re-arming the forts on the Dniestr and the Danube. Under these circumstances the Reiss Effendi, Vasiff Effendi, asked the Russian Ambassador to discontinue the passage

---

[10] Goriainow, S. M., Le Bosphore et les Dardanelles, Paris 1910, p. 1.

of Russian vessels through the Straits, explaining that he was doing this out of fear of France, and in a note sent on April 26, 1806, the Porte argued that Article IV of the treaty of 1805 concerning the passage of Russian vessels was applicable only in case of a joint defensive war whereas Russia was conducting an offensive campaign against France in which Turkey was not involved. But two months later in June the Russian brig Jason arrived at Constantinople en route to Corfu and was followed a month later by the Russian frigate Kildum. Both vessels forced their way into the Mediterranean notwithstanding Turkish protests, and Ambassador Italinsky declared firmly that Russian warships would continue to do so whenever the necessity occurred. The Turks recoiled before this firm attitude and reiterated their friendly feeling for Russia placing the blame on France for their previous refusal. Italinsky received instructions to obtain the maintenance of the treaty or to ask for his passports and this issue together with the question of the Roumanian Hospodars brought on the war. Indeed, the Turks gave in with regard to the reinstatement of the Hospodars Muruzi and Ypsilanti but under advice from France refused to maintain the treaty of 1805. On December 23, 1806, the Porte ordered Italinsky to leave Constantinople within three days and the latter embarked for Malta on an English vessel and on December 27, Turkey declared war on Russia. In the armistice which followed the Treaty of Tilsit and the conclusion of the Franco-Russian alliance, Russia did not raise the issue of the Straits as the treaty of 1805 had been directed against France, now friendly with Russia. But Turkey signed a treaty in January 1809 with England in which the closing of the Straits was expressly stipulated. With the approach of Napoleon's invasion of Russia in 1812, Russia was not only anxious to terminate the war with Turkey but also to obtain an alliance with the Turks. Accordingly in a gesture of conciliation no mention of the Straits question was made in the treaty of peace, but the negotiations for an alliance carried on by Italinsky led to no results and the Straits question remained indefinite until the Russo-Turkish war of 1828-1829 opened the issue once more.

At the turn of the century and greatly as a result of defeat sustained in the wars against Russia, the Ottoman Empire had fallen upon evil days. The authority of the Sultan was challenged in many provinces by open rebellion or by the ambition of local governors; venality and corruption made for petty tyranny and as the annual appointment of Pashas and governors of provinces was dependent upon bribes, the Pashas virtually mortgaged their provinces to the rich Greek bankers of the Phanar in Constantinople. Not receiving any revenues from these virtually independent provinces, the government in Constantinople could not maintain an efficient military force and depended upon such medieval levies as the Janissaries of which there were 150,000 and mercenary troops, the Kaprikuli. Except for a force of artillery men, the "Topadjis" and the Sultan's guard, the "Bostadjis," the army was composed of provincial militias badly armed and called only in the event of hostilities. The Janissaries, once formidable soldiers, had now acquired a sinister reputation for lack of discipline, graft, and cruelty. They had neither modern armament, discipline nor drill and their methods of warfare were most primitive, every soldier being paid a bonus for each enemy head he could bring into camp.[11] Sultan Selim III made a brave effort to modernize the country and, following the example of Peter the Great of Russia, he started with the army. A renegade Turk, Omar Aga, who had served as lieutenant in the Russian army was commissioned to train some infantry in the Russian drill "to see how the infidels fought battles."[12] Very pleased with the results Selim attempted to impose these methods upon the rest of his forces and, Napoleon having now sent instructors, French methods of warfare replaced the Russian methods. But attempts to modernize the Janissaries led to a formidable insurrection and to the revolution of Constantinople in 1807 which cost Selim his life. However, Selim's successor Mahmoud II proved to be one of the ablest and most energetic Sultans in Turkish history and he vigorously pursued the course set by Selim. Against formidable obstacles including the Serbian and Greek Revolutions he rebuilt the might of Turkey and in 1826 by a wholesale massacre got rid of the unruly Janissaries, the greatest menace to his authority. It was with this resurgent Turkey under a strong and progressive ruler that Russia had to contend in the coming war.

---

[11]Creasy, Sir Edward S., History of the Ottoman Turks, New York, 1877, p. 455.

[12]Creasy, op. cit., p. 459.

CHAPTER II

RUSSO-TURKISH WAR 1828-29

I

The new Turkish army built up by Sultan Mahmoud II was to prove itself a very formidable opponent in the coming war. It had all the courage and fighting ability which had made the Turks such a terror to Christendom in the past and it had gained, in addition, discipline and the knowledge of modern warfare. Opposing this army and designed for action in the Balkans was the Russian 2nd Army composed of 113,920 men with 384 guns.[1] The plan of campaign worked out by the Russian General Staff was to co-ordinate the operations of the army with those of the Black Sea Fleet. As the fleet had an unquestionable control over the sea its task was twofold: (1) to protect the left flank of the advancing army and (2) to bring up supplies to the coast, thereby eliminating the necessity of hauling them over the bad roads of Moldavia. But to obtain this co-operation the army had to advance as closely to the sea-coast as possible.

The military operations started on May 7, 1828, with the crossing of the river Pruth by the 6th and 7th Corps. Bucharest, Jassy, Galatz and Craiova were occupied without firing a shot and the 7th Corps invested the important Turkish fortress of Braila on the Danube. At the same time Count Pahlen took over the civil administration of both Principalities. The next important task ahead was the crossing of the Danube. In pursuance of the plan of following the sea-coast, the point selected was opposite the Turkish fort of Isakcha near the delta of the Danube. Accordingly, the 3rd Corps under General Rudzevich was concentrated in Bessarabia around Bolgrad. However, the spring floods made the lower Danube impassable and delayed the operations for a whole month. To gain time it was decided to attempt to cross further up stream opposite

---

[1] Polievktov, M., Imperator Nikolai, Moscow, p. 105. Official report of the Ministry of War.

RUSSO-TURKISH WAR 1828-29

Turtukai but the scheme was abandoned owing to the difficulties of the task as well as the undesirability of transferring the line of communications of the army to the interior of Bulgaria. On May 19, the Czar arrived at Braila where he inspected the troops before proceeding to witness the operations of forcing the Danube. His arrival coincided with an important historical event. When the independent Cossack Republic of Zaporog Setch on the Dnieper had been destroyed by Catherine the Great, several thousand Cossacks had moved into Turkey where they had been given privileges and special rights by the Sultans and had established a new Setch. Now on May 24, as a result of tactful negotiations conducted by General Tuchkov, Military Commandant of Ismail, the Cossacks decided to return to Russia. The Koshevoi (hetman) Gladky, all the subordinate hetmans and essauls (officers) and 1,000 Cossacks arrived on boats down the Danube bringing with them their standards and insignia. They were interned in quarantine camps in Ismail and Kilia, after which they were enrolled in the army. Later Nicholas I showed remarkable insight and courage when, during the operations of the crossing of the Danube, he went to inspect the Turkish works on the other side of the river in a boat manned by the Hetman Gladky and a crew of his Cossacks. They had been bitter enemies of Russia and might easily have captured the Czar or rowed him under Turkish guns, but instead, flattered by the confidence shown them they remained thoroughly loyal.

On June 8 the Russian 3rd Corps forced its way across the Danube and defeated a force of 10,000 Turks holding the opposite bank. The Russians lost 112 men in the operation. Three days later the Turks surrendered the fortress of Isakcha thus permitting the Russians to gain a foothold on the right bank. The fall of Isakcha gave the Russians 85 guns, 18 colours and an immense amount of war material. Moltke, speaking of this crossing, says that conditions were such as to make the forcing of the river at this point impossible, since a causeway had to be built on this left bank to approach the river and this causeway was under the direct fire of the heavy guns of Isakcha, whereas on the heights beyond the river a powerful Turkish corps occupied a strong defensive position. But 10,000 Turks offered no resistance to a handful of Cossacks and infantry who forced their way across the river on boats and made it possible for the pontoon bridge to be thrown across.

Meanwhile, however, the force besieging Braila sustained a heavy reverse on June 3 and lost 3,000 men in an unsuccessful assault. Braila surrendered, nevertheless, on June 19, releasing much needed forces, while the other Turkish forts of Hirsov, Kustendji and Tulcha capitulated in turn during the following two weeks. But under the terms of the capitulation the garrisons of these fortresses were permitted to rejoin the Turkish field army. Thus the garrison of Braila alone had increased the latter by 17,000 men. However, the main result had been achieved, the bank of the Danube had been cleared of the enemy except for the important fortress of Silistria, commanding the middle course of the river, which remained in Turkish hands. The fall of Kustendji, in particular, permitted the use of this important harbour on the Black Sea for supplying the army. The main advantage gained by the fall of Braila was the releasing of the 7th Corps for further operations. Already at this stage it became woefully clear that the Russians had not put enough men into the field and subsequent events were to prove this. However, as Moltke says, "Up to this time the Russians had been successful in all their undertakings. They had forced an almost impossible passage over the Danube and in six weeks they had taken six Turkish fortresses. The belief that it was impossible to resist their arms preceded them and was sure to have an incalculable influence on adversaries like the Turks, provided this prestige was not destroyed by subsequent engagements."[2]

After crossing the Danube the main Russian Army composed of 40,000 men with 194 guns [3] started to advance into Bulgaria along the line Silistria-Kustendji. Silistria, being not yet taken, could not be safely left in the rear and hence the 6th Corps was sent to besiege it. The delay caused by the coming up of the 7th Corps from Braila made the army lose a precious week and the advance started only on July 7. After the first serious engagement in the field the Turks were driven back and the Russians occupied Bazardjik. However, at this point so many detachments had to be made that by the middle of July the advancing army had been reduced to some 24,000 men at Bazardjik and an advance-guard of 6,000 men at Kosludja. The rest of the forces had to be employed to garrison Wallachia, escort the Danube flotilla and guard the lines of communication. Silistria required another 10,750 men whereas there were 5,000 men observing the fortress of Varna on the Black Sea coast. An attempt to capture Varna with merely 2,500 men had failed, the place being defended by a garrison of 12,000 to 15,000 Turks. This blocked the best road across the Balkans. There remained two other roads, one from Shumla and the other from Pravadi. Accordingly, a force under General

---

[2]Moltke, Baron von. The Russians in Bulgaria and Rumelia in 1828 and 1829, London, 1854, p. 105.

[3]68 battalions, 52 squadrons, 4 regiments of Cossacks. See Moltke, op. cit., p. 109.

Benckendorff was detached to secure Pravadi. The Turks on the other hand had assembled their army at Shumla. Consequently the main Russian army marched toward Shumla. The insufficiency of numbers became so pronounced that the Guards Corps from St. Petersburg as well as the 2nd Corps were ordered to move up from Russia, but these forces could not arrive until the end of August or the beginning of September. Meanwhile, the two separate detachments before Varna and Pravadi were too weak to attempt the capture of these places. The main body, now 30,000 strong and led by the Emperor himself, after an indecisive engagement with the enemy at Yenibazar on July 20, advanced toward Shumla.

Pending the arrival of reinforcements from Russia the war resolved itself into a series of sieges of which the most important and the most costly was to be the siege of Shumla. Lying in a gorge walled in by precipitous mountains, Shumla was inaccessible except from one side which was protected by powerful lines of fortifications and defended by a Turkish army 40,000 strong under Hussein Pasha. Moreover, the routes leading toward the rear from which the Turks could get reinforcements in men and ammunition were by the nature of the mountainous country, beyond the reach of the Russians. Under these circumstances there was no possibility of attempting an assault on this strong place with an army so inferior in numbers to the defending force. Hence the Russians invested it as closely as they could and entrenched themselves in front of the enemy lines by erecting a line of redoubts. For a while both sides indulged in occassional attacks, feeling each other out, and the Russians made attempts to extend their lines on their left flank toward Rasgrad so as to close that approach to Shumla. This meant a dangerous scattering of their forces further weakened by the necessity of sending reinforcements to Varna. The Turks, aware of the numerical weakness of the enemy, decided upon a bold coup and on August 27, after capturing one of the Russian forts by a night attack, fell upon the 7th Corps now under the command of Prince Eugene of Württemberg. This corps had been so scattered and so reduced by detachments that Prince Eugene, at his head-quarters at Marash, had merely 3,800 men under his orders. However, though faced with compact masses of charging Turks, he succeeded in beating them back but was too weak to pursue them. Presently another Turkish column 15,000 strong came down a side valley to menace the Russian hospitals and rear institutions at Marash. Once more the Russians beat the Turks back but these attacks revealed the danger of the Russian position. Moreover, with temperatures on the plateau reaching 120 F at noon and the troops living merely on biscuits and beef spoiled through long transportation, disease set in which further reduced the army. The loss in horses was such that two thirds of the cavalry had to be dismounted. This gave the

Turkish cavalry, which was suffering no such hardships in its enclosed camp, the opportunity of making, without punishment, deep foraging expeditions into the Russian rear. On September 8, the Turks, after having received important reinforcements, once more attacked the Russian positions. The attack was repulsed with great loss on both sides. Thus the siege dragged on and, in Moltke's words, "Putting all these circumstances together, there can be no doubt that the Russian Army was in a most critical position during the whole of the months of August and September and that had the Turkish generals shown greater activity, and had their troops been more to be depended on, the results of the campaign would have been disastrous to the Russians."[4]

The turn of the tide came with the fall of Varna in October. This fortress was particularly important because it commanded the road to the Balkans and because through its harbour the fleet could supply the army and bring up reinforcements hastily. It had powerful defences and an enceinte consisting of an earthen wall defended by 10 bastions with an artillery of 162 guns and held by a garrison of 15,000 men. Against these forces the Russians had first 2,500 men, then 5,000 and finally by reinforcements brought up from the army before Shumla and from Anapa by way of the sea, 9,000 men.[5] The Black Sea Fleet under Admiral Greig, consisting of 8 ships-of-line, 5 frigates, cutters and gunboats, reached Varna at the beginning of August bringing with it a brigade of infantry. It cruised 7 miles off the coast. Throughout the next two months the Russians methodically approached the fortress with their works and by August 18, were able to open the first parallel at a distance of 300 paces from the enemy's lines.

In September the long delayed reinforcements arrived from Russia composed of two divisions of the Guards Infantry and one of Guards Cavalry and thus the besieging force was brought to about 20,000 men (34 battalions and 28 squadrons). The Czar himself arrived before the fortress, remaining on board the "Parizh" cruising off coast. By this time the Russian batteries had succeeded in silencing the fire of 4 bastions. But the Russians were weakened by dividing their forces in an attempt to surround the south side of the fortress. 5,000 men were sent to occupy a precarious position between the Turkish garrison on the fortress and the reinforcements which the Turks had gathered in the hills to the south. Meanwhile the Russians started laying mines which blew up great portions of Turkish defences. The Turks held on to their crumbling defences

---

[4] Moltke, op. cit., p. 137.

[5] 18 battalions, 29 squadrons, see Moltke, op. cit.

with obstinate courage and just as the Russians started a series of general assaults to capture the weakened remaining bastions, a new danger arose in the approach of a Turkish relieving army of 25,000 to 30,000 strong under Omar Vrione. A weak Russian detachment sent to reconnoitre this approaching enemy stumbled against it in a forest and lost 700 men out of 1,500 including its commander, General Harting. In these circumstances a corps 6,000 strong under General Bistrom was sent to block the enemy's approach and troops were collected hastily from wherever available. At Kurt Tepe the two forces clashed in one of the bloodiest battles of the war. On September 30, the Chief of Staff, General Diebitch, arrived from the Emperor's Headquarters with the order for the little force to attack immediately even though the enemy far outnumbered it. But as there was no position for the artillery, and the mountainous country made the use of cavalry impractical, the infantry attacked unsupported, the Azov regiment distinguishing itself by boldly charging the Turkish force alone. After a fierce hand to hand struggle, the Russians were unable to enter the Turkish camp and the Turks, realizing the smallness of the enemy forces, counter attacked. The engagement came to an end by the Russians falling back to a plateau nearby and the Turks remaining in their camp. The Russians had lost 1,400 men including the commander and two generals. "The action at Kurt Tepe was one of the most brilliant of the campaign although the attack failed, the moral effect which the courage of the Russian troops produced upon the Turks did much toward bringing the campaign to a successful issue".[6]

The most important result of the battle of Kurt Tepe was, that although Omar Vrione was close enough to Varna to hear the explosion of Russian mines and might easily have brushed aside the remaining forces which were obstructing his way, he did not venture any further. He remained in his camp and left Varna to its fate. Meanwhile, in Varna, the Russian infantry kept storming the separate works, while the Guards Sappers blasted them with mines, reached down into them with saps and fought hand to hand struggles in the darkness of underground mine tunnels. The result was that by the first week of October the whole front of the Turkish works had crumbled in ruins leaving the way open to the city. For 14 days the relieving Turkish army remained at a distance of merely 5 miles from the city not venturing further. The defenders of Varna became completely demoralized and finally on October 10 the commander of the fortress, Yussuf Pasha, surrendered it to the Russians. The place had resisted 89 days after the first investment, 70 days after the beginning of the siege and 27 days

---

[6]Moltke, op. cit., p. 203.

after the first breach in its fortifications.[7] The garrison and the besieging army at the end of the siege were brought to about the same size, 20,000 men, though the Russians had merely 65 guns as against the Turkish 162. The Russians fired 50,000 shells in all, lost 5,000 to 6,000 men and took 7,000 prisoners.[8] They not only fought an equal force entrenched behind most powerful fortifications but in addition warded off the attack of the relieving army of 30,000 men. Thus the siege of Varna remains one of the spectacular achievements of the Russian Army.

As for the third siege, that of Silistria, it was by contrast most ineffectual. Defended by a garrison of 22,000 men according to Russian sources, a figure which Moltke considers exaggerated,[9] it was at first opposed by 10,000 Russians. With the arrival of the 2nd Corps the besieging force was increased to some 30,000 men. Notwithstanding the undoubted superiority of the Russians in numbers, with the exception of a few sharp encounters, nothing effective was done, partly through lack of siege artillery and partly through the heavy toll of disease in the Russian ranks, 500 cases of cholera being reported there in one day. After two months of investment the trenches were flooded by heavy rains followed by snow. Accordingly, after two days of ineffective bombardment of the fortress, on November 10 the siege was raised and the troops put into winter quarters. There remained Shumla where the besieging force was reduced through detachments and disease to 10,000 men, a wholly inadequate figure for such a task.

There were further some military operations in Wallachia, garrisoned by Russian troops, where flying columns of Turks engaged in marauding expeditions. A Turkish army 26,000 strong, chiefly cavalry and 30 guns, working its way out of the fortress of Viddin, on September 26 fell upon a Russian column 4,500 strong with 14 guns under General Geismar. The latter, fearing for his communications, decided to attack at once, notwithstanding the disparity of numbers, and routed the enemy completely. The Turkish camp with several hundred wagons of provisions, 24 standards and the Vizier's correspondance was captured and the Turks fled in disorder across the Danube. This victory put an end to serious fighting in Wallachia, and with the approach of winter the first campaign of the war came to an end.

Except for desultory fighting at Shumla and the capture of a

---

[7] Moltke, op. cit., p. 216.
[8] Moltke, op. cit., p. 217.
[9] Moltke, op. cit., p. 20.

small fort and a bridgehead on the Danube at Nicopolis, all military activities ceased. The Russian General Head-quarters were moved back to Jassy, the Guards Corps went to Bessarabia and the 2nd and 3rd Corps wintered in Wallachia and Moldavia. The 6th and 7th Corps remained around Varna holding the line of the Balkans. Summing up the results of the campaign we find as positive results the clearing of Moldavia of all Turkish troops and the capture of 7 Turkish fortresses, of which two (Braila and Varna) were first class fortresses. However, Silistria still remained in Turkish hands, a dangerous wedge into the Russian positions scattered on both sides of the lower Danube, and Shumla was still resisting. Before both these forts the Russians had been defeated and the operations before Silistria call for the greatest criticism, Moltke calling the siege "an ill planned, feebly executed, and wholly unsuccessful attempt."[10] "It is possible", he adds, "that more accurate information might explain and justify much that seems like want of vigour, a fault of which we do not find the Russians guilty on any other occasion during this campaign."[11] In general he has a high opinion of the conduct of the Russian troops as shown in this campaign though he considers, "the preparations were insufficient, the campaign began too late, and the direction of the main army was not likely to ensure a successful result. But all these faults were atoned for by the innate excellence of the Russian troops. The self-sacrificing obedience of the commanders, the steadiness of the common soldiers, their power of endurance and unshaken bravery, were the qualities that enabled them to avert the dangers of their position before Shumla and hold the Seraskier, (Commander-in-Chief of the Turkish Army) in check, to make up for all deficiencies and overcome all resistance at Varna; and to strike such terror into Omar Vrione that even after defeating the Russians he remained 10 days in his camp..... while Varna, the bulwark of the kingdom, fell before his eyes."[12] But he continues, "If we consider the enormous sacrifices that the war cost the Russians in the year 1828 it is difficult to say whether they or the Turks won or lost it."[13]

The Turks were by no means disheartened. They had held out against a very much more powerful foe, and the mountainous Balkans with its forests and rocks offered advantages for the undisciplined but impetuous Turkish irregulars, accustomed to such country,

---

[10] Moltke, op. cit., p. 229.
[11] Moltke, op. cit., p. 232.
[12] Moltke, op. cit., p. 257.
[13] Moltke, op. cit., p. 288.

over the European tactics of more disciplined troops. Moreover all European military experts agreed that the Balkan range could not be crossed by a modern army. On the diplomatic front the Turks were secretly encouraged to further resistance both by Britain and Austria. It is true that the obstinate refusal of the Sultan to accede to the Treaty of London of 1827 with regard to Greece, which the British and French insisted upon, hindered any effective aid from Great Britain. Furthermore, the Russian fleet was there to make the approach of any British squadron very difficult. Indeed, the Russians had full control of the Black Sea with their 11 ships-of-line, 8 frigates and 12 corvettes and brigs of war totaling 1,800 guns.[14] Furthermore, on the Mediterranean side, Admiral Heyden, fresh from Navarino, cruised off the Dardanelles with 8 ships-of-line, 7 frigates and 20 small vessels, totaling 1,500 guns. To these forces the Turks could oppose 8 ships-of-line, 2 frigates, 5 corvettes and 3 brigs with 1,000 guns. The hope that Mehemet Ali's Egyptian fleet or Admiral Malcolm's British squadron would come to the aid of the Turkish fleet never materialized. Nevertheless, the Turks felt reasonably secure and believed that the campaign of 1828 had exhausted Russia.

During the winter both sides reorganized their forces. With a new Commander-in-Chief, Reshid Mohammed Pasha, and replacements brought up from Asia, by the spring of 1829 the Turkish Army was about in the same condition as at the beginning of the war.

On the Russian side General Diebitch, the former Chief-of-Staff, replaced the old and ineffectual Count Wittgenstein in supreme command. Diebitch was energetic and able; moreover after the Emperor and his court returned to Russia, the army gained by the absence of court intrigues and by the establishment of a single command. However the army was not increased, it was even reduced. The Guards were recalled to Russia and did not participate further in the military operations. Paradoxically, it was during the months of winter inactivity that the army suffered its greatest losses. The country had been so thoroughly ravaged by both armies that the food supplies had to be brought up from Russia. The overcrowding of winter quarters and the change in the climate from extreme heat to extreme cold were contributing causes for waves of epidemics: bubonic plague, cholera, dissentery and scurvy took a toll estimated at 40,000 men or approximately half the army. During the 10 months from May 1828 to February 1829 the hospitals took care of 210,108 cases of which 134,882 were serious, this high figure being accounted for by the fact that the men were sick several times in succession and on an average every man in the army was hospitalized

---

[14] Moltke, op. cit., p. 256.

twice during this period.[15] Diebitch laboured energetically to reorganize the army; he remounted the cavalry, organized the commissariat and with replacements, brought up the effectives for the spring campaign of 1829 to 68,000 men with increased artillery and light cavalry (48,000 infantry, 16,000 cavalry and 300 guns).

The next task lying ahead for the army was the crossing of the Balkans and as thus far the army had been supplied by sea it became imperative to secure a harbour on the Bulgarian coast south of the Balkan range. The little port of Sizeboli, not far from Burgas, possessing one of the finest harbours on the coast was selected. In February a Russian squadron under Vice-Admiral Kumani, with a regiment of infantry on board suddenly attacked the city and took possession of it. Infuriated, the Sultan ordered the recapture of the port and after much delay a Turkish force of 4,000 infantry and 1,500 cavalry attacked the Russian entrenchments held by 3,000 men and two field guns under General Wachten. Notwithstanding the fierceness of the Turkish onslaught, the Turks were driven back and the Russians kept Sizeboli. Next the Turkish Fleet composed of 6 ships-of-line, 3 frigates, 5 corvettes and 3 brigs set out to sea. So unexpected was the appearance of Turkish vessels that the Russian ship-of-line Raphael and the brig Merkurii, meeting the fleet during the night, thought it to be Russian and joined it. Great was the surprise of the Turks next morning to find two more vessels in their columns. Upon discovery of their plight, the Raphael surrendered, but the commander of the Merkurii ordered the flag nailed to the mast and taking an oath from his men that the vessel would be blown up rather than surrendered he made a dash and escaped. The Turkish Fleet appeared before Sizeboli, cruised at large but did not attack the Russian squadron in port and finally sailed away. This was its last cruise for Admiral Greig blockaded the Bosphorus while Admiral Heyden closed the Dardanelles and the Turkish fleet remained blocked till the end of the war.

II

The campaign of 1829 opened in May and lasted 4 months. Before the army could think of an advance it was imperative to neutralize Silistria where a powerful Turkish garrison was assembled right on the flank of the Russian lines of communication at a distance of merely two day's march. Accordingly, whereas the troops wintering in Wallachia crossed the Danube and joined the 6th and 7th Corps which were centered at Varna, General Diebitch himself advanced from the crossing at Czernavoda with portion of the 2nd and

---

[15] Moltke, op. cit., p. 466.

3rd Corps against Silistria, and 96 guns were brought up as well as material for the siege which was sent up-stream by boats. Furthermore 11 vessels of the river flotilla were moored below and 5 above the fortress so as to cut it off completely by water. This time the siege was conducted systematically and vigorously. First the Turks had to be driven out of the Russian trenches which had been left undestroyed the preceeding year and this was done by a strong Russian attack on May 17 which cost the Turks 800 and the Russians 240 men. Though the Turks, 15,000 strong, showed great courage in the defence of the fortress and made frequent sorties to hinder the enemy, the Russians advanced their works speedily under the protection of batteries established on both sides of the river. Early in June the parallels were laid from which saps and mine galleries were pushed forward. As at Varna, mines were used extensively and demoralized the Turks who finally, after the failure of a last counter-attack, surrendered the fortress on June 26. The Russians took 9,000 prisoners, 261 pieces of artillery of which 31 guns were mounted on gunboats, and 40 standards. Meanwhile on June 5 Diebitch, alarmed by the movements of the enemy, had left Silistria and marched with the 2nd Corps leaving 8,000 men to complete the capture of the crumbling fortress. The Russian losses at Silistria amounted to 115 officers and 2,566 men killed and wounded.

The reason why General Diebitch so hurriedly left Silistria with the 2nd Corps leaving the siege operations to be conducted by General Krassovsky, was that powerful Turkish field forces had started operations endangering the position of the 6th and 7th Corps. Indeed the new Turkish Commander-in-Chief, Reshid Mohammed Pasha, had restored the fighting ability of the Turkish units at Shumla, opened new communications, reorganized the commissariat and tightened the discipline of the troops. A Turkish corps was being organized at the same time at Rustchuk under Hussein Pasha and the plan was to get these two forces to operate jointly; thus a total of 60,000 men could fall upon the Russians who were scattered in Bulgaria. The 6th and 7th Corps separated by the Danube from the rest of the army, had been so weakened by disease and detachments that together they could put into the field only some 12,000 to 14,000 men against the Turkish 60,000.

The Turks started their advance from Shumla on May 10 with a corps some 20,000 strong and advanced in two columns, one marching upon Pravadi and the other through Jenibazar to cut the Russians off from the Danube. Opposing the column marching on Pravadi were only 3,000 Russians. General Roth, commanding the 6th Corps hastened to send reinforcements but before these had arrived the Russians had repelled a Turkish attack of some 10,000 men. This success made General Roth send a force of 4 battalions and 6 guns against the retreating enemy, later supported by one regiment of infantry and another battalion. This pursuing column however found itself trapped in a narrow mountain gorge surrounded by Turks in such numbers that practically the whole force was cut down except for two battalions in reserve which were rescued by a bold counter attack.

The column marching on Jenibazar stormed the town in vain and fell back. With Russian reinforcements coming up by forced marches to the aid of the hard pressed troops, the Grand Vizier thought it prudent to fall back to Shumla, well contented with the results of his raid. The Russians had lost over 1,000 killed which represented one seventh of the forces at hand. Meanwhile, Hussein Pasha started his advance from Rustchuk and marched upon Razgrad. Covering Razgrad was one division of infantry and a few cavalry units under General Kreutz, who succeeded nevertheless in dispersing the enemy. However the Vizier, hearing of Hussein's advance, started a new offensive from Shumla against General Roth, this time with 40,000 men (May 28). It was upon receiving intelligence of this advance that Diebitch, taking with him whatever troops he could spare, marched to the aid of the 6th and 7th Corps. He sent 4 battalions and 16 squadrons of the 3rd Corps to strengthen the forces holding Pravadi and himself marched with the 2nd Corps to a junction with General Roth with the intention of subsequently marching upon Shumla. The Russians had now 21,000 infantry and 7,000 cavalry against 40,000 Turks but these forces were scattered over a curved front 25 miles long.

With the detachment at Pravadi Diebitch had all told 31,000 men and 146 guns on the right bank of the Danube. He deemed this army sufficient to cope with the Turks and was prepared to meet them in a decisive engagement. But owing to the extreme heat the movements of the Russians had been very slow and though Diebitch had started his march on June 5 from Silistria, five days later his forces were still scattered whereas the Grand Vizier had encamped on a plateau in the center of the curve of the Russian line and at an equal distance from both Shumla and Pravadi. He thus was three or four times stronger than any single sector of the Russian army, the nearest force being the 12,000 men of the 6th and 7th Corps; and any attempt of the separate columns to join each other involved perilous marches over mountain passes with their flanks exposed to a Turkish attack.

As the 2nd Corps came up from Silistria it advanced toward Jenibazar while General Roth with the 6th and 7th Corps, leaving his fires burning in camp, executed a perilous flank movement to converge with the 2nd Corps which in turn veered to the left to come closer to Pravadi. These night movements made in complete silence and under cover of fog passed unobserved by the Turks. With his army thus in hand, Diebitch on June 11 had placed himself in a position to bar the Turkish retreat to Shumla on the three roads available for the Grand Vizier to reach his base; this made a battle inevitable and it was fought the same day at Kulevtcha. It involved an attack on a high rocky ledge and in narrow mountain valleys which by their nature tended to separate the Russian column. The Russian advance-guard under General Ostroshenko, finding itself in a narrow gorge a mile ahead of its corps, was fallen upon by the Turks and almost annihilated; but when the main body of the 2nd Corps came up and the Russian attacks began developing, the Turks lost courage, were seized with panic and ran away. The battle was over before even the 6th and 7th Corps were engaged. The Russians lost 2 generals, 261 officers, 1,500 men killed and 1,000 men wounded but the Turkish army was completely dispersed. The Grand Vizier fled to Shumla by a circuitous route followed by only 600 cavalry and during the next two weeks disorganized remnants of his army trickled through into Shumla by various routes.

This battle, so easily won, opened the way over the Balkans. But the undertaking was a foolhardy one; for as we have seen, foreign experts declared the Balkans could not be crossed by a modern army. In modern times the range had been crossed only once before in the XVth century by the Hungarian hero Hunyadi. Moreover Shumla remained in Turkish hands and with the Turkish troops being reorganized there they could menace both the flank and the rear of the army while it was engaged over the mountain passes. Further the necessity of detaching 10,000 men to observe Shumla would leave only 15,000 to 20,000 men for the crossing. There was also a menace that Hussein's army at Rustchuk might advance on Silistria where the beseiging force had been greatly reduced and, finally, the troops were exhausted. For these reasons Diebitch decided to await the fall of Silistria which would permit him to bring up the portion of the 3rd Corps left there under General Krassovsky as much needed reinforcements. Meanwhile to gain time negotiations for a truce were begun. At the same time the Russian Army was manoeuvred into position preparatory for an advance over the Balkans or for quick aid to be given to Silistria if necessary, and Shumla was invested. Thus, except for small foraging movements and occasional engagements at the outposts, there was a lull of 4 weeks in the operations. As for the truce, without refusing to negotiate it, the Turks adopted dilatory tactics and left things open. Meanwhile the fall of Silistria released General Krassovsky who came up to Shumla with the 3rd Corps and was left there to observe it. The other forces were to cross the Balkans as follows: the 6th Corps was to follow the road from Varna to Burgas, the 7th Corps the road from Pravadi to Aidos and the 2nd Corps was to follow with the Headquarters and act as general reserve for both columns.

Before setting out on this perilous expedition a religious service was held for the whole army. Ahead lay 100 miles of difficult mountain roads, little more than trails. The Balkans slope gently on the northern side but fall in abrupt cliffs on the southern side. From 4,000 to 5,000 feet the mountains rise to 6,000 feet as they approach the coast. It was therefore not so much their height as a cumulation of other obstacles which made their passage difficult. The road from Varna to Burgas, after crossing two streams at which point the Turks had erected forts, reaches the summit by a gradual ascent and traverses "an almost impenetrable forest..... the forest everywhere so thick, that it would be impossible for troops to fall into order and the roads form continuous defiles."[16] It further "traverses the deep valley of the Kosaakderch, besides several smaller dells which are very troublesome to cross especially in wet weather."[17] The road from Pravadi to Aidos passes through a very narrow defile with points of rocks jutting out and forming natural forts and both the Pravadi and Kadishoi rivers present difficult crossings. There follows a narrow gorge where one can only advance single file for 15 miles and the valley narrows to a point only 50 paces wide between two perpendicular walls of rock. An alternate route crosses the Kamtchik river but after that rises very steeply and can easily be blocked. The two roads meet on a wide plateau at the summit between two "rocky hollows" which can easily be fortified. The descent is abrupt.

The army took 9 days to cross the Balkans. Marching as we have seen on two parallel roads, the 6th and 7th Corps met a determined stand of the enemy, as might have been expected, at the crossing of the Kamtchik. But the Turkish columns were routed and the Russians pushed on. The main difficulty was less the resistance of the Turks than the condition of the road which had to be cut through the thicket with axes. The wagons of the train had to be dragged by hand by working parties of infantry in a heat which late in the evening showed 82F and then the weather changing, the thermometer suddenly fell to 54F. As the Russians were making their way over the crest, descending toward the sea, they met the opposition of a Turkish division 7,000 strong. This force was put to flight leaving behind 2 guns, 9 standards and 800 prisoners. The remnants locked themselves up in the fortress of Missivri which was invested and forced to surrender, giving the Russians 2,000 prisoners, 10 colours and 12 guns. The Russians, as they approached the sea, were cheered to see Admiral Greig's squadron lying in the bay of Burgas. While General Roth had thus reached

---

[16] Moltke, op. cit., p. 52.
[17] Moltke, op. cit., p. 52.

his destination, General Rudiger, commanding the 7th Corps, decided to abandon the march toward Aidos in order to avoid passing through the narrow gorge already mentioned in which his corps might be easily trapped. Accordingly, he made for Burgas where he rejoined the 6th Corps. The 2nd Corps and the Head-quarters having come up the next day, the whole army was now assembled and Diebitch had 25,000 men and 96 guns with which to carry out the invasion of Turkey proper. Meanwhile, with the exception of small detachments 3,000-7,000 strong, which attempted to oppose the Russians, the bulk of the Turkish army remained inactive at Shumla. Apparently believing that the Balkans were impassable, Reshid Pasha had decided that the Russian movements were directed against Shumla and kept his army there.

From Burgas, following the coast, the army reached the city of Aidos where some 10,000 Turks were concentrated. The city was taken by an attack of the vanguard and the Turks fled in disorder leaving a great quantity of military stores. The road to Adrianople was now open. In the meanwhile the Russians met a friendlier welcome from the important Christian minorities residing in the cities. In Roumania and Bulgaria the necessity for the army to live on the country, which inevitably led to depredations and looting, had antagonized the local populations, but the Greeks living south of the Balkans met the Russians rapturously. As for the Turkish population, it fled before the invader. But General Diebitch issued a decree that the Turkish magistrates should remain in office, that the mosques should remain open and the name of the Sultan should be mentioned in prayers and promised to pay in cash for all requisitions. These measures gradually reconciled the Turks to the presence of the enemy and the local population caused no trouble to the army. However, ahead was the city of Slivno where General Diebitch was expecting serious resistance for he had received intelligence that the Seraskier, having finally abandoned Shumla, was marching by forced marches to Slivno. The Turkish Commander-in-Chief now replied to the offer of armistice made by Diebitch at Shumla and offered an armistice himself. But Diebitch waited until Slivno should be captured to give a reply.

It was now a race between the two to reach Slivno; the Russians got there first. The 6th Corps, totally unsuspected by the garrison, crept up to within 5 miles of the city, and it was decided to attack immediately under cover of the night. So unexpected was this attack that the city was captured at a cost of 1 officer and 12 men killed and the infantry did not fire a shot. The Turks were now utterly demoralized and Diebitch resolved to advance without delay upon Adrianople, the second capital of the Empire. The Russians had to cross a rocky desert and one more very difficult mountain defile, Bujuk Derbent (Great Pass), but there were no Turks defending it. However the march was extermely strenous in the great heat, and disease took a heavy toll. At last on August 19, four weeks after the army had crossed the Balkans, it came within sight of Adrianople. The army at this point had dwindled to some 15,000 to 20,000 men and was still facing an enemy much superior in numbers, the Turkish corps from Shumla and a fresh Turkish army converging upon Adrianople. Moreover, the city itself could oppose as many armed inhabitants as the whole Russian army. In these circumstances, General Diebitch's march upon Adrianople must be regarded as a foolhardy gamble. But he won; the city which had never seen an invasion since Byzantine days, surrendered the same day. A week later, negotiations for peace were opened and the campaign was at an end. However, the position of Diebitch, with a mere handful of men might at any moment have become very critical but he bluffed well and he assumed such an attitude of quiet superiority and strength toward the Turkish negotiators who had arrived at Adrianople, that even the European diplomats and observers in Constantinople were convinced that the Russian army was at least 60,000 strong. It was this belief in numbers which forced the hand of the strong-willed Sultan to sign terms of peace virtually dictated by Russia.

The campaign cost Russia 100 million roubles. The loss in battle according to an official report of the Russian Minister of War amounted to slightly below 20,000 men (the total figure including all the fighting the Russians did between 1826 and 1850 is 26 generals, 1,206 officers and 30,233 men, but this includes three more minor campaigns, the Polish, the Persian and the Hungarian). The death from disease in the campaign of 1828-29 is given at 89,897, in other words nearly three times the loss in battle.[18] Summing up, we may say with Moltke about Diebitch, "He besieged one fortress and fought one battle, but this brought him into the very heart of the hostile empire. He arrived there followed by the shadow of an army, but with the reputation of irresistible success. To the sagacious, bold and prudent conduct of General Diebitch at Adrianople, Russia owes the fortunate issue of a campaign which would have led to far different results if the Sultan and the European diplomats had been at all aware of the real state of things."[19]

When the peace negotiations were opened with Turkey, Count

---

[18]Sbornik, Imperatorskogo Russkogo Istoricheskogo Obshchestva, St. Petersburg, 1864-1916, 148 vols. Vol. 98, p. 303-306, Report of the War Ministry in Connection with the 25th Anniversary of the Reign of Nicholas I in 1850.

[19]Moltke, op. cit., p. 476.

Alexis Orlov and Count Pahlen were appointed as Russian negotiators by the Czar. Pending the arrival of these diplomats Russia was still preparing for the continuation of the war. Reserves were called up amounting to 90,000 men, the second half of the war loan of 42,000,000 florins floated in Holland was raised and the Mediterranean squadron of Admiral Heyden was strengthened by the addition of three ships-of-line and a number of frigates. Diebitch on his side was still facing the reserve army of 30,000 strong in Constantinople, whereas portions of Bulgaria were still occupied by a force of 30,000 Albanians and the fortresses on the Danube, Viddin, Nicopolis, Rustchuk and Sistovo were still in Turkish hands. But the Turks were demoralized and they, as well as the foreign diplomats, were impressed by the bold bluff of Diebitch and believed that his small forces were the vanguard of a much greater army and not the army itself. Furthermore, Prussia, supporting Russia, sent General Baron von Müffling to Constantinople and the latter persuaded the Turks to give in. Also the naval activity of the Russians worried the Turks; indeed, Admiral Greig occupied the ports of Ajeboli, Wasiliko and Iniada on the Black Sea while Heyden brought his squadron to Enos to co-operate with the detachment of Diebitch's army composed of 8,000 men which had marched to occupy the line of Enos-Midia and left the main army in Adrianople only 5,000 strong. The negotiations were opened at Adrianople on September 1 and concluded two weeks later; but even after the signing of peace the Turkish commandant of Rustchuk, Achmet Pasha, refused to surrender the fortress. Diebitch therefore remained in Adrianople till Achmet surrendered and only evacuated his headquarters in November, moving them to Burgas and leaving 5,000 Russians sick in hospitals behind him.

III

The treaty signed at Adrianople was of far reaching importance and concerned itself with the future relations between Russia and Turkey and the rights and privileges granted to Moldavia, Wallachia, Serbia and Greece. The river Pruth was to remain the frontier between Russia and Turkey, but Russia obtained the channel of St. George in the Danube delta. The Turkish fortresses of Giurgevo and Braila were to be dismantled and both nations were to have the privilege of free commercial navigation on the river, though Russian men-of-war were not to proceed beyond the confluence of the Pruth and the Danube. Turkey also ceded the portion of the Caucasian coast on the Black Sea extending south of the river Kuban to a point beyond Poti, as well as the Pashalik of Akhaltsik. Furthermore, she was to recognize the Russian acquisitions in Persia, pay a contribution of war of 10,000,000 Dutch ducats and 1 1/2 million ducats for losses to Russian trade. The Russians further obtained extra-territoriality and entire freedom of trade in Turkey as well as in Turkish waters, Russian ships to be exempt from inspection by Turkish authorities. The Straits were to remain open to merchant vessels of all nations. Separate acts covered the new rights of the Christian population in the Principalities and in Serbia and as for Greece, Turkey recognized the London treaty of June, 1827 and the Protocol of the London Conference of March 10, 1829. [20]

The results of the war far exceeded the acquisition of some portions of territory along the Caucasian Coast of the Black Sea. The new Turkish armament which Mahmoud II had so painstakingly built up was not only destroyed but worse still discredited in Turkish eyes; the efforts toward modernization were abandoned and a weak Turkey was to become the prey of Egyptians and Kurds, thus foreshadowing the day when a Russian alliance would, 4 years later, amount to a virtual protectorate. The revelation of this weakness encouraged the French to start the conquest of Algeria, the first real attempt at the dismemberment of the Ottoman Empire. Virtual master of the Balkans, dominating Turkey, Russia reached a high point in her power and prestige and the policy which Catherine II had initiated was brought to a successful conclusion by Nicholas I. But there was danger in such success. Whereas the "sick man" of Europe was forced to abandon his last efforts to recover his health and was going gradually towards further disintegration, his fate was too closely linked with the interests of the other major powers of Europe to allow this process to develop unhindered and not to create powerful rivalries and jealousies. Thus it may be said that in the success of 1829 lay the seeds of the Crimean War and of the Russo-Turkish War of 1877-78.

Equally important were the immediate effects of the war; that it would inevitably deeply affect the fate of the Balkan nations was a foregone conclusion. The independence of Greece was secured by the Treaty of Adrianople, and as for the Danubian Principalities and Serbia, the undoubted betterment of their lot was obtained at the cost of the establishment of a Russian protectorate. Russia, however, now discovered that it was easier to obtain privileges from the Turks, even at the cost of a war, than to maintain her hold over these young and turbulent nations. Russian diplomacy was faced, now that it had fulfilled its mission with regard to the Balkan Christians, with an increasing hostility of the very peoples it had aided so much. Jealous of their complete independence and coming more and more under the liberal and democratic ideas of the West, the Greek, Roumanians, and Serbs began objecting to the Russian tutelage and turned against their benefactor. The Czar, embittered, called this "ingratitude" and as the liberal western powers, England

---

[20] Polievktov, op. cit., p. 111-112.

and France, were backing these aspirations of newly won freedom, once more the situation resolved itself into a duel, between Russia on the one hand and the western powers on the other, over the heads of the Balkan nations. Greece, by her geographical position and by the fact that the war had come out of her struggle for independence, was the first and most vitally affected, and the internal situation in Greece must now be studied in more detail.

The Greek National Assembly of Troezene, which had met in April 1827, therefore a year before these events, had elected Capo d'Istria as first president of Greece for a period of 7 years. This was a signal victory for the Czar considering the earlier associations of that statesman with Russia. Before accepting the offer Capo d'Istria, who had been residing in Switzerland ever since his dismissal by Alexander I from the Russian service, went to St. Petersburg and obtained from Nicholas I the formal approval of his new position. On January 18, 1828 the newly elected president of Greece arrived at Nauplia on a British warship, escorted by a British and Russian squadron.

Admiral Codrington in a speech of congratulation expressed the idea that, as a Britisher, he would like to see Greece institute a liberal form of government patterned after Great Britain. But Capo d'Istria had different ideas: he deemed it necessary to establish first a strong centralized government which would avoid the factionalism and division which had done so much harm to the Greek cause. Accordingly he created a Council of State, the Panhellenion, which was composed of his personal nominees thereby creating a great deal of jealousy and enmity. In this policy he had the support of Admiral Lazarev commanding the Russian squadron and of the Russian Consular Agent, Bulgary, appointed to the newly established government. Thus, clearly etched from the beginning, appeared the irreconcilable oppositon of British and Russian ideas concerning the welfare of Greece. The Sultan, anxious about these developments decided to send a delegation of Greek bishops to Nauplia who were to seek grounds for an understanding. These bishops were carrying a letter written by the Patriarch of Constantinople, advising the Greek people to offer submission and ask for the clemency of the Sultan. Capo d'Istria received this delegation at Porros and haughtily turned it down declaring that it had come too late. He might have considered such an offer before 1821 but not now. Once more Admiral Lazarev, who was present at the meeting, gave his full approval to this attitude. With the opening of the hostilities between Russia and Turkey, Russia, busy in the northern Balkans, left the field of Greece open to the action of France which so far had been negligible in the Greek Revolution. Russian diplomacy welcomed the idea of a French military expedition into Morea as a diversion for the Turkish Army. England, thus far opposed to French intrusion in Greece, now welcomed it as a counterbalance to the

Russian penetration on the Danube. Thus, for diverging and contradictory reasons, the three powers came to an agreement in London where a protocol to this effect was signed on July 19, 1828 and in September the French expeditionary force landed in Morea. Ibrahim Pasha evacuated Greece and the French expedition served to fortify Capo d'Istria's position. For this very reason a violent protest was issued by the liberal Greeks headed by the Mavromichalis brothers who complained to General Maison, the commander of the expedition, that France was supporting the power of a "Rusisian regent, a despot and not a president." Ibrahim Pasha's depredations had been forgotten

Meanwhile the ambassadors of England, Russia and France, having left Constantinople, arrived at Corfu. It was there that they decided to attempt to negotiate the details of the future settlement of Greece and for this purpose to renew contacts with a Turkish representative-a delicate situation considering the war between Russia and Turkey. For this purpose the island of Porros in the Archipelago was selected as a convenient and relatively neutral ground and an invitation was extended through the Dutch minister in Constantinople to the Reiss Effendi to send plenipotentiaries. But the Turks, encouraged by the stalemate which had developed on the Russian front on the Danube, became présumptuous and refused to do so. The result was that perforce the conference developed into a unilateral affair between Stratford Canning, Ribeaupierre and Guilleminot with Capo d'Istria as consultant. Moreover, the three ambassadors spent most of their time jealously watching each other's moves. Capo d'Istria presented two memorandums, one on the future delimitation of the frontiers of Greece and the other on the situation of the Greek treasury. He suggested the line of Volo-Sayada as the minimum demand of Greece but stated that the more desirable and sound frontier should run from Mount Olympus to the Adriatic, north of Corfu, thus including Thessaly and Epirus as well as the islands of Eubea and Crete. With regard to the financial difficulties of Greece, the new Greek Government had thus far been receiving a monthly subsidy of 500,000 francs paid jointly by Russia and France. Capo d'Istria demanded the continuation of this monthly subsidy and the loan of a million francs a year for 10 years for the immediate needs of Greece and a large loan later.

The financial question, as may have been expected, caused no trouble but not so the question of frontiers. France suspected England of wanting the islands of Crete, Rhodes, Cyprus and Milos for a chain of naval and military bases directed against Egypt. France and England both saw a grave complication in the naval blockade of the Dardanelles declared by Russia. Admiral Heyden had detached Admiral Ricord from his squadron to put this blockade into effect. England complained bitterly that Russia had promised to remain neutral in the Mediterranean but that Russian warships were mingled with the French and British vessels in the Archipelago and thereby could provoke an incident which would involve both powers in the war The issue was finally settled by the Russians limiting the blockade strictly to the entrance of the Dardanelles and promising to consider the waters of the Archipelago and particularly of Crete as neutral. Finally, after much wrangling, the ambassadors agreed upon a series of memoranda signed on December 12, which formed the basis for the ultimate status of Greece and embodied most of the technical problems concerning this future status. Having terminated this preliminary task the three ambassadors left for Naples to await the time for their return to Constantinople; but their consular agents accredited to Capo d'Istria's government remained as their representatives on the spot. As already stated this function was carried out for Russia by Count Bulgary, himself of Greek extraction, for France by Baron Juchereau de Saint Denis and for England by Edward J. Dawkins who treated Capo d'Istria with contempt and rudeness, threatening him occasionally with the use of British naval forces if he did not comply.

Czar Nicholas, meanwhile, had realized "the impossibility of attempting to persuade the Turks to deal with Russian negotiators concerning the Greek question, so long as the war was on." [21] He therefore left the matter in the hands of France and England, but conditional to agreements to be reached at London between the three powers. Accordingly the staff of the Russian embassy in London was increased by the sending of Count Matussewich to assist Prince Lieven. As a result of pressure by the Russian and French ambassadors, the Duke of Wellington and Lord Aberdeen finally accepted, not without some misgivings, the terms worked out at Porros and these were in turn embodied in the Protocol of March 22, 1829, and became the virtual charter of the new Greece. According to this Protocol the frontier of the new state was to run from Volo to the Gulf of Arta and the islands of Eubea, while the Cyclades archipelago were to be given to Greece. Greece was to pay the Sultan an annual tribute amounting to 1,500,000 Turkish piastres, but though remaining under Turkish suzerainty was to enjoy complete authonomy and freedom of internal administration. A monarchical form of government was to be appointed, under a Christian ruler whose rule would be hereditary, but who would remain a vassal of the Sultan and under no circumstances could he be selected from the ruling houses of the three powers concerned. Russia gave France and England full powers to conduct negotiations on her behalf

---

[21]Driault et L'heritier, <u>Histoire Diplomatique de la Grece de 1921 a nos Jours.</u>, Paris 1925, Vol. I., p. 436.

with Turkey, but on condition that no demand to exclude Russia directly or indirectly from the negotiations should be raised. The other clauses dealt with purely technical matters concerning trade, exchange or citizens, etc.

Capo d'Istria protested this Protocol because it failed to give Crete and Samos to Greece, but finally accepted it with certain reservations such as the necessity of the new ruler accepting the Orthodox faith, the granting of a constitution to Greece, etc. Following the signing of the Protocol the French expeditionary force was recalled leaving in Greece a small detachment of 5,000 men under General Schneider. Turkey, still confident of victory, held out and in the tedious negotiations which followed found one excuse after another to postpone the acceptance of the Protocol. The pressure of the war had forced "Reshid Pasha to leave Continental Greece and Epirus almost destitute of troops,"[22] and this was a real service which the Russian army had rendered the Greek cause. It was to render a still greater service by forcing Turkey to accept the Protocol of March 22. When the defeat of Turkey became apparent as the Russian Army crossed the Balkans, Capo d'Istria summoned a national assembly at Argos which opened on July 23. The assembly ratified all Capo d'Istria's administrative measures and gave him the powers he desired. Accordingly a Senate was created which was to be a consultative body in the hands of the President and a regency was formed in the event of Capo d'Istria's death.

Meanwhile, terrified by the approach of the Russian army, the Turks showed the first signs of yielding on the Greek issue. On August 5, the Reiss Effendi invited the British and French ambassadors to a confidential meeting where he declared that Turkey was prepared to grant Morea a regime similar to the one existing in the Danubian Principalities on condition that Turkish garrisons should be maintained in fortified places. The ambassadors declared these conditions to be insufficient and insisted that the Treaty of London of 1827 be made the base of further discussions. M. Guilleminot, according to instruction received, wanted the Turks to accept the Protocol of March 22 but met with the opposition of his British colleague, and the Turks were quick to discern and capitalize upon the lack of unanimity in the councils of the powers.

With the usual dilatory tactics the Reiss Effendi kept on delaying and giving in only step by step as news from the front became increasingly bad. Finally on August 11, the Porte accepted the conditions of the Treaty of London and subscribed to them officially.

---

[22]Finlay, G., History of the Greek Revolution, London, 1861, Vol. II. p. 205.

Great Britain declared herself satisfied and as far as she was concerned the Greek question was settled. But not Russia. Russia insisted that Turkey should recognize the clauses of the March protocol as well and this was duly inserted into the Treaty of Adrianople which, in Article X with regard to Greece, read as follows: "the Porte gives its full adhesion to the Treaty of London of July 6, 1827, and to the Protocol of March 22, 1829." [23] "The policy of the British cabinet received a severe rebuke..... the courts of England and France felt humiliated by the position in which Russia had placed them. The Sultan was obsequious, the Greeks were grateful. Capo d'Istria perhaps expected with secret trepidation, to hear that he was named hospodar of the Morea. To give the negotiations a new turn, and to neutralize the credit of Russia, a decisive step was taken in a different direction." [24]

Russia had achieved by the sword what Great Britain had been trying to do by financial pressure and a somewhat devious diplomacy the situation was to repeat itself in the Balkans, and once more secret diplomacy was coming to the foreground. Scarcely had the Treaty of Adrianople been signed when Turkey addressed a note to the powers on September 25 requesting them to replace the projected borders of Greece, as indicated in the Protocol of March 22, by those of the proposed Protocol which thereby would limit Greece to Morea and the Cyclades alone. By a striking coincidence this frontier had been advocated by the British all along. At the same time Great Britain declared that she was reserving her attitude with regard to the recognition of Article X of the Treaty of Adrianople on the ground that Russia had no right to impose, unilateraly, the Protocol of March 22 upon Turkey. Diebitch replied diplomatically that his victory was a victory for the powers and therefore the acceptance by the Turks of Article X was a success for the three powers. Confirming this point of view, Russia suggested that the issue should be brought up for discussion at the conference in London. Thus the first shots were fired in the diplomatic war which once more was to be centered in London. Meanwhile, after a searching examination of the situation as created by the Russian victory, Britain decided to modify her Greek policy to an extent which amounted to a virtual diplomatic revolution. In a communication from Lord Aberdeen on November 10, addressed to Sir Robert Gordon, Britain's envoy in Constantinople at the time, these new principles based on a realistic acceptance of the changed situation were made clear: the war had revealed the weakness of

---

[23] Driault et L'heritier, op. cit., Vol. I., p. 453.
[24] Finlay, op. cit., Vol. II, p. 223.

Turkey, hence it was in Britain's interest to uphold "This clumsy fabrick of barbarous power." (Someone wrote on the margin of the document at this point "Our ancient ally.") [25] Therefore it would be better to create and make possible the existence of an independent Greece, as powerful as possible, which would replace Turkey in the Eastern Mediterranean and which if properly handled would serve as a buffer against Russia just at the time Turkey was being reduced to virtual Russian vassalage. Such were the new lines of British action as the conference opened in London.

Thus, if we compare the situation as it existed at this point with the one at the time of the signing of the Protocol of St. Petersburg we find the attitude of the two powers, Russia and England, completely reversed. France came out with a compromise solution which was to reduce the territorial size of Greece in exchange for complete independence. This made possible the agreement which was reached on November 30, but it was only by the Protocol of February 3, 1830, that the issue, "after long and difficult negotiations was finally settled." Greece became independent but with frontiers reduced as compared to those fixed by the Protocol of March 22 thereby meeting the Turkish demands. The new frontier ran from the Gulf of Aspro-Potamo to that of Sperchios and included the islands of the Cyclades, Eubea and Skyros. A foreign prince was to be made ruler of Greece with the title of Prince and he was not to belong to the reigning families of the three powers. Similarly, no troops of these powers could occupy Greece without the assent of the two other signatories. French, Russian and British commissioners were to be appointed to trace the new frontier. The protocol was to be converted later into a formal treaty. When the terms became known Greece protested for she failed to obtain as much Greek territory as previously acceded to her. But in the meanwhile the question of the internal regime in Greece, under the proposed monarchy, was absorbing the attention of the powers and was going to lead to new and increasingly serious difficulties.

Now that their revolution was coming to an end the Greeks conceived it to be more and more a revolution and less and less a struggle for independence. They wanted independence to be coupled with liberty and democracy, and in this they were going to clash with Capo d'Istria's policy and with the policy of the protecting powers, particularly Russia. Count Bulgary, the Russian Commissioner, wrote a memorandum jointly with Capo d'Istria which expressed clearly the stand of Russia. Opposing the liberties demanded by the Greeks and such local institutions worked out by the previous assemblies,

---

[25] Driault et L'heritier, op. cit., Vol. I, p. 460.

which had led to 7 years of anarchy, the memorandum stated explicitly that "the sacrifices which the powers have made and are still making give them the incontestable right to intervene actively in the establishment of the form of its (Greek) government. President Capo d'Istria goes even further: he recognizes the right of the allied powers not only to demand from Greece guarantees of order and stability, but to establish a monarchial government."[26] This memorandum had been attached to the Protocol of March 22, 1829 and showed clearly Russia's desire, and Capo d'Istria's acquiescence with the idea of bringing Greece into the fold of the Holy Alliance principles.

These principles had been imposed by Capo d'Istria at the National Assembly of Argos. Because this assembly met just at the time of the collapse of Turkey at the hands of Russia (July 23, 1829) and because of the association of the cause of the liberation of Greece with Russia's victory and with the Russian background of Capo d'Istria, the President enjoyed overpowering prestige and had his way. But the republican and democratic minority were only temporarily hushed up and when the question of the candidature of Prince Leopold of Saxe-Coburg to the throne of Greece was raised, a petition was circulated in Greece against the establishment of a monarchy and in favour of a republic. To this was added the bitterness caused in Greece by the mutilation of Greek territory owing to the reduced frontiers and the order of the protecting powers to evacuate Greek troops from the territories to be given back to Turkey. Capo d'Istria's popularity was being seriously undermined by these factors.

Meanwhile Prince Leopold, realizing the difficulties he would encounter in Greece and not without persuasion by Capo d'Istria, decided to withdraw his candidature. This occurred just as the July revolution was breaking out in France.

This revolution had the most ominous results for Greece. On one side it gave a powerful stimulus to the republican and democratic trends in the country and on the other it left Greece without the support of the powers just at the time when she most needed it. Indeed, it put an end to the triple alliance and Russia became reconciled with Austria, thus reconstituting the new Holy Alliance. Russian armies menaced France, while the Belgian and Polish issues so absorbed the attention of the Great Powers that Greece was virtually forgotten. For over a year the status of Greece remained unsolved and during this period Crete and Samos, both claimed by the Greeks, were disposed of by the Sultan

---

[26] Driault et L'heritier, op. cit., Vol. II, p. 7.

who rewarded Mehemet Ali with Crete and restored his authority over Samos. The conference in London did not occupy itself with Greek matters again until the 26th of September, 1831.

Coming at such a critical time, this long period of stagnation and uncertainty placed Capo d'Istria in a dangerous position with which he was unable to cope and the cumulation of explosive forces was so great in the country that it finally led to a serious and dangerous insurrection against his dictatorship. The popularity which he had enjoyed vanished and he was accused of having mishandled the situation and held responsible for the predicament in which Greece found herself. He was further suspected of aspiring to power for himself, and to achieve this purpose, he was accused of wanting to make Greece so small that no foreign prince would want to become its ruler. A definite insurrectionary movement came into existence led by the powerful Mavromichalis family and supported by the islands, particularly Hydra and Spezzia. Following the excitement produced by the revolutionary news coming from France, this insurrection crystallized itself in August, 1830, and assumed the character of a struggle for liberty against the "tyrant" supported by Russia. Thus the movement though aiming at the President, through him aimed at Russia as well, and Capo d'Istria was accused of being merely a Russian agent. The former leaders of the revolution—Mavrocordatos, Tricoupis, Miaoulis, Coundouriottis, Tombazis and significantly, a British emissary General Church—assembled at Hydra to organize the insurrection. Russia was now the main enemy; always pro-British and anti-Russian, these men however had welcomed Russian aid in their struggle against Turkey. Now that this was accomplished they saw in Russia the counter-revolutionary power of Europe attempting to crush liberty and democracy. Russia, on her side, gave the weight of her support to the dictatorial regime of Capo d'Istria, and thus the lines were drawn for a new struggle. Capo d"istria, however, was still powerful and had the support of a large conservative and pro-Russian group. Thus Greece was divided into two factions and the situation was ripe for civil war, a war in which, behind each faction, we find Russia and Britain once more aligned against each other as elsewhere in the Balkans and the Near East.

Capo d'Istria did not wait for the storm to break, but struck first. He restricted the liberty of the press, established a passport system for internal communications between cities and had the powerful Petro Bey Mavromichalis arrested. The Mavromichalis family was all powerful in the district of Maina which was already in a state of insurrection. Now the island of Hydra proclaimed its own liberal government and took to arms. The insurrection rapidly spread to the island of Syra which was the center of Greek commerce. The loss of Syra would take away from the rebels the main source of revenue. Accordingly Capo d'Istria decided to outfit an expedition against the island. He mobilized those ships of the Greek Fleet which had remained faithful to his cause and turned for support to the Russian naval squadron of Admiral Ricord. But the insurrectionists at Hydra decided to forestall this move by capturing the base of the Greek Fleet at Poros. On the night of July 27, 1831, Miaoulis, commanding the Hydra expedition, seized the arsenal at Poros and captured Capo d'Istria's ships. Capo d'Istria immediately ordered a battalion of troops to march by land to Poros and appealed to Ricord for aid on the sea. Admiral Ricord sailed to Poros and summoned Miaoulis to surrender the captured vessels. Miaoulis refused and the Russian Admiral blocked the entrance to the port. Meanwhile the British and French squadron had arrived at Poros, impeding any hostile action on the part of the Russians. The residents of France and England at Nauplia suggested to Capo d'Istria a conciliatory policy involving negotiations with the rebels as well as the calling of a new national assembly. It was obvious that neither France nor England were supporting Capo d'Istria's stand; he must rely therefore wholly upon Russia. On August 6 a small boat of the Russian brig, Telemachus, guarding the entrance to Poros, forced a Greek ship bringing provisions to the rebels to turn back. The affair resulted in some shooting and a few casualties occurred on both sides. Following this, Capo d'Istria issued an order to Admiral Ricord to attack Poros jointly with the Greek land forces. Ricord took charge of the operations and established a battery of his guns in a position to cut off the access to the city. Then the Russians attacked and gained possession of the seized ships while the Greek troops occupied Fort Heidick. Victory was complete and Poros capitulated.

On August 13, while a small Greek force of government troops occupied the city, Miaoulis on his flagship, the Hellas, observed that the Russian vessels had now manoeuvred themselves into a position which placed the insurgent ships under their guns. He sent an officer on board the Russian flagship to request the Russians to return to their old stations until the arrival of the allied squadrons which were due back; otherwise, if the Russians should start hostilities he would blow up his own ships. A request to wait was also made by the commander of a French brig which had come into port. Ricord flatly refused and continued to manoeuvre into position and Miaoulis blew up his ships. At the noise of the explosion the troops of Capo d'Istria rushed into Poros and sacked the city. Meanwhile, to aggravate matters, a bitter feud had developed between the Mavromichalies family and Capo d'Istria, and on October 9, 1831, as Capo d'Istria was leaving a church he was assassinated by two members of the Mavromichalis clan.

Following the death of Capo d'Istria a regency composed of three members, the late President's brother Count Agostino Capo d'Istria, Kolokotrones and Kolettes was established with Agostino Capo d'Istria as President. A second national assembly was convened at Argos and the Capodistrian party, still supported by Ricord, fought for control. Ricord kept Hydra blockaded with his ships. The Capodistrians openly accused the French and the British of being party to the assassination of the president and, in his hatred of the French, Agostino Capo d'Istria dismissed the French general, Gerard, who had taken service in the Greek Army. Meanwhile an insurrection of Romeliots was faced with vigour by the new government, and a Russian lieutenant, Raikov, made colonel in the Greek army, was summoned with a detachment of artillery to Argos which was taken after a battle of two days. Civil war was now raging and anarchy rampant. The Romeliots, after a fierce struggle, succeeded in turning the tide of battle and by April 1832 Agostino's position became so hopeless that he resigned and left Greece on a Russian warship with the body of his brother. Confused events which are of little concern to us followed. The Russian Resident wanted to maintain the existence of the Senate established by Capo d'Istria as the basis for the stability of Greece, but was opposed in this by his French and British colleagues. A new regency of five members was created but enjoyed little power and no prestige; the rebels were making rapid headway in dominating the whole of Greece. The seat of the government and assembly were transferred from Nauplia to Argos in rebel territory and it may be said that this triumph of the insurrectionists marks not only the end of a regime in Greece, but the end of Russian influence as well, since the latter had been inextricably associated with the Capodistrian party. Only the election of Prince Otto of Bavaria as the new ruler of Greece finally put an end to the civil war and ushered in a period of relative stability. He was elected by the conference of London and his candidature had received the endorsement of the three protecting powers by the treaty of London of May 7, 1832. This treaty is the final diplomatic document establishing the status of Greece. Prince Otto was made King of Greece and Greece was declared to be a sovereign and independent state. The three powers made a loan to the new kingdom of 20 million francs each. All allied forces in Greece were to be evacuated and replaced by a corps of 3,500 men enrolled in Bavaria. As for the question of the frontiers, negotiations were now transferred to Constantinople and after much hard bargaining with the Turks this issue was settled by a protocol, signed on July 21, giving Greece the frontier from Volo to the gulf of Arta. Samos and Crete remained outside the new kingdom.

With the arrival of King Otto in Greece on January 30, 1833, the Greek issue, as an international question, had come to an end and the sponsorship of the three powers was terminated. Admiral Ricord was recalled and the Russian Resident, Baron Ruckman was replaced by a regularly appointed Minister. But the new government in Greece, playing up to the mood now prevailing in the country, assumed a distinctly anti-Russian attitude. The Regency which had been appointed pending the coming of age of the King, leaned heavily on France and Britain and the complete absence of a pro-Russian party was noticeable. The departing Admiral Ricord as well as the new Russian Minister, Kalakazi, were treated by the Regency with marked coldness, and relations with Russia became relatively strained. Thus Greece fades out of the picture of Russian diplomacy and the attitude of the Greek Government was interpreted by Czar Nicholas as one more triumph of the revolutionary spirit in Europe and was partly responsible for his policy of turning toward a friendship with Turkey as marked by the forthcoming treaty of Unkiar Skelessi.

IV

As the war had been fought to a great extent on Roumanian soil, it was to be expected that the Principalities would be deeply affected by the outcome of hostilities. The Convention of Akkerman and the Treaty of Adrianople established a virtual Russian protectorate over Moldavia and Wallachia. Under the clauses of the Treaty of Adrianople the Turks were to evacuate all forts on the left bank of the Danube whereas Russia obtained the right to keep garrisons in the Principalities until the full payment of the war indemnity by Turkey. The Turks guaranteed complete internal independence of the Principalities and the Sultan pledged himself to ratify all administrative measures promulgated by the Russian or local authorities. The sole remaining token of Turkish sovereignty was the payment of a tribute by the Principalities to Constantinople. The Hospodars were to be elected for life by the people in national assemblies. But already during the war the Russians had set up an administrative mechanism of their own which was to be carried through into peace times as well. Indeed, on February 10, 1828, Count Theodore Pahlen was appointed from St. Petersburg, Plenipotentiary President of the Divans of Moldavia and Wallachia, with Minciaky acting as counsellor and Pisani head of the Ordnance and Supply Services. A committee of 7 pro-Russian Boyars called the "General Divan" was formed and was complemented by a National Assembly summoned at will by the Russian High Command. These bodies became the government particularly after the flight of the Hospodars at the entry of Russians into Jassy and

Bucharest. Pahlen was superseded by General Zholtukhin, who alienated the Boyars by his disregard for their punctilious ceremonials and their insistence upon their social position. Zholtukhin's death brought to power a man of a very different caliber and temperament, Count Paul Kisselev, one of Russia's most successful pro-consuls. With a great deal of zeal and devotion he set himself the task of introducing better conditions of life and of developing the country. While the Russian troops were in occupation he used Russian military engineers to plan and build cities in the place of the destoyed Turkish fortresses; thus the cities of Giurgiu, Turnu-Magurele and Braila, were founded by the Russians, Braila becoming one of Roumania's principal ports. He further built highways, laid out parks and avenues and introduced sanitation thus putting an end to constant epidemics. The city of Jassy saw its first stone pavements and sanitation system. Finding the Divan unwieldy he replaced it by a council of experienced functionaries and then established a commission which jointly with this council was to work out a new constitution under his personal supervision. This work was completed by April 1830 and the National Assemblies in their respective Principalities having approved them, these charters were sent for endorsement to St. Petersburg and were put into effect under the name of Réglements Organiques. The principle introduced was aristocratic; the boyars obtained the power of making laws, of electing the hospodars and appointing the main military officers whereas the taxes fell on the lower classes. But for the first time in Roumanian history judges were made irremovable and litigations were limited by law. Moreover by the identity and similarity of institutions introduced into both Principalities a step was taken toward their ultimate unification; the Russian consuls were to continue to act as arbitrators in any quarrels arising between the hospodars and the boyars and were to have the last word. The next important measure undertaken by Kisselev was the forming of a national militia organized on the Russian pattern and drilled by Russian officers. In 1834, as the Turks had fulfilled their obligations, the Russian occupationary forces evacuated the Principalities. Count Kisselev's departure was the object of touching demonstrations of affection on the part of the population which followed him right up to the border on the Pruth; one of the important thoroughfares of Bucharest has since been given his name. Writing 20 years later a Roumanian historian said that the administration of Count Kisselev had been blessed by all classes of the Roumanian people during its exercise and for a long time afterwards. [27]

---

[27] Iorga, Neculaī, Histoire des relations russo-roumaines, Jassy, 1917, p. 275.

Kisselev's zeal was undoubtedly prompted by the conviction that the Principalities were predestined ultimately to belong to Russia. It is the more ironical that his very enlightened policy in the long run produced the reverse result for it fostered the development of Roumanian nationalism. But for the time being Russia's hold was virtually complete not only politically but intellectually. The reigning Hospodar, who was in power during the time of the Russian occupation, Michael Sturdza, was not only pro-Russian but served Russian interests to the point of censoring an uncomplimentary reference in the press to Russia's climate. The officers of the Moldavian-Wallachian militia went to Russia for their military studies. The Roumanian clergy closely cooperated with the Russian Orthodox Church. Prince Koltzov-Masalski, a member of the higher Russian aristocracy, married a member of a prominent Roumanian Boyar family, Dora d'Istria, this being incidentally the only such union between the two aristocracies. Roumanian writers of the period spoke the Russian language freely, modelled their poetry on Russian works or translated them into Roumanian; such was the case of Constantin Negruzzi who was influenced by Pushkin, Alecu Donici who translated Krylov and finally Constantin Stamati. This intellectual cooperation was largely due to the fact that the Roumanians still used the same Slavonic script as in Russia. But a movement was now developing in Transylvania sponsored by the Roman Catholic Church to introduce the Latin script; this movement spread across the mountains into the Principalities and with it came the theory of the Latin origin of the Roumanian people and culture. With the triumph of these ideas the young Roumanian intellectuals began turning to France and England for both political and literary inspiration. A new generation came into the political life of the country at the turn of the forties. These were French educated intellectuals imbued with the liberal, nationalist and democratic spirit of the times who hated Russia as the autocratic protector and creator of the aristocratic regime which they were fighting in their own countries. They also accused Russia of having designs on the independence of the Principalities. Headed by Kagolniceanu this group was encouraged by the revolution of 1848 in France to stage a revolution at home.

Kagolniceanu was not only a democrat, he was also a nationalist. He advocated the creation of a greater Roumania which would incorporate Transylvania, Bucovina and Bessarabia. This made him doubly obnoxious to Russia. When the Revolution of 1848 broke out in France and was followed by a revolution in Hungary, Kagolniceanu staged a military coup in Wallachia which drove out the pro-Russian Hospodar, Bibescu, and resulted in the establishment in Bucharest of a provisional revolutionary government

(June 9, 1848). But Russia acted swiftly and reversing her usual
policy offered to co-operate with Turkey. While Turkish troops
crossed the Danube and the Porte ordered the dissolution of the
revolutionary government, a Russian army under General Ivin
marched once more on Bucharest. The revolutionary government
collapsed and its leaders were forced to flee. By the Russo-
Turkish Convention of Balta-Liman, the Réglement Organique
was cancelled and the National Assembles in the Principalities
were replaced by Councils or Divans composed of boyars selected
from "the most notable and the most worthy of confidence" and
members of the higher clergy. New Hospodars were appointed
for 7 years jointly by the Czar and the Sultan: Gregory Ghica for
Moldavia and Barbe Stirbeiu for Wallachia. They were to carry
on their administration under the guidance of Commissioner-
Generals and with the forces of occupation guaranteeing order.
But in 1850 the Principalities had quieted down to a point where
General Ivin evacuated his army. However, three years later
with the coming of the Crimean War two Russian army corps under
General Danenberg and later Prince Gorchakov once more reoccupied them. Hospodar Ghica, ordered by the Turks to have nothing
to do with the Russians, preferred flight and his functions were
handed over to General Ouroussov (Sept. 28, 1853).

This was the last of the long series of Russian occupations
and lasted one year. In September 1854 with the allies carrying
the war into Crimea and Austria menacingly assembling an army
under Baron von Hess on the Russian flank in Moldavia, the Russians finally evacuated the Principalities which were immediately
occupied by the Austrians. By the Treaty of Paris in 1856 Russia
renounced the right of protection over Moldavia and Wallachia,
returned Bessarabia and pledged herself not to interfere any longer
in the internal affairs of the two Principalities. Thus the period of
Russian tutelage of the Principalities had come to an end and with
the sympathetic support of Emperor Napoleon the way was paved
for the unification of Moldavia and Wallachia by their joint election
of Alexander Couza as Prince of united Roumania.

V

Once more what happened in Roumania was to some extent
paralleled by the situation in Serbia. By the Treaty of Adrianople
the Turks undertook to evacuate all Serb territory within the
boundaries of 1813 and to put into effect the clauses of the Convention of Akkerman. The following year the Hatti Sheriff of
1830, drawn up by the Russian Ambassador in Constantinople,
officially recognized Prince Milosh as hereditary Prince of Serbia
and acknowledged other privileges, such as the single tax and the

freedom of religious service including the right to ring church bells, an issue which had caused much friction with the Muslim population. Furthermore the Orthodox Church in Serbia became independent of the Greek Patriarch in Constantinople by the right granted the Serbs to elect their own bishops and metropolitans. Four years later a second Hatti Sheriff of 1834 solved the vexatious issue of the Turkish garrisons in Serbian fortresses; with the single exception of the fortress of Belgrade, the Turkish troops were to evacuate all Serbian fortresses. Thus step by step Turkish rule became merely nominal, and under the protection of Russia and through the agency of Russia, Serbia had gained virtual independence. But Russia, as in Greece, discovered that it was far easier to obtain privileges from the Turks for her protegés than to run them under her protection.

Trouble was brewing in Serbia with a rising opposition against Milosh's headstrong and tyrannical government with its strong tendency toward centralization. The leader of the opposition, Milosh's brother Ephrem, obtained support from Russia who "was pursuing the time honoured policy in the Balkan peninsula, which consists in allowing the various states to acquire sufficient power to make them independent of Turkey, but not sufficient to enable them to stand alone without Russian aid."[28] Milosh replied in 1835 by issuing an organic statute or constitution which met with the opposition of the leaders and chieftains and thereby was unworkable. This constitution was deemed too liberal and democratic by Russia and Austria; furthermore Russia and Turkey objected that as protecting powers they had not been consulted before its issuance. The increasing influence of Britain in Serbia was immediately noticed in St. Petersburg and Russia realized that she had no diplomatic representative in Belgrade. Accordingly the Russian Consul-General in Wallachia, Baron P. Ruckman was appointed Special Russian Commissioner to Serbia. He did not get along with Milosh and sharply demanded the abrogation of the constitution. This led to an open quarrel with Milosh and Ruckman left Serbia without achieving any results. The following year, 1836, he returned to Serbia with a constitution worked out by the Ministry of Foreign Affairs in St. Petersburg under the name of the "Basis for a Statute in Serbia" which Milosh refused to accept, considering this a personal attack on his own powers. In taking such a stand he was warmly supported by the newly appointed British consul, Colonel Hodges; thus once more over the body of a Balkan state, England and Russia were fighting out their great duel in the East. In October, 1837, Prince V. A. Dolgoruky,

---

[28] Miller, William, The Balkans: Roumania, Bulgaria, Servia, Montenegro, London, 1923, p. 323.

A. D. C. to the Czar, arrived in Serbia on a special mission with the purpose of imposing upon Milosh the acceptance of the Russian constitution. Milosh was forced to yield and agreed to the establishment of a Senate or Council of Elders of 17 members, irremovable and with full legislative powers as demanded by Russia. Thus the autocratic power of Milosh was curtailed. This made possible the resumption of good relations with Russia and in February, 1838, the first Russian Consul to Belgrade, Vashtchenko was appointed. Meanwhile a bitter diplomatic battle was fought over the issue in Constantinople. With the approval of Russia, Turkey demanded that a Serbian mission should be sent to Constantinople to discuss the constitutional issue. Austria and England through their embassies fought tooth and nail for the maintenance of Milosh's power but Buteniev insisted upon the limitation of the Prince's authority and carried his point. The Hatti Sheriff of 1839 officially acknowledged the establishment of the Council of Elders. Milosh "had relied on the support of England in resisting the Constitution and demanding absolute authority," [29] but had been defeated and was now faced with a Council hostile to him. There remained nothing else for him to do but to abdicate in favour of his son, Michael (July 1839). Michael's accession was confirmed by the Sultan but the Sultan appointed two councillors, the senators Voutchich and Petroujevich as defenders of the constitution. Michael soon quarrelled with his councillors and banished them. Russia protested and insisted upon the recall of Voutchich. Voutchich returned and organized a rebellion against Michael in favour of Prince Alexander Karageorgievitch. This led to the abdication of Michael in his turn and the election of Alexander as Prince (1842). Russia protested these elections as being illegal and new elections were held on June 15, 1843, which confirmed the popular will of having the Karageorgievitch dynasty back in power and Alexander remained on the throne. This opposition alienated Alexander from Russia and he turned to Austria and Turkey for support in his future policies. There is here a striking similarity with the events which were to occur half a century later in Bulgaria with Ferdinand Coburg in the place of Alexander and Stambulov in the place of Voutchich. The consistently anti-Russian policy of Karageorgievitch was due not only to spite, but to the rise of a powerful liberal democratic current in Serbia, looking toward the West. At the time of the beginning of the Crimean War the Prince appointed a liberal anti-Russian

---

[29] Lazarovich-Hrebelianovich, Prince S., *The Servian People, Their Past Glory and Their Destiny*, New York, 1910, Vol. II, p. 861.

Minister, Elia Garashanin, and Russia issued an ultimatum demanding his recall within 24 hours. The Prince obeyed but turned to Austria for support and, as a result of Austria's pressure, Serbia, during the war, adopted a policy of "masterly inactivity" which helped the allied cause considerably. Following the war and at the Congress of Paris, Serbia was placed under the collective guarantee of the powers which abolished the Russian protectorate. But the pro-Russian elements remained strong in the country and these eventually accusing the Prince of servility to Austria, organized a conspiracy which forced him to abdicate in 1858 in favour of the now elderly Milosh. After the death of Milosh (1860) Michael Obrenovich once more came to the throne and proved to be the best monarch Serbia had had to date. But when in 1862 a new crisis arose, and the Turks bombarded Belgrade, the issue was settled in favour of Serbia by the joint action of the powers, mainly Austria and England, and not by the unilateral action of Russia. The assassination of Michael in 1868 by a Karageorgievitch plotter brought to power Milan IV Obrenovitch, a cousin of the former ruler, whose capricious rule opens a new chapter in the history of Serbia.

CHAPTER III

THE EASTERN QUESTION AFTER THE WAR OF 1828-29

I

When Diebitch was negotiating the Treaty of Adrianople a secret committee was functioning in St. Petersburg for the purpose of revising Russia's policy in the Eastern Question and in September 1829 took cognizance of a report drawn up by the Minister of Justice, Dashkov, who was regarded as an expert on Turkish affairs. Dashkov pointed out that no alliance between Russia and Turkey had ever been successful because of the hostility and distrust of the Turks who secretly continued to regard Russia as their main enemy, and he pointed to the fate of the alliance of 1798 as proof of this fact. There were therefore two alternate solutions- 1) the dissolution of the Turkish Empire and 2) the maintenance of a weak and dependent Turkey. Capo d'Istria had proposed to make Constantinople a free city with adjoining territory along the Black Sea and the Sea of Marmara, and to include two fortified points on the Asiatic banks of the Bosphorus as well as the Island of Tenedos covering the entrance to the Dardanelles. Dashkov in turn suggested that if Russia could not obtain control of Constantinople she should have possession of points on each side of the Bosphorus which should be fortified so as to protect the entrance to the Black Sea. But in view of the difficulties which would inevitably arise, the committee decided that it was in the best interests of Russia to maintain the Turkish Empire in existence, provided the control of the Straits should not pass out of weak Turkish hands into those of any other stronger power. Count Nesselrode wanted further to obtain permission for Russian warships to pass through the Straits, but he did not succeed in having this clause inserted in the peace treaty which made no mention of the Straits and hence left things as they were before. Nevertheless the affirmative decision of the committee on the desirability of maintaining Turkey in existence is of great historical importance for it became the cornerstone of Russia's policy for the next quarter of a century.

Barely three years later this policy was to be put to a crucial test by the rather unexpected projection of Egypt into the field of

Russia's interests. Indeed, it was from Egypt that developed the menace which Russian diplomacy had feared: an alien domination of Constantinople and the Straits. Egypt had been the first country in the Near East to become westernized through the impact of Napoleon's invasion. However, the transformation was due to the genius of a man with a Napoleonic temperament and destiny, Mehemet Ali, who became not only the sole ruler of Egypt but was sufficiently powerful to challenge the authority of his suzerain, the Sultan. Having made himself master of Egypt he established a strong and able government and, with the aid of French experts, built up a powerful army and fleet and modernized the administration. During the Greek Revolution the Sultan appealed to this powerful vassal for aid, and the role played by the Egyptian military and naval forces in Greece under Ibrahim Pasha has already been told. The battle of Navarino, which destroyed 3 large ships of the line, 15 frigates and 70 smaller craft which Mehemet Ali had so painstakingly assembled, roused in his soul a lifelong hatred for the British and the Russians; but he maintained his friendliness toward France which dated from impressions of his early youth when, as a wandering boy, he had received his first education at the hands of a French merchant in Cavalla. This feeling toward France increased after Navarino for the French helped him to rebuild his fleet. When the fleet was ready he reminded Mahmoud II of his promise, given to him at the time of the Greek Revolution, to cede him Crete and Syria with Damascus in return for assistance, but the Sultan ignored this demand.

Hence on November 1, 1831, he moved 9,000 Egyptian infantry and 2,000 cavalry into Syria and this force under Ibrahim Pasha operated a junction with the new Egyptian fleet at Jaffa. By the middle of 1833 Ibrahim had captured Jerusalem, Damascus, Aleppo and Gaza and by August had crossed the Taurus into Asia Minor. The situation was becoming serious for Mahmoud II and in St. Petersburg it was rightly appraised that back of Mehemet Ali was France, hence his success meant the triumph of France. It was imperative for Russia that this should not happen. Mahmoud II, in August, appealed for aid to the Western Powers. Stratford Canning urged England to sign an alliance with Turkey but Lord Palmerston declared that "the Turk was neither desirable as a friend in his present state of civilisation nor capable of regeneration," [1] a point of view which he was to disavow completely in the days of the Crimean War.

This gave a chance for Russian diplomacy to step in. Nesselrode

---

[1] Weigall, A. Brome, A History of Egypt from 1798-1914. New York 1915, p. 67.

in October, wrote to Buteniev, the Russian envoy in Constantinople stating that the Emperor was anxious to put an end to the insurrection by exerting pressure on Mehemet Ali. [2] Accordingly General Muraviev was sent to negotiate with Mehemet Ali whereas Admiral Greigh was ordered to put the Black Sea Fleet in a state of preparedness. The directions given by Nesselrode to Muraviev made Russia's apprehensions clear: "The successes of Mehemet Ali are preparing an ominous catastrophe for the Ottoman Empire and whatever the consequences of such an event they will affect Russia because the advantages gained by Russia as a result of the Treaty of Adrianople would be jeopardized. With Mehemet Ali's triumph, French influence would increase in Constantinople which would become a center of refuge for men without principle or country who are conspiring against Russia..... To sum up.... it suffices to say that with Mehemet Ali, Russia would see the appearance of a powerful and victorious neighbour in the place of a weak and defeated neighbour." [3]

On December 21, on the very day that Mehemet Ali inflicted a smashing defeat upon the Turks at Konieh, Muraviev arrived at Constantinople and offered Russian aid to Turkey which the Porte at the time, thought it more prudent to decline. However, a month later as Mehemet Ali's troops were marching on Brussa, the Reiss Effendi officially approached Buteniev with a request for the aid of a Russian squadron and an expeditionary corps 30,000 strong. Muraviev in the meantime had proceeded to Alexandria and obtained from Mehemet Ali a pledge that he would not advance further. At the news of this development and as a result of strong pressure put on the Porte by the energetic French Ambassador in Constantinople, Admiral Roussin, Turkey recoiled and withdrew her demand for Russian aid (January 27, 1833). However, the Sultan not having mentioned this officially in an audience with Buteniev, Russia went ahead. On February 8 a Russian squadron composed of 9 vessels under Admiral Lazarev anchored in the Bosphorus at Buyuk Dere while in March a force of 5,000 men were landed and encamped in the valley of Unkiar Skelessi. Additional troops were assembled at Odessa ready for immediate embarcation and an army corps moved up to the Danube. Count Orlov was placed in supreme command of the expedition with full powers to carry on all diplomatic negotiations required. The Russian force was to remain in Turkey

---

[2] Nesselrode to Buteniev October 28, 1932, quoted Goriainow B. Le Bosphore et Les Dardanelles. Paris 1910, p. 29.

[3] Goriainow, op. cit. p. 29. 30.

until Mehemet Ali had recrossed the Taurus and reached an agreement with the Sultan. Orlov was further instructed to act in such a way as to win the confidence of the Turks, avoid antagonizing Austria and offset British and French intrigues in Constantinople. He was further to maintain an attitude of complete independence and not to associate his policies with those of any other power. Orlov's position was a difficult one for it was easy for Admiral Roussin to persuade the Turks that the Russians had come to stay. The frightened Turkish ministers told Orlov that if the Russians did not leave, the Egyptians would refuse to retreat, to which Orlov replied that in such case he would bring additional troops from Odessa and force Ibrahim to withdraw. Similarly, when the French attempted to send their warship "la Messange" through the Dardanelles, it was at Orlov's insistence that the Turkish forts opened fire and forced the French to abandon their attempt. His policy, as he put it to Nesselrode, "of patting the Turks with one hand and showing a fist with the other" proved to be the right one and he made sufficient headway to raise the main issue of his mission, the proposal of a Russo-Turkish military alliance.

Orlov's task was considerably facilitated by the steadfast attitude of the Sultan, Mahmoud II, who did not share the vacillations of his ministers and remained faithful to his new pro-Russian policy. The question of an alliance was raised in the first interview between the Sultan and Orlov on April 30, five days after the latter's arrival in Constantinople. Nesselrode had informed Orlov that the Emperor favoured the alliance because it would stop Mehemet Ali, it would eliminate French influence and it would render Turkey peaceful and powerless. On June 26 the treaty of alliance was duly signed at Unkiar Skelessi and two days later Ibrahim Pasha began his much delayed retreat. Having thus achieved his purpose, Orlov ordered the Russian forces to be embarked for Russia. The treaty, valid for 8 years, was composed of 6 articles providing for mutual military aid in the event of a menace to the integrity of the territories of the contracting parties. In Article 3, Russia declared that as a result of her sincere desire to assure "the duration, maintenance and the independence of the Sublime Porte" she would furnish Turkey with such naval and land forces as the contracting parties would judge necessary. In return for which, in a secret article, the Sublime Porte pledged itself "in lieu of the aid she was to have furnished in accordance with the principle of reciprocity, to limit her action.....to the closing of the Straits of the Dardanelles, so as not to permit the entrance of any foreign warships under any pretence whatsoever."[4]

---

[4]Goriainow, op. cit. p. 42, 43.

No mention of the right of passage for Russian warships was made, Russia assuming that this had been provided for by the treaty of 1805. To all effects the new treaty gave a very definite strategical preponderance to the powerful Russian Black Sea Fleet over the fleets of England and France in the Eastern Mediterranean for, by using the Black Sea as closed harbour, the Russians were in a position to intercept the lines of British and French communications in the Mediterranean and return to the Black Sea without the British or French being able to pursue them. Equally important was the hold that Russia had obtained over Turkey; Russian engineers were employed to erect the fortifications on the Bosphorus and Russian officers were invited to reorganize the Turkish Army.

Though the treaty remained secret and the Russian Government did not communicate it officially until the spring of the following year, the main clauses appeared, through Turkish indiscretion, in the Morning Herald of London on August 21. The impression produced abroad was tremendous. Writing in October 1833, the French Minister of Foreign Affairs, the Duc de Broglie, summed it up by declaring that Russia "has determined, in the face of Europe, to proclaim openly, to erect into a principle of international law, its exclusive, exceptional preponderance, in the affairs of the Ottoman Empire." [5] France and England assembled their fleets at Tenedos in a naval demonstration which scared the Turks but failed to make any impression on Russia. Palmerston instructed Lord Ponsonby in March 1834 to inform the Porte that Turkey could count on the assistance of the British Fleet in place of the Russian Fleet should she so desire. Meanwhile at Münchengraetz in September 1833, Russia obtained a sanction of her policy from her two allies, Austria and Prussia, and Metternich's thinly veiled hostility to the treaty was placated by a promise given by the Czar not to invoke the treaty without previously consulting Austria. But in 1835 there occurred an incident which tested the validity of the treaty and showed that the Turks were abiding by it. The American frigate, "The United States" requested permission of the Porte to pass through the Straits into the Black Sea. The Reiss Effendi immediately consulted the Russian Ambassador who advised him not to give the permission in order to avoid setting a precedent.

---

[5] Guizot, F., Memoires to Illustrate the History of My Time. London 1861, Vol. IV, p. 384.

II

A superficial quietness came over the situation in the Near East after the signing of the Treaty of Unkiar Skelessi which however did not deceive the Russian Government. Mehemet Ali had been humbled but not defeated and was biding his time before challenging Turkey anew. Turkey was reorganizing her military forces with the aid of a mission of Prussian officers and was visited in 1835 by a young captain of the Prussian General Staff, Freiherr von Moltke, who used a six month's stay in the East not only to learn the Turkish language but to write a competent history of the campaign of 1828-29, thereby laying the foundations for a career which was to make him the greatest soldier of his day. In 1838 he was officially appointed advisor to the Turkish general in command of the troops in Armenia, which were to be used in the campaign against Mehemet Ali. The Russian Government could not but view with displeasure this displacing of Russian instructors by Germans in the Turkish Army, so soon after the conclusion of the alliance. On the other hand it was in the better interests of Russia to have Turkey sufficiently strong to be able to hold Mehemet Ali in check, the more so as Nicholas I was watching with alarm the growth and spread of what he termed the "French spirit," meaning by that not only the French influence in the East but the general spirit of revolutionary unrest. Furthermore, with the hostility of the French and English so visible through their action both in Poland and in Turkey, it was not surprising to find the Russian Government once more vigilantly preparing for war in the East. The military forces concentrated on the coast of the Black Sea during the 1833 crisis were retained there. The 5th Corps was stationed permanently at Sebastopol and the troops were assigned to constructing the gigantic forts around that city which stood Russia in good stead during the Crimean War. Unfortunately, however, only the approaches to the city by sea were fortified, leaving the inland routes open. The 5th Corps, together with the 2nd Corps, was to form an expeditionary force to be transported across the Black Sea to Constantinople, while the 3rd Corps was to invade Moldavia or Wallachia and make its way overland toward the Turkish capital. The Black Sea Fleet was brought up to full complement and a question of purchase of steamers in America was under consideration. These preparations had the object of meeting any untoward event in Turkey which, in the opinion of Nicholas, would probably lead to a war with England and France. Russia thus had an expeditionary force of 80,000 men concentrated in Sebastopol and in Kherson whereas England, it was estimated, had only 40,000 men available, the rest being sent to face the Canadian rebellion and to watch the United States. "Let

England and France stew, we are ready," said Nicholas.[6]

When the Russian Consul-General in Alexandria, Baron Medem, reported to Nesselrode[7] that Mehemet Ali had informed him of his decision to proclaim his independence from Turkey, the crisis had come. Nicholas received this report while he was at Toeplitz and wrote on the margin "It is extremely suspicious and the future appears to me very uncertain but we are ready."[8] He immediately ordered his Minister of War, Count Chernyshev, (July 15) to have the 5th Corps in readiness to move. Chernyshev and Paskevich however were of the opinion that the sending of the 3rd Corps through the Principalities would be a mistake for, on one hand it would arouse the suspicion of Austria and on the other raise the difficult problem of supplying the corps while in Moldavia. The British were watching closely, and ten days earlier the British Chargé d'Affaires in St. Petersburg called at the Ministry of Foreign Affairs to ask for an explanation of Russia's amassing war supplies in the Principalities. Paskevitch suggested that the occupation of the entrance of the Bosphorus should be the sole method of coming to the aid of Turkey and should Turkey object to this, under pressure from England and France, the Bosphorus should be seized by force.[9] The French Ambassador in St. Petersburg, Baron Barante, on his side, expressed the conviction that Russia could easily take Constantinople and the Straits. However, in the event of a general war, the possibility of a direct French attack on Russia across Germany had to be considered. Accordingly Nicholas, on his way back from Toeplitz, visited Bavaria, Württemberg, and Prussia, sounding out the attitude of the rulers bound to him by family ties. The war-like King of Württemberg alone responded with enthusiasm and, at an interview in his summer palace at Friedrichshafen, depicted the role Württemberg would play in the event of a war with France. The other monarchs showed no desire to get involved in a conflict which did not concern them. Nicholas further made a surprise visit to Stockholm, reviving the old friendship which had somewhat fallen on bad days. Sweden by her geographic position, if not her military power, could not be overlooked in the Russian scheme of defense. But nobody wanted war and Metternich also fully shared with the cabinets of Paris and London

---

[6] Mosely, Philip E., Russian Diplomacy and the Opening of the Eastern Question in 1838 and 1839. Cambridge 1934, p. 41.

[7] Medem to Nesselrode June 16/28, 1838

[8] Mosely, op. cit., p. 36 footnote

[9] Sbornik, Imperatorskogo Russkogo Istoricheskogo Obshchestva. St. Petersburg 1864-1916. Vol. CXXII, p. 383-385.

their dislike of seeing Russia being given a chance to put the Treaty of Unkiar Skelessi into effect. The easiest way out was to put pressure on Mehemet Ali and this was done by the powers so effectively that Mehemet Ali, impressed, decided to postpone his declaration of independence for a while at least.

The diplomatic shadow fencing produced by this crisis revealed to what an extent the various issues in Europe were intertwined. Dissatisfied with the position of isolation in which she found herself in the Belgian crisis, France showed signs of coming to terms with Russia, and Nicholas did not turn an entirely deaf ear to these overtures. Palmerston was greatly worried and wrote to Granville on June 8, 1838, "It must not be forgotten that one great danger to Europe (read England) is the possibility of a combination between France and Russia which although prevented at present by the personal feelings of the Emperor may not always be as impossible as it is now; and it would be well to fix the policy of France on the right track with respect to affairs of the Levant while we have the power to do so." [10]

It was known that the conservative policies of Count de Molé, the French Prime Minister, were being appreciated by Nesselrode and the Czar, and Nicholas I during his stay in Berlin in the summer of 1838 said a few gracious words about Louis Philippe which were passed on to the King. These small indices were picked up both in Paris and in London. Accordingly France offered to restrain Mehemet Ali if Russia would agree to put pressure on the Sultan to moderate his policy. For this purpose Molé agreed with the British Cabinet that a Franco-British naval demonstration would impress Mehemet Ali sufficiently to achieve this end. At the same time, however, France insisted that the Powers should guarantee to the Egyptian Pasha the terms which he had asked from Turkey. But, as Pozzo di Borgo pointed out from London, this apparently conciliatory policy was a conciliation at the expense of the Sultan and furthermore the presence of the naval forces of the two western powers in the Eastern Mediterranean might turn out to be a menace for Russia. After conferring with Austria, Russia came out with a different suggestion. She proposed that a simultaneous and identical declaration should be addressed to Mehemet Ali by all the Great Powers. She also stressed the desirability of maintaining the Viceroy of Egypt in his present relations with the Sultan, and gave the assurance that she would view without suspicion any measures which would insure the maintenance of

---

[10] Bulver Lytton, Henry. Life of Henry John Temple, Viscount Palmerston. London 1871-74. Vol. II, p. 269, quoted Mosely, op. cit., p. 51.

the status quo but warned that in the event Mehemet Ali should embark on "an unjust aggression" Russia would be forced to intervene and to grant "the aid and assistance which the Sultan could demand of him," (the Emperor). Thus Russia was reasserting the Treaty of Unkiar Skelessi. This communication was made first to the Cabinet in London and then, after a delay to see what effect it had produced there, to the Cabinet in Paris. Palmerston saw in this declaration a threat to invade Syria but Molé preferred to give it a peaceful interpretation and declared that it was not provocative, Russia being justified in standing by her ally. Thus a certain divergence of views had occurred between the western allies whereas Metternich concurred entirely with the Russian démarche. Molé, by his conservative views, was inclining towards Russia and, on the Russian side, Pozzo di Borgo was working steadily for a Franco-Russian rapprochement. Molé made a cautious but definite bid by asking Russia to give France moral support in European questions and offering to come to an understanding in Eastern affairs which would be satisfactory to both parties. The offer however met with no response in St. Petersburg--Nicholas was too rigid to change entirely from hostility to friendship, and Nesselrode's purpose was to go only far enough to separate England from France and to block the unwelcome suggestion of a possible European conference over the Eastern issue. Quite obviously a conference would lead to the discussion of the Treaty of Unkiar Skelessi and Russia's position in the Straits. For this very reason Palmerston was anxious to have a conference, and on June 8 he suggested to France that he favoured a "short convention between England and France on the one hand and Turkey on the other, by which the two former should bind themselves for a limited time to afford to the latter naval assistance in the event of her demanding it to protect her territory against attack; and the wording might be so framed as to include either Russia or Mohamet Ali." [11] In other words an Unkiar Skelessi in reverse. At the same time he approached the Austrian Ambassador (June 24) with a suggestion that the Austrian Army should render military assistance to the Sultan. Metternich was at first agreeable to these suggestions and Palmerston early in July proposed a conference to discuss this project. In August Palmerston revived the issue but Nesselrode won Metternich over to his view and obtained the somewhat hesitant support of Molé, after which he informed Palmerston that he saw no need for a conference. A somewhat acrid exchange of notes between England and Russia, interspersed by war scares, followed throughout the

---

[11] Bulver Lytton, op. cit., p. 269-271.

year but Nesselrode had obtained his aim and the idea of a conference was finally abandoned.

If by the autumn Mehemet Ali's virtual renouncement of his aggressive intentions had relieved the situation, particularly since he set out on a journey during the winter to inspect gold mines in Senaar, it did not eliminate the danger of war but merely reversed the situation. This was because the more Mehemet Ali showed moderation, the more warlike the Sultan became since he fiercely hated his vassal and was prepared to avenge past humiliations at the first opportunity. Thus the center of the crisis was transferred from Alexandria to Constantinople and the stress gradually shifted from the Egyptian question to the Straits question. The two questions were linked into one when the energetic and violently anti-Russian British Ambassador in Constantinople, Lord Ponsonby, started a drive to destroy Russia's predominance in Turkey by playing up to the warlike intentions of Sultan Mahmoud. Ponsonby's aim was to replace the Russo-Turkish Alliance by an Anglo-Turkish entente and now, profiting by a temporary absence of Buteniev from the city, he had the field virtually to himself. Ponsonby pursued his drive along three lines: to persuade Reshid Pasha, the Reiss Effendi, to come to London; to arrange a treaty of commerce; and to obtain Turko-British naval co-operation. The treaty of commerce was negotiated in great secrecy and signed on August 16, 1838. It contained clauses which dealt a virtual death blow to Turkish economy and further abolished the monopolies which were the principal source of revenue for the Sultan. The Turks, however, hoped that by granting these privileges they would obtain political support and possibly military support from England. Reshid left for London immediately after signing the treaty and the European chancelleries were quick to associate the two events. Pozzo di Borgo, in particular, was alarmed and saw as inevitable an alliance between Britain and Turkey which would be directed against Russia. The announcement which followed to the effect that the Turkish and British Fleets would engage in joint manoeuvres and that British officers would be placed aboard Turkish vessels, seemed to substantiate fully Pozzo's alarm. Not only Russia but France became uneasy as well. In these circumstances Buteniev returned post haste to Constantinople on September 3 and set himself the immediate task of undoing everything that Ponsonby had done. He found the Sultan much less cordial to him than previously and he waited for an opportunity to make a bold move. This was provided by a rumour which spread in Constantinople that the British Fleet was about to enter the Dardanelles under pretence of refueling. Buteniev asked for an explanation and made it clear that it was his duty....."to warn his Highness against any action or surprise which might be intended to introduce even for a moment, any English warships into the Dardanelles: that such a fact, whatever pretext might be adopted to lend it colour, was of a nature to furnish the most just motives of surprise and dissatisfaction to the Imperial Court (of Russia) and to provoke.... consequences so serious that it might become the signal for that conflagration of the Orient which the Porte and the powers were so anxious to prevent by all means in their power"...... [12] The warning had its effect and the Sultan replied two days later that under no circumstances would he allow any English warships to enter the Straits. This was Ponsonby's first setback.

Having achieved this, Buteniev next set himself the task of obtaining the recall of the Turkish squadron operating jointly with the British, and on October 23 he was able to report to Nesselrode that the Sultan had ordered the Turkish Fleet back to winter in the Bosphorus. The Sultan had been disgruntled that the combined fleets had never approached the coast of Egypt, as promised by Admiral Stopford, but had merely cruised between Smyrna and the Dardanelles. Following Nesselrode's instructions, Buteniev had played on the Sultan's vanity by asking him "Is it becoming to the interests and dignity of the Sultan to leave his Fleet in the hands of the English and to render it, so to speak, hostage to the capricious and passionate policy of Lord Palmerston?" [13] Next Buteniev dropped a hint that if British officers remained in Turkish service Russia would demand a similar privilege and the British officers were sent home. Thus Russia had regained most of her positions.

There still remained the treaty of commerce. Nesselrode was worried for fear it contained some secret clauses. Early in December Buteniev reported that according to his information, which corroborated that obtained by the French Embassy, no such clauses existed. There remained, however, the danger that Reshid Pasha might conclude some such agreement in London. There was also the danger that Reshid might be induced to accept the idea of the conference on eastern affairs which Palmerston was so anxious to obtain and which Turkey might accept as giving her a means of gaining the support of the Great Powers. Nesselrode instructed Buteniev to draw up a memorandum for presentation to the Sultan which pointed out that international conferences were always fatal for weaker states, as in the case of Greece and Belgium, and that, furthermore, Mehemet Ali would become the equal of the Sultan by

---

[12] Buteniev to Nesselrode, Sept. 21/Oct. 2, 1838. Folio 50. No. 11, quoted Mosely, op. cit., p. 106-7.

[13] Nesselrode to Buteniev Oct. 27, 1838 Folio 50, No. 1441, quoted Mosely op. cit., p. 109.

the fact that both would have the same voice at the conference table. The Sultan, very impressed, ordered Reshid to steer clear of any conference. As the negotiations between Palmerston and Reshid dragged on throughout the winter, Buteniev managed to secure a further restriction of Reshid's activities by the Sultan's order that he should not sign anything without referring the matter to the Porte and that he should not accept anything detrimental to Russia. This made the negotiations in London drag on fruitlessly until Palmerston in April 1839 offered his final terms for an Anglo-Turkish alliance. Once more he offered Anglo-Turkish naval cooperation in the event Mehemet Ali went to war. The two fleets were to act off the coasts of Syria and Egypt and the Turks were to declare a blockade against Egyptian shipping. Disgruntled by the paucity of these offers in return for the valuable economic advantages already given to England, the Sultan ordered Reshid to terminate the negotiations. Anxious now to regain the entire support of Russia and to destroy the impression produced by his negotiations with England, he placed all the secret materials concerning the progress of the latter at the disposal of the Russian Embassy. At the same time he ordered Hafiz Pasha, the commander of his army assembled against Mehemet Ali, to advance into Syrian territory. Thus the last results of Ponsonby's drive had been nullified and Russia had gained a signal diplomatic victory in Constantinople. But psychologically one important result was gained by the British--Russia had her faith in the alliance with Turkey seriously impaired by these events and this was one of the contributing factors which made Russia decide not to put the Treaty of Unkiar Skelessi into effect when hostilities did break out.

III

The Turkish Army crossed the Euphrates in April 1839, and attacked the Egyptian forces of Ibrahim Pasha. The French Cabinet immediately sent two officers, Callier to Alexandria and Foltz to Constantinople, to persuade both sides to desist from further action, while Buteniev warned the Porte of the dangers to which this precipitate move might lead. The Foltz mission in Constantinople was a complete failure but Mehemet Ali, who received Callier on June 15 and 16, was persuaded to issue an order to his son to cease any further advance. Callier left Alexandria for Ibrahim Pasha's headquarters with Mehemet Ali's order, but before he was able to reach Syria, Ibrahim had fought the battle of Nesib and crushed the Turkish Army. When Callier did reach his destination he found the Egyptian Army advancing rapidly toward Konieh. After a violent dispute with the French negotiator, Ibrahim was finally persuaded to obey his father's instructions and to occupy a line running from Marach to Orfa, agreeing to cross the Taurus only in the event of any further Turkish aggression and to leave to French diplomacy the task of fulfilling Mehemet Ali's ambitions. Meanwhile came the news of the sudden death of Sultan Mahmud and the accession to power on June 30 of his successor Abdul Medjid. Two weeks later the Turkish Fleet under the command of Ahmed Fewzi Pasha, composed of 8 ships of the line, 12 frigates and 2 brigs sailed into the harbour of Alexandria and surrendered to Mehemet Ali. Thus, according to the words of Guizot, Turkey, in three weeks, had lost her sovereign, her army and her fleet. Overwhelmed by so many misfortunes the Turkish Grand Vizir, Khosrew Pasha, made a move to terminate the conflict and on July 5 sent a letter to the Viceroy of Egypt offering him the hereditary dominion of Egypt. Mehemet Ali replied to this message by declaring that he would consider peace if Turkey added to Egypt the hereditary possession of the territories at present occupied by his forces. These terms, when known, were deemed moderate by Metternich and by the ambassadors of the Great Powers, but Lord Ponsonby was of a different opinion.

These rapid developments had placed Russia in a ticklish position. The events of the preceding year had made her lose faith in the value of her Turkish alliance and yet she might be called upon to fulfil her obligations under the Treaty of Unkiar Skelessi, which would lead to an armed conflict or at best a diplomatic clash with the other powers. She would find herself isolated and the powers would acquire the long sought opportunity of being able to interfere in her relations with Turkey. It was therefore with great relief that Russia learned of the direct negotiations proceeding between Turkey and Egypt--the best possible solution for her since it eliminated the necessity of her own action under her alliance and kept the rival powers out of the conflict. No wonder therefore that Nesselrode said to the Duc de Barante, the French Ambassador in St. Petersburg, "Be assured that we will readily give our approbation to any arrangement made between Turkey and Egypt,"[14] to which the Ambassador replied "What will be settled between Turkey and Egypt would have neither value nor stability so long as this arrangement is not placed under the guarantee of the Powers."[15] By these words he had touched the crux of the situation. Left to themselves the Turks and Egyptians would have settled the quarrel but it was not in the interest of the Western Powers that this should occur for they were anxious to use this

---

[14] Sabry, M., L'Empire Egyptien sous Mohamed Ali et la Question d'Orient, Paris 1930.

[15] Sabry, op. cit., p. 448.

conflict as a lever directed against Russian preponderance in Turkey. Marshal Soult in writing to his ambassador in London, Baron Bourqueney, on July 26 made this plain: "For England as well as for us and Austria, though she does not proclaim it openly, the main, the real object of the concert of powers is to restrain Russia and to accustom her to negotiating in common in the affairs of the Orient. I believe therefore that the powers should give full approbation to the conciliatory sentiments shown by the Porte but at the same time should invite the Porte not to precipitate matters and to negotiate with the Viceroy only through the intermediary of the allies."[16] The Ambassador replied that Lord Palmerston concurred entirely with these views. "He (Lord Palmerston) is very afraid that the Russian Cabinet might strive in Constantinople for a direct settlement between the Sultan and Mohamed Ali..... but he thinks that even in the event of a direct settlement, we should continue our efforts to achieve by moral co-operation of the four courts a settlement to which the fifth will be forced to accede."[17]

Meanwhile, at the instigation of France and Britain, Metternich suggested a conference in Vienna to discuss the question of military aid to Turkey and more particularly the sending of an allied squadron to the coast of Turkey and the Dardanelles, a move to which Russia objected violently. In his instructions to Buteniev, Nesselrode laid down the principles of Russia's policy as approved by the Czar, 1) The decision to maintain the integrity of Turkey and to oppose any attempts to endanger this integrity, 2) To consult with Austria concerning measures to be taken to achieve this end and to refuse the recognition of any order which would endanger the present independence of Turkey. A copy of this message was sent to Novikov in Vienna to be shown to Metternich. As for the stand to be taken by Turkey, Nesselrode suggested that the settlement should run along the following lines: hereditary possession by Mehemet Ali of the territories now occupied by his forces in return for the payment of a tribute to Turkey and the return of her fleet. In the meantime, between July 21 and 27, three councils (divans) were deliberating the issue in the Turkish capital, one of which was presided over by the Grand Vizier and the Sheikh ul Islam, and it was decided to accept the conditions of Mehemet Ali. But European diplomacy was not going to allow peace to come to Turkey at so cheap a price. The very next day, July 28, under instructions from Metternich, the Austrian Ambassador, after consulting his colleagues, forwarded a note to the

---

[16]Sabry, op. cit., p. 449.
[17]Sabry, op. cit., p. 450.

Porte stating that "the five undersigned ambassadors, acting in conformity with instructions received yesterday from their respective courts are happy to inform the Sublime Porte that accord between the five Powers relative to the Eastern Question is assured and they request the Sublime Porte.....to make no final decisions on the aforesaid question without their endorsement."[18] This note marked the end of the unilateral action of Russia and also kept the wound open in Turkey purely for the egotistic benefit of the Powers. But the accord of the five Powers existed only on paper. Nicholas I openly expressed his displeasure at the way the Powers had interfered in the settlement of the question which had practically been consumated. Furthermore, Nesselrode obdurately refused to accede to a guarantee to be given by the five Powers for the integrity of Turkey. Instead, he kept on proposing that the direct settlement between Turkey and Egypt should be permitted, provided it concerned the Egyptian question alone and did not cover any other parts of the territory of the Ottoman Empire. Then early in August the British squadron, under Admiral Stopford, having joined the French Fleet, under Admiral Lalande, in the Aegean Sea, the allied ambassadors raised the issue of the fleets entering the Dardanelles. The indignant protests of Russia, supported this time by Austria, made the Turkish Government request the departure of the allied fleets from its waters. But above all, Mehemet Ali, furious at the intervention of the Powers which deprived him of the fruits of his victory, ordered Ibrahim Pasha to prepare for an advance of his forces into Asia Minor and openly challenge the Great Powers. This in turn put a severe strain on Franco-British relations. Ever since the French, in return for a pledge of moderation on the part of Mehemet Ali, had taken over the defense of his case, the divergence of views between Paris and London had been increasing. The British wanted Ibrahim Pasha out of Syria and a further difficulty developed over the question of the return of the Turkish Fleet which had surrendered at Alexandria. On the other hand, Metternich was coming closer to England and abandoning Russia. Thus the Eastern situation was hitting back on the Powers and accentuating their differences. One thing became clear--only a regrouping of powers would solve the issue and in this re-orientation it became apparent that just as Austria was drawn toward England by their common interest of putting an end to Russia's hold over Turkey, so England and Russia were being drawn together by their common interest of blocking France's support of Mehemet Ali. Thus, paradoxically, these three powers came

---

[18]Sabry, op. cit., p. 457.

together for divergent reasons and by so doing made Prussia, the friend of both Russia and Austria, follow suit.

This diplomatic revolution took place in August and September and made London the center of events. On September 15 the Russian Minister to Stuttgart, Baron Brunnow, regarded as one of Russia's most able diplomats, arrived in London on a special mission to start negotiations with Palmerston. Brunnow was to prepare a settlement along the following lines: Russia would not renew the Treaty of Unkiar Skelessi and would guarantee the settlement, concluded between Turkey and Egypt, if France and England would consent to the permanent closure of the Straits and abandon the idea of a guarantee covering the whole territory of the Ottoman Empire. Further, should Turkey call for the aid of Russian forces under the Treaty of Unkiar Skelessi, Britain and France would abstain from sending their fleets into the Straits and would concentrate their military action in Syria and Egypt. Palmerston, suspicious, insisted upon the presence of British naval forces wherever the Russians might be. Furthermore, he asked Russia to guarantee the integrity of Turkey and to accept the closing of the Straits as a principle of international law. A convention signed by the five Powers was to replace any unilateral action between Turkey and Russia. The negotiations broke down and Brunnow left London in October. However, he returned in December with specific instructions to come to an agreement and protracted discussions followed along the lines mentioned above until a final agreement was reached in July 1840. In their first phase these negotiations amounted to a regular contest between the French Ambassador Sebastiani and Baron Brunnow. "Sebastiani was firm, calm, sagacious but a little slow..... imperturabable, however and far seeing. Brunnow, nourished in the traditions and designs of the Russian Chancellery, was well instructed, adroit, persevering without obstinacy--never exacting or impatient--an abundant and spirited talker--a well trained and prompt writer of dispatches--clever at seeing the aims of other people while enveloping his own under a dense mantle of conceptions, reserves and comments. Here is a picture of two of the most expert diplomatists of the nineteenth century." [19]

In March the fall of Marshal Soult's cabinet in Paris brought Thiers to power and Guizot as the new French Ambassador to London. In April the Turkish Ambassador in Paris, Nouri Effendi, arrived in England with moderate proposals for a five power settlement of the crisis, but which implied the limiting of Mehemet Ali's hereditary power to Egypt alone without Syria, a condition

---

[19] Mowat, R. B., History of European Diplomacy 1815-1914. London 1927, p. 61.

not acceptable to France. Two days later Guizot was told privately that the British, Russian, Austrian and Prussian negotiators were prepared to accept Nouri Effendi's terms. Guizot also noticed how studiously Brunnow was keeping out of his way while the other two ambassadors showed unusual reserve--Guizot was beginning to sense the isolation of France. In May and June insurrections broke out in Syria revealing how precarious was the hold of Ibrahim Pasha over that province and both Austria and Prussia were impressed by the dark picture of conditions there as painted by British agents on the spot. These reports, according to Metternich "decided everything and brought on the signing of the convention." In Turkey itself a dangerous effervescence was becoming evident. In June the Russophile Grand Vizier, Khosrew Pasha fell, leaving Reshid Pasha alone in charge of affairs.

These events in the East hastened the desire of the Powers to settle the issue. Guizot alone, apparently busy extending his relations in the influential circles of London society, remained on the fringes of the issue, unaware of the true state of affairs. On July 10 Palmerston offered his final terms to Brunnow who accepted them after some modifications. These terms implied that the combined fleets of the Powers, both in the Black Sea and in the Mediterranean, would furnish aid to Turkey should Mehemet Ali's actions render such aid necessary. This co-operation of naval forces was to be regarded as an exceptional measure and the Sultan maintained the right of closing the Straits to all warships, particularly in time of peace. Five days later Mehemet Ali, as a result of encouragements given by Count Walewski, sent on a mission from Paris to Egypt, rejected the peace terms proffered by Turkey, and the same day in London, the so-called Four Power Treaty, settling the issue, was signed between England, Russia, Austria and Prussia. Guizot only learned about this treaty two days later from a British note saying that, in view of the French refusal to join with the Powers, the latter had undertaken the settlement of the crisis without France.

Under this agreement the four Powers offered the hereditary dominion of Egypt, Acre and Southern Syria to Mehemet Ali provided he accepted this offer within ten days, after which the offer was reduced to Egypt alone and was to hold good for twenty days. Mehemet Ali, having refused these terms, the British squadron bombarded Beyrout in September. A British expeditionary force landed in Syria and raised an insurrection against Ibrahim Pasha who was forced to retreat into Egypt. But it was not until February 1841 that Mehemet Ali acknowledged his defeat and the issue was finally settled by granting him the hereditary rulership of Egypt alone. In the meantime France, wounded in her pride and seeing in the treaty of July 1840 the revival of the dreaded Chaumont coalition of the four Powers against her, gave vent to her anger and disappointment by the rise of war fever which plunged Europe into a serious war crisis. Conscripts were called to the colours and the issue was transmuted into a threat against her hereditary enemy on the Rhine--Prussia.

Russia had no direct concern in these events and since the defeat of Mehemet Ali, Russian diplomacy had lost interest in him. What was, however, of direct concern to Russia was the part of the treaty of July 1840 which dealt with the status of Turkey. No guarantee of the Ottoman Empire, as sought by England, was included in the treaty but in the preamble it was stated explicitly that the Powers were "animated by the desire of maintaining the Integrity and Independence of the Ottoman Empire as a Security for the Peace of Europe." [20] After the war crisis had blown over and France had been forced to accept the settlement, a new convention supplementing the treaty of 1840 was negotiated by the five Powers with Turkey and was signed on July 13, 1841, dealing specifically with the Straits question. Article I stipulated that the "ancient rule" concerning the closing of the Straits to all warships should be applied at all times with the sole exception (Art. II) of light vessels in the service of the foreign legations in Constantinople which should be allowed to pass the Straits by express authorization of the Sultan.

This crisis affords the rare instance of a settlement which pleased all parties concerned. England and France had obtained the annulment of the Treaty of Unkiar Skelessi and the five power control of the affairs of Turkey. Russia was not displeased for though she gave up her treaty, the settlement fulfilled the very purpose for which the treaty had been drawn up, namely the defeat of Mehemet Ali and the limitation of French influence in the Orient. Furthermore, an accord with England had been reached which paved the way for better relations with that country and it was along these lines, to eliminate the pernicious effects of the Anglo-Russian rivalry in the East, that Russian diplomacy was next to develop its activity.

IV

The crisis of 1840-41 foreshadowed the possibilty of an important shift in the balance of power of Europe. England and France had come to grips over the Egyptian issue and their relations were to be further strained by the question of the Spanish marriages and the Pritchard affair in Tahiti. On the other hand Russia and England had co-operated in the settlement of the Near

---

[20] Mowat, op. cit., p. 65, footnote I.

THE EASTERN QUESTION 81

Eastern menace and thus the way was paved for a possible further rapprochement. As Nesselrode had written in a memorandum "On land Russia exercises a preponderant influence over Turkey, on the sea England occupies the same position. Isolated, the action of both these powers could do a lot of harm, combined it could do a substantial good." [21] On the other hand, writing to Lieven as early as 1830, Nesselrode had declared explicitly that the Czar considered Russia to have the same right to protect the entrance into the Black Sea as England had to do the same with regard to the Mediterranean and therefore that Russia had the right to dominate the Bosphorus just as England did the Straits of Gibraltar. Some compromise between these contradictory views had to be found before a sound friendship with England could be achieved. Commercial relations offered a certain point of contact and a treaty of commerce "on a footing of liberal reciprocity" was concluded between Russia and England in 1843. Thus the ground had been prepared for the forthcoming negotiations to settle the Eastern Question when they were ushered in dramatically by the somewhat sudden and unexpected visit of Nicholas I to England in 1844.

A few months earlier Nicholas had hinted to Lord Bloomfield in St. Petersburg that he would like to visit London. In March, acting upon these hints, the British Government extended the Czar an official invitation. Nicholas accepted, stating however that he did not know when he could avail himself of the invitation. Then, acting with an impulsive suddenness, Nicholas left his capital so hurriedly that he did not even have time to inform Lord Bloomfield of his departure and a special courier had to be sent to London, the latter arriving only 24 hours before the Czar. On May 31, 1844 Nicholas landed at Woolwich accompanied by a suite of only four persons. Nesselrode had been instructed to meet him in Germany after his return from London. The Czar remained ten days in England during which time, after staying two days in the Russian Embassy, he became the official guest of Queen Victoria at Buckingham Palace. Every evening official banquets were given in his honour, a great military review was held at Windsor and he twice attended the races at Ascot where he was cheered most enthusiastically. Hearing of these cheers Palmerston commented sarcastically: "If we can purchase his goodwill by civility, without any sacrifice of national interest, it would be folly not to do so." [22] However, amidst these festivities, Nicholas met

---

[21] Puryear, V. J., England, Russia and the Straits Question 1844-1856. Berkeley 1931, appendix.

Lords Aberdeen, Melbourne, Palmerston, the Duke of Wellington, and Sir Robert Peel, and spoke to them with a frankness which caused a sensation in London. He was outspoken in his dislike of King Louis Philippe and he based his arguments for British-Russian co-operation on the fact that French imperialism in the Mediterranean and the Near East was equally menacing to both countries, particularly in view of the condition in Turkey. "Turkey is a dying man. We may endeavour to keep him alive but we shall not succeed..... I foresee that I shall have to put my armies into motion and Austria must do the same. I fear nobody in the matter but France."[23] Peel agreed with this and after having discussed possible Anglo-Russian co-operation in Poland, Belgium and Persia, the question of Turkey and the Straits became the main issue at stake. Nicholas stated that he did not want to take Constantinople but that he would never permit England or France to do so and therefore he wanted to maintain the status quo. However, should Turkey fall to pieces England and Russia were to agree upon what course to follow jointly. Discussions proceeded along these lines and led to a definite agreement between Sir Robert Peel and Lord Aberdeen on one side and the Czar on the other.

It was decided that so long as it was possible the present status quo of the Ottoman Empire should be maintained but should Turkey crumble, in a common understanding with Austria and leaving France out, they were to carry out a peaceful partition of Turkey. It was also decided to discuss the terms of the partition in advance so as to be ready for this eventuality. Thus far the agreement was merely oral but both sides considered it binding and, writing to Queen Victoria, Lord Melbourne said, "It is extremely fortunate that Nicholas, with whom it is probable that Great Britain will have such near and intimate relations, should also be a man upon whose honour and veracity strong reliance may be safely and securely placed." Nicholas left London well pleased with the results obtained, one of which was to be henceforth the complete solidarity of action by both countries in Persia. Rushing home to the bedside of his sick daughter, Nicholas sent Nesselrode to London to work out the technical terms of the newly concluded agreement. The business-like Nesselrode, arriving in September at the English capital, after interviews with Lord Aberdeen, set down in a memorandum which was approved by the British Government the points agreed upon. These were formulated to follow closely the ideas expressed by the Czar: England and Russia would 1) endeavour to maintain the existence of the Ottoman Empire in its present state as long as this political combination remair

---

[23] Denkwürdigkeiten aus den Papieren des Freiherrn Christian Friedrich von Stockmar. Braunschweig, 1872, Vol. II, p. 106.

possible; 2) if it becomes apparent that the Ottoman Empire is crumbling they are "to concert with each other previously with regard to the establishment of a new order, destined to replace the existing one, and to take such joint measures that the changes which might occur in the internal structure of that Empire would not endanger the security of their respective states, the rights which are assured by treaties or the maintenance of European equilibrium." [24] Upon returning to Russia on December 28, Nesselrode wrote to Lord Aberdeen stating that "the Emperor feels that the memorandum completely fills this purpose, that it embodies the most exact resumé of his conversations with you and your colleagues" to which Aberdeen replied on January 21, 1845 stating "it gives me much pleasure to find that no differences exist respecting the accuracy of your statement to which I already had borne my humble testimony." [25] Thus both sides had endorsed this agreement. However, it was a fatal mistake of Nicholas to have attached too much value to it. He overlooked the elements of discord and resistance which were not overcome. These were both psychological and economic and were of prime importance.

Nicholas had always been an admirer of England--his early visits to that country had left an indelible mark upon him. But it was the old Tory England he liked while for the England of the Whigs, the Reform Bill and Chartism he had the greatest antipathy. This warmth was reciprocated on the British side. Lord Aberdeen had been completely won over by the frankness and loyalty of the Czar and remained a staunch supporter of the new agreement. The Queen and even the Prince Consort had been favourably impressed. Writing to her uncle, Leopold of Belgium, during the visit of the Czar, Victoria gave the following portrait of her guest in a famous letter: "He is stern and serene with fixed principles of duty which nothing on earth will make him change; very clever, I do not think him and his mind is an uncivilized one. His education has been neglected, politics and military concerns are the only things he takes great interest in..... He is I should say too frank for he talks so openly before which he should not do and with great difficulty restrains himself..... He is bald now but in his chevalier garde uniform he is magnificent still, and very striking." [26]

---

[24] Martens, Fedor Fedorovich. <u>Recueil des traités et conventions conclus par la Russie avec les puissances étrangères.</u> St. Petersburg, 1874-1909. Vol. XV, p. 517-519.

[25] Puryear, op. cit. Appendix F and G.

[26] <u>Letters of Queen Victoria.</u> First Series. New York, 1907. Vol. II, p. 14.

Peel too was impressed by his frankness and trusted him. But Palmerston and Granville were caustic and behind them the great mass of liberals hated Russia as the embodiment of autocracy, and when the Cracow affair and later Russia's aid to Austria in the Hungarian revolt resulted in the worsting of the Poles and Hungarians, the two Whig protégés, this hatred became hysterical. Also must be mentioned the animosity of King Leopold of Belgium and of his personal secretary, the ubiquitous Stockmar who had a great influence on the Prince Consort and the Queen. Thus there was a psychological gulf which was ever widening and the small group of British statesmen in favour of the rapprochement with Russia was helpless to bridge it.

Had the trade relations with Russia been favourable to England this factor, so important in moulding Whig opinion, might have helped to remove this hostility, but at this juncture the reverse was true. The importance of the Anglo-Russian trade relations may be seen by the fact that between 1831 and 1850 England imported about 50% of all Russia's exports. In 1842 England purchased 261,000 quarters of Russian grain exported through Russia's Black Sea ports as compared to 214,000 quarters from Canada. In 1852 the corresponding figures for Russia and Canada had risen to 957,000 and 126,000 respectively.[27] In return for grain, lumber, flax and other raw materials constituting Russian exports to England, of which grain was by far the most important, England sold to Russia manufactured goods and machinery, which however never made up for her imports. Thus the trade balance remained consistently and impressively in favour of Russia. In 1843 Russia exported $56,000,000 and imported $48,000,000 worth. In 1847 the corresponding figures amounted to $121,000,000 and $71,000,000 (of the exports $57,000,000 were accounted for by grain). Thus England was consistently the loser in her trade with Russia. But there were other unfavourable factors. The rise in importance of the Black Sea trade took place during the decade of the 1840's and to a great extent was due to the after effect of the Treaties of Adrianople and Unkiar Skelessi. In the Black Sea, however, British shipping represented only 10% of the whole in 1842, which development also was unfavourable to England. Lastly the Russians competed very closely with British shipping in Turkey as seen by the fact that of the 470 steam vessels which entered Constantinople in 1841, 16% were British and 11% Russian as compared to 3 1/2% French.[28] Thus while all the increase in trade between Russia and England was to the advantage of Russia, trade

---

[27] Puryear, op. cit., p. 128.
[28] Puryear, op. cit., p. 93-125.

between England and Turkey was increasing equally, offsetting the loss resulting from the Russian trade. Thus Turkey was becoming a better customer for England than Russia and, needless to say, the policies and sympathies of an essentially trading nation were to be on the side of the best customer. Furthermore, whereas no industrial competition or development of any kind was to be feared in Turkey, the 1840's saw the rise in Russia of an increasingly important textile industry. Imports of cotton into Russia increased fourfold between 1830 and 1842 and by 1850, 350,000 spindles produced 9,600,000 pounds of cotton yarn and the total value of Russian textiles was estimated at 40,000,000 roubles. These textiles and wools could not compete effectively with British textiles in Europe but did so very successfully in Persia, Central Asia and China, and the British complained that the Russians were selling their cloth at Tabriz 10% to 20% cheaper than British produce cost at Manchester. These factors together with the dislike of the autocratic policies of Russia particularly in the revolution of 1848-49 made the secret agreement of 1844 so illusory that by 1849, in the affair of the Hungarian prisoners in Turkey, the British Fleet was once more appearing near the Dardanelles in a spirit of hostility toward Russia.

CHAPTER IV

THE REVOLUTION OF 1830 AND THE
ALLIANCE OF THE THREE NORTHERN COURTS

I

The deaths of Louis XVIII and Alexander I just a year apart in 1824 and 1825 did not affect Franco-Russian relations greatly. In Russia the change of ruler meant a more definite and resolute foreign policy; in France thus far it meant little change since the all-powerful Villèle remained in control of foreign affairs. Pozzo di Borgo reported not only an increase in the Minister's power through the rising influence of the Jesuits and the Congregations but also a tendency to concentrate the various branches of the administration in his hands. While still heir to the throne, on August 24, 1824, some three weeks before the death of Louis XVIII, the future Charles X said to the Russian Ambassador: "I hope to remain a long while next to the throne, but if God calls me to the throne, I would like the Emperor (of Russia) to know that I will change nothing, neither my system, nor my ministers." [1] At the first audience given to Pozzo di Borgo, the new King reiterated his adherence to the principle of the European Alliance and regretted the policy of England in abandoning it. [2] As for his personal attitude toward Russia, it was expressed in an audience in February 1825 granted to Prince Volkonsky, who had been sent by the Czar to congratulate the new King on his accession to the throne: "I will never forget", said the King, "what the Emperor (Alexander) has done for my family in delivering France," [3] and added later as Volkonsky was leaving for Russia: "Please assure the Emperor that I am anxious to conserve the good intelligence

---

[1] Martens, Fedor Fedorovich, Recueil des traités et conventions conclus par la Russie avec les puissances étrangères. St. Petersburg, 1874-1909. Vol. XV, p. 40.
[2] Report of Pozzo di Borgo, 5/17 October, 1824 ibidem.
[3] Martens, op. cit., Vol. XV, p. 45.

existing between France and Russia and that all my efforts will tend toward this goal." [4] Thus was apparently answered, to Russia's satisfaction, the major question which Pozzo was instructed to elucidate, namely: would France remain in the European Alliance or would she join Canning in his efforts to stem the interventionist policy of the Three Northern Courts in the major questions of the day concerning Spain, Portugal and Greece. However Pozzo soon noticed a discrepancy between words and acts in Paris and furthermore he did not believe in the stability of the new regime. The Greek question served as a test case of France's policy toward Russia. Pozzo di Borgo was unable to pin Villèle down to any definite attitude and found him procrastinating and evasive. He concluded that France was unwilling to commit herself to the increasingly aggressive stand taken by Russia with regard to Turkey. But early in 1826 Pozzo noticed a tendency to come closer to Russia and the King even went so far as to suggest France's readiness to act jointly with Russia in a naval demonstration against Turkey. Just as this mood was ripening in Paris came the news of the signing of the Protocol of St. Petersburg and produced the impression of a bombshell. France was particularly sensitive to the fear of isolation and here an important diplomatic move had been carried out without French diplomacy being informed. Villèle called a session of his cabinet to discuss the issue and Pozzo was informed that the Protocol had given such a blow to the prestige of France, both external and internal, that France was thereby being pushed toward becoming a revolutionary power which would be obliged to make use of the "compressed passions of Continental Europe." [5]

Though Pozzo noticed the utmost dejection in government circles he was not impressed by this veiled threat and he was right. Indeed, in May France gave her adhesion to this Protocol and in June 1827 became co-signatory of the London Convention relative to Greece. But Russia remained suspicious of France particularly in view of the activities of the French Ambassador in London, Prince Polignac, who attempted to block the signing of the convention by all means available. Polignac revealed himself a persistent enemy of Russia and was regarded in Russia as a British agent. Hence when Polignac was to have been appointed as Ambassador to Russia in the place of Count La Ferronays, who was persona grata with the Czar, Nicholas informed the French Government of his refusal to accept the new Ambassador. At the

---

[4] Report of Prince Volkonsky, March 2, 1825, ibidem p. **44**.
[5] Martens, op. cit., Vol. XV, p. 53.

same time Pozzo di Borgo received instructions which qualified the French court as being "uncertain of its aims and attempting to spread to others the timidity and the suspicions which do not allow her to proceed with firm steps along honorable and worthy ways,"[6] and in the same letter the Ambassador was instructed to remind the French Government of the dangers of alienating the "only power which had rendered great services and is still interested in so doing."[7] The stern warning had its effect and France instructed her diplomatic agents abroad to support Russia's stand against Turkey. Pozzo now began to report the increasing seriousness of the internal conditions in France though he did not foresee immediate trouble. When the government of Villèle fell in January 1828, Count La Ferronays, a staunch friend of Russia, became Minister of Foreign Affairs in the succeeding cabinet of Count de Chabrol. Complete understanding was established between the new Minister and Pozzo di Borgo with regard to a joint policy in Greece, while Nicholas, who was considering war with Turkey, felt confident he had France on his side. A cordial exchange of letters between the two sovereigns strengthened these ties and the words "sincere friend and loyal ally" were used by King Charles in his letter. Furthermore, Charles instructed his Ambassador in St. Petersburg, the Duc de Mortemart, to tell the Emperor that he was firmly resolved to maintain a concerted action of the two governments. And indeed throughout the first year of the Russo-Turkish War France maintained her attitude of loyalty to Russia, thereby discouraging any British schemes of hostile intervention in the war. Throughout the war French public opinion remained on the side of Russia, partly through the influence of a powerful philhellenic movement and, though a passing cloud appeared in Franco-Russian relations when France joined in a move of mediation suggested by Great Britain, the King nevertheless spoke continuously of the "unshakable alliance" with Russia. The Treaty of Adrianople produced a great impression in Paris and was received with signs of unmitigated joy by the King. Under these circumstances the coming to power in August 1829 of the anti-Russian Polignac was considered by Pozzo to be a real catastrophe. However, though the relations of the Ambassador with the new government became decidedly strained even Polignac did not dare alter his course too abruptly and declared, through Mortemart to Nesselrode, that there would be no change in Franco-Russian relations. The King however, under the influence of his new Prime

---

[6]Nesselrode to Pozzo di Borgo, July 28, 1827, Martens, op. cit., Vol. XV, p. 56-57.
[7]Ibidem, p. 56, 57.

Minister grew colder to Russia. Polignac nevertheless was credited with working out a grandiose scheme of European re-adjustment suggested to him by Rayneval, his Ambassador in Vienna, and based on the continued alliance with Russia. Under this scheme Russia was to get Constantinople, France the Rhineland, Prussia a part of Hanover and Saxony, and Austria Serbia and a portion of Dalmatia. [8] Russia in turn showed a warm approval of France's conquest of Algeria on the grounds that this move weakened both Turkey and Great Britain and was useful in getting the French people's thoughts away from their internal problems. Obdurate and ultra reactionary, the very name of Polignac was a symbol of anti-liberalism and his appointment was taken to be a sign that the King was intending to get rid of the constitution. Though Pozzo's reports were inevitably coloured by his dislike of the man, he nevertheless showed insight when he stated that the appointment of Polignac would cost Charles X his throne. In February 1830 he became more explicit, predicted the ordinances which would do away with the constitution and spoke of the inevitable overthrow of the monarchy This alarming news produced a great impression in St. Petersburg and completely overshadowed the advantages which Russia thought she had gained from her unofficial alliance with France. In April Nesselrode wrote to Pozzo that in view of the uncertainty of the internal conditions in France the Emperor "desires the peace and the happiness of France, and consequently seeks the triumph of a wise moderation." [9] At the same time Pozzo was secretly instructed to do everything in his power to bring moderate influences to bear upon the King. Even more explicit was the Czar when he told Mortemart that Russia would not countenance any measures taken by the King in violation of the Charter.

II

While Russia was beginning to lose faith in her French alliance the advent of Nicholas I to the throne was the cause of the strengthening and crystallization of a trend which eventually was to become sufficiently solidified to form the main axis of Russia's foreign policy. This was the growing friendship between Russia and Prussia which eventually extended to most of the other German states. There were several reasons for this. The complete harmony of mutual interests and of political systems was one. But perhaps

---

[8] Blanc, Louis, *History of Ten Years*, 1830-1840, London 1844, Vol. I, p. 74.
[9] Martens, op. cit., Vol. XV, p. 91.

even more important were sentimental reasons: first, the confraternity of arms in the wars against Napoleon, particularly in 1813, and second, family ties through marriage between the ruling families. The confraternity of arms linked not only both officers' corps but extended such a strong influence on both Courts that the future Czars Nicholas I and Alexander II remained faithful to it, whereas in Prussia, Prince Wilhelm, later King of Prussia and Emperor of Germany, made of the friendship with Russia a cardinal principle of his life and policy up to his very death. This mutual respect and friendship created by the feats of arms of the two armies in their struggle against Napoleon proved to be not only of advantage to both nations but on a nation reared in military ideals such as Prussia it was to produce a more permanent impression than on any other. "In 1813 his (Alexander's) army surprised Germany by its splendid aspect, in 1814 he entered Paris, in 1815 he put in the field a second army of 300,000 combattants with 2,000 cannons, such was the power of Alexander to whom Napoleon had left Europe in legacy." [10]

This military aspect, by a curious twist of fate, became entwined with a romantic issue, and both were predestined to appeal to the two strongest emotions of Nicholas I, about to succeed his brother: his love of military things and his love for his wife and family. Indeed Grand Duke Nicholas had gone on a tour of Europe for the first time in 1814, anxious to participate in the war, but had reached Paris only after its occupation by the Russians. On his way home he passed through Berlin where he first made the acquaintance of his future wife, Princess Charlotte of Prussia, daughter of King Friedrich Wilhelm III. On his second visit abroad he happened to be in Berlin just as the Russian Guards were passing through the Prussian capital in their triumphant march home from France and it was in this atmosphere of military glory, so dear to the heart of the future autocrat of Russia, that his betrothal to Princess Charlotte took place. The marriage was celebrated with great pomp in St. Petersburg on July 13, 1817, and the young bride, on conversion to the Greek Church, took the name of Alexandra Feodorovna. She was accompanied to Russia by her brother, Prince Wilhelm who returned from his stay in the Russian capital a staunch and everlasting friend of that country. After the birth of their first child in 1818 (the future Alexander II) Nicholas and his young wife visited Berlin once more in 1820-21 and carefully studied the organization of the Prussian Army. In 1823 the betrothal of Nicholas's younger brother, Grand Duke Michael to Princess Charlotte Frederica of Württemberg (daughter

---

[10] Chateaubriand, Congrés de Verone. Oeuvres Complètes, Vol. XII, Paris without date, p. 91.

of Prince Paul, brother of Empress Maria Fedorovna) resulted
in another family reunion with the Hohenzollerns and Prince Wilhelm of Prussia made a second extended stay in Russia. Thus
came into existence the regular family meetings either in Berlin
or in St. Petersburg which were to shape the international policies
of both countries and thereby to have a great influence on the affairs of Europe. The family ties thus created became strong
enough to override the first serious difficulties between the two
countries arising from a conflict of economic interests.

From the 1820's Prussia, developing rapidly economically,
began striving to corner the trade with Russia and obtain the
virtual monopoly in supplying Russia with manufactured goods.
But the government of the Russian Kingdom of Poland complained
that thereby Polish industry and trade were suffering. By an additional act in the Treaty of Vienna, drawn in 1818, special tariffs
were to operate between the three former sections of partitioned
Poland. But in 1821 Russia insisted on cancelling this act as
being profitable to Prussia at the expense of Russia, for as a part
of former Poland was in the hands of Prussia, it permitted Prussian goods not only to flood Poland, profiting by the franchise,
but from Poland to penetrate into Russia proper. Nesselrode
raised a cry of alarm to his Minister in Berlin, Alopeus, "Our
agriculture is falling...our nascent industry will perish in the
cradle, for with the franchises of 1818, foreign industries are
creating a competition which it cannot yet sustain." [11] Accordingly Alopeus, in January 1822, approached the Berlin government which however refused to yield the advantages obtained by
the act of 1818. The failure of his mission induced Alopeus to
suggest the threat of diverting to Austria the Russian mail, an important source of Prussian revenue, by re-routing it via Cracow.
On February 15, 1822, Czar Alexander wrote a personal letter to
King Friedrich Wilhelm III about the issue, couched in terms which
revealed his displeasure and at the same time the Russian Government decided unilaterally to revoke the act of 1818 and in March a
new protective tariff was officially announced, the Prussians however being exempt for a year from application of the same. This
move produced a sensation in Berlin and Prussia protested. She
retaliated in April, 1823 by raising her tariff and the negotiations
which had started between the two governments in July, 1822
dragged on until the fall of 1823, when they broke down completely.
Alexander then sent to Berlin a special envoy, Baron Mohrenheim,
who carried on negotiations from January 1824 to October and
finally succeeded in persuading the Prussians to yield. A new

---

[11] Nesselrode to Alopeus, Martens, op. cit., Vol. VIII, p. 2.

convention safeguarding Russia's interests was drawn up and signed in March 1825 and the customs war came to an end. The visit to Russia of Prince Wilhelm in 1823 and the exchange of cordial messages resulting from it did much to relieve the growing strain resulting from this economic conflict.

But the rapidly developing crisis in the Near East, which was leading up to the Russo-Turkish War in 1828, placed Prussia in the singularly difficult position of having to keep a balance between her Russian and Austrian friendships, and to maintain complete neutrality. Accordingly Prussia warmly supported the Protocol of St. Petersburg but, as a result of Austrian pressure, refused to take part in the London Conference. With the approach of hostilities Nicholas, now reigning, wrote a personal letter explaining to the King of Prussia the causes of the coming war and in his reply the King stressed his hope for peace and suggested a joint action of the three allied powers to induce Turkey to yield. But when Prince Wilhelm wanted to join the Russian Army in the Balkans, the King refused to grant him the permission. Nevertheless when Austria in the fall of 1828 proposed a joint mediation to save Turkey from complete defeat, Prussia refused to associate herself with this anti-Russian move. Again in May, 1829 when Czar Nicholas brought his family to Berlin on the occasion of the marriage of Prince Wilhelm with Princess Augusta of Saxe Weimar (niece of Nicholas I), as a special courtesy, the 6th Cuirassier regiment of which the Czar was the "chef" was sent specially to meet the Czar half way through Prussia at Sibillenort and Nicholas indulged his love for parades by having the regiment march past him. In Berlin he carried on negotiations with the King which resulted in the dispatching of General Müffling to Constantinople on a secret mission which very materially influenced the outcome of the war in favour of Russia. The Peace of Adrianople caused genuine rejoicing in Berlin both because it was a Russian victory and because it put an end to a situation fraught with dangerous potentialities for Prussia. Prussian diplomacy by carefully husbanding her relations with Russia came out of this dangerous crisis having fully retained the friendship of Russia and without losing the goodwill of Austria.

III

The news of the revolution of 1830 in France hit St. Petersburg like a thunderbolt. "So long as we live, dear Princess," wrote Nesselrode to Princess Lieven, "there will not be another moment of tranquility in the world."[12] It meant for Russia something infinitely more than a change of regime in France, which brought to an end the policy of close co-operation with Charles X. It meant a challenge to the fundamentals of Russian diplomacy which aimed at maintaining in existence the old order in accordance with the principles of Metternich. "In practice it pursued the purpose of blocking the new political strengthening of France and opposing the growth of the world power of England."[13] Hence for Nicholas I the growth of democratic ideas increased the influence of France and England whereas conservatism stood for the defence of the interests of Russia as a world power. Hence also this revolution was viewed as a double challenge, - a challenge to the internal stability of Europe and Russia and a challenge to the international position of Russia as a power. Furthermore it meant that a wave of revolutionary agitation starting from Paris and passing through Belgium and Italy was to eventually reach Russian Poland where Russia was to face an open insurrection which soon developed into a real war. It finally meant the first open attempt to annul the clauses of the Treaty of Vienna which for Russia was the cornerstone of the existing European order.

Perhaps no better analysis of the implications of this revolution may be found than in the instructions given to the French Ambassador in St. Petersburg, Marshal Marquis Maison, by the Duc de Broglie, Foreign Minister of France under King Louis Philippe. "Before the events of 1830 France and Russia were united in an alliance which seemed to draw them closer from day to day... The Emperor Nicholas who showed himself less suspicious, less impassioned, than his predecessor... had moreover learned... the frankness and efficacy of our co-operation. This important circumstance, by raising France from the position of inferiority in which she found herself as regards Russia... gave additional strength and solidity to an alliance which, between two states of the first rank could, as was evident, only exist on the footing of perfect equality. The July Revolution has completely altered this situation ... It has raised in Belgium questions in which the interests and

---

[12] Nesselrode to Princess Lieven, Feb. 11, 1831. <u>Lettres et papiers du Chancelier Comte de Nesselrode</u>, Paris 1908, Vol. VII, p. 175.

[13] Polievktov M. <u>Imperator Nikolai I</u>, Moscow 1918, p. 90.

inclinations of the Cabinet of St. Petersburg are in absolute opposition to those of France. Finally this revolution being a powerful reaction against the spirit of the treaties of 1815 and of the Holy Alliance, or rather against those doctrines and facts which during the past ten years have invested Russia with a sort of European dictatorship, attacked that power in all the most susceptible points of her ambitions and pride." [14] Nicholas lost no time in acting. He sent Field Marshal Diebitch to Berlin on a confidential mission to attempt to persuade the Prussians to mobilize along the Rhine for joint action, should the need arise, with a Russian army 150,000 strong which was ordered to assemble in Poland. In Russia itself council was divided with regard to these warlike schemes--the military intervention in the revolution in France or subsequently in Belgium was supported by the Minister of War, Chernyshev, and Generals Diebitch and Orlov, but strenuously opposed by Grand Duke Constantine, Counts Nesselrode and Kankrin. Nesselrode declared it impossible to return to the policy of 1813-15 while Kankrin, as Minister of Finance, stated that a new war would bankrupt Russia and pointed out the impossibility of obtaining loans for it. The more reasonable view thus prevailed, particularly after the complete failure of Diebitch's mission to Berlin.

Prussia bordered on both France and Belgium, hence any military operations carried out as a consequence of the revolution would inevitably be fought on her soil and, furthermore, there was manifest a dangerous revolutionary spirit both in the Prussian Rhineland and in Prussian Poland. It was therefore imperative for King Friedrich Wilhelm to maintain a spirit of cautious neutrality and this was precisely what his Imperial son-in-law, the Czar, in a spirit of bellicose anti-revolutionary crusading, was not prepared to do. Diebitch arrived in Berlin on August 26 where he was received the next morning by the King in an audience which lasted an hour and a half. The King agreed entirely that the situation looked ominous and a general war appeared imminent, but he declared that he was forced to follow the precedent set by both England and Austria in recognizing the new government in France. As a precautionary measure he ordered the assembling of an army 80,000 strong on the Rhine and arranged a secret conference between Diebitch and his two generals Witzleben and Krausenek, but beyond that he would not go and Prussia carefully avoided giving any offence to France or creating any border incidents. He refused even to increase the garrison of the fortress of Luxemburg, a step which

---

[14] Guizot, F., <u>Memoires to Illustrate the History of My Time</u>, London 1861, Vol. IV, p. 355, 356. Broglie to Maison, Oct. 28, 1833.

Emperor Nicholas considered a vital strategic necessity. Following Diebitch, General Neidgart was sent to Berlin with more specific plans for joint co-operation. Neidgart was instructed to say that Russia was prepared to move an army 200,000 strong and that this army was to form the center between the Prussian and Austrian armies. The Russian and Prussian Guards were to be pooled and for this purpose a division of Russian Guards would be sent by sea to Stettin to join the Prussian Guards Corps, but the King showed extreme reserve and at the audience given him talked with Neidgart about trivial matters avoiding the main issue. By order of Nicholas, Neidgart feigned illness to remain longer in the Prussian capital, but to no avail. Thus the envoys returned virtually empty handed except for a vague memorandum given by the Prussian Government stipulating an alliance of four powers to hold France at bay.

Nevertheless the Russian army assembled in Poland remained there hanging as a menacing cloud over the revolution torn countries of Western Europe. At the same time, however, Pozzo di Borgo in Paris was notified to order all Russians home from France, not to issue any visas to Frenchmen coming to Russia, to give up the house of the Russian Embassy and to inform the French Government of the closure of Russian ports to French ships. Pozzo's position became very difficult, the more so that the British Ambassador Lord Stewart had already presented his letters of credence to the new government of King Louis Philippe, and Austria and Prussia had signified their intention of doing the same. Pozzo decided on a course of moderation and prudence and was warmly seconded in this by Nesselrode who disapproved of the Czar's impulsiveness. Thus the Ambassador took it upon himself to remain in the building of the Embassy, and even when the latter was the object of a hostile mob demonstration incited by the fact that the liberal Lafayette was living on the same street, Pozzo played down the incident, overlooking the broken window panes and did not ask for his passports as he was urged to do by his staff. He maintained secret contacts with the new government and the King expressed his desire to have a confidential interview with the Russian Ambassador. At this interview Louis Philippe tried to justify his course of action and said that he needed the confidence of Europe to maintain peace and "particularly the benevolence of the Emperor to whom he abandons himself without any reservations."[15] Reporting this conversation Pozzo strongly advised acknowledging the accomplished fact and to grant confidence to

---

[15] Maggiolo, Vicomte Adrien de, Corse, France et Russie, Pozzo di Borgo, 1764-1842. Paris 1890, p. 329.

the new government. Nevertheless Russia alone, of all the powers, withheld official recognition for four months.

Louis Philippe had been terrified by the stand taken by Russia and the menace of the Russian army in Poland, for above all he needed peace to maintain his newly acquired and still shaky throne. Therefore, following his conversation with Pozzo di Borgo he wrote a personal letter on August 19 to the Czar notifying the latter of his accession and giving an explanatory account of the events. "The substance of the letter, every expression of which seemed carefully weighed showed through all the forms of timorous obsequiousness what was to be the attitude of the new government." [16] Indeed the King flattered the Czar, lauded the Charte as a gift of Emperor Alexander I to the French people, asked for the support of the Holy Alliance and intimated that he would not modify the policy of the previous reign toward Russia. Nicholas answered coldly and omitted in his reply the customary address to a King, "Monsieur mon Frère." Nevertheless after Russia had recognized the new regime, Louis Philippe was anxious to establish good relations with Russia; hence having learned that the Czar once said that the Duc de Mortemart was the only person he would accept as Ambassador, the King appointed the latter as his first Ambassador to Russia in January 1831. The Duke's obstinate refusal was only overcome by "the fear of seeing war break out between Russia and France if the Emperor's wish had not been complied with." [17]

In the meanwhile the revolution which broke out in Russian Poland removed the menace of the Russian army which was now used to fight the insurrection, but at the same time the relations between France and Russia were further strained by this revolution. Indeed, the revolution in Poland like the revolution in Belgium, had been an offshoot of the events in Paris and occurred at a time when the revolutionary passions in France had not yet cooled off. Hence the wild enthusiasm which it produced in Paris. Lafayette said: "The whole of France is Polish," and Louis Blanc added "We are living mainly in Poland." The government of Louis Philippe was in an embarrassing position--it could not take an aggressive stand in the matter yet was afraid of losing its precarious popularity if it did not heed the outcry of public opinion. Hence it steered a somewhat contradictory middle course. Through Mortemart Russia was notified of France's strict neutrality in the crisis, and at the same time France initiated a diplomatic campaign in favour of the Poles. But in this campaign it met with complete failure. Prussia was actively helping Russia by sequestering Polish funds

---

[16] Blanc, Louis, op. cit., Vol. I, p. 285.
[17] Ibidem, p. 378.

THE REVOLUTION OF 1830

in Berlin and by supplying Russia with munitions and by mobilizing four army corps on the Polish border. Metternich openly declared the Russian cause to be justified and Lord Palmerston instructed his Ambassador in St. Petersburg to avoid any step which might be construed as unfriendly to Russia. The Poles themselves rendered the French championship of their cause difficult by proclaiming as their goal, not the reinstatement of their rights under the Treaty of Vienna, but the downfall of the Romanov dynasty and the creation of a Greater Poland which would include the Russian provinces which had once formed a part of the old Kingdom of Poland. Any power which sponsored their cause was thereby proclaiming itself in agreement with this program of dismemberment of Russia. When however the cautious Lafitte was replaced by the more energetic Casimir Perier as head of the French Cabinet, French diplomatic action stiffened under pressure of the popular excitement and carried out what was termed a "moral intervention." A protest was lodged in St. Petersburg in May 1831. At the same time Perier proposed to England and Prussia to join with France in offering to mediate between Russia and the Polish insurgents. Berlin refused and Palmerston declared that nothing authorized England to "act against a ruler whose rights were not subject to discussion in the matter." [18] Russia reacted aggressively to French interference and on June 9 Nesselrode expressed "his surprise and regret" at seeing the French Government meddling in Polish affairs after pledging itself to the contrary. France persisting in her attitude, on August 5 Nesselrode in a sharp statement declared that "the Emperor has been disagreeably affected by the renewing of the démarches of France and that he could not, without prejudicing his rights and failing in his duty towards his subjects, grant to anyone the right of meddling in the internal affairs of his country." [19] At the same time the Duc de Mortemart was bluntly told by Nesselrode: "I request you, my dear Duke, that this should be the last time that you make us such observations for we intend to be masters in our own country."[20] The French Ambassador in Vienna attempted to gain the sympathy of Austria for the Poles but Metternich writing to Count Apponyi said "I sent him flying" and added that he had no explanation to give to those who have no right to ask for one. [21] Thus meeting

---

[18] Thureau-Dangin, P., Histoire de la Monarchie de Juillet, Paris 1897, Vol. I, p. 484.
[19] Ibidem, p. 485.
[20] Ibidem, p. 485.,
[21] Metternich, Memoires, documents et ecrits divers laissés par le prince de Metternich, chancelier de cour et d'Etat. Paris 1880-1884, Vol. V, p. 144.

with rebuffs all around French intervention fizzled down to violent speeches in the Chamber of Deputies in Paris. On September 7, meanwhile, the energetic Field Marshal Count Paskevich had crushed the insurrection by capturing Warsaw.

The net result was that France was singled out in her hostility toward Russia and this added to the implacable hatred which Nicholas developed for the "renegade house of Orleans" and thwarted all subsequent attempts at reconciliation made by French diplomacy.

As a sign of displeasure toward France, shortly after the Polish crisis came to an end, Pozzo di Borgo was transferred from the Paris Embassy to that of London. Pozzo had been in Paris for nearly two decades and his activities were as we have seen most beneficial and helpful to France. He was replaced by an obscure diplomat, his former Chargé d'Affaires, Count Medem. Thus without actually breaking off relations with France this gesture of Russia's in a veiled way came close to it. The Czar's hostility caused real trouble to Louis Philippe and affected even his family affairs. When the King, anxious to unite his family with some leading dynasty, in 1836 raised the question of a marriage between his son, the Duke of Orleans, and Princess Theresa, the daughter of Archduke Charles of Austria, the marriage scheme was blocked by the joint opposition of Archduchess Sophie, the Czar and Metternich. The cordial reception given in Berlin to the Duke of Orleans immediately brought forth angry protests from Count Pahlen, the Russian Minister at the Prussian Court. King Louis Philippe was forced to content himself with a much more modest matrimonial alliance, Grand Duchess Helena of Mecklenburg-Schwerin. Even so he had to overcome a virtual matrimonial blockade organized by the Czar and when the marriage did take place it was the cause of tremendous rejoicing in Paris. A witty observer saw in this marriage supported by Prussia a set back for Russian influence in Germany: "Six months ago the Russian vanguard was at Saarbrucken, now it is the French vanguard which is at Memel." [22] By a curious twist of fate from this marriage two generations later was to be born Prince Ferdinand Coburg who was to play so nefarious a role for Russia in Bulgaria.

---

[22] Bourgeois, Emile, Manuel Historique des Politiques Etrangères, Paris 1915, Vol. III, p. 137.

IV

The revolution of 1830 was not confined as we have seen to France alone but to Poland and Belgium as well. The Polish issue however by this time had become a question of Russian internal policy. With Belgium the case was different--it did not affect Russia directly but the revolution in Brussels, following upon the July days in Paris, was so closely linked with events in France as to make of it a twin issue for Russian diplomacy. Moreover, by its proclamation of independence from Holland, Belgium had been the first to violate openly the Treaty of Vienna. For these reasons the Belgian question was given precedence in St. Petersburg over all other questions, except the events in France and in Greece. Apart from the principle of fighting revolutions and maintaining legitimacy Russia obviously had no interests in Belgium. Hence after the first flurry of excitement, the idea of armed Russian intervention in the Netherlands was abandoned for the more conservative view of supporting King William of Holland in his attempts to restore his authority over the Belgian provinces. When the Conference of London opened in November, 1830 to settle the Belgian question it was obvious that the Powers did not want war and Russia least of all since the opening of the Conference coincided with the beginning of the rebellion in Poland. However this meant recognizing the fait accompli in Belgium which was highly displeasing to the Czar. Lord Palmerston, who was directing the Conference, on his side used it as a lever to detach France from the united front presented by the Three Northern Courts. It was in this early period of manoeuvring for the final line-up in the coming struggle, that the Russian delegate, Count Matussevich, wrote to Nesselrode on November 15 suggesting that the only means of safeguarding the peace of Europe was to have the powers "guarantee jointly the existence of the Belgian Kingdom, and declare that under no circumstances could any one of them invade or annex (Belgium) without the consent of the other four." [23]   The idea of Belgian neutrality was born.

The next stage was reached in December of the same year when the Conference of London admitted officially the failure of the union of Belgium with Holland and recognized the "future independence" of Belgium provided it met the stipulations of the treaties and the interests and security of the other powers." This raised the question of the candidates for the new throne and whereas France put forward the name of the Duc de Nemours, second son

---

[23] Pirenne, H., <u>Histoire de Belgique</u>, Brussels 1928, Vol. VII, p. 1-46.

of King Louis Philippe, Russia favoured Karl Augustus, Duke of Leuchtenberg, the eldest son of Prince Eugene Beauharnais. The reason for the support of this candidate was that the descendants of Josephine's first marriage had, through a curious twist of fate, linked their future with Russia.

It will be recalled that Alexander I had developed a real friendship with Prince Eugene Beauharnais. After the fall of the Napoleonic Empire the latter went to reside in Bavaria, the kingdom of his father-in-law. His second son, Maximillian, who took the title of the Duke of Leuchtenberg, after the death of his elder brother, Karl Augustus, subsequently married in 1839 Grand Duchess Marie Nicolaevna, the eldest daughter of Nicholas I and went to reside in Russia. His descendants became Russian and assumed the double name of Dukes of Leuchtenberg and Princes Romanovsky. The closeness of these family ties, already apparent, explains Russia's attitude. However, vetoed by France, the Leuchtenberg candidature met with little support and was voted down from the outset. The Conference having further decided that no candidate should be considered who belonged to the reigning dynasties of the five great powers, the Duc de Nemours found himself excluded in turn. Thus the field was left open for the British nominee, Leopold of Saxe-Coburg, a candidate who at that time was not displeasing to Russia. Indeed the future King of Belgium had served as an officer in the Russian Army and had taken part with the Russians in the battles of Lutzen, Bautzen, Kulm and Leipzig. Moreover, his sister Julia had married Grand Duke Constantine.

After Leopold had been elected King of the Belgians by the Belgian National Congress, the London Conference in the so-called Treaty of XVIII Articles established the basis for the settlement of the Belgian question by defining in a general way the frontiers of the new kingdom and providing for her neutrality. Thereupon King William I of Holland marched his forces into Belgium. This led to a counter invasion by a French army of 50,000 and the retreat of the Dutch. The speedy withdrawal of the French troops after the Dutch had gone solved that crisis and gave the London Conference the opportunity of drawing the Protocol of XXIV Articles which gave Belgium a portion of Luxemburg and Limburg, thereby defining the frontiers more precisely. In the face of the obdurate opposition of King William the protocol was converted into the Treaty of London (November 15, 1831) which was signed by the Great Powers, including Russia. But Russia, in sympathy with the King of Holland, very effectively blocked all further progress along these lines by delaying, in concert with her allies, the ratification of the treaty. There remained only one solution that of trying to obtain the voluntary adhesion of King William to this treaty and Russia made the gesture of sending Count Orlov to the Hague to persuade the King. Upon his refusal Russia declared officially that she would not take part in any military coercion to force Holland to yield. Thus encouraged, the Dutch held out. Finally Austria and Prussia ratified the treaty on April 18, 1832, followed by Russia on May 4. But Russia made the vital reservation that the ratification was conditional on the "modifications of Articles IX, XII and XIII by agreement with Holland."

Pending this agreement everything was thereby blocked and the treaty could not be put into effect. The fury of the Belgians against Russia reached a virtual climax. To force the hand of the recalcitrant King of Holland, a French army invaded Belgium for a second time and besieged the fortress of Antwerp, held by a Dutch garrison. The presence of French troops on Belgian soil started a war fever in Prussia and the old King Friedrich Wilhelm though peacefully inclined, ordered the Prussian army to march toward the Meuse. But afraid of tackling France alone, he ascertained whether he could count on the co-operation of his allies. Austria was disinclined to act and the Czar replied he needed six months to get ready. The intervening fall of Antwerp (December 2, 1832) brought an end to the crisis by a treaty signed between Holland and Belgium in May, 1833, not to resort to hostilities. The issue however was revived once more at the conference of Münchengraetz the following September where it was decided that the independence and neutrality of Belgium should be respected provided the interests of the Germanic Confederation, particularly with regard to the Duchy of Luxemburg, should not be affected. If this failed to occur, Prussia was entitled to start a war and was to obtain the support of 120,000 men from Russia. From this point, however, Russia's interest in the issue waned with the danger of war having subsequently been averted, and the Belgian issue gradually became a mere maze of technicalities. Finally in 1839 Russia was co-signatory of the final series of treaties which guaranteed both the independence and neutrality of Belgium. However, the bitter resentment in St. Petersburg toward the Belgians remained, and under pretence that Belgium had given refuge to and accepted in her army, in commanding positions, the leaders of the Polish rebellion against Russia, Russia refused to establish regular diplomatic relations with Belgium and it was only in 1852 that Russia finally accredited a minister to Brussels. [24]

Across the map of Europe another country was attracting the

---

[24] Révue d'Histoire Diplomatique. Paris 1923. See article by Thirlingen, Etablissement des Relations Diplomatiques entre la Russie et la Belgique.

vigilant attention of the Russian Government. The revolution of 1830 had given a powerful stimulus to the revolutionary movements in Italy as testified by the outbreaks in the Papal States, in Parma and Modena. Mazzini and his recently founded Giovine Italia movement were rapidly gaining ground. The political philosophy of Mazzini with its ardent democratic and nationalist ideals was the very essence of what the great counter-revolutionary alliance of the Three Northern Courts was fighting. Furthermore in his ill fated and foolhardy attempt to invade Sardinia in 1834 Mazzini had enrolled many Polish exiles of the rebellion of 1831-32. All this was enough to mark Mazzini in the eyes of the St. Petersburg government as a most dangerous radical and agitator.

In 1830 the able and energetic Ferdinand II mounted the throne of Naples, but after a few enlightened measures he soon drifted into a policy of reactionary repression of liberalism in his kingdom. Therefore the traditional support and to some extent patronage of the Court of Two Sicilies became the fundamental issue in Russia's Italian policy.

The other parts of Italy were considered to be more or less the preserve of Austria, hence Russian action asserted itself in conjunction with Austria. A note dated May 21, 1831 and signed by England, France, Russia, Prussia and Austria suggested, as the best means for re-establishing tranquility in Central Italy, the revision of the Papal administration in a liberal sense. The principle of popular elections in communal and provincial assemblies as well as the admission of laymen into the administration of the Church Estates were two of the suggestions which the Pope forthwith rejected. But when the revolutionary outbreaks occurred, the Three Northern Courts promised Pope Gregory XVI their aid. However, this being a matter for Austrian troops, Russia viewed indifferently the subsequent Austrian occupation and the French landing of an occupationary force at Ancona. In Tuscany however Russian action was more direct and Austro-Russian pressure brought about the suppression in 1833, of a reference to the treatment of Polish exiles in Siberia, in an issue of the "Antologia", a liberal periodical founded in imitation of the British Edinburgh Review. Small in circulation (only 350 copies) the review had a tremendous influence due to the fact that the leading Risorgimento writers, including Mazzini, contributed to it. In Piedmont, when Charles Felix died in April 1831, by the law of salic succession, the throne should have passed to Duke Francis of Modena who had married the daughter of Victor Emmanuel. It was however as a result of pressure by France and Russia, whose support Charles Albert had previously enlisted, that the latter mounted the throne. Mistakenly considered a liberal, Charles Albert, known for his indecision as King Wobble, was at heart an absolutist and the

Russian Government was aware of this.

Beyond the Pyrenees the bloody Carlist Wars waged at this time, represented in Spain the same struggle between liberalism and reaction. As expected, the Three Northern Courts gave full moral support and some indirect aid to the reactionary Don Carlos though hesitating to recognize him officially or to intervene actively on his side. [25]

V

The close conformity of views developed between Russia, Austria and Prussia brought on by the events of 1830 marks the second most important after effect of the July Revolution and amounted to a revival of the Holy Alliance. It is the more striking after the nearly complete estrangement of St. Petersburg and Vienna caused by the Russo-Turkish war of 1828-29, the annoyance of Metternich at this Russian venture and his open siding with the enemies of Russia. However the crushing of Turkey by the Treaty of Adrianople made the realistic Metternich revise his position and decide that it was more profitable to be on the side of Russia than against her. Thus it was that in January 1830 Metternich made overtures to Russia, declaring to the Russian Ambassador in Vienna that he was seeking a rapprochement with Russia which would eventually be extended to include Prussia and thus become the "basis" of an alliance for the preservation of European peace. As a bait to Russia he promised to do everything in his power for a speedy settlement of the Greek question. But the attitude of the Russian Government was reserved. However Count Nesselrode met Metternich at Carlsbad in July 1830 and renewed a personal friendship dating from 1823. The two statesmen here laid the basis for the alliance and Metternich put down the main principles in his "Chiffon de Carlsbad." That there was still considerable distrust may be seen by the report that Metternich made concerning this meeting to Emperor Francis wherein he writes: "Count Nesselrode was anxious, he was afraid of an interview with myself."[26] Metternich enumerated his grievances against Nesselrode: first that he had worked to undermine the close relations between Russia and Austria and second that he had given encouragement to the

---

[25] Lafuente, M., Historia general de España, desde los tiempos más remotos hasta nuestros dias. Madrid 1840-1867, Vol. XX, p. 51.

[26] Metternich to Emperor Francis, Metternich Memoires, Vol. V, p. 10.

enemies of order by abandoning the political principles which he deemed to be right. The revolution of 1830 having thereupon started, this wrangling was laid aside and the two powers quickly got together. In pursuance of the policies established at Carlsbad, Metternich suggested a conference of the allies to meet at Vienna in 1831 but failed to get the acceptance of Russia. Nicholas I wrote a marginal note on his Ambassador's report: "We now have the great ambition of Metternich clearly and concisely expressed; as we know how much we can rely upon him by his past antecedents, I will only agree if Prussia so desires and makes us a similar proposal from her side." [27]

Nevertheless two years later the first meeting of the allied sovereigns did take place at Münchengraetz in Bohemia and followed the lines of the former Holy Alliance. This resemblance will not only appear in the decision to confer regularly at intervals, as after the Congress of Vienna, but also in the spirit of these meetings, the topics discussed and remedies suggested which revive the ideas of Troppau-Laibach and Verona.

King Friedrich Wilhelm III of Prussia used to go regularly for a cure to Toeplitz in Bohemia and Nicholas I announced he would arrive there also. The Czar decided to go to Germany by sea but owing to bad weather had to return to St. Petersburg and pursue his journey by land. This delayed him for nearly a month. Friedrich Wilhelm waited for him as long as he could but manoeuvres had been scheduled in Prussia which could not be postponed. Hence he left, leaving the Prince Royal of Prussia (future Friedrich Wilhelm IV) to serve as his deputy for the interview which finally took place in September at Münchengraetz and not at Toeplitz. Princess Metternich writes in her diary that the first words of Czar Nicholas to Metternich upon his arrival were: "I have come here to place myself at the orders of my chief," [28] a compliment which greatly flattered the old statesman. The meeting of the sovereigns gave an occasion for manifestation of sympathy and real fraternization between the Russian and Austrian officers present and, to quote Princess Metternich, everyone was delighted. So was Metternich--he had achieved his main purposes: the policy of the three powers with regard to Belgium had been co-ordinated; the thorny question arising from the Treaty of Unkiar-Skelessi, which gave Russia such predominance in Turkey that it became dangerous for Austria, was ironed out by an agreement in which both parties pledged themselves to maintain the existence of Turkey, and the

---

[27] Martens, op. cit., Vol. IV, p. 45.
[28] Metternich Mémoires, Vol. V, p. 446.

Czar promised further not to apply the Treaty of Unkiar-Skelessi without first seeking the mediation of Austria; with regard to Poland the two powers mutually guaranteed the tranquil and peaceful possession of their respective parts of Poland. Thus all the pending Austro-Russian issues were settled. The Prince Royal of Prussia not having the authority to sign treaties, Nesselrode and Count Ficquelmont were ordered to Berlin by the two Emperors to put into treaty form the matters which had been discussed. The result, after several weeks of negotiations, was the drafting at Berlin of the treaty of October 15, 1833, under which the three powers, in view of the revolutionary menace in Europe and the dangers to the existence of the treaties of 1815, pledged themselves to strengthen the conservative alliance as forming the basis of their policy of mutual support. By Article I the three courts gave the right to any independent sovereign who found himself menaced by internal troubles or dangers of external aggression to appeal for aid to any other sovereign. This latter would be free to accede to the demand or to refuse aid according to his judgement and interests, but no other sovereign not appealed to would be permitted to interfere in this matter either in the sense of giving the aid requested or in the contrary sense. By Article II it was stipulated that should one of the three signatories of this treaty be the recipient of such an appeal and find a third power attempting to oppose such aid by force the three allied powers would act jointly and would consider any such hostile act as being directed against them. The treaty was to remain secret.

Thus the very spirit of the Protocol of Troppau-Laibach was recreated by this mutual pledge of fighting jointly any revolution or outside aggression. With the revival of the Holy Alliance thus secured and the regular meetings of the allied sovereigns decided upon, the next conference took place two years later at Toeplitz.

VI

The alliance of the Three Northern Courts cemented at the meeting of Münchengraetz had once more divided Europe into two camps. France and England on their side had concluded an alliance with Portugal and Spain which Palmerston hailed as the counterpart of the Conservative Alliance. However it proved to be less enduring whereas the death of Emperor Francis in March 1835 further strengthened the bonds between the Courts of St. Petersburg and Vienna. The new Emperor Ferdinand wrote to Nicholas that his father on his deathbed had counselled him that "outside of hope in God he should put his faith in the maintenace of the close alliance with Russia." [29] But above all a sensation was produced in the capitals of Europe by an outstanding and unique testimony of military solidarity between Prussia and Russia as exhibited by the joint manoeuvres of the armies of both countries preceding the next meeting of the sovereigns of the Three Northern Courts; this was to be held in September 1835 at Toeplitz. On his way to this meeting the Czar stopped to witness the joint Russo-Prussian manoeuvres.

The idea had been suggested by Czar Nicholas. Kalish in Russian Poland was selected as being only five miles from the German frontier. The Russian 3rd Army Corps was assembled there while a selected detachment 5,000 strong, representing the Guards infantry regiments was shipped by sea on transports to Danzig (August 4, 1835) escorted by the Baltic Fleet. From Danzig this detachment made its way overland to Kalish, where it met the Guard cavalry and artillery which had come directly through Poland. All told, a Russian army composed of 57 1/2 battalions of infantry, 54 squadrons of cavalry and 128 guns was assembled. The Prussians sent a detachment also representing the various units of the Guards and of regiments whose honorary commanders were members of the Russian Imperial family, 3 1/2 battalions of infantry, 13 1/2 squadrons of cavalry and 8 guns. The grand total of the combined forces amounted to 58,347 men and this army was placed under the command of the Russian Field Marshal Prince Paskevich.

Emperor Nicholas accompanied by his daughter, Grand Duchess Olga and his brother Grand Duke Constantine went by sea from Cronstadt to Danzig where he was met by Prince Wilhelm and thence to Kalish. The King of Prussia, accompanied by 12 members of his family met the Czar at Kalish. The occasion attracted such wide attention that Austria sent Archduke Franz Karl and Archduke Johann (brother and uncle of the late Emperor Ferdinand). A host of members of lesser royalty were present--amongst these the Grand Dukes of Mecklenburg-Schwerin and Hesse-Darmstadt, the Duke Eugene of Wurttemberg, the Duke of Cumberland (brother of the King of England and future King of Hanover), the Princes of Netherlands and Schleswig-Holstein-Sonderburg-Glucksburg and in addition the Marquis of Douro (son of the Duke of Wellington), the Chief of the Prussian General Staff, a number of diplomats and others. Amidst great pomp and endless festivities the military manoeuvres of the allied army were carried on from September 11 to September 22 and two days after their termination, Czar Nicholas left Kalish to attend the meeting of the monarchs at Toeplitz. Nothing of the kind had been seen in Europe before and the impression

---

[29] Tatishchev, S. S., _Imperator Nikolai i Inostrannye Dvory_. St. Petersburg 1889, p. 80.

produced by this military demonstration was the more striking, followed as it was by the display of diplomatic solidarity of the Three Northern Courts given at Toeplitz.

Five questions were considered at Toeplitz resulting in an exchange of diplomatic memoranda. In regard to England and France it was decided to let things be, but to recognize immediately the legitimist candidate in the event of a new revolution in France. It was further decided not to accept the British suggestion for a renewal of the London Conference on the Belgo-Dutch situation until England and France showed signs of yielding to the conservative point of view. Similarly in the Spanish Civil War it was decided to support Don Carlos and in the event of his success to acknowledge him as King. Later in the subsidiary protocol signed in Vienna, Russia joined Austria in giving Don Carlos financial aid. Thus in short, on the three outstanding issues in Western Europe, a united front was formed to deal with the liberal block. The more thorny questions in Eastern Europe offered less possibility for unanimity. In the Turkish question the suggestion made by Metternich to inform London and Paris of the decisions reached at Münchengraetz was heatedly turned down by Russia, who suspected this move to be a manoeuvre in the direction of an alliance between the Western Powers and Austria against Russian's interests in Turkey. Similarly the fate of the little Polish republic of Cracow offered elements which, while bringing Russia and Austria together, also revealed a possible clash of interests and policies. Though subsequently a protocol was signed in Berlin concerning the decision taken at Toeplitz to dispose of the independence of this free city, the issue was deemed so delicate as to require further negotiations. Nothing was to be done for the time being. Indeed both Turkey and Poland offered a fertile ground for complications between Russia and Austria.

In July 1838 a second visit of Czar Nicholas to Toeplitz resulted in a meeting with Archduke Franz Karl, the brother of Ferdinand, and with Friedrich Wilhelm III of Prussia. During this meeting again the issue of Cracow was discussed but once more a decision was postponed, other more important matters looming. Indeed, the crisis in the Near East, caused by Mehemet Ali's ambition, was to produce the severest strain yet experienced between Russia and Austria. Already in 1839 the Russian Chargé d'Affaires in Vienna, Prince Gorchakov, had written to warn Nesselrode that Metternich would not abide by the decisions taken at Münchengraetz in the event of a crisis in the Near East, and should Turkey come to war with Russia, Metternich would give Russia only apparent and insincere aid. But Nesselrode, disliking Gorchakov, paid no heed to this warning. Now the crisis had come and Metternich, on his side, watched jealously the incipient rapprochement between Russia and England which made possible the treaty of August 15, 1841.

During the negotiations of this treaty Metternich insisted upon the closing of the Straits and a guarantee of the Ottoman Empire, both issues at variance with Russia's policy. And even though Nesselrode kept on regarding the alliance of the Three Northern Courts as "the corner-stone of the social structure of Europe", [30] Metternich came out with violent diatribes against Russia, writing in April 1842 to his Ambassador in St. Petersburg, Voina, that in many issues Austria and Russia were treading different paths. Other issues were increasing the strain: the question of the abolition of the Uniat Church in Russia was one which caused Metternich to declare that the religious persecution in Russia was preparing a dreadful storm; in Serbia the support of Michael Obrenovich by Austria was displeasing to Russia; the refusal of Metternich to consent to the entry of Russian troops into Moldavia to quell the revolutionary agitation, -all these issues caused serious ill will and mutual small offences started.

The new King of Prussia, Friedrich Wilhelm IV, who succeeded Friedrich Wilhelm III in 1840, was not on as intimate terms with Nicholas as his father and began gravitating toward a closer relationship with Austria. These signs of the renewed importance of Vienna as a center for European diplomatic intrigue made Metternich feel more independent toward Russia than heretofore, and in 1842 he declined an invitation of the Czar to come to Warsaw to see him, sending Count Ficquelmont, former Ambassador to Russia and now Vice-Chancellor, in his stead. Nicholas retorted by a demonstrative snub. While on his way to Palermo where he was taking the Empress for the winter, Nicholas in 1845 avoided Vienna and went through Bavaria, notwithstanding that preparations had been made for his reception in the Austrian capital. He merely sent Nesselrode in his place with desultory apologies. On his way back, after calling upon Field Marshal Radetzky in Milan, he stayed for three days in Vienna but refused the hospitality of the Hofburg and remained in the Russian Embassy. His whole attitude was stiff and cold. In the meanwhile another personal issue had arisen to increase this coldness: the failure of the projected marriage between Archduke Stephen, the son of the Palatine of Hungary and Grand Duchess Olga, due to religious differences. Metternich became apprehensive. Writing in her diary on New Year's Day in 1846, Princess Metternich says: "God the Holy Virgin, and the Saints grant us their compassionate aid... No new year has begun under such ominous auspices. Emperor Nicholas still maintains his severe attitude." [31] Similarly a strain

---

[30] Tatishchev, op. cit., p. 99.
[31] Metternich Memoires, Vol. VII, p. 145.

developed between Russia and Prussia.

There was a rising tide of liberal public opinion in Prussia which was becoming bitterly critical of so close an alliance with Russian autocracy. Regarding the Kalish meeting it spoke of "playing with toy soldiers" and Stockmar, the close friend and confident of the Prince Consort, consequently himself anglophile and liberal, spoke scathingly of "one of those fêtes which were staged at the time of Catherine II". He stated that the King of Prussia had taken part in the meeting because he could not refuse to do so out of political considerations and out of "weakness toward a too polite ally and son-in-law." [32] King Friedrich Wilhelm IV, a romantic and richly endowed nature, came more and more under these liberal influences of which Nicholas disapproved to the extent that he observed in 1841, "My Prussian brother will destroy himself." Through the influence of liberals and particularly of such men as Bunsen, Stockmar and the Prince Consort, the new King showed tendencies to come closer to England and he subscribed to a scheme for establishing in the Near East a general protectorate of all the powers over the Christians-- both very distasteful to Russia. His visit to London in 1842 where he was showered with honours, produced such a bad impression on Nicholas that, to right the balance, Friedrich Wilhelm went to Russia to be present at the silver wedding of the Czar. Nevertheless the next year on his return visit to Berlin, Nicholas showed himself more reserved than usual, and in 1845 when he accompanied the Czarina on her way to Palermo, he avoided Berlin altogether, going by way of Munich. The Emperor was thus signifying his disapproval of the constitutional experiments in Prussia and the following year as Prince Wilhelm visited Russia, Nicholas quite outspokenly criticized the policies of the King. Picqued, the King said "My brother (the Czar) has no right to interfere with what is not his business, let the Emperor care for his own possessions." [33] Thus in the first years of the 1840's the Alliance of the Three Northern Courts had been seriously imperilled by the strain between Russia and Austria and the parallel strain between Russia and Prussia, but it sufficed for the Polish issue to come to life again with a new revolutionary menace for these strains to vanish immediately. The otherwise obscure issue of the Free City of Cracow thus at this juncture assumes a role of historical importance through its influence on the diplomacy of its powerful neighbours and guarantors, and therefore must be studied in more detail.

---

[32] Stockmar, Denkwürdigkeiten aus den Papieren des Freiherrn Christian Friedrich von Stockmar. Braunschweig 1872, p. 299 quoted by Tatishchev, op. cit., p. 258.
[33] Tatishchev, op. cit., p. 269.

VII

The republic of Cracow was the last piece of Polish territory remaining independent, at least nominally, after the fourth partition of Poland in 1815. It was also the product of the mutual jealousies of the allies, particularly of Austria and Russia at the Congress of Vienna. As such the elements which constituted the reason for its future existence were precarious even though the guarantee given the new republic in the Treaty of Vienna was explicit and binding. "The city of Cracow and its territory is to be forever free, independent, and neutral, under the protection of the three courts." [34] Modelled along the lines of the Hanseatic cities, the city republic of Cracow had its boundaries delimited by an international commission to include the Wieliczka salt mines, but excluding the neighbouring city of Podgorce. The administration and affairs of the republic were closely supervised by the Resident Commissioners of Austria, Russia and Prussia in whose hands the real fate of Cracow lay. One important provision of the Constitution has to be mentioned. Cracow was not to harbour any political refugees at any time (Article IX of the Constitution). The commission terminated its work only in 1818 and it is from that year that the history of the city republic properly begins. The first years were relatively smooth and it was not until the outbreak of the Polish rebellion of 1830 that a serious issue was created with the protecting powers. When the Polish revolution was crushed in Russian Poland, and Polish refugees swarmed into the neighbouring countries, making their way to Paris, Brussels and London, Cracow was filled with refugees. Furthermore the center for maintaining the struggle for Polish independence having moved to Paris, from where organizations carried on propaganda and sent money to branches all over Europe, Cracow reverberated passionately to the action of the Paris center and was the obvious observation post and spring-board for any further campaign in Russian Poland. Accordingly, Field Marshal Prince Paskevich, pursuing the mopping up campaign, occupied Cracow on the ground that a new uprising was to take place in March 1832, starting from that city. Neither Austria nor Prussia protested this occupation merely expressing hope that it was temporary and due to military necessities.

Already during the campaign Paskevich advocated the idea of letting Austria have Cracow in exchange for the district of Tarnopol to be given to Russia. On the other hand, perhaps as a result of pressure by Paskevich, a petition signed by ten leading citizens of

---

[34] Martens, K., <u>Causes Célèbres du droit des gens</u>. Leipzig 1861, Vol. V, p. 359.

Cracow was presented demanding its annexation to Russia. If these schemes were for the time being not productive of any results, the revolution in Poland had sufficiently frightened the guarantors that they decided upon a modification in the Cracow constitution. On May 30, 1833, the new status of the city was published and, as may have been expected, was much less liberal. The powers of the legislative bodies were curtailed, whereas the power of the President of the Senate increased, conditional however on the approval of his appointment by the three guarantor states. This was followed up at the conference of Münchengraetz by further restrictions of a purely technical nature, such as the question of political criminals, the interdiction of patriotic societies in the city and the abolition of free trade with Podgorce. But more important, following the precedent set by Paskevich, it was decided to occupy the city whenever circumstances warranted it.

The next step was taken at Toeplitz. Emperor Nicholas complained bitterly to his allies that not only was Cracow giving asylum to some of the leaders of the Polish revolution, but that it was becoming a source of agitation endangering the peace of Russian Poland. The result was the signing by Metternich, Nesselrode and Ancillon of the secret treaty of October 1835, under the clauses of which Cracow was to be united to Austria, and Prussia was to receive a rectification of her boundaries in Silesia. However the actual annexation was postponed until a time when the international situation would make such a move safe. Nevertheless the following year, under the pretence of a hostile demonstration which had taken place in Cracow on the day of the Czar's birthday, and with the official reason of ousting the revolutionary elements from the city, Cracow was once more temporarily occupied by the three protecting powers. From now on the city maintained merely a shadow of independence. Martial law was enforced by the Austrian General Kauffmann, the police force and militia were put under the control of an Austrian commission and the subversive elements and refugees expelled. This brought sharp protests from France and England, and Palmerston declared in the House of Commons that, "The powers do not have the right to do what they have done. All the difficulties are not sufficient reason to justify intervention." [35] Palmerston further threatened to send a British consul to Cracow, to which Ancillon declared that he would not be recognized by the three powers. Indeed, the latter were not much impressed and Palmerston after a while was forced to declare that "it was one thing to express an

---

[35] Lutostanski, K., Les Partages de la Pologne et la Lutte pour l'Independence. Paris 1918, p. 540, 541.

an opinion, and another thing to take hostile steps... and especially in a case where, from local and geographical circumstances, there were no means of enforcing the opinion of England..."[36] Thus gradually the hubbub died down and with the Near Eastern crisis absorbing the attention of the powers, the Cracow question faded out of the picture.

With the settling of the Egyptian crisis, Metternich once more raised the issue of Cracow in 1842, suggesting that the republic should be brought into the Austrian customs system. This move was motivated by the fact that Cracow had become a center for smuggling from Prussian Silesia. But this was the time when Austro-Russian relations were becoming strained and hence Russia did not support Austria's plea. Nesselrode wrote to Meyendorff in Berlin that if Austria would drop this project, Russia had no intention of insisting on any scheme displeasing to Prussia.[37] Once more the issue was postponed. However with the ominous sign of a great storm already brewing in Western Europe, the Revolution of 1848, revolutionary agitation in Poland was again ripe and the following year the Czar on his return from Berlin was fired at while travelling through Posen. Though the Prussian Government insisted that the shot had been merely an accidental discharge by a sentry, Nicholas always considered it an attempt on his life at the hands of a Pole. Paskevich, now Viceroy of Poland, reported from Warsaw that the population was restless and that numerous arrests had had to be made. In Paris at the headquarters of the Polish revolutionary activities abroad, Ludwig Mieroslavski, the leader of Polish "Activists" was particularly aggressive and in 1845 he visited Posen to prepare the way for a great insurrection which was to be directed from Posen and Cracow, and meetings to this effect were held in both cities. A military organization was set up and the whole of Poland was divided into three sections. In Russian Poland the leadership of the insurrection was given to Broneslaw Dombrowski, in Cracow to Professor Gorezkowski and in Galicia to Count Wesselowski. But the Prussian police discovered the plot in Posen in Februar 1846 and when the insurrection broke out in March it was speedily quelled. Similarly in Russia, where Dombrowski had made grandiose plans for seizing not only Congress Poland but Russian territories in White Russia and Lithuania as well, without adequate mean for carrying out his plans, the whole thing fizzled down to an attempt at guerrilla warfare and marauding by a handful of followers, mostly students. Hearing of the end of the Prussian venture, Dombrowski fled, leaving his followers to the mercy of the Russian poli

---

[36]Bell, F. C. F., Lord Palmerston. New York 1936, Vol. I, p. 270.
[37]Nesselrode, op. cit., Vol. VIII, p. 185, 186.

But the story in Austrian Poland was different--here the insurrection developed into a peasants war and in Cracow, which now became the center of the revolution, a provisional government for the whole of Poland had been set up under a dictator, Jan Tyssowski, with strong socialist leanings. The Austrian General Collin, who was garrisoned in Cracow with a battalion of troops, retreated, abandoning the city, and his situation was becoming critical. Once more Nicholas acted swiftly and decisively. Under orders from Viceroy Paskevitch, General Paniutin, with a strong force of Russian troops, advanced on Cracow, reaching it on March 3, and issued a proclamation to the people which read as follows: "Inhabitants of Cracow! A powerful Russian army has come to re-establish peace which has been disturbed in your city. Make haste to receive it within your walls so that it may protect the innocent. Everybody who lays down his arms will be spared. But whoever is seized with arms will be put to death; and if the defence of the city is persevered in, it will be mercilessly delivered over to fire and sword." [38] The city capitulated and Tissovsky was interned in the fortress of Königstein. Thus came to an end the independence of Cracow.

The next question was what was to be done with the city. Nicholas did not want it; as far as he was concerned his purpose had been achieved and the Russian troops were ordered to withdraw when the Austrians reoccupied the city. But the diplomatic situation created by the Russian coup de force remained acute. Indeed now that Metternich had been faced with a fait accompli, he showed extraordinary hesitancy in availing himself of the opportunity. He found that Austria was in some respects between the grindstones of Russia on one side and the Franco-British entente on the other. Before acting decisively he wanted to make sure that France at least would not offer too much opposition and thus he waited for the French elections to return Guizot to office, as well as for the development of the crisis between France and England, caused by the affair of the Spanish marriages. He had also to overcome the opposition of Prussia, who while objecting to the method employed, found the change in the status of the city was bringing lucrative trade between Breslau and Cracow, made possible because of low customs duties between Prussian Poland and the free city. The incorporation of the city into Austria would bring with it the application of the higher Austrian tariff. Canitz accordingly demanded, in return for Prussia's consent to the annexation, not only the maintenance of the customs status quo but building of a railway line between the two cities of Breslau and Cracow. This issue resulted in protracted negotiations and Nicholas became so

---

[38] Morfill, W., <u>A History of Russia from the Birth of Peter the Great Till the Death of Alexander III</u>, London 1902, p. 395.

exasperated at these delays that he threatened to take Cracow if Austria refused to do so promptly. A conference was held in Berlin in April to put pressure on Prussia with General Count Berg representing Russia, and in a secret protocol it was decided to first settle the outstanding issues between the three powers before the final incorporation of the city. It was not until November that these issues having been dealt with, the document of annexation was signed followed by letters of patent signed by Kaiser Ferdinand to the effect that "the city of Cracow and its territory is hereby annexed and inseparably incorporated into the Austrian Empire." [39] In a long note justifying the action, Metternich informed both France and England. As may have been expected during these proceedings bitter protests were voiced in Paris and in London on the grounds of the violation of the Treaty of Vienna.

Palmerston declared, "I am sure that it cannot have escaped the perspicacity of those (German) powers that if the Treaty of Vienna is not suitable on the Vistula it must be equally bad on the Rhine and on the Po," [40] and Queen Victoria stated in a speech in Parliament: "... The extinction of the Free Republic of Cracow has appeared to me, to be so manifest a violation of the Treaty of Vienna that I have commanded that a protest against that act should be delivered to the courts of Vienna, Prussia, and Russia, which were parties to it..." [41] But platonic protests did not impress the Three Northern Courts very much, and Nesselrode summed up the situation by saying that England and France would not fight over Cracow. Indeed the situation was soon accepted and forgotten and the storm in a tea cup had blown over. The Cracow affair had nevertheless the important result of bringing Russia and Austria together once more after the period of relative estrangement in the first half of the 1840's. Indeed the old cordiality was entirely restored and when the menace of the tide of Italian nationalisms faced Austria next, Nicholas gave Austria his whole-hearted support, granting to her in January 1848 a secret loan of six million roubles. In February Nesselrode wrote to Metternich that in the event of a French and Sardinian attack on the Austrian possessions in Italy, "all our forces will be ready to support you", [42] but this was the last diplomatic victory of

---

[39] Lutostanski, op. cit., p. 54-56.
[40] Rambaud, A., History of Russia. New York 1882, Vol. III, p. 70.
[41] Hertslet, E., The Map of Europe by Treaty: showing the Various Political and Territorial Changes which Have Taken Place Since the General Peace of Vienna. London 1875-1891, Vol. II, p. 1068.
[42] Martens, op. cit., Vol. IV, p. 581.

Metternich. A month later he was ousted from office by the revolution breaking out in Vienna, and Russia had to face an entirely new situation developing on the western borders.

CHAPTER V

THE REVOLUTION OF 1848

I

The news that the revolution had broken out in Paris reached St. Petersburg on March 5, 1848, on the last day of carnival week, preceding Lent. A large reception and dance were being given by Grand Duke Alexander (the heir apparent) at the Anichkov Palace. About 5 P.M. in the midst of the festivities Emperor Nicholas entered the ballroom and, holding in his hand an urgent message from the Russian Ambassador in Berlin announcing the events in Paris, said to the officers present: "Saddle your horses, gentlemen, a republic has been proclaimed in France." The Emperor then retired to an adjoining room to discuss the situation with the statesmen present. Nicholas was delighted at the news of the fall of Louis Philippe and was quite outspoken about it. "For eighteen years I have been considered a fool," he said, "because I have been saying that his crime would reap its punishment and now my prediction has been fulfilled; he got what he deserved and he is going out by way of the same door through which he came in."[1] But on the other hand he felt that the revolutionary disease might spread to Germany and from there to Poland and Russia. It was this fear that prompted him to think of military measures and, just as in the Revolution of 1830, his first impulse was to send 300,000 Russian troops to the Rhine as fast as possible. But more sober counsel around him prevailed. Prince Volkonsky, Count Paul Kisselev and Count Orlov opposed this scheme on the grounds of financial difficulties and the probable opposition to such a move on the part of Prussia and the other German States. Nevertheless, on March 7 the Czar addressed a rescript to the Minister of War, Count Chernyshev, which was published officially and which contained menacing words: "Events have occurred in Western Europe which foreshadow a criminal tendency to overthrow legally established powers. The treaties of

---

[1] Bapst, E., Les Origines de la Guerre de Crimée. Paris 1912, p. 3.

friendship and the conventions which unite Russia with neighbouring powers impose upon us the sacred duty of..... placing on a war footing a portion of our forces to be in condition, if circumstances made it necessary, to oppose a powerful wall to the destructive torrent of anarchy." [2] At the same time the diplomatic relations with France were officially broken off and Count Nicholas Kisselev, (the brother of Count P. Kisselev) who had been Chargé d'Affaires in Paris since 1841, was ordered to remain in the French capital solely in the capacity of a private observer. All Russians residing in the French capital were ordered to leave. As for the numerous French established in Russia they were informed by the Chief of the Gendarmes, Count Orlov, that they could remain in Russia provided they did not cause any trouble and abstained from political activities.

But events moved fast. On March 4 the Foreign Minister of the Revolutionary Government in Paris, the poet Lamartine, issued a circular declaring that France no longer recognized the Treaty of Vienna, thereby challenging the basic principles of Russia's diplomacy. Then came the news of a meeting of German liberals at Heidelberg who demanded the convocation of a national parliament and expressed a wish for the emancipation of Poland, as well as protesting the alliance of the King of Prussia with Russia. When finally came the news of the revolution in Austria and the fall of Metternich, followed by similar events in Prussia, the Czar felt the world crumbling around him. Writing to Metternich on March 26 Nicholas said that the fall of the Austrian Chancellor brought to an end "a whole system of ideas, interests and common action." Labouring thus under the emotional strain produced by the impact of these rapid developments, the Czar did a rash thing. Acting impulsively and against the cautious advice of his counsellors including Nesselrode, Nicholas issued a manifesto to his own people on March 26. "After the blessings of a long peace, Western Europe is now in the throes of troubles which are threatening to overthrow legitimate authority and social order. Rebellion and anarchy which first started in France have crossed the border into Germany, and, spreading like a destructive torrent the furore of which increases in proportion to the concessions made by the governments, have finally reached the Empire of Austria and the Kingdom of Prussia, our allies." [3] The manifesto goes on to say that Russia itself is now menaced and

---

[2] Bapst, op. cit., p. 4.
[3] Bapst, op. cit., p. 6, 7, also Schilder. Imperator Nikolai Pervyi appendix.

calls upon the Russian people to meet the foe, united and with trust in God, responding to the ancient slogan, "for faith, for Czar, for country." The Czar pledged not to spare himself in defending the inviolability of the Russian frontier and to lead his people to victory.

These bellicose sentiments publicly expressed produced a tremendous sensation in Western Europe and it became obvious that Russia was purposely envenoming the situation in France so as to discredit the Revolutionary Government, and in June one of its members, M. Caussidière, declared that "Cossack (sic) gold" was being spread amongst the 100,000 unemployed to start riots on the boulevards of Paris. Although such rumours were fantastic it was nevertheless true that, alarmed by the events in Austria and their repercussion on the Danubian Principalities and in Poland, a Russian army 420,000 strong had been quietly assembled on the western border of Russia. Though declaring herself strictly neutral, Russia nevertheless complained bitterly to Austria that the Austrian government was unable to keep order in Galicia, and Nesselrode on September 13, 1848, threatened to break off diplomatic relations should Austria allow the revolution to spread into Poland. Prince Schwarzenberg, worried by these demands of Russia, in November confidentially approached the Russian Government with a suggestion that Russia should occupy Galicia with her troops to maintain order, but this the Russian Government refused to do. Already in June Nesselrode had made a report to the Czar concerning the situation in Austria and particularly with regard to the agitation amongst the Slavs. He made the point that it was in the interest of Russia not to allow Austria to disintegrate and that it would be against the interest of Russia to desire the annexation of any Slav territory belonging to Austria for such a move would endanger the unity of the Russian nation. Thus there were to be no pan-Slavist tendencies and when a Croatian delegation presented itself to the Russian Chargé d'Affaires in Vienna, Fonton, in the name of Baron Jellachich, the newly appointed "Ban" of Croatia, to complain about the oppression of the Southern Slavs at the hands of the Hungarians, Fonton sharply put an end to the meeting by declaring that Russia would not meddle in the internal affairs of Austria.

Similarly, when Sardinia declared war upon Austria, Brunnow in London was instructed to inform Lord Palmerston that Russia's sympathies were on the side of Austria and that any support given by a foreign power to the other Italian states to attack Austria would result in a European war. It was largely through Russia's support that Austria refused the mediation of France and Britain concerning the cession of Lombardy until Field-Marshal Radetsky had turned the tables by crushing the Sardinians at Custozza. Russia's stand was once more based on the principle of legitimacy and she declared that Austria was the legitimate possessor of Lombardy and Venetia because these had been granted to her by the Treaty of Vienna. But Russia was prepared to accept the attribution to Sardinia of the Duchies of Parma and Piacenza, even though this meant the dispossessing of Bourbon princes. Similarly in Naples, which had always been the object of special benevolence on the part of Russia, her policies deviated from what was to have been expected. Indeed, at the outbreak of the revolution in France there had been a revolt against King Ferdinand in Sicily, fomented by France and Great Britain. France had sent a squadron in support of the Sicilian rebels, while Ferdinand, the notorious King Bomba, had provoked a rebellion in Naples by breaking his pledge on the issue of a constitution which he had previously granted. The French Minister demanded that Admiral Baudin, commanding the squadron should send landing parties ashore and bombard Naples, which the Admiral wisely refused to do. Wild rumours had spread over Naples, where it was believed that the King's reactionary policy was inspired by a secret committee which ruled the Kingdom and which was dominated by the Russian Minister Chreptovich, the Austrian diplomat Lebzeltern and the Queen, herself Austrian. Further rumours had it that the Czar had promised King Ferdinand a fleet to reconquer Sicily. But the official stand taken by the Russian legation on the Sicilian issue was exactly the reverse. In a communication to the French Minister, M. Sain de Boislecomte, Chreptovich on July 21 expressed his utter disapproval of the King's policy because he had broken his word. "We were of the opinion that since King Ferdinand had given the Constitution and sworn to it he should keep his promise religiously... The confidence of a people in their sovereign is today of supreme importance..." And he advocated the coming together of France and Russia to stave off the British menace of taking possession "morally and commercially" of Sicily, now virtually independent. [4] This slight overture to France on a secondary issue of no direct concern to Russia was made possible by the events which in the meanwhile had taken place in Paris. The crushing of the June Insurrection had resulted in the semi-dictatorship of General Cavaignac which was welcomed in St. Petersburg as a token of return to sanity. One of the first things Cavaignac did upon coming to power was to act upon this slight sign of better feeling in Russia and send a comrade-at-arms who had distinguished himself in Africa, General Le Flo, to St. Petersburg on a special mission endeavouring to obtain the recognition of the French Republic. Nicholas received him cordially and even conceded that republican institutions might be natural to France but withheld his recognition. Negotiations dragged on more or less futilely until the situation had

---

[4] Bapst, op. cit., p. 16, 17.

completely changed by the appearance on the French political stage of Prince Louis Napoleon.

In the meantime events nearer home had forced Russia to take the first step in active intervention in this revolution. The events in the Danubian Principalities, which have been discussed elsewhere, resulted in the military occupation of Moldavia and Wallachia and this occupation drew protests from both England and France who declared the move to be a violation of the autonomy granted by treaties to the Principalities. Justifying Russia's conduct, Nesselrode issued an important circular to his ambassadors abroad, for communication to the Courts to which they were accredited, (July 31, 1848) in which he declared that the Principalities placed under Russian protection by the Treaty of Adrianople formed a case apart. "Our principle of strict neutrality toward independent states remains invariably the same; and whatever may be the changes any of these states may desire to bring about in their social or political laws, so long as they do not endanger our security or our rights, we will continue to watch, armed, as we have done up to now, the spectacle of their internal revolutions." [5]

Thus the principle of armed non-intervention was solemnly proclaimed, but as the revolution developed it became more and more difficult to maintain it. Indeed, in January, 1849, the commander of the Austrian forces in Transylvania demanded military aid against the Hungarians from the headquarters of the Russian occupationary army in Moldavia. Two detachments under General Engelhardt and Colonel Skariatin, totalling 6,000 men in all, were moved into Transylvania. But in February the detachment of Colonel Skariatin was defeated by a force of Hungarians under the former Polish rebel leader, General Bem and both detachments were withdrawn from Transylvania. Skariatin's defeat particularly galled the Czar in view of the fact that it had been at the hands of one of the leaders of the Polish Revolution of 1831, and this was one of the motives for the coming Hungarian campaign. Meanwhile, even though Russia had expressly declared her neutrality and non-immixture into the affairs of the German states, the activities of the Frankfurt Parliament were being closely watched. In its enthusiasm for the unification of Germany the speakers at the Parliament had put forward claims on the Russian Baltic provinces, Poland and Schleswig-Holstein. In another circular note (June 1849) Nesselrode stressed the fact that these plans were endangering the peace of Europe. With remarkable prevision he denounced "the idea of material unity (in Germany) as dreamt of by a democracy avid for... aggrandizement and which sooner or later would infallibly result in a war

---

[5] Bapst, op. cit., p. 21.

between Germany and her neighbours."[6] Nicholas was bitterly opposed to the rising tide of nationalism in Europe, particularly with regard to the attempts at unification of Germany and Italy. In February he expressed his views about these two countries: "... "...Germany will destroy herself in the search for unity, the dream of a few professors. I do not forecast anything better for Italy; Italian unity is a chimera and as for Charles Albert, after having wallowed in dirt he will fall into the mud."[7] At the same time he once more expressed the view to the departing General Le Flo that he considered France had the right to govern herself as she wished and he would be willing to recognize the French Government if the latter gave serious guarantees of the maintenance of peace.[8] Thus the emphasis was gradually shifting toward a struggle against nationalism and this was to draw Russia into a serious war--the Hungarian campaign.

II

The revolutionary storm was still blowing full blast over the Hapsburg Monarchy when young Emperor Francis Joseph, 18 years of age, mounted the throne at Olmütz, whither the Austrian Court had gone to seek refuge. But there was now a powerful personality behind the Emperor to guide him and above all to dominate the unleashed forces of the revolution,--Prince Felix Schwarzenberg who, entering diplomacy under Metternich in 1824, had seen his first diplomatic service in St. Petersburg. Austria had found a new master six months after the fall of Metternich. Schwarzenberg imposed abdication upon the feeble-minded Ferdinand and the youthful Francis Joseph was proclaimed the new Emperor on December 2, 1848. No easy task lay ahead of him; true, Vienna proper had been recaptured from Jacobin democracy, the revolution had been crushed in Italy, Bohemia, Galicia and Croatia. But these results were virtually nullified by the dangerous turn the situation had taken in Hungary, where the forces under Prince Windishgraetz faced a veritable war of independence. Windishgraetz having failed to pacify Hungary, was superseded by General von Welden who, after a smashing defeat at Kapolna, was forced to evacuate Budapest, a shattering blow to Austrian prestige at home and more particularly abroad. The Hungarian national army under a young officer of the engineers, Arthur von Görgey, now took the offensive and raised the

---

[6] Polievktov, M., *Imperator Nikolai I*, Moscow 1918, p. 356.
[7] Bapst, *op. cit.*, p. 34.
[8] Bapst, *op. cit.*, p. 33, 34.

blockade of Komorn on his way to invade Austria proper whereas, on April 14, 1849, the Hungarian revolutionary government under Kossuth proclaimed the independence of Hungary excluding forever the house of Hapsburg from the Hungarian throne. The very existence of Austria and the safety of Francis Joseph were at stake. However reluctantly, both Schwarzenberg and Francis Joseph gradually were forced into the idea of asking for foreign aid. The archenemy of revolution and the most powerful ruler in Europe, pledged to a traditional friendship with Austria since the Holy Alliance, Nicholas was the obvious selection. True, it meant publicly acknowledging the humiliating weakness of Austria, it also meant acknowledging officially the moral right of the Czar to consider himself the protector of the Slav populations so badly oppressed by the Hungarians--a dangerous concession to the rising tide of pan-Slavis but there was no other course left. In a letter to Schwarzenberg, Francis Joseph wrote that he was "fully cognizant of Prince Schwarzenberg's feelings and knows well that he would never take this step if our own force were sufficient." [10] Nicholas had already been informed by the Russian Ambassador, who was then at Olmütz, of the impending request. He was ready to occupy Galicia and thereby protect his own Polish dominions from the danger of a revolution but, referring to an intervention in Hungary, he said in a letter to his wife "the Austrians want someone else to put out the fire for them. Not I." [11] But gradually he came to accept the idea of helping Austria in her Hungarian war. There were powerful motives for this. The year before there had been an insurrection in Austrian Poland which was subdued after Lemberg had been bombarded and after Count Stadion had played the Ruthenians against the Poles. Nicholas had nervously watched these events, so close to his frontier and now that the Hungarian situation seemed to be completely out of control and the flames of revolution were approaching perilously near his own border, Nicholas viewed the situation with increasing alarm.

There was the ever-present danger of the possibility of a new explosion in Russian Poland by detonation from Hungary. This danger was rendered all the more grave by the number of Russian Poles who had enrolled in the Hungarian revolutionary army. Two Polish leaders of the rebellion of 1831 against Russia had command positions in the Hungarian forces--Dembinsky was Commander-in-Chief before the appointment of Görgey--and Bem, as we have seen

---

[9]Leger, Louis, A History of Austria Hungary. London 1889, p. 523.

[10]Redlich, J., Emperor Francis Joseph of Austria, a biography. New York 1929, p. 57.

[11]Redlich, op. cit., p. 56.

was in charge of the Hungarian forces in Transylvania. He had conducted a brilliant campaign there and had occupied Hermannstadt after driving the Russians out of Transylvania. Such were the immediate considerations--there was also the mystical belief, so strong in Nicholas, that he was the instrument of Providence for maintaining law and established order against the tide of revolution and the dogged loyalty to his pledges under the Holy Alliance and to his friendships--a fact which puzzled foreign diplomats, unaccustomed to loyalty in politics, who therefore attributed it to barbarian instincts.

Hence the Czar was prepared to answer Austria's request favourably. It came in the form of a letter from Francis Joseph dated April 26, 1849, thanking the Czar for some distinctions bestowed by the latter upon Field-Marshal Radetsky. With rather too obvious flattery, the young Emperor wrote to Nicholas: "In showing this remarkable favour to an old soldier whose devotion has always been as great as his bravery, you Sire, win a new title to the fame that history can not deny you. At a period when the pillars of social order are shattered, you have the glory of having been the true appreciator and guardian of military honour, the last bulwark of a society that is about to perish, under the blows of ruthless foes..."[12] Five days later came the official request to which the Czar replied in the friendliest terms and the Russian armies were set in motion.

The plan of operations provided for a simultaneous invasion of Hungary by the Austrian and Russian armies converging toward the river Theiss. The Austrian Army, commanded by the able, energetic but brutal Haynau, entered from the west and secured some important victories. The Russians, 190,000 strong, entered through Galicia and through Transylvania. The main army under Field-Marshal Prince Paskevich, about 100,000 strong, was based on Dukla in Galicia while the Transylvanian army under General Luders numbered about 50,000. General Paniutin with a detached force was to march on Pressburg to link up with the Austrians while General Sass was to draw upon himself the Hungarians who had been pursuing the retreating Austrians, so as to give the latter time to reorganize their forces. The first contact with the Hungarians was established by the Russians on May 16. From then on Paskevich pushed ahead vigorously. General Paniutin defeated the Hungarians and occupied Pressburg on June 4, then as Görgey had placed two Austrian divisions in a critical position, Paniutin came up and relieved them by driving the enemy across the river Waag. Paskevich moved the bulk of his forces to Tokay and his cavalry swam across the Theiss and captured the city. From there he pressed his army

---

[12]Redlich, op. cit., p. 58.

towards the Danube with the object of keeping Görgey separated from his lieutenant Vysocky. Paniutin joined the Austrians, whom he assisted in the battle of Komorn, then subsequently defeated the enemy at Waitzen. Görgey, marching along the left bank of the Danube to escape the pincer drive of the Russians and Austrians, was stopped by the Russians at Tur, forced to retreat and once more defeated at Miskolcz by the latter. Finally on August 13 at Villagos he laid down his arms and surrendered to the Russian General Rudiger. The Russians took 23,000 prisoners, 130 guns and an historic relic of great sentimental value to the Hungarians--the sword of the national hero Rakoczy. This sword was kept in the Hermitage Museum in St. Petersburg until 1896 when by order of Nicholas II it was returned to Hungary on the occasion of the millenary celebrations of the existence of the kingdom.

Meanwhile Lüders, operating in Transylvania against Bem, had achieved equally brilliant successes. He captured Hermannstadt and marched on Segesvar, defeating Bem at Maros-Vasarhely in the heart of Transylvania. At Segesvar on July 31, the final defeat came to Bem, who was forced to escape to Turkey. In this battle fell the famous Hungarian poet Petöfi. Though the results of the war may have been considered as a foregone conclusion, in view of the fact that the Austro-Russians outnumbered the Hungarians two to one, it remained nevertheless true that the campaign had been a hard one, partly because of the fanatical bravery of the Hungarians and partly because of the ravages of cholera which took a heavy toll amongst the Russians. No wonder that after the capitulation of Villagos, Paskevich reported exultantly to the Czar: "Hungary lies at the foot of your Imperial Majesty."

Chivalrously, Nicholas I demanded nothing in payment for his services. He did even more. Reversing his own policy of brutality towards the defeated Poles, he appealed to the Austrian Government for clemency towards the Hungarians. What Hungary could expect from Haynau "the Butcher" once the Russian occupationary army had left the country was foreshadowed in the letter written by Paskevich, announcing his victory. "Görgey relies exclusively on the magnanimity of Your Majesty. Could I hand over to the gallows all those whose sole trust is in Your Majesty's mildness of heart, to be all the more severely punished because they surrendered to our troops?" [13] Nicholas was in Warsaw when this letter was brought to him by Paskevich's son acting as special courier. The Czar immediately dispatched his son, Grand Duke Michael, to Vienna to plead before Francis Joseph. The only result was that upon the Czar's insistance, Görgey's life was spared and he was allowed to

---

[13] Redlich, op. cit., p. 60.

go into exile. But once the Austrians had taken over the country, Haynau was given a free hand. The result was the bloody assize of Arad, when 13 leaders of the revolt were executed, some shot, some hanged. The elderly Count Batthyany, the first Prime Minister of the Hungarian revolutionary government, was hanged in a particularly brutal way, considering that in a previous attempt at suicide he had injured his neck. Prison terms of from 1 to 20 years were given 386 officers, and thousands of civilians, both men and women, were either jailed or flogged including the 72 year old mother of Kossuth, who was jailed. All Hungarian nobles who had fled abroad either during the rebellion or as a result of these persecutions, saw their estates and property confiscated by decree. Amongst these was young Count Julius Andrassy who had taken refuge in Turkey where he vainly attempted to raise the Turks against Russia during the war. Little could one foresee that this powerless exile whose estates were taken by the Austrian Government would one day steer Austrian diplomacy towards a dangerous hostility against her Slav benefactor. Not all the Hungarians, however, were so resentful and it is surprising to find that even during the campaign of 1849 there was a movement amongst certain officers of the Hungarian army for offering the crown of Hungary to the son of Nicholas I, presumably to Grand Duke Michael.

In the meantime the question of the Hungarian refugees in Turkey was to plunge Russia into a dangerous conflict with the Porte which foreshadowed the approaching Crimean War. In September, Austria and Russia had demanded that the Sultan should give up both the Polish and Hungarian refugees on his soil. Immediately the British Ambassador, Stratford Canning, assured the Sultan that Britain would support Turkey in refusing this demand. Palmerston on his side, seeing in this move not only the humanitarian side, but also a further step leading Russia toward the complete domination of Turkey, wrote a confidential letter to Ponsonby in Paris outlining his policy, which consisted in making representations jointly with France in Vienna and St. Petersburg and at the same time having British and French squadrons quietly take up positions outside the Dardanelles ready for action if necessary. Having obtained the support of his cabinet and of the French Government to carry through this policy, he speedily informed the Turkish Government that it might expect "moral" and "material" support from both France and England in this affair. Neither the Russians nor the Austrians were informed of any such move. Palmerston explained the reason in writing to Ponsonby: "The example (of sending vessels to Constantinople) might be turned to bad account by the Russians hereafter; and it would be too much of an open menace and the way to deal with the Emperor (of Russia) is not to put him on his mettle by open and public menace... The government have indeed resolved to support the Sultan at all events, but we must be able to show to Parliament that we have used all civility and forebearance and that if hostilities ensue, they have not been brought on by any fault or mistake of ours." [14] However, Nicholas' insistance on this issue was half-hearted and he withdrew his demand. Nesselrode wrote to Baron Meyendorff in Berlin: "Certainly I hate Palmerston as much as Prince Schwarzenberg can hate him...but Palmerston is not eternal and a war with England would be the worst of all wars." [15] The next time, however, that England tried the same policy in Turkey, the result was the Crimean War.

But even more ominous for Russia was the reaction to her Hungarian policy throughout the rest of Europe. The liberal public opinion, which was in sympathy with Hungary and in this openly supported by official France and England, received the news of the Russian success with awed fear, and hatred of Russia reached new heights--more than ever she was regarded as the "Gendarme de l'Europe." The French Minister of Foreign Affairs at this time, M. de Tocqueville, was to write two years later in his "Souvenirs": "As for myself, who believes that our West is due to fall earlier or later under the direct and irresistible influence of the Czars, I consider our most important task is to favour the union of the Germanic races to oppose them to the former...We must not be afraid to strengthen our neighbors so that they should be able to repulse, one day, together with us, our common enemy," i.e. Russia. [16]

III

Scarcely had the Hungarian issue been settled when another crisis arose in Central Europe in which Russia was called to play an equally important role. Francis Joseph and his energetic minister Prince Schwarzenberg, having re-established their authority over the Hapsburg Empire, were anxious to re-assert their power over Germany as well. Hence they invited the various German states to assemble at the reopening of the Frankfurt Diet under the presidency of Austria. But thereby they clashed with the ambitions of Prussia who, after the Revolution of 1848, had momentarily taken the lead in the movement for the unification of Germany by creating her own federation known as the Erfurt Union. The two competitive systems, which had divided between them the allegiance of the small German states were, bound to clash and the actual reason for the

---

[14] Bell, H. C. F., Lord Palmerston. New York 1936, Vol. II, p. 18.
[15] Bell, op. cit., Vol. II, p. 19.
[16] Bapst, op. cit., p. 78, 79.

conflict was created by the situation which developed in Hesse-Cassel, Mecklenburg and Schleswig.

The Elector of Hesse-Cassel, Friedrich Wilhelm I, was faced with an open rebellion of his diet and subjects. The situation was delicate for Hesse-Cassel since she was a member of the Erfurt Union and her territory was wedged in between Prussia and the Prussian Rhenish provinces. But the Elector turned for help to Schwarzenberg and to the Frankfurt Diet for here, alone, his reactionary policy would meet with sympathy. This gave Schwarzenberg a chance to interfere in the affairs of the Erfurt Union and take a strong stand against Prussia. This energetic policy was due in great part to the feeling that Austria had Russia behind her. Indeed, in the Schleswig-Holstein issue Russia made it clear that she did not approve of Prussia's policy and ambitions. In August 1850 Schwarzenberg had a conference at Ischl with Russian diplomats in which both parties came to a complete agreement concerning the Danish and German affairs. Sure of Russia's support, Schwarzenberg went ahead--the Diet, at his instigation, voted a federal execution in Hesse for October 25, whereas Prussia in return occupied the military roads across Hesse with her forces under a clause of a treaty giving her this right. A clash between the Prussian troops and the Bavarian Army, which was to carry out the execution, appeared inevitable and finally did occur. Austria on her side moved troops in Bohemia and Moravia. On October 11 at a meeting at Bregenz, the Kings of Bavaria and Wurttemberg pledged Emperor Francis Joseph their military support. Hanover and Saxony were to come in later. Thus Schwarzenberg had manoeuvred Prussia to face either the dissolution of the union and to see her Rhenish provinces cut off through the occupation by Bavaria of Hesse-Cassel or to face a war against the combined forces of Austria and the four German kingdoms. Vacillation and near panic reigned in Berlin. In desperation Prussia turned to Russia for help.

Nicholas had passed the summer in Warsaw watching the German situation closely, and convinced that he would have to interfere for the sake of the principles of the Holy Alliance. In Berlin the reactionary camarilla around the King's throne welcomed the idea of a Russian intervention even if directed against Prussia. "We ought to be happy at this affront to our fatherland," wrote General Gerlach, [17] and urged King Friedrich Wilhelm to go to Warsaw to plead with the Czar. Radowitz, now in power, feared the vacillations of the King, who might come under the complete influence of Nicholas. Hence Count Brandenburg was sent in his stead.

---

[17] Matter, P., Bismarck et son temps. Paris 1905-1908. Vol. I, p. 253.

Brandenburg in going to Warsaw had hoped that family ties and the long tradition of friendship would make certain the Czar's support for Prussia. But all such hopes were soon dashed to the ground. Arriving at Warsaw on October 17, Count Brandenburg was immediately received by the Czar who was very friendly, but made it plain that he was taking the side of Austria in the quarrel. From the very outset Nicholas made it clear that he placed the principles of the Holy Alliance above all considerations of family and friendship, as he had done in the Hungarian rebellion. He declared that he understood Prussia's desire to see the federal organization of Germany rejuvenated but at the same time he thought Prussia ought to start by demanding her re-admission into the Frankfurt Diet. He further refused to mediate in the quarrel (to leave Austria freedom of action) and declared that he entirely approved of the appeal for assistance made by the Elector of Hesse to the Diet. Brandenburg, having brought with him very moderate counter-proposals, appealed to Nesselrode, who was more amenable, and finally obtained permission to submit these Prussian proposals to Schwarzenberg through Baron Meyendorff, the Russian Ambassador to Austria.[18] At the same time Nicholas insisted during the subsequent negotiations that Prussia should also settle the Holstein affair as well.

On October 25 Francis Joseph and Schwarzenberg arrived in Warsaw. The very next day Bavaria was ordered by the Diet to invade Hesse, whereas Berlin had issued an order to the Prussian troops to occupy the military roads in the duchy, which was done by the Prussian commander on October 24. The situation was rapidly moving toward a climax and war fever had gripped Prussia, though the King was still hesitant. During the three subsequent days three-cornered negotiations proceeded in Warsaw between Austria, Prussia and Russia, but due to the adamant attitude taken by the Austrians, they got nowhere. Finally Russia made it clear that any attempt by Prussia to oppose a federal execution, would be regarded by Russia as a casus belli. Brandenburg left Warsaw on the 29th convinced that in case of war with Austria, Prussia would have to face Russia as well. In Berlin the news of what had taken place split the government into two parties, the one headed by Radowitz, insisting upon war for the sake of Prussia's honour, the other prepared to be more conciliatory and ready to yield to Austria. During the heated discussions, the Minister of War declared that mobilization would mean a war against both Austria and Russia and that the Prussian Army was not in a condition to face such an eventuality. The issue was up to the King, who finally threw

---

[18]Matter, op. cit., Vol. I, p. 254, 255.

in his lot with the peace party and the government of General Radowitz fell. The next day, November 3, Brandenburg fell ill with inflamation of the brain and died three days later, gossip immediately explaining his death as caused by the insolence of the Czar. But more justly Abeken, his subordinate, states in his "Ein Schlichtes Leben in Bewegter Zeit," [19] that the death was due "to the constant intellectual excitement of the past two years coupled with the fatigue of his journey to Warsaw and the dreadful tension he had undergone during the crisis."

Manteuffel replaced Brandenburg in charge of foreign affairs and his first move was to send conciliatory proposals to Austria; but when news came that the Bavarians were still advancing and that 30,000 Austrians had crossed into Bavaria and were marching on Prussia, there was nothing for Prussia to do but issue an order for general mobilization, which was issued on November 6, and two days later a clash occurred between the Prussian and Bavarian armies. Five Bavarians were wounded whereas on the Prussian side the only casualty was a trumpeter's horse, which thereby entered history. This incident played directly into the hands of Schwarzenberg who followed it up by demands for an apology, for the removal of the Prussian commander of the troops in Hesse and, more grave, the demand for the dissolution by Prussia of the Erfurt Union. At the same time, by chance or purposely, the new Russian Ambassador to the Frankfurt Diet, Prince Gorchakov, arrived in Frankfurt, thereby stressing the solidarity of his country with the position taken by Austria. The Prussians attempted further negotiations but, on November 25, Schwarzenberg issued an ultimatum with a time limit of 48 hours. In dismay Manteuffel asked for a personal meeting with Schwarzenberg. The meeting of the ministers took place at Olmütz where Schwarzenberg went on the 28th accompanied demonstratively by the Russian Ambassador, Baron Meyendorff. Schwarzenberg put the issue squarely--war or capitulation, and Manteuffel had no choice but to capitulate. A convention was drawn up, couched in diplomatic language, so as to take the form of a compromise agreement but in reality Manteuffel ceded every point to Austria. The King, upon Manteuffel's return to Berlin, first refused to sign the document but finally affixed his signature and the treaty was ratified by Prussia on December 2, 1850. Schwarzenberg's triumph had been complete and much of his success was due to Russia's attitude. Meyendorff attempted to mitigate the humiliation inflicted upon Prussia by declaring that the honour of Prussia was saved. The Prussian Government faced with turmoil at home as a result of its diplomatic defeat used

---

[19] Matter, op. cit., Vol. I, p. 260.

extensively this statement of the Russian Ambassador to placate public opinion. Bismarck, who was given the ungrateful task of being the government spokesman in parliament where a violent storm of oppostion had broken out, pointed out in his speech that Russia too, in the affair of the Polish refugees in Turkey, had given way in the face of a serious war. Gradually things settled down after Olmütz. The cumbersome Diet, of which Heine mockingly said "O Bund, du hund, du bist nich gesund", had received an unexpected new lease on life thanks to Schwarzenberg. Accordingly Frankfurt became once more a diplomatic center of great importance with foreign and German envoys, accredited to the Germanic Confederation, again filling the city. Two men were to meet in this brilliant corps diplomatique and here was to begin their long and momentous association. In the Germanic group, next in importance to the Austrian delegation was the Prussian delegation. It was headed by Baron von Rochow, Prussian Ambassador to St. Petersburg, transferred temporarily to Frankfurt because he was a "persona grata" with Czar Nicholas. His councillor of the legation was the 36 year old Otto von Bismarck-Schönhausen, who was to succeed him in a few months when von Rochow demanded his own reappointment to St. Petersburg. In the foreign group of diplomats, leading in importance and brilliancy was the Russian legation headed by a young diplomat of promise, Prince Gorchakov. Twenty years later both Bismarck and Gorchakov, as Chancellors, were to dominate the political life of Europe.

It was during this stay at Frankfurt that Bismarck's political views definitely crystallized: he gradually evolved a bitter antagonism towards Austria and conversely became the life-long friend of Russia. Meanwhile King Friedrich Wilhelm wisely decided to seek reconciliation with his powerful eastern neighbour and in 1851 travelled to Warsaw to meet the Czar. Here good relations were restored between the two countries and when the following year the Czar paid a return visit to Berlin, everything was done to please him and to win his goodwill. In striking contrast was the path which Austria was to follow.

On April 5, 1852, Schwarzenberg, after having presided over the Council of Ministers, was dressing for dinner when he was suddenly taken ill and died. This strong-willed Austrian statesman was the only one who might have opposed Bismarck. His death marked the beginning of a revolutionary change in Austro-Russian relations. Twice within two years Russia had come to the aid of Austria at critical moments: during the Hungarian rebellion when Russia saved Austria from destruction and at Olmütz where Austria secured her domination of Germany through Russian support. Schwarzenberg had already predicted that "Austria was going to surprise the world by her ingratitude." It was now his successor,

Count Buol, who was to veer Austro-Russian relations in an incredibly short time from warm cordiality to coolness and then to open enmity. "Nations are never so grateful as their benefactors expect" wrote Wellington to Canning (December 15, 1814.) Austria was to give the most spectacular confirmation in history of this truth, and to be punished by fate for her treachery in the most impressive way. For the Austro-Russian quarrel, caused by Buol, was to lead to the bitter rivalry between the two powers and to become one of the direct causes of the World War and the ultimate annihilation of Austria. There was nothing on the Russian side to warrant this change of attitude. Nicholas, always consistent, had remained thoroughly friendly to Francis Joseph. Indeed, on April 19, 1852, he wrote to the young Emperor: "If Thou will permit it, I shall visit Thee this time in Vienna. The hope of embracing Thee again gives me new life, and I feel more than ever the need of telling Thee how I love and prize Thee..." and commenting on the death of Schwarzenberg, "This man rendered Thee outstanding services and his devotion to Thee, like his other great noble characteristics, compel respect even from his adversaries." [20]

There were manifold influences at work to separate Austria from Russia. First the family, which exerted a powerful influence on the young Francis Joseph: the influence of his mother, Archduchess Sophia, a devoted and somewhat bigoted Roman Catholic, who looked upon Russians as schismatics and approved of the independence shown by her son in regard to the Czar; then, a little later, the influence of Empress Elizabeth with whom Francis Joseph was very much in love and who, particularly after her visit to Hungary in 1857, developed a life-long passionate romantic attachment to everything Hungarian and hence anti-Russian. There was also the jealousy of the army, which was bitter that Görgey had surrendered to the Russians and not to the Austrians. There were political considerations as well. For the past half century Austria had had to divert her whole attention and all her energies to German and Italian affairs and her policy in the Eastern Question had been purely passive, limiting itself to the maintenance of Turkish rule in the Balkans. She was viewing with increasing alarm the spread of Russian influence particularly in the Principalities which controlled the lower Danube, the vital trade way and life line of Austria. But Austria was further hampered by the fact that while she was stifling the rising pan-Slavist tendencies in her own Empire, she could not play the game that Russia was playing so successfully in the Balkans, namely, encouraging Slav and Roumanian aspirations against the Turks. Hence she watched Russia with impotent

---

[20]Redlich, op. cit., p. 125, 126.

jealousy and her only hope was to see Russian influence checked in the Balkans by some external pressure. The Crimean War was too good an occasion to miss. The successor of Schwarzenberg, Count Buol, as often happens, initiated a policy reversing the course of his predecessor and his openly avowed desire was to supersede Russian influence in Moldavia and Wallachia, thus securing control of the entire course of the Danube. Indeed, he occupied the Danubian Provinces the moment the Russians had evacuated them in the early stage of the war.

But in so doing Austria was throwing away the valuable support of Russia in her Western European policy and was making a dangerous enemy of her powerful northern neighbour. As Egon Corti puts it, "It was not seen till later that thanks to this he (Francis Joseph) would fall between two stools and lose all his friends. For the time being it looked as though Austria was strong enough to defy the Tzar." [21] The words of the Russian Ambassador, Baron Meyendorff, on leaving Vienna in 1854 were singularly prophetic: "I am sorry for the young Emperor, for his policy has wounded us Russians so deeply that he can be sure of not having another moment's peace as long as his reign lasts." [22]

The beginning of this anti-Russian drift may be traced as early as 1853, the time when Archduchess Sophia became definitely the head of the Court camarilla and dominated her son completely. But such a break in the traditions of Austrian diplomacy could not occur without a struggle and powerful influences fought the new anti-Russian policy. The most influential leaders of the pro-Russian party were the old Field-Marshals Windishgraetz and Radetsky, and the Emperor's personal aide-de-camp, Count Grünne, who was so powerful as to give rise to the witticism that the colours of the Austrian Army were not red and white, but green (Grunn.) With such leaders and with the support of most of the influential people at the Imperial Court, the Russophile party staged a bitter fight, which divided Court circles, the army and society. Baron Meyendorff was openly advised by these personages of their hostility to the Emperor's policy and the issue became a dangerous political conflict in the inner circles of Austria. [23] But the young Emperor had set his course, regarding it a matter of personal prestige and pride, and stuck to it. Buol merely echoed his master.

---

[21] Corti, Egon, Elizabeth Empress of Austria. Newhaven 1936, p. 55.
[22] From a dispatch of the Bavarian Minister to Vienna. Bavarian State Archives. Quoted by Corti, op. cit.
[23] Redlich, op. cit., p. 181.

This policy of Austria would not have been dangerous to Russia had not it echoed the growing wave of anti-Russian feeling all over Western Europe. The power and aggressiveness shown by Russia in dealing with the Revolution of 1848 and the post-revolutionary period, particularly the Hungarian War and the crisis of Olmütz, had stirred liberal public opinion to a pitch of hatred against Russia which was ominous. Russia was regarded as the enemy of progress and the extinguisher of liberty and civilization. Particularly strong was this mood in France and Napoleon III, anxious to play an increasingly important role, was to make it the corner-stone of his policy for motives of personal animosity toward Russia. Thus the relations with France after the Revolution of 1848 were to assume once more an importance they had not had for a long while and were to become the cause of a dangerous drift toward the next great war in Russian history--the Crimean War, and in this somewhat circuitous way the forebodings of the Czar concerning the evil effects upon Russia of the Revolution of 1848 in Paris were to be fully realized.

IV

The news of the election of Prince Louis Napoleon to the presidency of the French Republic was received with a sigh of relief in St. Petersburg, for it was expected to put an end to the dangerous revolutionary anarchy in Paris as exhibited in the June days. Speaking somewhat later to the French envoy in Russia, General de Castelbajac, Nicholas observed, "I believe that there remains in Europe only myself, your president and your minister (General de la Hitte, French Minister of Foreign Affairs) who have some common sense and loyalty; it is common sense that is most required." [24] But both Nesselrode in Russia and Drouyn de Lhuys, the new Minister of Foreign Affairs of the French Republic, were opposed to closer relations between the two countries and, in the Hungarian revolution, the sympathies of France were overtly on the side of the rebels. Nevertheless, both sides were anxious to regularize their relations and, after Russia had officially recognized the French Republic, Louis Napoleon made the next conciliatory gesture by sending an envoy to St. Petersburg. However, when General de la Moricière was appointed to Russia, Russia did not reciprocate by sending an envoy to Paris but merely appointed, as Chargé d'Affaires, Count Kisselev who had been in charge of the Paris embassy during the period of the breakdown of relations. Thus a shading of reserve

---

[24] Bapst., op. cit., p. 170.

and coldness remained and de la Morcière making himself unpopular in Russia, the relations continued strained. Sensing this Louis Napoleon replaced him by the General de Castelbajac, a man much more suited to please the Czar and Russian society. Castelbajac succeeded too well inasmuch as, won over by the charm and ascendancy of the Czar, he became too pro-Russian to suit the Prince President.

At the time of his arrival in St. Petersburg an opportunity presented itself not only to better the relations with Russia but actually to convert them into an alliance, and Castelbajac made the best use of this opportunity. This was the famous Don Pacifico incident in Greece which, following so closely on the affair of the Hungarian prisoners, once more revealed how precarious was the Anglo-Russian friendship. On the way back from what had amounted to a British naval demonstration against Russia in connection with the affair of the Hungarian prisoners, the British squadron, under Admiral Parker, composed of 13 vessels, put into the Bay of Salamin. Two vessels entered the port of Piraeus and five days later, on January 16, 1850, the British Minister in Athens presented the Greek Government with an ultimatum of 24 hours, threatening the opening of hostilities against Greece if reparations were not given for various hostile incidents which had damaged the interests of British subjects. Amongst these were the detention by Greek police of some sailors from the British vessel Phantom at Patras and the damages inflicted on a Gibraltar Jew, a naturalized British subject, Pacifico, whose house had been sacked by a mob in Athens three years earlier, in 1847. These issues had been the object of rather dilatory negotiations for some time and had not been pressed very hard by the British Government. Thus this sudden and unexpected show of force in what amounted to insignificantly small damages revealed at once that the issues at stake were not the ones raised but a serious matter of policy. Indeed, King Otto of Greece had for some time shown an inclination to come under the influence of Russia and France to the detriment of British influence and this had to be checked, as Lord Palmerston had made clear in Parliament. Thus it was apparent that this warlike gesture was aimed at Russia and France rather than at Greece proper. Terrified and claiming violation of the guarantee given to Greece by the London Treaty in 1832, the Greek Government appealed for aid to the two other co-guarantors of this treaty, Russia and France. The Russian Minister in Athens, Persiani, acting jointly with his French colleague, Thouvenel, obtained a 24 hour delay from the British, but upon the expiration of this time limit, the British Minister left the Greek capital and went aboard a British man-of-war. At the same time, the British took possession of all Greek vessels they could lay their hands on. The issue was now squarely up to Russia and

France, and their Minister in Athens jointly protested the seizure of the Greek vessels.

The news of the events in Greece caused a sensation in Russia, where it was considered that Russian prestige in the Balkans was at stake. Emperor Nicholas, who always considered that he had had the lion's share in the making of Greece, was profoundly indignant. He ordered Nesselrode to make a strong protest to England and to get into touch with the French Government for joint and energetic action. But Louis Napoleon, though disapproving British high-handedness, was not prepared to follow Russia in this matter; he was aware that Lord Palmerston was his main supporter and he could not forget the hospitality given to him by Britain in the days of his exile. Therefore he selected the course of sending Drouyn de Lhuys to London with an offer to mediate the Greek crisis single-handed. Anxious to keep Russia and France apart, Palmerston accepted without hesitation and the issue dragged on until a convention was negotiated in London between France and England, which the Greek Government was forced to accept. Russian diplomacy had sustained a defeat and Brunnow rather demonstratively refused to attend a diplomatic dinner given in honour of the Queen's birthday by Lord Palmerston. But the significance of the Greek incident transcended Russia's spite against England. It was a turning point in Louis Napoleon's diplomacy inasmuch as the crisis placed him at the crossroads: had he co-operated with Russia the way would have been paved for closer co-operation and even an alliance with that country. General de Castelbajac urged his government to follow this road and was working whole heartedly for the alliance, until restrained from Paris. The other road of closer co-operation with England, though more in line with French traditions, and more in accordance with Louis Napoleon's own sentiments, was nevertheless the road leading to a great war--the Crimean War. But in the meanwhile Castelbajac, restrained in his efforts to bring France and Russia closer, had achieved one important result. He had obtained the appointment of a Russian Ambassador to Paris in the person of Kisselev who was now promoted from Chargé d'Affaires to Minister Plenipotentiary, thus finally regularizing his diplomatic status. However this step did not serve to improve the relations with France because Nicholas, spiteful and more than ever suspicious of Louis Napoleon since the Greek affair, was to be faced with another token of his anti-Russian feelings. On May 28, 1850, the new French Ambassador to Constantinople, General Aupick, presented a note to the Turkish Government claiming a guarantee of the rights of Roman Catholics in Turkey under Article XXXIII of the so-called Capitulations of 1740. In line with the Catholic policy pursued by Louis Napoleon, it is possible that this step was not intended to be directed against Russia.

It is nevertheless true that it opened the long and tedious quarrel over the Holy Places which served as the occasion for the outbreak of the Crimean War.

Under these circumstances it was with a very mixed feeling that the news was received in St. Petersburg of the coup d'etat of December 2, 1851 making Louis Napoleon President for ten years. Indeed, though official felicitations were sent to Paris, Nicholas attempted to induce the Three Northern Courts to restrain Louis Napoleon. Russia appealed to Berlin and Vienna for joint action in accordance with the declaration made in 1814 by Alexander I in the name of the Allies which excluded the Bonapartes from the throne of France, a declaration which was confirmed by the Convention of March 30, 1814, and Article II of the Treaty of November 20, 1815. Prince Schwarzenberg's reply to the effect that times having changed, it was better to recognize the fait accompli, produced the most painful impression in St. Petersburg. Russia then turned once more to England in the hope of reconstituting the four power alliance of Chaumont, but Lord Granville made it clear that England would recognize the accession of Louis Napoleon. Thus Russia was the only power to show a spirit of hostility. Alarmed, Louis Napoleon dispatched to Russia on a secret mission with the object of bettering relations, one of his early followers whom he had recently named Senator, M. George Dantes. But the choice was unfortunate--true it was that Dantes, the adopted son of Baron Heeckeren, one time Minister of Holland to St. Petersburg, had seen service as an officer in the Russian Guards and had been presented to the Czar in this capacity, but it was this same Dantes who had killed the great Russian poet Pushkin in a duel and had been bitterly castigated by Lermontov in his famous poem on the death of a poet.

Nicholas received Dantes so coldly that the latter returned to France profoundly humiliated. Louis Napoleon did not hide his irritation, the more so that he was aware of the intrigues of Russian diplomats in Greece and elsewhere against him, and he attributed to these intrigues the increasing hostility of the Prussian Court which had aligned itself with Russia in the matter.

When finally on December 2, 1852, Louis Napoleon proclaimed himself Emperor Napoleon III, Russia, Austria and Prussia notified the French Government that they would consult between themselves as to their position with regard to this change. The Governments of Naples, Switzerland, Piedmont, Great Britain, Belgium, Spain, Holland and Denmark in this respective order had recognized the new regime within ten days following the coup d'état. But the Three Northern Courts debated the issue for a month and it was decided that Russia would move first, to be followed by the two other Courts which would model their action according to the

results of Russia's move. However, Nicholas I refused to use the
customary wording of My Dear Brother in the letters of credence
to be presented by his ambassador in Paris to the new sovereign.
Instead, the letters were addressed to the "Very serene, very excellent and very powerful Prince, our very dear friend Napoleon,
Emperor of the French," and signed "Your good friend, Nicholas."
Similarly Prussia, under the influence of Russia, had adopted the
same wording whereas Austria preferred to use the regular formula of Monsieur mon Frère. On January 3, 1853, Kisselev officially presented these letters together with a note stating that
Russia was prepared to recognize the new regime on condition
that it would respect existing treaties, but with reservations in
regard to the question of succession for the new dynasty. The
storm of indignation produced by the wording of the Russian letters
was so great in Paris that Drouyn de Lhuys observed caustically
to Kisselev that the Court of St. Petersburg was still very young
to aspire to establish a precedent in this question after the Bourbon, Saxon and Hapsburg dynasties had recognized the new sovereign as a "brother." Napoleon called a council of ministers to
decide whether the Russian letters were to be accepted or rejected,
but with the Austrian and Prussian Ambassadors withholding their
letters of credence until the Russian one had been acknowledged,
it was decided to overlook the issue and grant the Russian Ambassador the customary official audience. But in this audience, after
reading the letter carefully, Napoleon sarcastically requested
Kisselev to "thank his Majesty the Emperor Nicholas for his goodwill and especially for the words 'good friend' which he had used,
for if one must endure one's brothers, at least one can choose
one's friends." [25]

All these petty questions of protocol and minor irritations would
not have been important but for two factors: first, Napoleon believed
that military glory was a necessary prerequisite for the success of
a Bonaparte and, as he put it once, "he required a cheap war every
three years" and, second, hemmed in by the Treaty of Vienna,
which he was still not strong enough to violate, there was only one
section of Europe over which the clauses of the treaty did not extend, namely Turkey, and it was precisely there that a long drawn
out and irritating quarrel with Russia was dragging on. It was
therefore up to Napoleon either to show a conciliatory spirit or to
fan the quarrel into a major issue of European diplomacy leading
to war. He chose the latter course and the unimportant question
of the Holy Places became the direct cause of the Crimean War.

---

[25] Bapst., op. cit., p. 306.

CHAPTER VI

CAUSES OF THE CRIMEAN WAR

I

If the quarrel over the Holy Places in Jerusalem was the immediate and direct cause of the war, it occupied nevertheless a very subordinate place in the reasons for the hostility of the Western Powers towards Russia. As such it has to examined without giving it more importance than of being a pretext for bringing on a long maturing conflict. Jerusalem in 1850 had a population estimated at between 12,000 and 15,000 inhabitants. As a city it was completely insignificant, but as the capital of Christendom and a Holy City for the Muslims and Jews its importance obviously far transcended its size. There were 3,500 Christians residing in it of which 2,000 were Greek Orthodox, 1,000 Catholics and the balance Armenians, Nestorians etc. Furthermore about 12,000 pilgrims visited the city annually of which merely a few hundred were Catholics--the bulk coming from Orthodox countries, particularly Russia. Thus numerically speaking the majority of both the permanent and transient Christian population being Orthodox, Russia as the protector of the Orthodox faith was, more than any other power, vitally interested in anything which might occur in that city. Furthermore, as it was the Byzantine Empire which had been the defender of Jerusalem against the Persians and Arabs there was a tradition that Caliph Omar had given the Greeks the possession of the Christian sanctuaries in and around the city, the Catholics appearing on the scene only in the XI century at the time of the First Crusade. After the collapse of the Latin Kingdom of Jerusalem, the Greeks once more got possession of the city and it was only around the first quarter of the XIV century when, as a result of privileges granted in 1192 by Sultan Saladin of Egypt to the Roman Church that the first Catholic monks established themselves there. From the XVI century on the Turkish Sultans, ever since the alliance of Francis I with Suleiman the Magnificent, confirmed the privileges which made France the protector of the Catholics in the Near East without, however, specifying what those privileges were. The sanctuaries were divided into those common to all the Christian creeds and those belonging specifically to one particular creed. In the former the question as to who was to officiate first and such details as the right to light candles and lamps or to spread carpets, etc. were constant causes of conflict which sometimes led to bloodshed.

In 1808 the Church of the Saviour having been destroyed by fire, the Greeks obtained from the Sultan the right to rebuild it notwithstanding the vigorous protests of General Sebastiani, the French Ambassador in Turkey. This fact produced a bitter feud between the two denominations, and the Catholic clergy began an aggressive campaign for the restitution of what it deemed its historic rights. On the other hand, Russia since 1840 accused the Catholic organizations of carrying on anti-Russian political propaganda particularly on behalf of the Poles. In 1850, with relations between Greeks and Latins increasingly strained in Jerusalem itself, the whole issue was transferred to the plane of international diplomacy when Louis Napoleon, eager to receive the support of the Catholics in France, took official cognizance of their demands in Jerusalem and extended to them the protection of French diplomatic agents. Thereby what had been merely a quarrel of monks was being transformed into a dangerous issue of international rivalry between Russia and France. Conversely it envenomed the feud in Jerusalem, both sides encouraged by the support they were receiving. The new French Ambassador in Constantinople, General Aupick, was instructed to claim formally the privileges granted to the Catholics by the Firman of 1740, the last of the long series of instruments conferring upon France the rights of protector of the Roman Faith. Seeing a chance of conciliating France who had been hostile to Turkey on the Egyptian question, the Porte replied favourably and ordered the formation of a mixed commission of Orthodox and Catholic members to study the questions in dispute.

The arrival of a new French ambassador, M. de Lavalette, at Constantinople further stimulated French efforts--he declared that from 1690 to 1756 the Latins had been in possession of the sanctuaries and demanded the right to have control of three sanctuaries from which they had previously been excluded.

In September, 1851, Czar Nicholas wrote a personal letter to the Sultan Abdul Medjid in which he demanded the maintainance of the status quo, declaring that he had been painfully impressed by the negotiations between Turkey and France. The Sultan ordered the establishment of a commission of Muslim dignitaries (Oulemahs) under the Sheikh-ul-Islam to study the matter. The findings of this commission invalidated the French claims but, anxious to placate the French ambassador, the Porte suggested a compromise by which the Roman Catholic clergy would be allowed to officiate in the Grotto of Gethsemane whereas the Orthodox would have the same privilege in the Church of the Ascension. This compromise was accepted by the Russian Chargé d'Affaires, M. Titov, conditional on the right reserved to the Greeks to repair the dome of the Church of the Saviour. The Firman published by the Porte in January, 1852, accordingly granted these respective privileges but withheld the right from the Catholics to have the keys to the Grotto of Nativity at Bethlehem. As for the dome of the Church of the Saviour, its repairs were to be made at the expense of the Turkish Government under the supervision of the Greek Patriarch. The matter therefore appeared to be settled. But the rise to power of the liberal and Francophile Reshid Pasha as Grand Vizier, the strong impression produced by the accession to the throne of Napoleon and the rise of a new generation of Turks who were influenced by the Revolution of 1848 and showed intense hostility to Russia, gave the Russian Government the impression that the Firman would remain a dead letter. Russian diplomacy declared that it had secret information that Reshid Pasha had given positive assurances to France to this effect.

Another issue envenomed the situation. M. de Lavalette went on leave and returned on board a French man-of-war, the "Charlemagne", which entered the Dardanelles. Russia protested this as an infraction of the treaty of 1841 and Turkey replied that this was an exception which would not be repeated. Furthermore, Lavalette obtained additional privileges beyond those granted by the Firman, such as the key to the Church of Bethlehem and the replacing of the Silver Star in the Grotto of the Nativity which had been previously taken away by the Orthodox. Thus rightly or wrongly Russia refused to accept the Turkish stand at its face value and, acting under these circumstances, swiftly and decisively, Nicholas, who considered the accession of Reshid Pasha and his Foreign Minister Fuad Effendi as a victory for French influence over Russian, suddenly sprang a first-class diplomatic sensation on the world. At the same time as the Russian 5th Corps was ordered mobilized, Prince Menshikov was sent on a highly important special mission to Constantinople.

The very choice of Menshikov indicated the extraordinary importance of the mission. One of the highest dignitaries of the Empire, now Minister of the Marine, former Governor-General of Finland and a personal friend of the Czar, Menshikov was of the innermost circles of the Russian Government. Moreover, he did not proceed immediately to Constantinople, but on his way first inspected the 5th Corps and then went to Sebastopol where a great review of the Black Sea Fleet was held in his honour. Then he boarded a warship and, accompanied by Vice-Admiral Kornilov, the Chief-of-Staff of the 5th Corps, and a large retinue arrived in pomp at the Turkish capital on February 28th. Menshikov made a well nigh triumphant entry into Constantinople, the Greek population of the city and the Russian clergy awaiting him at the landing place and following him in a large crowd to the Russian Embassy. He informed the Reiss Effendi that he would call on the Sublime Porte on March 2 to arrange for the presentation of his credentials to the Sultan. But contrary to the established diplomatic usage he did not present himself to the Porte in full dress uniform but merely in civilian clothes, thereby stressing his disrespect for the Turkish Government, and worse was to follow. After having been received by the Grand Vizier, Menshikov refused to enter the adjoining room where Fuad Effendi, the Turkish Minister of Foreign Affairs, was ceremoniously awaiting him with his staff, and pointedly passing in front of the door, walked out of the building. This calculated insult forced Fuad Effendi, whom Russia had always considered of the anti-Russian clique, to resign and after some hesitation the Sultan accepted this resignation and appointed in his place Rifaat Pasha.

These events produced the greatest sensation in Europe, the more so that Menshikov's visit seemed to have been timed so as to find both the French and the British Ambassador absent from Constantinople. So terrified were the Turks that after the fall of Fuad Effendi, the Grand Vizier approached the Chargé d'Affaires of both France and England with a request for military aid against the Russian menace. The British Chargé d'Affaires, Colonel Rose, dispatched his stationnaire to Malta to request that the British Mediterranean Fleet should be sent to the Gulf of Smyrna. The French Chargé d'Affaires, equally disturbed, informed M. Drouyn de Lhuys of the urgency of "calculating the meaning and consequences of the Russian action."[1] Whereas the British Government threw cold water on Colonel Rose's alarm by ordering the fleet to remain in Malta, Napoleon, contrariwise ordered the French Fleet to proceed to the Bay of Salamin. Thus the French Fleet left Toulon on March 22 for Greek waters with orders to respond immediately to any demands made by the new French Ambassador to Con-

---

[1] Bapst, E., Les Origines de la Guerre de Crimée. Paris 1912, p. 351.

stantinople, M. de La Cour, who hastily returned to his post arriving on April 6th at Constantinople, a day after the arrival of Stratford Canning, now Lord Stratford de Redcliffe. Even though the British Government put pressure on the French Emperor to halt the French Fleet at Naples, these movements clearly illustrated the near panic produced by Menshikov's action in Constantinople. As for Turkey, she virtually abdicated and placed her foreign policy squarely in the hands of the French and British Ambassadors. Meanwhile Menshikov had embarked on the negotiations embodying the object of his visit. The Russian envoy had been instructed by his government to obtain, 1) the fall of Fuad-Effendi and the publication of a firman giving the possession of the church at Bethlehem to the Greeks, the repairs to the dome to be accomplished without Catholic participation, 2) the revocation of all concessions to the Roman Catholics which went beyond the Firman of January 30, 1852, and the official promulgation of said Firman, 3) guarantees for the future rights of the Orthodox Church to be embodied in a special Sened or separate act. If the Sultan refused to accede to these demands out of fear of France, Menshikov was to propose a secret alliance between Russia and Turkey with no other obligations to Turkey than the fulfilment of these three demands. Should Turkey refuse or try to avoid an answer Menshikov was to give three days for a definite reply after which he was to leave Constantinople with the staff of the Embassy. He was however given full latitude to act on his own judgement according to circumstances and was to report directly to the Czar, being thereby placed beyond the authority of Nesselrode. The instructions received by him were not mandatory but merely to serve as a guide for his actions.

In accordance with his instructions Menshikov, in the interviews he had with Rifaat Pasha between the 4th and 16th of May, demanded the acceptance by Turkey of the Russian claims. Acting upon the advice of Stratford de Redcliffe, Rifaat was conciliatory on the points concerning the situation in Jerusalem but extremely refractory in accepting any binding obligations of a more general nature and attempted to gain time by dragging out the negotiations. Finally the Porte submitted to Menshikov two Firmans accepting the first and second Russian demands. Having gone thus far Rifaat thought it safe, presumably acting upon Anglo-French advice, to turn down the demand for a special treaty concerning the future guarantees for the Orthodox Church. This being however the main issue at stake, Menshikov countered by a five-day ultimatum demanding that Turkey should declare that the Orthodox faith would receive the same rights enjoyed by the other churches, both within the limits of previous treaties and of any new privileges to be granted to the other churches, that the present status quo affecting the position and the properties of the Greek Church should be maintained by the scrupulous and textual execution of the above mentioned Firmans already granted and, finally, that Russia should be conceded the right to build a Russian church and a hostel for pilgrims in Jerusalem.[2]

The Porte replied to this ultimatum by a note couched in vague and general terms. Menshikov, considering this reply unsatisfactory, appealed directly to the Sultan. The latter promised a prompt reply but requested the extension of the ultimatum for five days more. During this time an extraordinary council of the Divan was convoked by the Sultan which decided to go no further, but to pledge the maintenance of the status quo in the Holy Places, which would not be modified without previously consulting both France and Russia, and to grant the Russian request for the construction of the church and hostel in Jerusalem. But on the major question of the rights of the Greek Church it was decided merely to issue a firman to the Greek Patriarch in Constantinople giving assurances as to the status of the Orthodox cult. Menshikov deemed this reply to be an evasion of the issue and, notwithstanding a conciliatory last minute move of the Austrian Chargé d'Affaires, threatened the immediate rupture of diplomatic relations unless Turkey in a note to Russia should officially declare she accepted the Russian demands. This the Porte refused to do and Russia accused Stratford Canning of being responsible for the unexpected obduracy shown by the Turks. Leaving merely a commercial attaché, Balabine, Menshikov accordingly left Constantinople on May 21 with the staff of the Russian Embassy and went to Odessa where he remained ready to return to Constantinople and renew negotiations should the Turks show signs of yielding. Meanwhile, Nesselrode on May 31 dispatched a note to the Reiss Effendi demanding that Turkey should accept Menshikov's ultimatum within 8 days. Otherwise, said the note, the Russian armies would cross the border into the Principalities, not to open hostilities but to secure a material gage to be held until Turkey acceded to the Russian demands. The Porte, having issued the Firman concerning the status of the Greek Church, replied to the ultimatum of Nesselrode stating that Menshikov's demands were inconsistent with the rights of a sovereign nation and declared that Turkey would mobilize in self defence to face a Russian invasion. But at the same time

---

[2]Jomini, A. G., Etude diplomatique sur la Guerre de Crimée (1852-1856). St. Petersburg 1878, p. 186, 187.

the Porte announced its willingness to send a special envoy to St. Petersburg to continue negotiations.

Just about this time Emperor Nicholas drew up secret instructions of a military nature which were forwarded by the Minister of War, Prince Dolgoruky, to the Commander-in-Chief of the Russian forces in the Caucasus, Prince Vorontsov.[3] The importance of this document lies in the fact that it reveals the Czar's secret thoughts in connection with the situation arising from the rupture of diplomatic relations with Turkey. Written by the hand of Nicholas himself, the memorandum is explicit. "The Emperor, not desiring a war owing to the nefarious action of the climate of Turkey on the one hand as well as owing to the indefinite aims with which our military operations would have to be pursued if we desire to avoid the final downfall of the Ottoman Empire, considers it necessary, in the event of unsuccessful results in attempting to bring the Ottoman Porte to accept our proposals, to resort to compulsory measures, the pressure of which will be increased according to circumstances in the following order." The Czar goes on to say that first the military forces assembled on the Moldavian border will cross the Pruth and occupy the Danubian Principalities without declaring war, using the Principalities as a hostage until Turkey accepts the Russian demands. For this purpose were to be ear-marked the 4th Corps, a part of the 15th Division, the 5th Cavalry Division and some Cossack units. These forces were not to cross the Danube and not to engage in hostilities unless they were attacked by the Turks. "In this situation with a chain of Cossack posts along the Danube supported by reserves...we will await what impression the occupation of the Danubian Principalities will produce upon the Turks."[4] Should these measures prove to be insufficient the next step would involve a blockade of the Bosphorus and the seizure of Turkish boats on the Black Sea by Russian cruisers, followed by a threat to declare the independence of the Danubian Principalities and of Serbia. "It would be desirable that the Austrians, sharing our views, should occupy Herzegovina and Serbia. The Russian army is nevertheless not to cross the Danube. Should the menace of declaring the independence of the Principalities and Serbia prove to be insufficient then would be the time to put this measure into effect, and this would

---

[3]Letter No. 893, dated June 30, 1853. Bogdanovich M. I. Vostochnaia Voina 1853-1856. St. Petersburg 1877, Vol. I, p. 88.

[4]Bogdanovich, op. cit., Vol. I, p. 89, 90.

doubtless be the beginning of the destruction of the Turkish Empire." This document reveals clearly that the Czar did not want war at this stage.

In pursuance of these plans, on June 26 an Imperial manifesto was issued announcing the occupation of the Principalities and 50,000 men with 196 guns under the command of General Prince Mikhail Gorchakov were set in motion. On July 3 the advance guard of the army under Count Anrep-Elmpt crossed the Pruth and marched on Bucharest. At the same time on July 2 a circular note was sent to the powers, signed by Nesselrode, declaring that the occupation of the Principalities was a temporary measure to be carried out only until the Turks accepted Russia's demands, that Russia was not motivated by any desire for territorial aggrandizement and pledged the integrity of the Ottoman Empire, that the Russians would not open hostilities unless attacked and finally that Russia would not stir the Christian populations to rebel against the authority of the Sultan. Simultaneously a bid was made for the co-operation of Austria. Baron Meyendorff, returning to his post in Vienna, was instructed to submit to Emperor Francis Joseph a plan for common action whereby Austria was to offer mediation and put pressure on Turkey to obtain the Porte's acceptance of Menshikov's terms, and should the Porte persist in refusing, to bring up to the Turkish border an army corps which would occupy, if need be, Herzegovina and Serbia.

Whether these measures would have been sufficient to bring Turkey to terms and avoid war, has today merely an academic interest. It is more than probable that left to herself the Porte would have submitted. However Russian diplomacy seems to have underestimated the role played by France and England both in Constantinople and in Vienna which transmuted the whole issue from merely a Russo-Turkish quarrel into a major international conflict.

II

While the situation in the Near East was beginning to look more and more ominous Nicholas turned once more to England to ascertain the position of that power in the growing conflict between France and Russia. This led to the famous Seymour conversations which were to have such an important bearing on subsequent events. The Czar in his customary direct manner, meeting the British Ambassador at a dance in January 1853 began a series of conversations in which he once more raised the question of the fate of Turkey, stressing the necessity of further maintaining the agreement between England and Russia in the spirit of 1844.

"When we are agreed I am quite without anxiety as to the West of Europe, what others think or do is immaterial. As to Turkey, that is another question... The affairs of Turkey are in a very disorganized condition; the country itself seems to be falling to pieces; that fall would be a great misfortune, and it is very important that England and Russia should come to a very good understanding upon these affairs, and that neither should take any decisive step of which the other is not appraised."[5] Then with regard to France, "God forbid," he said, "that I should accuse any one wrongfully, but there are circumstances at Constantinople and Montenegro which are extremely suspicious; it looks very much as if the French were endeavoring to embroil us all in the East, hoping in this way the better to arrive at their own objects one of which, no doubt, is the possession of Tunis."[6]

Therefore the aid of England in checking the ascendancy of French influence in Turkey would be useful to both parties. However, should Turkey crumble it would be necessary to avoid chaos, and the best way of so doing was to come to an agreement with regard to the disposal of the territory so as to avoid a scramble for spoils which would lead to an European war. With regard to Constantinople, Nicholas was outspoken: "Frankly, then, I will tell you plainly that if England thinks of establishing herself one of these days at Constantinople, I will not allow it...for my part I am equally disposed to take the engagement not to establish myself here..."[7] But, he added, if no previous provisions were made and things were left to chance, it might become necessary for Russia to occupy the city temporarily. Such were, in the main, the ideas propounded by the Czar to Lord Seymour. Nesselrode on his side addressed a note to Lord John Russell explaining that Russia's purpose was to be frank with England, so as to avoid a misunderstanding which would interfere with the common interest of both powers in preserving peace in the Near East. These overtures produced no alarm in England: "Lord Aberdeen does not think there is anything very new in this declaration of the Emperor. It is essentially the same language he has held for some years, although, perhaps, the present difficulties of Turkey have ren-

---

[5] Seymour to Russell Jan. 11, 1853. Folio Russia 424. 13 Eastern Papers V 1-3 quoted Puryear V. J. England, Russia and the Straits Question. 1844-1856. Berkeley 1931.
[6] Seymour to Russell Feb. 22, 1853. Quoted Bapst. op. cit., p. 335 footnote.
[7] Puryear, op. cit., p. 213.

dered him more anxious on the subject."[8] Seymour himself, reporting the matter, suggested the adoption of the Czar's idea so as to avoid the danger of war, should the Ottoman rule in Europe come to an end. Certainly if we view the words of the Czar in the light of the agreement of 1844 there was nothing startling in what he said, which resolved itself into the mere amplification of details on matters previously agreed upon.

Furthermore Lord John Russell himself had more than once acknowledged the weakness of Turkey and several pamphlets had appeared at the time proving the necessity for the partitioning of Turkey. Lastly, Lord John Russell had been informed by Lord Seymour that information had been received in St. Petersburg that Napoleon III was contemplating the sending of an expedition for the conquest of Syria. Under these circumstances, when the French made their first bid for an alliance with England in January, 1853, Lord John Russell replied that the British Government was "persuaded that the Emperor of Russia will not enter willingly, and certainly not without the consent of England, into any schemes for the subversion of the Ottoman power. Her Majesty's government has reasons quite satisfactory to it for this persuasion."[9] All the more startling was the publishing by the British Government in March of the Seymour conversations without the explanatory background, a move which created a tremendous sensation all over Europe and worked up British public opinion into hysteria. The purpose was obviously to create the impression of Russian territorial designs on Turkey and thereby may be regarded as an early attempt at the application of the "war guilt" method to Russia and it is difficult to exonerate the British statesmen from hypocrisy in this case. The publication of these conversations coincided with the arrival of Prince Menshikov on his momentous mission to Constantinople and obviously was inspired by the doings of the Russian diplomat in the Turkish capital.

When Menshikov arrived in Constantinople he had received orders to co-operate with the French Ambassador, but Nesselrode, in communicating the object of Menshikov's mission to the French, British and Austrian Ambassadors in St. Petersburg, omitted the fact that the main object of the visit was to obtain from Turkey a new convention. Both Russian Ambassadors, Brunnow in London and Kisselev in Paris gave assurances to

---

[8] Aberdeen to Queen Victoria, Feb. 8, 1853. Letters of Queen Victoria, Vol. II, p. 535.
[9] Puryear, op. cit., p. 220-221.

the respective governments that Menshikov's mission was not endangering the integrity of Turkey or pursuing bellicose aims. These assurances were accepted by the British Foreign Secretary Lord Clarendon at their face value and little emotion was shown at first in London. But in Paris it was different. Drouyn de Lhuys took a very grave view. On March 23 he stated definitely to Lord Clarendon: "The mission of Prince Menshikov in Constantinople would be in itself a grave event, but the assembling of three army corps in Southern Russia and the preparations taking place in Sebastopol indicate that if Emperor Nicholas hopes to intimidate the Porte, he also accepts the eventuality of a war with Turkey...We also desire to maintain peace but it is possible that the storm will break and the simplest prudence forces us to take our measures."[10] Thus French diplomacy from the outset was giving an alarmist complexion to the situation. A month later Lord Clarendon was still saying to Walewski at that time French envoy in London: "I am convinced that Emperor Nicholas wants peace." It was only therefore very gradually that the views of the British Government began veering toward the French warlike mood and, by the time Menshikov issued his ultimatum to the Porte, Lord Redcliffe was saying in Constantinople to his French colleague, M. LaCour, that it was necessary to oppose "a moral resistance to the Russian moral pressure,"[11] whereas Lord Clarendon wrote to Walewski (May 24, 1853) that it would be impossible for any British ministry to witness passively the fall of the Ottoman Empire.[12] Drouyn de Lhuys on his side was writing to London that if the question of the Holy Places had been settled, the real issue at stake was the independence of the Ottoman Empire.

By the end of May, Lord Cowley, the British Ambassador in Paris, was able to declare to Walewski that the interests of Britain and France were identical and early in June, just as Nesselrode's ultimatum was threatening the Porte with the occupation of the Principalities, the Anglo-French fleet was ordered to proceed to Besika Bay, near the island of Tenedos at the entrance to the Dardanelles. The Turks, who had seemed discouraged and, according to the French Ambassador's report dated May 27, about to give in to Russia, found new courage and a new spirit of resistance. Shortly after these

---

[10] Guichen Vicomte de: <u>La Guerre de Crimée et l'Attitude des Puissances Européennes</u>. Paris 1936, p. 21.
[11] Guichen, <u>op. cit.</u>, p. 39.
[12] Guichen, <u>op. cit.</u>, p. 38.

events, Buol confidentially informed the British and French Ambassadors in Vienna that he was fully in accord with the policies of France and England in the Orient--thus Austria was passing over to the side of the future allies (June 21). If the sending of the allied fleets to Besika Bay was in answer to Russia's military preparations, the Russians in turn declared that the occupation of the Principalities was partly in answer to the presence of the allied squadrons in Turkish waters. Such was the tenor of a circular note sent by the Russian Ministry of Foreign Affairs to the Russian representatives abroad and given wide publicity by its appearance in the official "Journal de Saint Petersbourg." It stated that the advance of the Russian troops into the Principalities was merely the taking up of military positions in view of the "naval occupation of the region of Constantinople" by the two naval powers.

Writing on July 2 to Meyendorff in Vienna, Nesselrode was even more emphatic: "We will not retreat before the demonstration of the naval powers, - they command the sea, we the land, the retreat must be simultaneous." Caught in this vicious circle of retaliations and counter-retaliations, the position of Austria was becoming more and more difficult. Secretly siding with the western powers but afraid yet to break with Russia too openly, Buol found refuge in a policy of no longer supporting Russia's position in Constantinople and weakly protesting in St. Petersburg the Russian occupation of the Principalities, covering the gradual shift in his policy by the impartial position of a mediator. Thus it was that the center of negotiations now shifted to Vienna. Indeed, on July 24 Buol took the initiative of inviting the French, British, Russian and Prussian Ambassadors in Vienna to examine with him and work out the project of a note which the special Turkish Ambassador, whom it will be recalled the Porte had offered to send to Russia, would carry with him for the final settlement of the crisis. The idea and the original version of such a note was submitted by Napoleon III.

The Russian Ambassador having refused to participate in these conferences, the three Ambassadors of France, England and Prussia with Buol drew up a note which they deemed would meet the Russian demands and be satisfactory to Turkey as well. This note was sent to St. Petersburg on July 28 for approval. But scarcely had the note been sent, than Buol received a letter from Reshid Pasha addressed to Nesselrode, which in view of the rupture of diplomatic relations between Russia and Turkey was to be forwarded through the agency of the Austrian Government. This letter had been written virtually at the dictation of Lord Stratford de Redcliffe and approved by the conference of Ambassadors in Constantinople. It was accompanied by a solemn declaration in the name of the Sultan that it represented the last word in Turkish concessions and that Turkey would go to war if this attempt at a peaceful settlement failed. As this note differed considerably from the note drafted in Vienna, by reducing appreciably the commitments of Turkey and being much more vague in the specific guarantees offered, Buol undertook on his own initiative the task of obtaining the assent of the Porte to the Vienna note, after receiving the approbation of the British and French Governments to this effect. Thus a courier left Vienna on August 1st instructing the four Ambassadors in Constantinople to join efforts to obtain from the Porte the acceptance of the text which the powers had already submitted to the Russian Government. Two days later came the consent by the Czar of the Vienna terms contingent however to their unconditional acceptance by Turkey.

Thus the crisis appeared to be satisfactorily settled. But war fever was gaining dangerous ground in Constantinople and the attitude of the foreign powers did nothing to discourage it. Indeed, the ambassadors, in the face of the obvious lack of desire on the part of the Porte to accept the Vienna version, showed no wish to impress the Porte with the necessity of so doing - quite the reverse. The British Ambassador after giving lip service to the instructions received, in private "had, to Lord Aberdeen's certain knowledge, called the conduct of the government infamous, and declared he would let the world know that his name was Canning."[13] The French Ambassador, reported likewise that Stratford de Redcliffe openly disapproved of his government's action and spoke of giving his demission. Encouraged by this attitude the Turkish Government replied that it would sign the note provided three further modifications would be accepted by Russia. This however, upon the advice of Nesselrode, the Czar refused to do and on September 7 a Russian note conveyed to the four governments, declared that the terms of the Vienna note were not Russian conditions but those worked out by the four powers, and therefore it was up to those powers to obtain the adhesion of the Porte. Whereas Russia had accepted these terms in a spirit of conciliation, the Porte had failed to do so. The note stated that as a further token of conciliation, Russia was prepared to evacuate the Principalities when and if the Turkish Ambassador arrived in St. Petersburg.

---

[13] Memorandum by the Prince Consort, Oct. 16, 1853. Letters of Queen Victoria, quoted by Bapst, op. cit., p. 435 footnote.

Accompanying this note was a lengthy memorandum discussing point by point the modifications suggested by the Turks and declaring that these changes abolished the right granted to Russia in the Vienna note to protect the Greek Orthodox in Turkey and, therefore, modified the whole tenor of the Turkish offer. In reply to this memorandum, Lord Clarendon declared that Russia had given an "unexpected interpretation" to the Vienna note, and therefore he could not any longer advise the Porte to sign it. France went even further and Drouyn de Lhuys proposed to the British Government that the Anglo-French squadron at Besika Bay should enter the Dardanelles under the pretence of protecting the Christians from the fanaticism of the war-mad Turks. This offer was accepted by the British in principle but Lord Aberdeen declared that, in accordance with the treaties, the Dardanelles could be opened to war vessels only in time of war, to which the French Government replied with the suggestion that Turkey be asked to declare war on Russia. Encouraged by this attitude and a joint note of France and England declaring that the two powers would give assistance to Turkey the Porte called a Grand Council on September 25 which declared its refusal to accept any amendments to its first proposals and declared itself ready for war. A weak and half hearted demarche of the four powers to obtain the adhesion of the Porte to the Vienna note was officially turned down.

Worried at seeing Austria and Prussia coming so close to France and England in Vienna and in a last effort toward conciliation, Czar Nicholas decided to take matters into his own hands. On September 24 he arrived at Olmütz to be present at the Austrian military manoeuvres and to talk things over personally with Francis Joseph and with the Prince Royal of Prussia. However, a French military mission under General Count Goyon had preceded the arrival of the Czar and the presence of this mission gave him the idea that he might try a conciliatory gesture towards France as well as an endeavour to detach France from England. Hence on September 26, selecting an appropriate moment, Nicholas approached the French general and after a few courtesies about the French, said: "I have in Warsaw an army corps which I intend to show in a few days to Emperor Francis Joseph. I should be happy to show it to you as well and invite you, gentlemen, to come."[14] Goyon having accepted the offer, Nicholas at a later meeting hinted that he would welcome a visit from Napoleon himself. However the news of this invitation produced the utmost irrita-

---

[14] Bapst, op. cit., p. 448.

tion in Paris and on September 30, just as General Goyon was about to leave for Warsaw, he was peremptorily recalled to France and lame excuses were forwarded to Nicholas in Warsaw, who had already made preparations for the reception of the French mission. This incident, more than anything else, opened the eyes of the Czar to the true disposition of France in the crisis.

The visit to Olmütz had however not been entirely fruitless. Though the Czar was unable to obtain what he desired from Prussia,-a written pledge of neutrality in the coming war, he did get from the Prince Royal verbal assurances to that effect, which were subsequently scrupulously honoured by Prussia. On the other hand, Buol and Nesselrode in their personal interviews at Olmütz worked out one more last minute formula for peace. This took the shape of a plan whereby Turkey would once more be invited by the four powers to sign the Vienna note without modifications, but appended to the note would be a written declaration by Russia, in which she would pledge not to interfere in the internal affairs of Turkey. But in Paris, Drouyn de Lhuys received the suggestion badly, declaring that a firm attitude of the powers would force Russia to recede, while England flatly refused to accept the suggestion, offering as counter-suggestion the submitting of the whole issue to the arbitration of the four powers. Meanwhile, on September 29, the Sultan ratified the advice of his Grand Council relative to war with Russia and on October 6, issued an order to the Turkish Commander-in-Chief, Omer Pasha, who had his headquarters at Shumla, to send a two week's ultimatum to Prince Gorchakov demanding that he evacuate the Principalities, after the expiration of which Turkey would consider herself in a state of war with Russia. The following day, October 7, after delivering the ultimatum the Porte officially requested the Ambassadors of France and England to order the allied fleet into the Dardanelles. The order was duly given on October 15 and a part of the allied squadron entered the Bosphorus and the rest anchored in the Sea of Marmora. A week later, on October 23, the Turkish batteries opened fire on a Russian flotilla sailing up the Danube and two days later the remaining staff of the Russian Embassy in Constantinople left for Odessa on an Austrian ship. The war had started.

Summing up the tangled webb of diplomatic intrigues which preceded the opening of hostilities, it may be impartially stated that Russia did not want this war, neither did she want to partition Turkey; claims to the contrary, often reiterated in history, belong to the clumsy fabric of subsequent war propaganda, which has to be dispelled by a better knowledge of the facts.

On the other hand, partly as a matter of prestige, partly for the sake of her interests in Turkey as well as from religious and other motives, Russia adamantly clung to the terms of Menshikov's ultimatum, even to the point of war. As for France whether Napoleon actually desired this war or not he, and particularly his Minister Drouyn de Lhuys, did everything to further the war crisis. In England, Lord Aberdeen was against war but Stratford de Redcliffe, violently anti-Russian was so bent on encouraging the Turks to resist Russia that he became the main force working for war. Subsequently and partly under his influence, the British Government seems to have reached the opinion that the destruction of Russian naval power in the Black Sea was worth a war--this change of view occurred sometime after the delivery of the Vienna note. The Turks at first scared, saw an unexpected boon in the support of the great Western powers and made the best of the good fortune which did not often come their way.

The outbreak of hostilities in the East forced Austria to take a definite stand. Already in the summer of 1853 Francis Joseph cancelled a projected visit to the Czar in St. Petersburg, but the day before the Russians crossed into Moldavia on July 2, Francis Joseph, with a touch of duplicity, wrote a letter so friendly that Nicholas answered enthusiastically: "With keen delight have I received Thy admirable letter at the hands of General Count Gyulai. Nothing gives me so much pleasure as the realization that Thou retainest that friendship for me, so dear to my heart, and the warm and close relations so happily developed between us." [15] Foreseeing a possible rising of the Christian populations in the Balkans, the Czar suggested united action with Austria. To this proposal Francis Joseph replied on July 21, stressing the danger of revolution should the Turkish Empire collapse. "...I am entirely of Thy opinion that we must act in the closest union to secure such a future organization of these territories as demanded by their position on our frontiers and by our mutual relation." But with regard to the suggestion of a common protectorate over Turkey, Francis Joseph raised two points: first, it would endanger the Austro-Russian friendship through the inevitable quarrels resulting from a condominum. [16] Second, the weakening of Tur-

---

[15] Redlich, J., Emperor Francis Joseph of Austria; a biography. New York 1929, p. 132.

[16] Francis Joseph, however, was to accept such a condominium with Prussia in Schleswig-Holstein though he was right in assuming that it would produce a war.

key would make the Balkans 'the playground for the democratic tendencies of the South Slavs, the focus of all the efforts of our opponents..." and he cited the fate of the republic of Cracow as an example. [17]

The Czar replied by a proposal to make Constantinople a free city, the Dardanelles to be held by Austria and the Bosphorus by Russia. This would permit such police supervision as would be sufficient to keep any revolutionary elements from making the city a center for propaganda. As for the partition of Turkey he added "Russia does not need that, and I should view it as a misfortune and a source of incalculable trouble. If however in the interest of Thy country Thou viewest this as necessary, I am ready to hear Thy views."[18] The meeting between the two Emperors at Olmütz and the subsequent visit of Francis Joseph to Warsaw further convinced Nicholas that Austria was still friendly.

III

The hostilities with Turkey began on October 23, both on land and on sea. The Turkish batteries at Isakcha on the lower Danube opened fire on the Russian river flotilla making its way up the river to Galatz. The same day a Russian squadron under Admiral Nakhimov composed of four ships of the line, one frigate and one brig put out to sea from the naval base at Sebastopol. The instructions given to Nakhimov, prior to the receipt of the news of the firing at Isakcha, were to the effect that the squadron was to patrol the Black Sea and watch the movements of the enemy, particularly between Constantinople and Batum, as it was feared that Turkish troops would be transported to the Caucasus to stir up a rebellion amongst the native tribes. However, Nakhimov was instructed not to open fire unless the enemy did so first. Upon receipt of news of the engagement on the Danube, a second squadron was formed in Sebastopol, under the command of Admiral Kornilov, composed of two steamships, six ships of the line and a brig which put out to sea early in November and made for the Bulgarian coast to track down the Turkish Fleet which was known to have left the Bosphorus. Kornilov informed Nakhimov that should he fail to find the enemy between Burgas and Varna, he would pro-

---

[17] Redlich, op. cit., p. 133-134.
[18] This disposes of the credit made by English historians concerning the Seymour conversations. See Redlich, op. cit., p. 137.

ceed to join his (Nakhimov's) squadron. The latter, in the meanwhile, had been carrying out his patrol duties under very trying conditions; the weather was stormy and cold, gales and rain alternated with fog and the rough seas did considerable damage to his vessels. But he persistently remained on observation of the Anatolian coast even though at times he had only three vessels. On November 12, Nakhimov received news of the official declaration of war and four days later hearing the sound of gunfire, he proceeded in the direction of the battle to find that one of Kornilov's steamers, the "Vladimir," had engaged and captured the Turkish steamship of line "Pervaz-Bakhra." The Turkish Fleet had in the meantime returned to cover in the Bosphorus. Kornilov, upon receipt of this intelligence, decided to return to Sebastopol with his squadron, leaving two of his ships of line with Nakhimov. But a particularly heavy gale did such damage to Nakhimov's squadron which kept on cruising that he had to send four of his vessels to Sebastopol for repairs.

Just at this time he received news from a Greek spy that a Turkish squadron under Osman Pasha had sought refuge from the gale in the bay of Sinope. It was composed of 7 frigates, two corvettes, two steamships and two transports with troops destined for the Caucasus. Nakhimov had only three ships with him but he bravely approached Sinope and investigated the strength of the enemy. He then sent a report to Sebastopol, asking for reinforcements and in the meanwhile kept on cruising in sight of Sinope. The reinforcements under Rear-Admiral Novossilsky joined Nakhimov's squadron on November 28, and he then had at his disposal 6 ships of line and two frigates (three ships of line of 120 cannons and three ships of 84 cannons--the frigates carried 44 and 56 cannons respectively, in all 712 guns). [19] Nakhimov considered that he was now strong enough to tackle the Turkish squadron which had remained motionless all the while, anchored under cover of the coastal batteries. On the 29th of November, he called a council of war and gave instructions for battle the next day. The Russian squadron was to enter the bay in two columns and approach the enemy as closely as possible. Except for the orders not to fire upon any vessels which might surrender and not to damage the foreign consulates in the city, which had their national flags raised, he left full latitude to the individual commanders.

The next morning, in rain and stormy weather, Nakhimov lined up his vessels in two columns headed by his own flagship

---

[19] Dubrovin, Colonel N. F., <u>Istoria Krymskoi Voiny i Oborony Sevastopoliya</u>. St. Petersburg 1900, Vol. I, p. 9.

"Imperatritsa Maria" and Admiral Novossilsky's flagship "Parizh." Two frigates were to remain outside the bay to intercept any fleeing enemy vessel. At 11 A.M. religious services were held on board the ships and at midday the squadron proceeded to advance into the bay. Twenty minutes later the Turks opened fire and the battle started. The Turkish land fortresses and naval guns aimed at the masts of the Russian vessels but were unable to stop their advance. Upon coming to within half a mile of the Turkish boats by 2:30 P.M. the Russians anchored and opened broadsides. The cannonading lasted till 4 P.M. and within this one hour and a half the Turkish squadron was virtually annihilated. Sixteen Turkish men of war, transports and merchant ships anchored in the harbour were destroyed as well as the whole Turkish landing force. The Turkish Admiral, Osman Pasha and two commanders of the frigates were made prisoners. The enemy losses in men were estimated at 4,000 whereas the Russians had 37 killed and 299 wounded. Whereas all the Turkish vessels were either blown up or set ablaze, the only damage to the Russian vessels was in the masts and rigging, particularly of the flagships leading both columns, but after thirty-six hours of repairs the squadron was able to put out to sea again and return to Sebastopol. Only one Turkish vessel, the steamer "Tariff" commanded by English officers, escaped by leaving the bay at the beginning of the action and, outdistancing the two Russian frigates left on watch outside, brought the news of the disaster to Constantinople. However important was the military significance of this victory, its international significance was far greater, for it was to result in the allied fleet entering the Black Sea.

Meanwhile in Constantinople the Ambassadors of the four powers kept on negotiating with the Porte concerning the possibility of re-establishing peace--"useless babble" to quote the French statesman, Emile Ollivier. A last minute exchange of letters was also taking place between Czar Nicholas and Queen Victoria. Knowing that Prince Albert was opposed to this war and the Queen hesitant, Nicholas had written her a personal appeal for peace, begging her to do all in her power to prevent a calamity which both countries had an interest in avoiding, and reminding her of the previous agreements to consult each other over the Near Eastern situation. This appeal was strengthened by a request to King Leopold of Belgium to interpose his influence for peace when he visited the British royal family. However the Queen's reply on November 14 was not encouraging and in a veiled way stipulated that peace could only be maintained on condition that Russia should renounce her protectorate over the Orthodox population and renounce the right of intervening in the Principalities resulting from the Treaty of Adrianople. Furthermore, the British Ambassador in St. Petersburg had previously informed the Russian Government of the order issued on October 7 to Admiral Dundas, commanding the British squadron, to defend from any Russian naval attack not only Constantinople but the whole Black Sea coast of Turkey, whereas the French fleet had been given similar instructions with regard to the coast of Bulgaria, from the Bosphorus up to Varna.

It was under these circumstances that the news of the battle of Sinope was received in London. Analyzing this battle after the war and in quieter mood, the British Admiral Sir Arthur Gordon wrote: "Looked at in the light of later years, there was nothing in the battle of Sinope to justify the outcry of horror which it called forth. Russia and Turkey were at war, declared not by Russia but by Turkey. When nations are at war, an attack of the fleet of one belligerent by another is to be expected. Nor does the number of ships sunk or the completeness of victory affect the legitimate character of the action." [20] But the emotion produced both in Paris and London by the news of this Turkish defeat was such that as Drouyn de Lhuys put it, this battle was a blow which struck not only at Turkey. The allies were mortified that the action had taken place within the waters defended by the Anglo-French fleet. Napoleon immediately proposed to the British Government that the allied fleets should be ordered to enter the Black Sea with the double mission of protecting the Turkish coast and convoying Turkish transports on their way to the Caucasus.

In England, the battle of Sinope was declared to be an insult to the British flag and Lord Clarendon said that Great Britain had been placed in a ridiculous position in view of the declaration of October 7. Lord Palmerston, under a transparent pretext which was in reality a protest against Lord Aberdeen's peaceful policy, left the cabinet. Violent popular resentment arose against the Prince Consort as being a foreigner. These manifestations of popular excitement and war fever forced the hand of Lord Aberdeen who not only acceded to Napoleon's proposal but went even farther. He suggested that the British and French Ambassadors in St. Petersburg should officially notify the Russian Government of the appearance of the allied fleets in the Black Sea and the object of this move. At the same time the British frigate "Retribution" was ordered to proceed

---

[20] Morfill, W., A History of Russia from the Birth of Peter the Great to the Death of Alexander III. London 1902, p. 404.

to Sebastopol with the purpose of conveying some information to the Commander-in-Chief of the Russian fleet. On January 6, the "Retribution" profiting by the fog managed to penetrate into the harbour of Sebastopol but was ordered out by the Russian authorities and had to deliver her message from the outer channel. The news of this incident reached St. Petersburg on January 14, just as the Ambassadors had delivered their verbal notes Nicholas was infuriated by what he termed "British arrogance" in the Black Sea. Forthwith instructions were sent to Kisselev and Brunnow to ask the French and British Governments for a pledge that they would restrain the Turkish fleet from attacking the Russian coast, just as they had resolved not to allow the Russians to attack the Turkish coast; and that they would offer the same security for the free movement of Russian transports from Russian port to port as they had pledged the Turks. Should the allied governments refuse, the two Ambassadors were immediately to demand their passports and leave. The allies decided, after mutual conversations, to answer the Russian demand jointly, accepting the first of the two demands and rejecting the second. Therefore on February 1, notes were delivered to the Russian Ambassadors refusing the freedom of the Black Sea for Russian convoys and on February 6, both Ambassadors, having demanded their passports, left their respective posts with the staffs of their Embassies. On the 13th the British and French Ambassadors in St. Petersburg received their passports. As a last token of good will, the day before, the Czar had granted the Grand Cross of Saint Alexander Nevsky to the French Ambassador, General de Castelbajac. Two weeks later, on February 27, after a last minute attempt at conciliation by Austria had failed, identical ultimatums were sent by France and England, for presentation to Nesselrode by their respective consuls, who had remained in the Russian capital after the departure of the Embassies. According to the ultimatum if Russia did not evacuate the Principalities by April 30, and had not pledged to do so within six days after the receipt of the ultimatum, England and France would consider themselves in a state of war with Russia. The ultimatum reached St. Petersburg on March 14 and four days later Nesselrode verbally notified the consuls that Emperor Nicholas did not consider it proper to reply to it, but he added, "we are not declaring war." By this time France and England had signed on March 12, an alliance with Turkey and on March 28, England and France officially declared war on Russia.

With the spreading of the war to the western powers, the position assumed by Austria and to a lesser degree by Prussia and the smaller German States was of paramount importance for, geographically speaking, the latter were hemmed in between the belligerent powers. There is no denying that Buol had earnestly laboured for peace but at the same time, as already has been noted, he imperceptibly and gradually was shifting Austria toward the side of the allies and against Russia. The key to Buol's policy was now beginning to reveal itself. He hoped that the war would give Austria a chance to oust Russia from the Danubian Principalities which would then fall prey to Austrian military occupation. The hesitant and indecisive course of the campaign on the Danube, in which the Russians showed little vigour, seemed to amply justify such hopes.

IV

"We shall not attack Turkey," said Nesselrode to Sir Hamilton Seymour.[21] We shall remain with folded arms resolved only to resist all aggression made against us in the Principalities or on our Asiatic frontier. We shall pass the winter ready to receive all overtures of peace which Turkey will offer." Accordingly Prince M. Gorchakov had, after the occupation of the Principalities, taken up purely defensive positions along the Danube, stringing our his army to cover all possible points of crossing. Opposing this army, some 60,000 to 70,000 strong, were the Turkish forces estimated at around 120,000. Of these only half were regulars but they were well trained by foreign instructors and provided with excellent artillery of British and Austrian manufacture. This army was under the command of Omer Pasha, an Austrian Croat by birth whose real name was Michael Lattas. The latter had been a cadet in the Austrian Army and was well versed in modern warfare. Omer Pasha was holding the line of the Danube with half his army, keeping the other half in reserve at Shumla and around Adrianople. Ten days after the firing on the Russian gunboats at Isakcha, which initiated the war, the Turks took the offensive and crossed the Danube at four points: Vidin, Rustchuk, Turtukai, and Silistria. The advances from Rustchuk and Silistria were intended to be demonstrations to cover up the main attack from Turtukai on Oltenitsa and from Vidin on Kalafat.

The first attack came from Turtukai. A force of 8,000 Turks under the command of Ismail Pasha moved along the Danube and captured the quarantine building at Oltenitsa. General Danenberg with a force composed of two regiments of infantry, 9 squadrons of cavalry and 18 guns was ordered to dislodge them

---

[21] Rambaud, A., *History of Russia*. New York, Vol. III, p. 127.

(November 4). He discovered that the Turkish positions were much stronger than he had expected, and moreover were protected by the fire of heavy guns from Turtukai, across the river. The Russian attack was beaten off and, losing heart, Danenberg ordered a retreat, leaving 1,200 men killed and wounded. The Turks however did not follow up their success and after burning the quarantine station at Oltenitsa were content merely to recross the Danube. Equally menacing was the second attack. Omer Pasha had assembled some 40,000 men at Vidin and in October a strong Turkish force had occupied Kalafat across the river. He was now in an excellent position to harass the Russian right flank composed of a detachment of 7,000 men, under the command of General Count Anrep-Elmpt, and strung out along a 25 mile front. In the first week of January a Turkish force 18,000 strong, with 24 guns, suddenly attacked the Russian detachment of Colonel Baumgarten, quartered at Tchetati and composed of one regiment of infantry, one squadron of cavalry, some Cossacks and 6 guns, all told 2,500 men. Baumgarten resisted desperately, lost half his men and had shot all his munition when, hearing of his plight, General Belgardt came to his rescue with a strong force and counter attacked the Turks, driving them away. The affair cost the Russians 2,000 men and the Turks 3,000, 6 guns and two colours. Omer retained Kalafat and further attempts to advance as well as to cross the river at Nicopolis and Sistovo were successfully checked. Nevertheless when the campaign of 1853 came to an end the Turks had been able to retain the initiative in the operations.

During the winter the Russian army, composed of the 3rd, 4th and 5th Corps held a line of some three hundred miles along the Danube. The Turks were content now merely to harass occasionally the long line of the Russian defence and carried out a series of short thrusts at Silistria, Turtukai, Rustchuk, Zimnitsa, Nicopolis and Giurgevo but failed to achieve any results. To put an end to these attacks, the work on the Russian batteries opposite Rustchuk was speeded up and by February these batteries were able to destroy the Turkish river flotillas which had been protected by the guns of the Turkish fortress. At Silistria the Turks had crossed the river in force in an attempt to interfere with the erection of the Russian batteries, but were thrown back into the river. Finally at Kalafat the Russians undertook a reconnoitring advance against the Turkish fortified positions. These operations were masking and distracting the attention of the enemy from a secret move Prince Gorchakov was carefully preparing. Having assembled at Ismail, Galatz and Braila, that is to say in the delta of the Danube, forces up to 50 battalions of infantry and 32 squadrons of cavalry, the Russians, in March, suddenly crossed the Danube in a surprise move and occupied Tulcha and Machin on the right bank. The Turks, after offering very slight resistance, fell back to Bazardjik, Varna and Shumla, abandoning the Dobrudja with Kustendji and Mangalia. The purpose of this Russian advance was to menace the Turkish army on the Danube and thus render necessary a diversion of the Anglo-French forces which had landed in Varna for a projected invasion of the Crimea. Indeed, already in February, the Russian General Staff had information that such a move against the Crimea was being contemplated.

The crossing of the Danube was however not followed up by an energetic advance. A new Commander-in-Chief, the elderly Prince Paskevich, had been appointed and was due to arrive at the Russian headquarters in Fokshani in April. Past seventy, the Field Marshal had lost the energy of his youth and, worried by the stand taken by Austria as well as by information that Omer Pasha in Shumla was awaiting the arrival at the end of April of an allied force 30,000 strong, he proceeded with extreme caution. He estimated that there were 70,000 to 80,000 Turks around Shumla and with the addition of 30,000 Anglo-French there would be an army of 100,000 in a position to attack the Russian bridges on the Danube and to cut the line of Russian communications. Accordingly he began preparing for a possible retreat behind the Seret and the Pruth and ordered the erection of defensive positions along these rivers, as well as the fortifying of Fokshani and Ismail. However, Nicholas I did not share in these fears and urged him to advance without losing any more valuable time. Faced with such peremptory instructions Paskevich was forced to advance, but he did it unwillingly and slowly, and decided upon a middle course of advancing along the right bank of the Danube toward Silistria. Accordingly, General Luders marched toward Czernavoda, whereas General Liprandi was ordered to fall back to Craiova and the main body of the army was brought up to 35 battalions, 16 squadrons and 104 guns. Luders reached Silistria and forced the Turks to take refuge in the fortress itself. Then he established contact with the Russian forces operating at Kalarash by building bridges across the river. But Paskevich had no intention of following up this first success; the retreat of the Turks partly into Silistria and partly from Bazardjik to Varna, he construed as a move on their part to join the French. Moreover he looked anxiously at the Austrian army mobilized on the border of Moldavia, which he deemed to be 200,000 strong and which could attack him from the rear. He thus visualized a simultaneous Franco-Turkish and Austrian attack which would place the army between two fires. Nicholas tried to cheer him up: "Do not be afraid of the Austrians and, with the aid of God and your heroes, beat anyone who appears before you."[22] Meanwhile the forces before Silistria had opened siege works. However the Turks, supervised by foreign engineers, were offering a stubborn resistance. An assault on the Turkish works attempted in the night of May 29 failed, but the engineering works were carried on and early in June one of the advanced forts was blown up. Such was the situation when, on June 20, a courier brought to Paskevich a letter from the Czar dated June 13, ordering him to cease all further operations and to evacuate the Principalities in view of the menacing stand taken by Austria: "The time has come," wrote the Czar, "to prepare to fight not only the Turks and the allies but to direct all our efforts against faithless Austria and to punish her severely for her shameless ingratitude. I have just received information that the Austrians will not be ready before July 13. It will be necessary to profit by this month to evacuate from the Principalities all heavy baggage such as artillery-trains and depots and especially such wounded and sick as can be transported without harm to themselves. If before receipt of this letter Silistria has not been taken, or if one can not estimate when it will be taken I think that prudence demands the raising of the siege, the siege material to be shipped to Ismail."[23] Upon receipt of these instructions Paskevich ordered the cessation of all further operations, and on June 26 the army crossed back to the left bank of the Danube and broke the bridges without losing a single man. While the evacuation of the Principalities was proceeding, feverish measures were taken to organize the defence of the south coast of Russia and particularly the Crimea, where it was obvious that an allied attack was pending.

---

[22]Imperial Rescript to Field Marshall Prince Paskevich. May 23, 1854 quoted Dubrovin, op. cit., Vol. I, p. 120.

[23]Nicholas I to Paskevich. June 13, 1854, quoted Dubrovin, op. cit., Vol. I, p. 121.

CHAPTER VII

THE CRIMEAN WAR

I

As early as July, 1853, Vice-Admiral Sir Charles Napier, later the Commander of the British Fleet operating in the Baltic, addressed a letter to Lord Aberdeen stating that in case of war with Russia, the latter power could attack the English coast with a fleet of some 27 vessels of the line and that "this country was not safe; that if Russia lost her fleet in a sudden attack on our shores she would care nothing for the loss; but that if we lost the few ships which could be opposed to her, the nation would be ruined."[1] The Prime Minister made a noncommital reply, but a year later, in the spring of 1854, the British Government came to realize the seriousness of this danger, after the bulk of the British Fleet had been sent to the Mediterranean. The reasons for this changed attitude were several. In January, 1854, the British learned that the Russian Fleet in the Gulf of Finland had been increased to 27 ships of the line, 8 or 10 frigates, 7 corvettes and brigs, 9 paddle steamers and 50 to 60 gun boats with a total complement of 3,160 guns and 33,750 men of the crew;[2] half of these ships were at Cronstadt and the other half at Sweaborg. Sir H. Seymour, the British Ambassador to Russia, warned that this fleet was not to be underestimated. The question of the neutrality of Sweden and Denmark assumed paramount importance in this respect. Indeed, in Denmark anti-English feeling still existed as a result of the British attacks on Copenhagen in 1806-7 and the British Minister at Copenhagen, Mr. Buchanan, had warned that the sympathies of the ruling classes in Denmark were with Russia. Should a Russian fleet reach Copenhagen before a British squadron, the Danes might be encouraged to join Russia openly. As for Sweden, she maintained a neutrality which opposed all British efforts to bring her into an alliance with England. Lastly, the Prussian and the German cities along the Baltic were the main sources from which war supplies

---

[1] Napier, Sir Charles,. The History of the Baltic Campaign of 1854. London 1857, p. 2.
[2] Napier, op. cit., p. 28.

came to Russia. Neutral ships brought goods to Lubeck, from where they were trans-shipped to Memel and Libau, or from Danzig up the Vistula to Warsaw. In this way important supplies of powder, lead, arms, percussion caps etc. were reaching Russia in sufficient quantities for her needs. When it became known that the ice was breaking up earlier than usual in the Baltic, that the Russian Fleet was being provisioned for six months and that Russian agents were negotiating for the purchase of steamers in New York, the British Admiralty ordered the assembling of a fleet to protect England, and Sir Charles Napier was placed in command of it. The vessels were collected from foreign and home ports. When assembled, the squadron consisted of 4 screw ships of the line with the Duke of Wellington as flagship, 4 block ships, 4 frigates and 3 steamers--the most powerful ships of the British Fleet. Three more vessels joined the Fleet later.

On March 11, 1854, consequently before war had been declared, the Fleet put to sea amidst pomp and circumstance. To stress the importance of the event the Queen herself in her yacht convoyed the outgoing ships, an unprecedented event in the naval annals of England. There was much jingoistic feeling both in the press and in speeches at the farewell banquets, and hope was expressed that the British would be at St. Petersburg within three weeks. Sir Charles Napier did not share these sanguine hopes and complained bitterly that his ships were under-manned and his crews ill trained; "The utter insufficiency of his badly manned squadrons as compared with the Russian fleet and forts...was not taken into account." [3] His misgivings were increased when he reached Copenhagen. "What is the condition of the Russian Fleet?" asked Sir Charles of the Danish Minister of Marine when at Copenhagen. "Their condition is good. They manoeuvre well and sail in close order," was the reply of the Danish Minister. The British Admiral was assigned the threefold task of bottling up the Russian fleet in the Baltic, of inducing Sweden to enter the war and of placing at British disposal the great number of gun boats which the Swedish navy possessed. For this purpose the Åland Islands were to serve as bait. The Russian Admiralty on its side had made plans for a defensive campaign and had mined the approach to Sweaborg, Reval and Cronstadt. In the event of an attack on Cronstadt, the Fleet was to remain in the harbour while coastal batteries disabled the British vessels, after which the warships were to come into action while the squadron based at Sweaborg was to attack the British Fleet from the rear. In the

---

[3] Napier, op. cit., p. 14.

event of an attack on Reval large ships were to be dragged into shoal waters, where the British vessels following them would run aground.

The attempt to win Sweden over produced no results. In an audience the King of Sweden told Sir Charles Napier that Sweden did not require the Aland Islands so long as her neutrality was secure. "It was true that Russia was a rather formidable neighbour, but he did not know how an alliance with the other Powers would mend his position." [4] The fleet having been forced to remain in Swedish waters owing to ice and fog, it was only in early May that the British were able to start their military operations in the Baltic, war having been declared in the interval. By this time the fleet had been increased by over 20 vessels arriving from England thus bringing the number of ships under command of Sir Charles to 45 plus some old steamers. [5]

Pending the arrival of the French Fleet, military operations marked time. The Russian Fleet remaining in port, the British exchanged some shells with the forts of Hangö. Some prizes were captured near Riga and Reval and on one occasion British vessels had a brush not only with Russian coastal batteries but with Russian infantry and cavalry operating along the beach. Both sides reported insignificant losses. The most important result of these activities was to immobilize some 60,000 to 80,000 of Russia's best troops, including the Guards Corps, in anticipation of large scale landing operations along the Baltic coast. The attempt to blockade the coast and stop the running of military supplies did not prove effective. From Lubeck and Memel the supplies were trans-shipped on flat bottom vessels which operated in shallow waters beyond the reach of British men-of-war. As for Russian ships, they evaded the blockade by being registered at neutral ports, particularly at Lubeck, and kept on plying under neutral flags. British consuls reported that 52 Russian ships had thus changed their registry. Much more important were the results of reconnaissance carried out with regard to the conditions of Russian defences. Under the impression of the data gathered, the British Admiral reported that he considered Cronstadt, Sweaborg and Reval to be impregnable and suggested that he would merely be in a position

---

[4] Napier, op. cit., p. 126.
[5] Sir Charles Napier states subsequently that at the time of the junction of his squadron with the French Fleet he had twenty-seven vessels under his command; however, in the course of his narrative he gives the names of twenty-six additional ships which had joined his fleet after the time it left its base. He does not explain this discrepancy.

to take the Aland Islands and Hangö. However, since Sweden had refused to act, the latter were deemed by the British Admiralty not worth the cost in men and in ships. Cronstadt, covering the entrance to St. Petersburg, was the most heavily fortified. The north passage into the harbour was "closed by a double row of piles with granite blocks between them, the whole being protected by batteries"...Mines, "infernal machines, as Napier calls them, electrically operated from the forts, had been scattered in all directions. "The Russians were making prodigious efforts to equip gunboats. Forty of these had left for the Gulf (of Finland). Seventy more would be ready within a week and 290 would be completed by August." These boats carried two guns and were manned by a crew of 80 men. [6] As for Sweaborg, the fortifications were built of granite blocks on small islands and mounted 2,000 guns of largest caliber "and altogether are of enormous strength...From the position and strength of these fortifications they must be considered as unassailable but at immense sacrifice of life and loss of ships.." And finally "Reval was reconnoitred the other day and the Russians made a great show." [8] The squadron was nevertheless ordered to anchor off Sweaborg and here on June 12, the junction with the French Fleet took place. The allied fleet was now of the following strength: French, 7 sailing ships of the line, 1 screw ship of the line, 6 sailing frigates, 1 steam frigate, 4 steamers, total 19 vessels; British, 13 screw steamers of the line, 6 sailing ships, 6 paddle steamers, surveying and hospital ships, total 27 ships. Thus the combined total of 46 ships was nearly double the size of the Russian Fleet. [9] The allied fleet still kept on doing sundry jobs, blockading the coast, reconnoitring the Åland Islands, taking possession of Uleaborg, a small town on the Gulf of Bothnia. The Russians managed nevertheless to get 24 gunboats into Sweaborg "under the nose of the British," as the Czar stated. These meagre results and delays excited public opinion in England and under its pressure the Admiralty ordered the fleet to proceed to Cronstadt.

Upon reaching Cronstadt the allied fleets anchored outside the range of the guns of the fortress and the Russians moved their ships in such a way that their broadsides would strengthen the fire of the forts. The total Russian force thus supporting the batteries of the forts was seen to be 22 ships of the line, 5 frigates, 4 corvettes, 7 paddle steamers and 25 gun boats. As

---

[6] Napier, op. cit., p. 165.
[7] Admiral Chad's report dated June 14, 1854. Napier, op. cit., p. 189.
[8] Napier, op. cit., p. 163.
[9] Napier, op. cit., p. 181.

for the forts, they were lined with 1,000 heavy guns and "everything about the forts was in first rate order."[10] Sir Charles Napier refers to them as "the strongest fortification in the world."[11] Hence with cholera breaking out on board the ships, the allied squadrons stood idly before Cronstadt for a week, then sailed away. The failure to do anything at Cronstadt produced a very bad impression in England and wild recriminations arose against Sir Charles' lack of energy. The British Admiralty then wrote to the Commanding Admiral: "We have collected also from the various reports that with 10,000 men Bomarsund and the Åland Islands may be taken and being of opinion that the presence of the Allied fleet in the Baltic must be marked by some result, we determined to propose to the Emperor of the French to send there forthwith 6,000 soldiers, and these in addition to your marines and to the troops now on board the French line-of-battle ships will raise the effectual military force at your disposal to 10,000 men."[12] Thus the task was assigned of capturing the Åland Islands. Sir Charles Napier's suggestion of trying an attack on Sweaborg was turned down as being too costly. When the French landing forces amounting to 10,000 men arrived, the fleet, early in August, laid siege to Bomarsund, the fortified city on the Åland Islands. These islands had a population of some 6,000 fishermen and a weak Russian garrison of 2,000 men concentrated at Bomarsund. A combined attack of the fleet and the landing parties carried the place and after some fighting the little garrison surrendered and was taken to England. After the capture of the Åland Islands, the French recalled their fleet and their expeditionary force. The British lingered on for a month making plans for further military operations but carrying out none. Finally with bad weather setting in, the whole campaign was called off in September and October and the English Fleet left the Baltic to return to its base at Kiel. So incensed was public opinion in England over the pitiful results of this campaign that Sir Charles Napier was dismissed from his command and during the next years became the object of violent attacks both in Parliament and in the press.

The results of the naval operations in the Black Sea during this same period were not more fruitful. The British had concentrated the remainder of their fleet in that sea, viz: 10 sail of the line ships, 9 frigates, 3 corvettes and 11 steamers, supported, as in the Baltic, by a powerful French squadron. On April 12, 1854, a British vessel reconnoitred Odessa. This

---

[10] Napier, op. cit., p. 272.
[11] Napier, op. cit., p. 263.
[12] Napier, op. cit., p. 289.

great commercial metropolis of Southern Russia had no permanent fortifications and an attack on that city was a violation of the code of war. However a few batteries had been erected, after the declaration of war, housing 40 guns. Furthermore, the garrison of the city was composed of 16 reserve battalions with 50 additional guns. On April 20, an allied fleet of 27 vessels appeared off the city and two days later opened fire on a battery of 4 guns. Notwithstanding the disparity in numbers, these guns replied and succeeded in disabling one of the vessels. An attempted landing of British forces was beaten off by the fire of Russian guns and the bombardment of the other batteries produced no material results. The city suffered little though, ironically, an enemy shell imbedded itself in a monument to the Duc de Richelieu, erected in the heart of the city. The total Russian losses amounted to 50 men and 9 merchant ships which were burnt in the harbour. The enemy had 4 frigates disabled which were towed back to Varna. Commenting upon this fruitless assault on a great city, Sir Charles Napier writes: "In the Black Sea our army gained no satisfactory victory whilst our navy....suffered a defeat at Odessa, having there made a demand upon the Russian authorities which was not acceded to and which we failed to enforce." [13]

On June 12, the British screwship of the line "Tiger" (Captain Gifford) ran aground and the crew of 225 surrendered to the Russians. These were the first British prisoners to be captured by the Russians and they were treated with great courtesy, witness the narrative of one of these prisoners, Lieutenant Royer.

A word must also be said of operations in the White Sea where a British squadron under Captain Hall occupied itself mainly with capturing prizes--small commercial craft. However, like Admiral Plumridge in the Baltic (second in command to Sir Charles Napier), he burned, destroyed and looted defenceless villages and private residences and topped this off by twice bombarding the venerated Solovetski Monastery, merely scaring the monks and arousing the religious fanaticism of the Russians. The bombardment of the arctic city of Kola produced no results.

Thus we see that notwithstanding the fact that the whole naval might of Great Britian, seconded by that of France, had been drafted against Russia, during six months of warfare no appreciable result had been gained in any one of the three seas in which these forces were operating, and not the slightest indention had been made in the defences of Russia. To achieve

---

[13] Napier, op. cit., p. 73.

any results, the war had to be carried out on land. Such was the opinion gaining ground both in England and in France, where public opinion was getting exasperated at the poor results achieved.

II

Two schools of thought prevailed in England--the one argued that this was an European war, hence it ought to be fought in Europe. The main attack ought to be delivered in the Baltic where the allied armies would land and, in co-operation with the fleet, advance on St. Petersburg. Sir Charles Napier belonged to this school. The other wished to narrow the whole issue down to the Eastern Question and advocated merely the military support of Turkey in her struggle against Russia. The British newspapers stressed the necessity of returning the Crimea to the Turks, liberating the Caucasus from Russian domination for the benefit of Turkey and protecting the Balkan Slavs from Russia, blissfully ignoring history and political realities. The Government sided with this school considering the main object of the war the destruction of Russia's naval armament and power in the Black Sea, which had been such a thorn in England's side ever since the Treaties of Adrianople and Unkiar-Skelessi. To achieve this end the great naval base at Sebastopol had to be destroyed--hence the Crimea was to be invaded. The French, with no interests in the Baltic but with vital interests in the Eastern Mediterranean, were agreeable to this plan. A further consideration was that an attack on Russia's main defences would require a far greater effort than an invasion of a relatively remote and outlying region such as the Crimea appeared to be and would inevitably lead to a major war, taxing the whole strength of the belligerents. Whilst the allied general staffs were debating these issues, Russia on her side was systematizing her defences and these reveal strikingly both her fears and the relative value she attached to the various fronts. Toward the end of 1854 the disposition of the Russian forces had been definitely crystallized. The whole western and southern frontier had been divided into 6 zones, each under the command of a general with the rights of a commander-in-chief of a field army. 1) The Baltic coast with 179 battalions of infantry, 144 squadrons and 384 guns (exclusive of fortresses), 2)Poland and the Ukraine bordering Austria and Roumania, 146 battalions, 100 squadrons and 308 guns, 3)from the Danube to the Bug river 182 battalions, 285 squadrons and 612 guns, 4)from the Bug to the Sea of Azov, including the Crimea, 27 battalions, 19 squadrons and 48 guns, 5)the coast of the Sea of Azov and the northern Black Sea region, 31 battalions, 140 squadrons and 54 guns and, finally, 6)Transcaucasia, 152 battalions, 281 squadrons and 289 guns. A small force of 2 1/2 battalions was assembled along the coast of the White Sea. Sections two and three, in other words the western frontier from Poland along the Pruth to the Bug, were under the command of Field-Marshal Paskevich and totalled 328 battalions, 385 squadrons and 920 guns. Thus Paskevich, with by far the largest army, was to face Austria in the event she came into the war. True, subsequently some of these units were drafted into the Crimea, but this disposition is indicative of the menace Austria presented to Russia. The forces in zone 3 were also to block any advance of the allied armies should they proceed along the coast from their point of concentration in Bulgaria and attempt an invasion through Moldavia and Bessarabia, singly or in co-operation with the Austrian armies.

However, on June 29, 1854, the Duke of Newcastle, the British Secretary of War, wrote to Lord Raglan, the Commander-in-Chief of the British army assembled in Bulgaria, "I have to instruct your Lordship to concert measures for the siege of Sebastopol, unless, with the information in your possession, but unknown in this country, you should be decidedly of opinion that it could not be undertaken with a reasonable prospect of success." [14] It will be noticed that these instructions are positive and differ from the vague ones given to Sir Charles Napier in the Baltic with regard to Cronstadt or Sweaborg, the latter having been given latitude to decide the course of action on the spot. However, General Sir Edward Hamley observed that, "A siege, then was in the programme, but it is certain that even a probability that it would last through the winter would have put an end to the project." [15] Cholera had been raging in the allied forces, the French having lost some 10,000 men and the British between 500 and 600 from the disease. This and the difficulty of bringing up transports delayed the decision until well into August, when it had become clearly apparent that naval operations alone without support of land forces were predestined to failure. It was therefore only after the virtual conclusion of the naval operations in the Baltic that, on August 25, the expedition was officially announced and the embarcation of troops at Varna started on September 5. Delayed by contrary winds the expedition finally set sail on September 7, and was escorted by a formidable naval force including 10 line-of-battle ships, 2 screw steamers, 2 fifty-gun frigates and 13 smaller armed vessels of the British squadron; also 15 line-of-battle

---

[14] Hamley, General Sir Edward, <u>The War in the Crimea</u>. London 1910, p. 26.

[15] Hamley, <u>op. cit.</u>, p. 27.

ships and 12 war steamers of the French squadron and 8 Turkish line-of-battle ships and 3 war steamers. In the face of this combined fleet of 65 ships, the Russian Black Sea Fleet consisting of 15 sailing line-of-battle ships, 1 steamer, a few frigates and brigs and 11 small vessels remained in port at Sebastopol. Hence the allied expedition reached the coast of Crimea without being molested and cruised off shore until a suitable landing place had been selected. The spot decided upon was the Bay of Eupatoria, some twenty-five miles northeast of Sebastopol, which was reached by the advance guard on September 9. By the 18th the whole force had been landed, meeting with no resistance as Russian troops were absent at this point. The British Army was comprised of 26,000 infantry, a light brigade of cavalry (about 1,000 sabres) and 60 guns; the French had 28,000 infantry and no cavalry and the Turks 7,000 infantry and also no cavalry--the Franco-Turkish forces had 68 guns between them. Thus the total amounted to 61,000 infantry, 1,000 cavalry, 128 guns and sundry services. No transports being on hand, some 350 Tartar arabas (wagons) were requisitioned.

The relative smallness of this army indicated clearly that the allied command completely underestimated the task assigned to it; indeed before the allies succeeded in reducing Sebastopol they were forced to send close to a half million men into the Crimea. True, at the outset the difficulties appeared not to be so challenging. The Russian field army in the Crimea, commanded by Prince Menshikov, was as we have seen only a small fraction of the forces Russia had mobilized--some 35,000 men with 48 guns. As for Sebastopol itself it was garrisoned merely by one battalion of regular infantry (750 men) and 5 battalions of militia, hence it was left to the navy to man the defences. Lieutenant-Colonel Todleben, who was in charge of the engineering works of the fortress, states unequivocally that had the allies shown more initiative and boldness at the outset they might have captured the city in two days. He put the size of the garrison at that time at 16,000 men. This figure is disputed by General Hamley, who places it at 35,000, but one can not help feeling that in his desire to explain why the allies did not attack the fortress, Hamley somewhat stretches the power of the defending forces--indeed he includes as combatants 5,000 civilian workers of the arsenal, all the seamen of the fleet, including those who remained on the ships in the harbour or were employed at the base in non-combatant capacity and finally, more understandably, the five battalions of militia. These were never regarded in the Russian army as regular troops and were mostly employed for rear activities but, in an emergency like the one occurring in Sebastopol, they may have been thrown into the defences, though their fighting value would have been negligible. Discounting these facts, Todleben's statement comes nearer the truth. As for the actual state of the defences, they were at that time prepared to face an attack from the sea but not from the land side. Indeed the entrance to the deep harbour of Sebastopol was flanked by powerful forts: Fort Quarantine, Fort Alexander, Fort Nicholas and Fort Paul. On a height beyond the harbour, on the north side, was a permanent work known to the British as Star Fort, which could sweep with its guns not only the coast but a section of the inland harbour. But beyond these fortifications on the eastern and the southern side of the city there were no defences of any kind and the trenches and other earthworks which were being thrown up were not yet completed. The city therefore was entirely vulnerable from the land. One of the main assets of the defending garrison was the quality of its leadership. The navy provided men of strong determination and courage who by their example maintained the morale of the defenders in the face of increasing odds and hardships. Such were the Admirals Kornilov, Nakhimov (the victor of Sinope), Istomin and Lazarev. The army, on its side, produced an engineer of genius, Lieutenant-Colonel Todleben who, as Chief Engineer of the fortress, was responsible for the stubbornness of the defence and the technical skill with which it was conducted.

Born in Mittau (Courland) in 1818 Todleben had graduated from the School of Military Engineers in St. Petersburg in 1836 and first saw active service in the conquest of the Caucasus. In the early stages of the Crimean War he distinguished himself at the siege of Silistria and had just been attached to the staff of Prince Menshikov, who loaned him to the fortress of Sebastopol. Thirty-six years of age, he was in full mental and bodily vigour and he not only became the soul of the defence but made important contributions to the science of military engineering. These men greatly counteracted the mediocrity of the commanders of the field army, first Prince Menshikov and later Prince Gorchakov (the brother of the future Chancellor). On the allied side, however, the high command was not more remarkable--Lord Raglan showed himself to be average and the French Commander-in-Chief, Marshal St. Arnaud, died at the outset of the campaign. He was succeeded by the weak-willed and irresolute General Canrobert and it was not until the latter, in the final stage of the war, had handed over his command to the determined General Pelissier that operations were conducted in a more vigorous and successful way.

We have seen that the landing operations of the allied armies had been successfully completed at Eupatoria on September 18. The next day their advance on Sebastopol began, along the post road from Eupatoria to Sebastopol. On the same afternoon, whilst crossing a stream, the Bulganak, they first sighted the Russian vanguard, a mixed force some 8,000 strong which retreated without giving battle. The next day the advance was resumed over undulating flat highlands with hard soil over which the armies could march easily cross-country. The British were marching in columns astride the post road. To their right and nearer to the sea, came the French followed by the Turks.

Coming to the valley of the river Alma they found the Russian army awaiting them on the heights on the opposite side of the valley. Menshikov had there under his command 33,000 infantry, 3,400 cavalry and 120 guns.[16] It will be noticed that according to the figures given in the disposition of the Russian armies, the Crimean Army had only 48 guns. General Hamley, who was himself present at the battle, does not explain from where the additional Russian guns came, assuming that his figures are correct. This small Russian army of some 37,000 men was preparing to bar the way of 24,000 British and 35,000 French and Turks. It is difficult to conceive the reasons that guided Menshikov in giving this battle unless he wanted thereby to delay the enemy advance so as to give time to strengthen the land defences of Sebastopol. If so his purpose was partly achieved. As for the battle itself, the result was a foregone conclusion. The heights occupied by the Russians were situated to the west of the little village of Bourliuk on the Alma which became, by the nature of the course of the river, the dividing line between the British and the French sectors. Hence the major portion of the Russian army, 21,000 infantry, 3,000 cavalry and 84 guns, faced the British whereas 12,000 infantry, 400 cavalry and 36 guns faced the flanking movement of the French.

When the allied armies deployed for battle, their front so far outflanked the short Russian line that the French right wing never even came under Russian fire. Here Bosquet's brigade and a Turkish division crossed the Alma at its mouth and under protection of the guns of the French fleet, which were sweeping the plateau held by the Russians, proceeded methodically to encircle Menshikov's left flank and cut him off from the road to Sebastopol. Meanwhile the British and the remaining French forces some 50,000 strong attacked the Russian position frontally and on the immediate flank. After being delayed and thrown into

---

[16] Hamley, op. cit., p. 52.

some confusion by the burning of the village of Burliuk, the English attack concentrated on the center of the Russian position. Here a twelve-gun heavy battery on Kurgan Hill inflicted serious casualties on the attacking columns and held back the British, permitting the Russians to counter-attack. But when General Codrington's brigade succeeded in reaching the battery, Menshikov ordered the hurried withdrawal of the guns. Though a Russian infantry counter-attack drove Codrington back with severe losses, this appeared to be the turning point of the battle. The whole British army was brought to bear on the Russian columns, whereas the French occupied Telegraph Hill in the left rear of the Russian line; while further to the right Bosquet and the Turks were pursuing their enveloping movements. Unde these circumstances Menshikov ordered a retreat and the day cost the Russians 5,709 men, the British 2,002 men and the French 1,340. Tactically little credit was earned by either side. Menshikov has been criticized first, for not having fortified his positions, second for having withdrawn his battery on Kurgan Hill at the decisive moment, and third for not having brought all his reserves into action. It may be argued that he could not afford the loss of heavy guns, of which he had such a limited number, and neither could he afford the loss of his reserves in such a small army. As for the lack of any trenche or earthworks on his position, except for two small trenchworks, this might have indicated either negligence or the lack of time or the intention not to hold this position beyond a certain cost. At any rate, Menshikov's resistance was half-hearted. On the allied side, the British Commander-in-Chief rode out on his right flank so close to the French that he left his own divisional commanders to take care of themselves and, lastly, the sweep of the French enveloping movement was so vast that only a minor portion of their troops supported the British attack.

But one important result accrued to the Russians. The enemy stayed two days more on the Alma, resting after the battle, and resumed their march only on September 23. Thus three extremely valuable days had been gained for the strengthening of the defences of Sebastopol.

Upon retreating from the battlefield of the Alma, Menshikov did not lead his army into Sebastopol but marched past to take up a position east of the city beyond the river Chernaya which flows into the deep inland bay of Sebastopol. In so doing he did a wise thing. Though apparently lacking in energy and tactical skill, Menshikov had a good grasp of strategical problems and his march beyond the Chernaya placed him in the rear of the investing armies. He was thus able not only to harass and menace the enemy's rear while not losing his communications with the interior of Russia, but he was also in a position to keep a door open into the besieged city as well and thus not permit the complete investment of it.

Following rather sluggishly behind the retreating Russians, the allied armies came within sight of the northern defences of Sebastopol on September 25. Thus 12 days had elapsed since the enemy was first sighted off the coast of Crimea and a week since it had landed. During this interval Todleben and the navy had achieved the miracle of transforming Sebastopol into a fortress capable of withstanding a prolonged siege from inland as well as from the sea. Seven ships of the Black Sea Fleet were sunk on the night of the 22nd to form a boom to bar the entrance to the harbour from the sea. The remaining vessels of the fleet, now blocked in the harbour took up such strategic positions on the inland side of the bay and near the creeks on the south side of it, that their guns could effectively co-operate with the land batteries. As for the land defences, they were extended in a semi-circle around the bay to surround the city. On the north side, that is to say from the sea near Careenage Bay to the upper end of the Bay of Sebastopol an uninterrupted chain of bastions, redoubts and batteries had been erected and armed with 172 pieces of artillery taken either from the sunken vessels or the arsenal. The key position on this side which was to become the key of the whole defence was the famous Malakhov Kurgan with a tower 28 feet high and 50 feet in diameter with 5 guns on the top and surrounded by trenches and other works. Flanking Malakhov on both sides were the Redan and the Little Redan. To the south of the bay a similar series of defences covered the south side of the city. Here the most important centers were the Flagstaff Bastion, Central Bastion and finally close to the sea the Quarantine Bastion. Thus the defences encircled the city and the harbour stretching from one bay north of the city, the Careenage Bay, to another bay south of the city, the Quarantine Bay. The line was 7 miles long and during the later days of the siege was equipped with 800 guns. The whole system of works was made more and more elaborate as the siege progressed and the total mileage of trenches was brought up to 15 miles and the strength of the defending garrison reached 115,000 men.

Upon reaching the northern outskirts of the city the allies stopped and held a council of war to decide whether or not to attack Sebastopol from the north. It was found that the defences were already too strong and the cost of an assault would be too heavy. Hence the decision was made to besiege the city and the allied armies started their encircling movement by marching around the Bay of Sebastopol. In so doing they were paralleling the march of the Russian field army, and here an incident occurred illustrative of the way this war was conducted. The advance of the British forces toward a point beyond the inner end of the harbour, known as Mackenzie's Farm, started on the 25th. As the vanguard was nearing this point it was stopped by some confusion caused by the fact that a troop of horse artillery found itself leading the column. Lord Raglan rode up to straighten out the situation and as the column started to move, the Commander-in-Chief with his staff found themselves leading the way followed by 30 guns of artillery and then the other troops--needless to say a formation which was contrary to all rules since the artillery thus alone in front was helpless in the face of an enemy. Presently as the column reached an open space it stumbled against a Russian column moving at right angles. The Commanders-in-Chief of both sides had been absolutely unaware of the presence of the other army marching across their respective fronts, though the main bodies were merely some four miles distant from one another. Both sides were equally anxious to avoid battle, hence no serious engagement resulted. With the French following behind, the British next day crossed the river Chernaya and turned south, cutting across the Chersonese peninsula. Thus they reached the sea once more, due south of Sebastopol at Balaclava.

This little city was held by a garrison of some 70 men; hence with the co-operation of men-of-war firing from the sea the town was easily captured. The same day the French, advance guard crossed the Chernaya. Thus the front began shaping itself. It was divided into two sectors, the northern and the southern, by the Bay of Sebastopol or Inner Harbour--four miles long. Half way up this bay, which runs east-west, was a creek a mile and a half long, branching out at right angles with the harbour on its southern shore. This was known as Men-of-War Harbour, and the city of Sebastopol nestled between this creek and the sea on the south side of the main harbour. On the opposite side, that is to say on the north side, was the Korabelnaya suburb with docks, warehouses and barracks. Paralleling the Bay of Sebastopol a couple of miles to the north and also to the south of the city along the coast of the Black Sea were two more bays--Careenage Creek to the north and Quarantine Bay to the south. The French held the northern sector facing the Little Redan and Malakhov. Beyond Malakhov the British sector ran along the inner harbour up to its eastern end and beyond. The British sector was thus astride the main highway leading into Sebastopol, known as the Vorontsov Road. The Great Ravine, which was prolongation on land of the end of the harbour, marked the beginning of the second French sector which

spread toward Quarantine Bay. Thus the French were on the
flanks of the line and the British in the middle; the total length
of all the works of this line was 52 miles and was held toward
the end of the siege by the combined total of 229,000 men with
827 guns.

    The weakness in the allied line lay in the fact that it was
too extended and was cut by deep perpendicular ravines. This
made the complete investment of the city impossible, with the
forces which the allies had and the menace of the Russian field
army in the rear, and at no time during the siege were the allies able to bar the Russians from access to the city. This
brings us to the major problem confronting both sides--that of
organizing the transportation of reinforcements and of supplies.
It was not an easy task. The Russian forces in the Crimea
were insignificant compared to the size of the army which had
been assembled in the Bug-Dniester zone, that is to say around
Odessa. Since the war had been definitely centralized in the
Crimea, the units which could be spared from Paskevich's army
facing Austria had to be transported to join Menshikov's army.
But with the sea barred by the presence of the allied fleets,
these units had to undertake a march of some 1,000 miles along
the coast over the dreary and at times waterless steppes to the
Isthmus of Perekop and then down the Crimean peninsula. Even
worse was the fate of the reserves and replacements coming
from the interior of Russia. The Russian railway system at
that time did not go beyond some 200 miles south of Moscow.
Hence the troops had to march more than a thousand miles over
the great south Russian steppe before reaching their destination.
More than anything else this hindered the successful conduct of
the war. The casualties from exhaustion and disease (particularly dissentery), during these marches, equalled if not sur-
passed the Russian losses on the battle front. Some alleviation
was found by using the waterways. The main line of supplies
and to some extent of transportation of troops was organized
down the Don river, to the Sea of Azov, thence across this sea
to Kerch, from where a relatively short distance separated them
from the front. On the allied side the problem was equally complex with all supplies and reinforcements being brought up by sea.
The question of a landing base became of paramount importance.
Eupatoria being too far north, the British, tempted by the deep
fiord-like bay of Balaclava, selected the latter. The French,
more practical as it turned out, chose the open bay of Kamish,
much closer to their lines. It was merely some four miles
from their front and, after building a paved road from their
landing base to their line, the French had no trouble with the
problem of bringing up supplies and reserves and evacuating

their wounded. Not so the British. Balaclava was eight to nine miles away from the British positions. True, the Vorontsov Road, a good paved highway, descended into the valley of Balaclava some three to four miles from Balaclava itself, and therefore could be used for transportation purposes. But Menshikov was quick to see his chance. His advanced parties crossed the Chernaya, followed by the main force detailed for the operation totalling 22,000 infantry, 3,400 cavalry and 78 guns under the command of General Liprandi. On October 25, this force attacked the trenches and batteries, held by the Turks, covering Balaclava and captured them. Realizing the menace, the allied command threw into action two British infantry divisions, two French brigades and all available cavalry taken from the front around Sebastopol.

Thus a major engagement developed on a ridge overlooking Balaclava. A Russian cavalry charge swept on the recently arrived British Heavy Brigade which counter-charged, pending the arrival of the two infantry divisions hastening to the scene of action. As the Light Brigade had remained so far inactive, Lord Raglan ordered it to advance to recover the heights, supported by the advancing infantry divisions and a French brigade of cavalry on the left rear. Interpreting this order as indicating the front directly ahead of him, Lord Cardigan led the Light Brigade straight ahead, thereby losing touch with the infantry. As the Brigade advanced ahead at a trot it found itself within the range of fire of a battery of 12 Russian guns. Losing 247 men out of 670, the Brigade broke and the men retreated, trickling back by groups of two's and threes's. Such was the Charge of the Light Brigade. The French, seeing the plight of their allies, charged in their turn and the 4th Chasseurs d'Afrique succeeded in silencing a Russian battery on the flank of the Light Brigade, thereby facilitating the retreat of the survivors. Meanwhile, the British infantry divisions had come up, but were not brought into action and returned to their camps during the night. The day finished with the Russians not only retaining the conquered field works and captured guns but, more important, having obtained control of the Vorontsov Road near Balaclava. This was the main strategic significance of the action and was to cause untold misery to the British. Indeed this meant the loss of the only road connecting the British positions with the Balaclava base just at a time when wet and stormy autumn weather was about to set in. Indeed three weeks later the warm sunny weather, which had facilitated operations, broke and a fierce gale on November 14 destroyed stores at the base and sank supply ships in the harbour. Twenty-one ships were dashed to pieces and eight disabled. The army remained without warm clothing, medical supplies or forage for horses. It began snowing, the ground became soggy and transports were bogged as they made their way cross-country in the absence of a road. The difficulty of bringing up food and fuel to the front line caused a tremendous increase in disease and at the end of November the British had 8,000 men in hospitals, or approximately one-third of the army. "Yet at this very time there was a sufficiency of fuel stored at Balaclava and rice, flour, vegetables, and tea such as might have rendered the diet wholesome. Here then, seven or eight miles from the camps were supplies which would have enabled the army to meet on much better terms the evils of overwork and exposure to wet and cold." [17] Such were the effects of the loss of the Vorontsov Road and conditions went from bad to worse during the succeeding months. On the other hand the reduction of effectives caused by sickness made it impossible to detach sufficient men from the front to build a road, hence no relief could be expected until the Vorontsov Road was recaptured. The evil consequences did not even stop there but led to a major political crisis in England. The indignation caused in England by the news of the happenings in Crimea led to a series of letters written from December on, by the Secretary of War censuring Lord Raglan and his staff, with the Quarter-master-general being made the scapegoat. When a motion was made and carried in Parliament for a committee of inquiry into the conditions of the army before Sebastopol, the government of Lord Aberdeen fell to be replaced by that of Lord Palmerston. In April, 1856, already after the war, a board of generals sat in Chelsea for the court-martial of the Quarter-master-general and of the two cavalry Generals, Lord Lucan and Lord Cardigan, who were responsible for the defeat at Balaclava. Such, in the last analysis, were the consequences of this engagement.

III

It is now necessary to turn to the events around Sebastopol proper, before examining the next operations of the Russian field army. It was not until the allies could bring up their siege guns and their ammunition that the siege operations could really be undertaken. This occurred on the night of the 9th of October, when a north-east wind prevented the Russians from hearing the men at work. When this was accomplished the allies had 126 siege guns as opposed to the Russian 118. On the morning of the 17th, that is to say a week before the battle of

---

[17] Hamley, op. cit., p. 168.

Balaclava, the allies opened a fierce bombardment to precede the general attack on the city, which it was confidently believed would end the war. The allied navies were to attack in co-operation with the land forces. It was decided that the French fleet, anchored 1,600-1,800 yards off the coast would open fire on Forts Quarantine and Alexander, whereas the British would extend their line to bear their fire on Fort Constantine and the batteries beyond. On land both sides had increased their strength in prevision of the coming struggle, Menshikov strengthening the garrison of the city by 25,000 men taken from the field army and the allies landing marines and seamen. The cannonade was opened on the 17th by the allies at 6:30 in the morning and, the Russian batteries replying, a furious artillery duel raged for four hours. The British succeeded in ruining Malakhov Tower and silencing the guns on it but the Russians scored a direct hit on the French batteries on Mount Rodolphe and blew up their ammunition magazine. By 10:30 the concentrated fire of Russian batteries succeeded in silencing the French artillery. This so demoralized the allies that they abandoned the idea of an attack and the bombardment ceased. Not more successful was the action of the fleet which bombarded the forts with 1,100 guns, the Russian forts replying with 152 guns. After four hours of firing the ships withdrew. The French navy lost 203, the English 317, and the Russians 138 men.[18] However, during this bombardment Admiral Kornilov was mortally wounded. The next day the British resumed the bombarding but the French batteries were still unable to join. "But dawn had disclosed a new feature in the problem. At nightfall we had looked on works reduced to shapeless heaps, on ruined batteries and disabled guns. Before morning the parapets had been rebuilt, the batteries repaired and fresh guns from the inexhaustible supplies of the ships and arsenals had occupied the embrasure; and the Allies could now begin to realize how formidable was the opponent, who could thus, as chief engineer, wield the resources of the place."[19]

The importance of the failure of the allies to attack on October 17 resided in the fact that the initiative of the operations thus slipped out of their hands. Indeed they had postponed indefinitely any further assault on the city and the Russian command felt free to act,--hence the battle of Balaclava, hence also an attempt at a combined operation by the field army and the garrison of Sebastopol which followed shortly afterwards.

---

[18] Hamley, op. cit., p. 107.
[19] Hamley, op. cit., p. 108.

There was a point in the allied lines where there was a wide gap--namely at the junction of the British right flank and the French left flank around two ravines, the Dock and the Careenage. These ravines cut through the Chersonese plateau from the Bay of Sebastopol near where it descends into the valley of the Chernaya. Beyond this river rose a cliff which, owing to a formation of rocks resembling a ruined city, was known as the "Ruins of Inkerman", a name which was also given to a neighbouring plateau. Through this gap contact could be maintained between the besieged and the field army on the Chernaya. The British accused the French of not doing their share in closing this gap, but owing to the divided command nothing was done.

Meanwhile the Field Army had been reinforced by an army corps, which had arrived from Odessa. The allied armies were also reinforced and the French, anxious to retrieve the disaster of October 17, were preparing for an attack on Flagstaff Bastion. A council of war was held by the allies to arrange for a concerted action the next day but Menshikov, who knew of this coming assault, struck first on November 5 and the Battle of Inkerman was on. On the Russian side the operation brought into action 16,000 men of the field army under General Pavlov and 19,000 men under General Soimonov, from the garrison of Sebastopol. The combined artillery amounted to 54 heavy guns and 81 field guns. The troops of Liprandi's corps, which had fought at Balaclava and now were commanded by Prince Gorchakov, were in reserve on the left flank since their task was to hold the captured positions at Balaclava. The plan of battle worked out by Menshikov provided for a simultaneous advance of General Soimonov through the Careenage Ravine and of General Pavlov across the Chernaya. After the two forces operated their junction they were to attack the British while Gorchakov was to attempt to draw the enemy upon himself. Such complicated plans require perfect timing and co-ordination and in conditions of actual warfare they rarely succeed, because of unforeseen factors which come to disturb the timing. This is precisely what happened at Inkerman. Instead of a co-ordinated and concentric attack the battle degenerated into a series of isolated assaults. Soimonov at dawn led his column to the heights of Inkerman and, coming from the ravine, he immediately attacked the enemy without waiting for Pavlov. Pavlov, seeing this, attacked without waiting for his whole column to come up. The nature of the ground was such that the Russians could not deploy and had to advance in columns. Hence they sustained heavier losses than the defenders.

Just as the British succeeded in repulsing this attack, General Dannenberg, now in charge of all the troops in action, launched the second attack, throwing in the units of the two columns which had not been engaged. This attack conducted with vigour on the British center and right resulted in the capture of a part of the enemy positions. It was followed by a series of attacks on Sand Bay battery followed by British counter-charges, during which Sir George Cathcart, who had been designated as successor to Lord Raglan, met his death. Demoralized by the death of their commander, the British 4th Division scattered, and Fore Ridge, an important strategic point, was occupied by the Russians. It was only through a timely French attack of Bosquet's corps on the Russian flank that a disaster was averted for the British. The Russians, driven back by this flank movement, launched a third determined attack which this time was met by the combined effort of the British and the French which were coming up in great numbers. Up to this point the French had been held back by the menace of Gorchakov's corps on their flank. Toward evening the attacking Russian columns withdrew to their respective positions along the Chernaya and within the fortifications of Sebastopol, and the battle came to an end leaving things very much as they were before it started. The Russian losses were estimated by the British to be 11,000; the British lost 2,357 or 27.7 per cent of forces engaged and the French 932 men. However one result had been obtained by this otherwise inconsequential battle namely,-the projected French assault on Flagstaff Bastion was once more postponed and Sebastopol received a possible lease on life of a few months. The Battle of Inkerman was the last major operation of the campaign of 1854. The coming winter put an end to any further actions of the field army. In December the Russians withdrew beyond the Chernaya except for a bridge-head at Traktir and two advanced posts at the villages of Kamara and Tchorgun. In January a Franco-British column attacked these posts and drove the Russians out of Tchorgun, thereby once more gaining access to the Vorontsov Road. The British now built a road connecting it with Balaclava and their position was notably ameliorated, but there were still 13,600 men lying in hospitals in February and during the four preceding months the British had lost 9,000 men from disease alone.

In February, the Russians attempted to gain possession of Eupatoria, which was the landing place for Turkish reinforcements. Eupatoria had been heavily fortified by the allies and was defended by 23,000 Turks with 34 heavy guns and by the men-of-war of the allied navies. Menshikov dispatched 19,000 men to carry these works and their failure to do so resulted in the appointment in his place of Prince Gorchakov as Commander-in-Chief. But these various operations throughout the winter were of a minor character, and both sides had concentrated during these months on the conduct of the siege of Sebastopol, to which we must now again turn.

On two occasions, as we have seen, on October 17, and November 5, the Russians had succeeded in forcing upon the allies a postponement of their contemplated attack on Sebastopol. After Inkerman the allies definitely gave up the idea of any further assault on the city and concentrated on increasing the strength of their lines and on a methodical carrying on of the siege. The Russians on their side, now that the field army's campaign had come to an end during the winter months, began using its resources in men and in supplies to strengthen the garrison of Sebastopol. Thus during the winter both sides concentrated on the siege, except for the minor operations we have already examined. On October 17 the plan of attack provided for an assault by the French on Flagstaff Bastion and by the British on the Redan. It was then deemed that the fall of these two forts would render the capture of the city inevitable. "But a great master of engineering science had been labouring on these works with unceasing energy and with formidable effect."[20] Indeed not only had Todleben strengthened the Bastion and the Redan, but also Malakhov, dominating the Redan, had been increasingly strengthened. The allies approached these works by laying parallels and the French had sapped up to within 180 yards of the Bastion and also dug a mine gallery. But Todleben blew it up by a counter mine and when the French tried to explode a second mine to prepare the ground for the attack, the Russians secured hold of the crater. In the meanwhile Todleben developed what was to become a new feature in engineering science. During the night parties of snipers would go out from the fortress to dig pits, holding one man, within easy range of the enemy from where they would fire into his trenches with deadly effect. Then during the subsequent nights these pits would be connected to form a new line which was then occupied by larger bodies and gradually made a permanent part of the defence system which thus was expanded closer and closer to the enemy's line.

This resulted in the unique situation of the besieged systematically gaining ground on the besiegers. In February the French made plans for gaining a conical hill about 500 yards from Malakhov which would dominate the latter work if they could place their batteries there. But the plan was thwarted by the Russians, who on February 22, developed works on ground gained during the night which flanked this hill, subse-

---

[20]Hamley, op. cit., p. 190.

quently known as the Mamelon. The French counter-attacked with five battalions but were repulsed with severe losses and Mamelon was encircled by the Malakhov defences. This was followed up by the seizure of a part of Mount Inkerman abandoned after the battle of the same name. These additional works had such importance that the allies held a conference on March 6, to plan an attack on the Mamelon, and Canrobert was urged to gain possession of it on the night of March 10, but once more Todleben thwarted the move by siezing the Mamelon the same night and crowning it with works which were integrated into the Malakhov system. This was followed up once more by throwing out pits which eventually were united into trenches. Now the Russians were in a position to fire into the sector of the British lines called the "Right Attack". Encouraged by these results the Russians struck once more on the night of March 20, when a sortie was made to destroy the French works which had been creeping up to the Mamelon, while three other assaults were directed against various sections of the British lines. These assaults, after bitter fighting, which cost the French 600 men on the Mamelon, were repulsed, but their main objective to disorganize the enemy line was achieved. Indeed the following night a new entrenched Russian line sprang up at a distance of 80 feet from the French.

So far the allies had been losing ground before Sebastopol. The political and economic reaction of the unsatisfactory march of events in the Crimea was becoming serious in Paris and the allied commanders were being urged to do something more decisive. The coming of spring permitted the resumption of large scale operations and enormous reinforcements both in men and in artillery had strengthened the fighting forces. Hence on April 9, Easter Monday, the allies opened a general bombardment on the Russian lines, which it was confidently believed on both sides was preparatory for an assault; 378 French heavy guns and 123 British at 6:30 in the morning opened a concentrated fire on the Malakhov, the Mamelon, the Flagstaff Bastion, and other major works. The Russians, taken by surprise, engaged their batteries twenty minutes later. This cannonade lasted uninterruptedly for ten days, and fire swept the city as well, causing terrible havoc. It was the greatest bombardment so far recorded in history and the Russian troops suffered heavily because, expecting an assault to follow, they had been brought out to man the defences. On the 19th the allied fire began to slacken and gradually ceased. No assault followed and the routine siege works were resumed in the allied lines. The Russians withdrew their infantry to places of shelter. Their losses during the ten days bombardment had been 6,000 men, those of the British 265, and of the French 1,585 men. Why the allies did not follow up their bombardment by an attack remained a mystery and may perhaps be explained by intrigues and changes in the French high command, and to some extent by the diplomatic negotiations which at that time were being carried on in Vienna.

Thoroughly discontented with the conduct of the war, Napoleon III resolved to go himself to the Crimea and to take command of his army. He had worked out a plan of operations reversing the previous strategy of the war and laying stress on the defeating of the Russian Field Army. Three armies were to be formed, of which two were to be engaged in this purpose and only one was to carry on the siege. The British opposed the Emperor's intention with all their might, for his arrival at the front would have placed them in a subordinate position. Serious discord reigned for a while amongst the allies and, to save the alliance, Napoleon finally announced on April 25 that he was abandoning his intention of going to Russia. But he insisted on his plan of strategy. On the other hand General Niel, chief engineer of the French forces and very influential with the Emperor, insisted upon the foremost task of investing Sebastopol and pursuing the siege by severing the connections of the Field Army with the garrison of the city. Caught between these contradictory schemes, Canrobert, always irresolute, did not want to risk an assault and finally, on May 16, sent in his resignation. He was replaced by the energetic Pelissier. The Emperor continued to insist upon his plan but Pelissier was a stubborn man with his own ideas and these he put into effect. The whole character of the war changed.

One of Pelissier's first moves was to sever the important Russian line of communication via the Azov Sea and Kerch. On May 24, a combined allied expedition of 15,000 men transported by sea appeared before the weakly defended city and captured it, after which the allied fleet passed into the Sea of Azov through the Straits of Kerch, destroyed a number of Russian vessels, laden with supplies, and pushed as far as Taganrog, destroying the supplies there. Pelissier was less fortunate with his first venture against Sebastopol. Todleben had pushed forward his works between the Central Bastion and Quarantine Bay around a graveyard which was partly occupied by the French. As the new works raked the French trenches, Pelissier ordered that the Russians should be ousted and accordingly on May 22, a force of 6,000 men attacked the Russian outworks, but after a night of attacks and counter-attacks the French were beaten off with a loss of 1,800 men. The next night a second attack gave the trench to the French, for meanwhile the Russians, interpreting the sailing of the allied squadrons for Kerch as an attempt to land forces against the Field Army, had withdrawn the garrison of this work which was needed elsewhere and left only a small guard. Just at this time the first contingents of the Sardinian Army of 15,000 arrived at the front and were assigned to a sector on the right of the French, facing the field army, whereas the Turkish Army, now very greatly strengthened, came up from Eupatoria to form the general reserve on the heights of Balaclava. With the capture of the village of Tchorgun, the second and last village held by the Russians on this side of the Chernaya, the front of the Field Army was straightened out along the northern bank of the river (May 25).

Whereas Napoleon still insisted on his plan to concentrate against the Field Army, Pelissier's intention was to throw his forces against Sebastopol. He was anxious to vindicate his strategy by a striking success and hence he was prepared to try the long postponed assault. At a conference of allied commanders it was decided that the objective of this attack would be the works which Todleben had pushed forward covering the Malakhov and the Redan, namely the so-called White Works, the Mamelon and the Quarry. On June 6, 544 heavy guns opened an artillery barrage on these works and maintained the fire for two days. The Russian defences crumbled under the concentrated cross fire of French and British guns and the batteries in the outworks were silenced while the batteries in the main line of defence continued to respond. At 6:30 P.M. on June 7, the signal for the attack was given, the French starting first, to be followed by a British attack on the Quarry, after the French had gained possession of the Mamelon. The French captured the Mamelon in their first attack, but a Russian counter-attack drove them back to their own trenches. French reserves were brought up and succeeded in capturing a lunette on this salient. The British in the meanwhile stormed their objective but the combat swayed to and fro, attacks and counter-attacks succeeding each other throughout the night. By next morning both French and British had maintained their gains. The artillery duel continued till June 10. The Russian losses were 5,000 men and 73 disabled guns left in the outworks; the French lost 5,440 men and the British 693 men. Encouraged by this success, Pelissier and Lord Raglan decided to follow it up by an attack on the Redan, the Malakhov and dependent batteries on June 18.

Once more the allied artillery opened its preparations on the 17th whereas the attack itself was scheduled on the 18th. At dawn the French columns, 25,000 strong, began their attack on Malakhov, but during the night the Russians had been able to repair the damage produced by the bombardment of the previous day, and met the advancing foe with such a withering fire that the French could not advance any further and contented themselves with merely an exchange of rifle fire. Meanwhile the British, who started their advance on the Redan, met with the same fate and after their advance columns had been almost annihilated, the attack was abandoned and between 7 and 8 o'clock in the morning the troops were recalled to their trenches. The allied losses had been extremely severe, the French losing 3,500 and the British 1,500 men. Four of the six generals leading the attacking columns had been killed and one wounded. The attack had been a disastrous failure.

Ten days later Lord Raglan died suddenly after a short illness; a few days before his death a British staff officer wrote referring to the failure of the attack: "I fear it has affected Lord Raglan's health; he looks far from well and has grown very much aged lately." [21] Todleben had been wounded and was evacuated, not to return again to Sebastopol, and ten days earlier, on July 10, Admiral Nakhimov, the victor of Sinope, was killed. Thus the garrison had lost all the leading spirits of its defence. The end was approaching. The constant artillery fire had reduced the defence works to shambles notwithstanding the heroic efforts of the garrison to rebuild them after each bombardment. The daily loss of the garrison, outside of battles, averaged 800 men. On August 9, Gorchakov convened a council of war to discuss the next step. It was decided that the Field Army should attack the allies on the upper Chernaya, held by the French and the Sardinians, with the Turks in reserve. The total allied force occupying this sector or immediately available as reserves amounted to 60,000 men. The Russian forces detailed for this operation amounted to 29,000 with 27,000 in reserve. Gorchakov's plan was to drive on the Sardinian outposts which were holding the Russian side of the Chernaya around Tchorgun and then to determine whether the main attack was to be directed against the Sardinians or the French. General Liprandi succeeded in driving the Sardinians back, though they held the last height on the bank of the river. In the meantime General Read, commanding the Russian right flank, misinterpreting his orders, attacked the French prematurely with two divisions and without artillery preparation and was driven back across the river. Reforming his troops he launched a second attack by capturing the Traktir bridge and bridgehead, but was repulsed a second time and was killed in this engagement. A third attack followed, once more across

---

[21]Hamley, op. cit., p. 265.

the stream, but the French brought up powerful reserves and Gorchakov withdrew his troops and formed a line across the valley, waiting the remainder of the day for a French counter-attack which never materialized. The Russians lost 2,369 killed and 5,700 in wounded and prisoners; the French lost 1,500 and the Sardinians, whose only engagement this was to be, around 200. After the Battle of Traktir, Gorchakov visited Sebastopol and decided that the city could not hold out very much longer.

"There was no longer either a city or a suburb to defend, for both were heaps of rubbish and cinders. The parapet of works, dried in the heat of summer and split in huge fragments by the shot, were crumbling into ditches. The interior space was honey-combed with holes made by shells. Gabions and sandbags could not be procured to repair the embrasures...Many of the dismounted guns could no longer be repaired...the gunners lay dead in heaps on the batteries, the wounded could not be removed by day..." [22] Gorchakov gave orders to prepare the evacuation of the place but resolved to defend it till the last extremity "for it is the only honourable course which remains to us" as he wrote to the Minister of War. For this purpose 25,000 men were to be brought into the city from the Field Army, leaving 20,000 outside. The French resumed their cannonade, the Russian batteries replying feebly, and under protection of this bombardment the French pushed up their field works to within 25 feet of Malakhov. Now everything was ready for the final assault, which was to be carried before Russian reinforcements reached the garrison. Once more the French were to attempt to take Malakhov, the Central Bastion, the Little Redan and the Curtain, while the British were to concentrate on the Redan. The final bombardment of Sebastopol opened on September 5, all the allied batteries coming into action and sweeping the city with a circle of fire and the "feu d'enfer" was sustained uninterruptedly for four days. The Russians manned their last defences and loaded their remaining guns with grape shot awaiting the coming attack.

Pelissier selected as zero hour for the assault September 8 at noon because it was known that the relief of the troops took place at noon and hence Malakhov momentarily would be destitute of defenders. Indeed, profiting by this short relaxing of the defence, the French made a dash and got a foothold in Malakhov. When the Russians realized what had happened, they brought up their last reserves and for four hours a desperate hand to hand struggle was waged within the walls and in

---

[22]Hamley, op. cit., p. 274, 275.

the trenches of the work. Every traverse was taken and retaken, and it was only when the fresh French Brigade (of General Vinoy), turning the work, succeeded in breaking into it from the rear and combined its onslaught with the Zouaves of the Guards, who were fighting within Malakhov, that the work was finally captured. Meanwhile St. Pol's brigade which was attacking the Little Redan and Bourbaki's brigade assaulting the Curtain, were thrown back in two successive attacks and could not make any further progress. Similarly, further to the left two French brigades attacked the works flanking the Central Bastion but were driven back with heavy losses. When the second attack also failed Pelissier called off the assault. The French losses for the day had been extremely heavy amounting to 7,567 men, with 6 generals killed and 4 wounded.

In the meantime the British attack on the Redan met with a disastrous defeat. As their columns emerged into the open space they were met with such a fire from the work that, except for a few who pushed on further, the bulk lay down and opened fire instead of advancing. Presently their morale broke and they fell back in a disorderly retreat which the British "Engineer Journal" explains as being caused by the fact that "They found themselves without any officers of rank to command them". Indeed Colonel Windham, leading the column, left his troops to go back into the rear. This attack cost the British 2,271 men.

The day cost the Russians 12,900 men and the allies around 10,000; these figures in themselves speak of the extremely heavy fighting which took place. The Russians repulsed all the attacks except those on Malakhov, but Malakhov dominated the defences to such an extent that its loss made the situation untenable for the garrison of Sebastopol. Hamley gives a graphic description of this stronghold: "Huge subterranean barracks had been dug under the ramparts, the earth above being supported on the trunks of trees... it was here that the troops destined to oppose assaults found all the repose that could be given to them when not immediately called on to face the unrelenting iron storm which swept across the open space of the interior. Phrases can hardly do justice to the constancy, the military spirit, of a soldiery that could under such circumstances readily obey the call which brought them to the last struggle, and so bear themselves on it that their enemies had everywhere recoiled, except in one point." [23] But this one point was all important and Pelissier well earned the title of Duc de Malakhov which was given him later. Consequently the evacuation of Sebastopol was

---

[23] Hamley, op. cit., p. 287.

decided upon and the next day the Russians blew up the Fort Paul and other defences, sank the remaining vessels of the Black Sea Fleet, and under cover of night the garrison crossed the Bay to the north side. The allies were too exhausted to interfere. "The Times" of London gave the following account of the evacuation: "Covering his rear by the flames of the burning city and by tremendous explosions which spoke in tones of portentous warning to those who might have wished to cut off his retreat he [the Russian Commander-in-Chief] led his battalions in narrow files across a deep arm of the sea which ought to have been commanded by our guns and in the face of a most powerful fleet. He actually paraded them in our sight as they crossed and carried off all his most useful stores and munitions of war. He left us few trophies and many bitter memories." [24]

After the fall of Sebastopol the question of what to do next was of paramount importance for the allies. The Russian army took up a position on the north side and Gorchakov revealed no inclination to cease fighting. Czar Alexander II announced to his army that he would not voluntarily abandon the Crimea, and he visited the theater of war, speaking of carrying on the struggle.

The Russians were partly encouraged in this stand by the failure of the Second Baltic campaign and the success of their operations in Transcaucasia. With the opening of navigation on the Baltic a new Anglo-French armada once more made its appearance under the respective commands of Admirals Dundas and Penaud. This fleet was composed of 109 vessels and was well equipped with mortar boats and gun boats which Sir Charles Napier had vainly demanded the preceding year. In August the armada appeared before Cronstadt, exchanged fire with the fortress, but had to withdraw without achieving anything. After this, Dundas left a few vessels to observe Cronstadt and the Anglo-French fleet proceeded to Sweaborg. Afger placing mortar batteries on the outlying islands, the allies attacked Sweaborg, but after two days' fighting they were beaten off and sailed away baffled.

In Transcaucasia the tide of war definitely turned in favor of the Russians in June, 1855; their operations were crowned on the following November 25, by a brilliant military feat--the capture of the main Turkish fortress of Kars which had been stubbornly defended by the British Colonel Fenwick Williams.

The operations in the Crimea were however gradually coming to a standstill. Napoleon was still insisting that Pelissier

---

[24] Rambaud, A., History of Russia. New York 1882. Vol. III, p. 197.

should advance, making use of the fine October weather, and threaten Russian communications by his right flank moving toward Simpheropol. But Pelissier found the Russian positions to be too strong and reported that the Russians had "made them more difficult to force than the ramparts of Sebastopol."[25] Hence he merely contented himself with taking up a line along the Chernaya. At the same time a French corps was sent to Eupatoria to co-operate with the Turks in defending the city from a Russian attack. A diversion was also made against Kinburn on the Dnieper estuary and a combined Anglo-French division, composed of British and French brigades under Bazaine attacked this fortified city from the sea and, in co-operation with the navy, succeeded in capturing it.

In the meantime and subsequently the British were engaged in pursuing their real objective of the war, the destruction of Russia's naval power in the Black Sea. Hence they systematically blew up all the forts and the docks of Sebastopol. Both allied commands decided that before winter the Russians had to be driven out of the Crimea. Lord Clarendon wrote on October 31 to the Commander-in-Chief that "the military honour and the political interests of France and England require this triumph and this guarantee; we must have it at any price."[26] The insistency of the British on this point was to be explained by the fact that their forces had been gradually reinforced to a total at this time of 81,000 men (51,000 British, 20,000 Turks of the Turkish Legion and 10,000 Germans of the German Legion, both maintained by the British). But notwithstanding these orders no further military operations took place after the capture of Kinburn. Thus the two armies remained facing each other along the Chernaya, for virtually five months, until the conclusion of peace.

It is now necessary to estimate the cost of this war. Marshall Vaillant, Minister of War, in his report to the French Emperor, indicates that France sent 309,268 men to Sebastopol, of which 70,000 died or were missing. The Russian losses have been variously estimated between 110,000 and 153,000. Professor Sorokin in his study of Wars [27] places the figure at 128,000. The British losses have been put between 22,000 and 27,000 but Professor Sorokin places them as low as 18,000.[28] The Sardinians lost, including those who died from cholera,

---

[25] Hamley, op. cit., p. 290.
[26] Hamley, op. cit., p. 293.
[27] Sorokin, P., Social and Cultural Dynamics. New York 1937, Vol. III, p. 558.
[28] Sorokin, op. cit., Vol. III, p. 563.

2,200 and the Turkish losses have been estimated at around 35,000. The siege of Sebastopol was by far the most important siege of the Nineteenth Century as it lasted 334 days as compared to 72 for the siege of Metz, 142 days for the siege of Paris and 100 days for the siege of Plevna; the assailants used 827 guns and the defenders 800. By September, 1855, the allied forces in the Crimea had risen to 126,000 French, 47,000 British, 40,000 Turks and 16,000 Sardinians, a total of 229,000 not counting the foreign legions. [29]

---

[29]Rousset, Camille, Histoire de la Guerre de Crimée. Paris 1887. Vol. II, p. 412.

CHAPTER VIII

CONGRESS OF PARIS

I

In the Crimean War Russia, for the first time since 1812, single-handed faced a coalition of European powers. Once more it became a test of the military strength of Russia as against the military strength of the major armies of Europe. Though Russia was defeated and exhausted by the struggle, exhaustion had set in amongst the allies as well and they were unable to impose a sufficiently clear-cut decision to bring on a cessation of hostilities through military action alone; it was brought about largely through diplomatic pressure in the secret negotiations which were carried on in Vienna throughout the greater part of the war. Hence the importance of the role played by Austria. It was indeed Austria, who did not venture to go openly into the military struggle and yet kept on unheroically "blowing loud her paper trumpet", who was responsible for bringing Russia to terms. It will be recalled that at the beginning of the hostilities Nicholas I still sincerely believed that Austria was siding with Russia, when actually Buol was gradually and secretly veering toward the allies. It was when France and England came openly into the war that both Emperor Francis Joseph and Buol felt strong enough to lay their cards on the table and become, under guise of mediation, openly hostile to Russia.

Indeed, desiring to clarify his position, Nicholas in January, 1854, sent special ambassadors, Baron Budberg to Berlin and Count Orlov to Vienna with personal letters to Frederick William IV and Francis Joseph. Budberg brought back from Prussia the assurance of strict neutrality; but Orlov's mission demanding unconditional neutrality was rejected. Orlov had been instructed to obtain a treaty whereby Austria would pledge herself to complete neutrality not only in the war between Russia and Turkey but in the eventuality of a war between Russia and the Western Powers as well. Even more important, just as Orlov had left for Vienna, Buol forwarded a note to Russia suggesting a conference to put an end to the war. The conference was to be preceded by the immediate evacuation of the Danubian Principalities by Russia, but not the evacuation of the Black Sea by the allied fleets. These conditions were turned down by Orlov who declared that the evacuation of the Principalities was to be the consequence and not the preliminary condition of the negotiation. Whereupon on February 2, Buol having assembled the Ministers of France, England and Prussia, officially declared the mediation of the four powers to be at an end. Thus Orlov not only returned to Russia with empty hands, but with the tangible evidence of Austria leaguing herself with the Western Powers.

Austria was nevertheless to maintain the role of mediator throughout the war, but by the inexorable logic of the course she had set herself, she was drifting towards active hostility with Russia. It suffices for our purpose merely to indicate the main steps in this evolution. On June 3, 1854, Austria addressed a summons to Russia demanding the evacuation of Moldavia and Wallachia and refusing permission for the Russian Army to cross the Danube. On August 8, Austria signed a note drawn up in Vienna by the Western Powers known as the Note of Four Points. By this note England, France and Austria formulated the following demands as basis for the negotiations to end the war: 1) replacement of the protectorate of Russia in the Danubian provinces by a collective guarantee of the powers, 2) freedom of navigation on the Danube, 3) the revision of the Treaty of 1841, 4) renunciation by Russia of any protection over the Orthodox Christians in Turkey. Meanwhile military measures had been taken by Austria; in the winter of 1853 three army corps were mobilized in southern Hungary and on May 15, a second army of four corps had been ordered to assemble in Galicia while a general call of conscripts over the whole Empire was issued. A huge forced loan had to be raised to meet these military expenditures and the Austrian currency fell. Finally in October, 1854, Francis Joseph issued the order of general mobilization and 450,000 men menacingly lined the Russian frontier forcing a diversion from Crimea of at least half the Russian Army.

But Francis Joseph was not prepared to fight Russia and on November 18, Napoleon received a letter from him speaking once more of his neutrality. Exasperated, Napoleon, who had been expecting Austrian entry into the war for a long while, menaced Austria with a rupture of diplomatic relations. The result was the alliance concluded on December 2, with France and England by which Austria pledged to enter the war on the side of the allies if peace was not concluded within the year, on the basis of the acceptance by Russia of the four points stipulated on August 8. In such an eventuality "the sovereigns of France, Austria and Great Britain will deliberate without delay on the efficacious means of achieving the purpose of their alliance."[1] Thus the cycle had been completed and Austria had become an open foe of Russia. Should hostilities break out between Austria and Russia the treaty of alliance was to guarantee Austria the military support of both England and France. Having gone thus far, Austria refused to proceed further and preferred to camouflage her position by re-assuming the role of mediator. Russia, having agreed to discuss peace on the basis of the four points, a second series of diplomatic conferences was started under Buol's auspices in Vienna on March 15, 1855, and lasted two and a half months. Prince A. M. Gorchakov and V. P. Titov were appointed Russian delegates to these negotiations with instructions from Nesselrode to adhere strictly to the letter of the four points. "Russia will feel it deeply and the whole of Europe will have to acknowledge that the hope to restore peace would remain fruitless if the conditions of the agreement to be concluded go beyond the limits indicated sine qua non to our August sovereign by the realization of the dignity of his crown"[2] wrote Nesselrode in his circular of March 10, 1855.

But the third point proved to be the stumbling block of the negotiations: the allies interpreted it as a clause demilitarizing the Black Sea and consequently implying the obligation for Russia not to maintain any naval forces on that sea. Gorchakov observed "a great power only consents to the limitation of its forces after a great reverse and we have not come to that."[3] The Czar on his side in a letter to Prince Paskevich observed that Russia had gone to the limit of her concessions for the sake of peace and that yielding any further would not only be incompatible with her dignity but would encourage Austria to become more and more immoderate in her demands.[4] Gorchakov accordingly proposed either to open the Black Sea to the fleets of all nations or to close it to all. Both France and England refused to accept Gorchakov's counter-proposal and thereupon the conference broke up. However, after the fall of Sebastopol in October, 1855, Napoleon himself opened feelers for peace, partly because of the refusal of England to countenance

---

[1] Matter, P., Bismarck et son Temps. Paris 1905-1908. Vol. I, p. 392.

[2] Tatischev, S. S., Imperator Aleksandr II Ego Zhizn i Tsarstvovanie. St. Petersburg, 1903, Vol. I, p. 49.

[3] Mowat, R. B., History of European Diplomacy 1815-1914 1914. London 1927, p. 108.

[4] Alexander II to Paskevich, May 20, 1855. Tatishchev, op. cit., Vol. I, p. 149, 150.

his scheme of the re-creation of Poland and partly because his military ambitions having been satisfied, he was unwilling to jeopardize them by the indefinite prolongation of the war. A discreet hint came from Paris through the Courts of Prussia and of the minor German States that France would welcome a move for peace if Russia made the first step. Gorchakov observed that Russian diplomacy "would be mute but not deaf."

Secret negotiations were initiated between Napoleon's half brother, the Duke of Morny and Gorchakov, but by order of Nesselrode these were interrupted so as not to intefere with parallel negotiations carried on more discreetly in Paris between the French Minister of Foreign Affairs, Count Walewski, and the Saxon Minister, Seebach, who was Nesselrode's brother-in-law. In October, 1855, Beust, at that time Prime Minister of Saxony, proceeded to Paris to visit the Exposition. On his way he had an interview with Brunnow, who told him Russia was prepared to make peace provided the conditions offered by the allies did not involve any cession of territory or payment of any indemnity. These words were carried by Beust to Napoleon who insisted that Russia should agree to the neutralization of the Black Sea. Nesselrode thereupon observed that a nation of 80 million cannot be forbidden to maintain warships in her own waters but empowered Seebach to conduct negotiations with Walewski. The latter suggested, as a solution acceptable to both France and England, that Russia and Turkey should negotiate between themselves a mutual limitation of naval forces on the Black Sea. Nesselrode, through Seebach, offered as counter-proposals the closing of the Straits to all warships and that no warships of any powers should be permitted in the Black Sea except for a small number to be agreed upon by direct negotiation between Russia and Turkey. Once more this issue proved the stumbling block, and Walewski, refusing to proceed further, declared that Austria should now be consulted again in the matter. Thus once again, the issue was brought squarely back to Buol, who had been kept secretly informed of the negotiations by Walewski. It was Austria's chance for a spectacular coup and she did not miss it. In December the Austrian Ambassador in St. Petersburg, Count Esterhazy, delivered to Nesselrode an ultimatum supported by a personal letter of Francis Joseph to the Czar. The ultimatum demanded the acceptance of the four points but very much extended in scope. A strip of Bessarabia along the Danube was to be ceded by Russia to Moldavia under the extended interpretation of the first point, whereas the third point was to involve not only the neutralization of the Black Sea but the dismantling of arsenals and coastal defences as well. In addition the Powers reserved the right to present further demands in the interest of Europe. The refusal by Russia to adhere to these demands as stated in the Austrian note would lead to serious consequences. Napoleon in turn declared these conditions to be the minimum demands of the allies, and the King of Prussia, carefully avoiding consideration of the merits of the case, wrote to the Czar urging him to accept them in the name of humanity and peace. The Czar convoked a council of the highest dignitaries of the Empire including Grand Duke Constantine, Nesselrode, Counts Orlov, Vorontsov and Kisselev and Baron Meyendorf, the former Ambassador to Vienna. All except one urged acceptance of the ultimatum and Nesselrode read a note he had prepared which was to be delivered to Vienna accepting the terms "conditionally" but rejecting the cession of Bessarabia and the vague fifth point. Gorchakov presented the note to Buol who refused to allow any modifications and gave Russia six days for the unconditional acceptance of Austria's demands, declaring that otherwise the Austrian Ambassador would leave St. Petersburg. He yielded, however, on two minor points: the issue of the cession of Bessarabia would be left to be debated at the coming peace conference and point five would not involve any further territorial demands or payment of any indemnity.

A second meeting of the council was called by the Czar at the Winter Palace on January 15, 1856, and in view of the unmistakable menace of war on the part of Austria the council accepted the ultimatum unconditionally as amended, and two weeks later the representatives of the warring powers assembled in Vienna and signed a protocol, whereby a peace conference was to meet within three weeks in Paris. Thus it had been Austria's action which brought on the surrender of Russia and Buol had scored a signal diplomatic victory. But had the Austrian Government looked further ahead, it would have realized that this unheroic victory was to be repaid by the unremitting bitterness and hatred of Russia. Already Czar Nicholas had given to his valet the bust of Francis Joseph which he had in his study; and upon receiving Count Esterhazy he asked caustically who had been the two stupidest Kings of Poland, adding in reply to his own question: "the first was John Sobieski who liberated Vienna from the siege laid by the Turks, the second am I. For both of us...saved the House of Hapsburg." [5]

Four years later Bismarck wrote from St. Petersburg to his wife (April 4, 1859): "one has no idea how the Austrians are regarded here. No mangy dog would accept a single piece

---

[5] Redlich, J., Emperor Francis Joseph of Austria, a biography. New York, 1929, p. 159.

of meat from them... The hatred of the Austrians is boundless and exceeds all my expectations."[6] What Austria had sown in the Crimean War she was to reap on the bloody battlefields of Galicia in 1914.

II

The attitude taken by Prussia in the conflict appeared to Russian eyes in striking contrast to the hostility shown by Austria. Since the Revolution of 1848 there was in Prussia the same splitting of responsible political circles into two camps-- pro-Russian and anti-Russian, but the latter trend was much less pronounced than in Austria. Moreover, the Court and the King remained faithful to their Russian alliance. For this there were several reasons. There were the sentimental memories and traditions already referred to which influenced the members of the older generation of statesmen, such as Gerlach; there was the family tie as a result of the marriage of Nicholas I to Princess Charlotte of Prussia, and there was also the political testament of Friedrich William III, which emphasized the necessity for the continued friendship with Russia in no uncertain terms: "...above all", he wrote for the guidance of his successor, "try to maintain good understanding between Prussia, Russia and Austria. Their union is the cornerstone of the great European alliance." There was also the tremendous prestige and fear of the Czar, who alone was not affected by the revolutionary turmoil of 1848 at a time when the Emperor of Austria and the Pope were forced to flee, the King of France dethroned and the King of Prussia forced to bow to the revolution. "He had given in a haughty and authoritative manner his opinion on the question of Schleswig-Holstein and Prussia had obeyed. During the crisis of Olmütz...he had convoked the contending parties to Warsaw and had dictated them their will; one of them, not submitting promptly enough, he had growled and Prussia had obeyed. Since then he had appeared in Berlin, superb, enigmatic, dominating, admired by some, hated by others, feared by all."[8] The Court camarilla was completely under the spell of the Czar, preaching a real cult of Nicholas as the saviour of Europe from revolution; Prince Charles of Prussia, two ministers and many influential generals including General von Gerlach demanded the active intervention of Prussia on the side of Russia in the Crimean War. Leading the anti-

---

[6] Matter, op. cit., Vol. I, p. 366.
[7] Matter, op. cit., Vol. I, p. 366.
[8] Matter, op. cit., Vol. I, p. 391.

Russian camp, as may have been expected, were the liberals--
those who had had any connection with the Frankfurt Parliament
or any other parliamentary movements looked to England for
support. A fairly important group of conservatives had similar
views; these were the bureaucrats and diplomats whose ideas
were expressed in the "Wochenblatt", amongst whom the most
influential were the Counts Goltz and Pourtales, and the Councillors Bethman-Hollweg and Mathis. This group had immense
and utopian ambitions. They wanted to partition Russia between
Prussia and Sweden, thereby making Prussia the mightiest state
in Europe. As for the King, he hesitated between these divergent tendencies, at times listening to Gerlach and preaching a
holy war with Russia against Turkey, at another time (December 1853) sending Count Pourtales to London to offer an alliance
to maintain an armed neutrality. All those who had resented
the anti-Prussian stand taken by Nicholas at Olmütz or were
pro-Austrian supported the King in this move, the most notable
amongst them being the head of the government, Manteuffel,
and the Minister of War, Bonin. But these conflicting and
somewhat hesitating opinions in reality counted less than the
titanic will of a man who at that time was still in the seemingly
relatively minor but strategically important position of Prussian
envoy at the Diet of Frankfurt--Otto von Bismarck-Schönhausen.
He had no hesitations and had thrown in the weight of his influence and personality on the side of Russia.

Bismarck's idea was that intervention on behalf of Russia
would be too dangerous, the more so that it might lead to a
Polish insurrection. But to take the side of Austria would be
for Prussia to play second fiddle to that country and strengthen
the latter's position in Germany. Hence he advocated a strict
neutrality benevolent to Russia. On January 8, 1854, Austria
made a move to win the co-operation of Prussia in her anti-
Russian policies by offering Prussia a treaty of neutrality, but
reserving liberty of action for protection of common interests.
Then came the offer to join the alliance with France and England. On April 9, Count Arnim, Prussian Ambassador to Vienna, signed with the representatives of Austria, France and
England a protocol in which Prussia acknowledged the principle
of the integrity of Turkey and the evacuation of the Danubian
Principalities by Russia, and consented not to enter into any
deliberations with Russia without previously consulting the allies. On April 20, 1854, an alliance was concluded between
Austria and Prussia including a military convention obligating
both powers to mobilize if their territories or those of any
other German states were attacked by any power. Thus officially, Prussia was seemingly drawn into the orbit of Austria

notwithstanding the vehement protests of Bismarck. Encouraged, Buol put pressure on Prussia and the German States of the Confederation to join Austria's alliance with the Western powers concluded on December 2, and demanding the mobilization of Prussia and the sundry German States. Bismarck had already been fulminating, "Austria terrorized us in 1850 with Russian bayonets and in 1854 with French bayonets to force us to submit to her will" in a letter to Gerlach on November 22.[9] But this time Prussia refused to join the alliance. As for the little German States, it was Bismarck who, in his capacity of Prussian envoy to Frankfurt, had to deal with them, and he put in the way of Austria every obstacle conceivable and delayed the matter as long as he could. Finally in February, the German States joined Prussia in their refusal to adhere to the alliance and to mobilize their armies on the ground that no danger of Russian aggression was menacing Germany. This was Bismarck's victory. Thus if Prussia had platonically acquiesced to Austrian policy, when it came to act against Russia, she refused.

The result was that the friendly feelings between Russia and Prussia were not impaired and were to develop into a virtual alliance which was to prove so beneficial to both sides.

III

The line up of European powers in the Crimean War would not be complete without the mention of Sardinia. This small and hitherto insignificant state, like Prussia, was being driven by the will, power and the genius of one man, Cavour, to assume in the struggle a role of ever increasing importance. Furthermore her geographical position, menacing Austria in her Italian possessions, had a great deal to do with the hesitancy shown by Buol in coming out openly against Russia until Sardinia herself had become an ally of the Western powers.

Contrary to the marked cordiality of the friendship between Russia and Naples, Russia's relations with Sardinia could not have been worse since the severing of diplomatic ties in 1848. To Nicholas, Sardinia was nothing more than a dangerous center of revolutionary agitation, and Russian diplomacy considered Sardinia too insignificant a factor to deserve much consideration, thereby making a bad mistake; for Cavour was to transform Sardinia into the powerful Kingdom of Italy, and in the delicate balance of power existing in Europe, Sardinia could become the straw which broke the camel's back. This

---

[9]Matter, op. cit., Vol. I, p. 391.

Sardinia achieved not so much through the military aid given to the allies against Russia in the Crimean War, which was negligible, but by forcing Austria out of Italy and thereby shifting Austria's center of gravity towards the Balkans. Already in 1844 Balbo in his work "Speranze d'Italia" had predicted the possibility of such a shift as the result of a war in the Near East, a contingency beneficial to the Italian cause, but very dangerous for Russia. Also Russian diplomacy had forgotten that during Catherine's struggle with Turkey, Sardinia had supported Turkey against Russia. Thus the snub administered in 1848 to the government of Turin by Russia was near-sighted, particularly if we consider the very active commercial relations which seemed not to have suffered from the breakdown of political relations. Indeed the number of Sardinian vessels which entered the Black Sea was exceeded only by British ships. These Sardinian vessels carried to Russia silks, textiles and jewelry and exported from Russia grain and livestock. Large numbers of Italian merchants had settled in the Black Sea ports, investing their money there in real estate. The center of this trade in Sardinia was Genoa, which thereby had renewed the lost tradition of the Middle Ages and the splendour of Azov and Kaffa.

Hence the excitement which was caused by the approach of the Crimean War in Turin may be understood. At Turin it was, so far, taken for granted that Austria would become Russia's ally, hence though full of hopes for such an eventuality, Cavour remained strictly noncommital during the first months of the hostilities, waiting to see clearly which way the wind was blowing. The only active step he took was to authorize Captain Govone and a few other officers to enroll in the Turkish Army after having been given a leave of absence from the Sardinian Army.

When it became clear that Austria would not stand by Russia but on the contrary was veering towards the allies, nowhere was disappointment keener than in Turin. Owing to Cavour's endeavours the army was in good shape and finances in satisfactory condition. Was the great chance offered by the Crimean War for the advancement of the Italian cause to be lost? In January, 1854, Cavour's mind was made up: if he could not fight Austria he would fight Russia, gambling on the success of the allies, and the possibility of receiving from them some "tip" for Sardinia in the forthcoming peace conference in return for the military aid offered. But Cavour met with the staunch and unanimous opposition of his whole cabinet, of the Parliament and the greater part of public opinion. Particularly violent in opposing entry into this war were Ratazzi, Minister of Interior and powerful left wing leader, and General La Marmora, Minister of War, who did not want to see the army split. Outside the cabinet, the Army wanted a war with Austria, not with Russia; the conservatives held the so-called Little Piedmont view and were only concerned with the cost of the war to their country and were opposed to schemes of building up Italy, whereas the Republicans called this war an alliance with Sardinia's arch enemy, Austria. Brofferio, the extreme radical leader, denounced it as "economically reckless, militarily a folly, politically a crime"; he also declared he found no difference between the autocracy of St. Petersburg and the despotism of Paris.[10] But Cavour held out.

Meanwhile the war which was to be over in six weeks, according to the fatuous remark of Palmerston, was becoming a very grave matter for the allies and promising to become long and hard. Discouragement had set in in Paris, where it was realized that a lost war would mean the downfall of Napoleon III. M. Thouvenel, the Director of Political Affairs in the Foreign Ministry, wrote to Benedetti on November 7, 1854: "The slow progress, unfortunately too easily explained, of the siege of Sebastopol, has caused a panic on the Stock Exchange and all kind of sinister rumours are being spread about the city."[11] On the English side, there was growing "a conviction that numbers were urgently required if the war was to succeed and also the desire to lessen the large numerical superiority of the French." Lastly Austria, whose friendship the allies were courting so assiduously, was getting alarmed about the military preparations of Sardinia and through the intermediary of the Tuscan Government approached M. Scarlett, the British Chargé d'Affaires in Florence, on April 18, 1854, demanding the right to occupy with her troops the important fortress of Alessandria flanking Piedmont. M. Landucci, Minister of Interior of Tuscany and Austrian spokesman, added significantly that Austria knew that Sardinia's intention was to raise Italy against her should Austria get involved in the war. How could she declare herself openly against Russia, with an insurrection directed by King Victor Emmanuel menacing her rear? The sending of Sardinian contingents to Crimea would allay Austrian fears. For these reasons the allies brought pressure upon Cavour to have Sardinia join the allies, Sir James Hudson, British Minister in Turin, telling Cavour that Austrian fears would be at rest if a portion of the Sardinian Army were sent to Crimea.

---

[10] Martinengo-Cesaresco, Cavour, Foreign Statesmen Series, p. 85.
[11] Matter, op. cit., Vol. II, p. 297.

The pressure upon Cavour was exerted both by France and Great Britain. On February 22, 1854, the French official "Moniteur Universel" published an ominous warning to Cavour that France could not permit "with the colours of France and Austria united in the East, that attempts should be made to divide them along the Alps..." which statement brought from Cavour a demand for explanations. In June Cavour replied in vague terms to the notification of the alliance concluded between France and England against Russia, but the Duc de Guiche reported at the same time that the allies would probably be in a position to count upon 15,000 Sardinian troops if desired; however when on October 22, France confidentially asked Piedmont to lend her a few war vessels for service in the Black Sea, the Sardinian Government politely refused. The French having failed, England took up the question and on December 13, Sir James Hudson in Turin received an urgent message from London instructing him to approach the Sardinian Government with a view to obtaining a corps of Sardinian troops to be placed under Lord Raglan in the British forces in return for a loan granted to Piedmont of 20,000,000 pounds. After difficult negotiations, Cavour insisted that the Sardinian Army should not be incorporated into the British forces but remain independent, very much as in the case of the American Expeditionary Force during the 1st World War. The issue was finally settled according to Cavour's wish on January 10, 1855, when a military convention was duly signed with the allied powers. Russia, exasperated by this unexpected development which she termed an extraordinarily unwarranted attack, took the initial step of declaring war on Sardinia in February. Now Cavour had another worry, that his army would be kept in reserve in Constantinople and not see action, this being the wish of Napoleon, but he finally got the English to transport the 15,000 Sardinians to the Crimea. The force even then was held back and was badly decimated by cholera, which took a death toll of 65 cases a day with a total of 1,200. Quarrels broke out between the Sardinian and the allied commands and Cavour wrote bitterly of Sardinian troops perishing of disease in the trenches while the allies advanced at the rate of a yard a month.[12] Finally however, they were brought into action and came out very creditably as will be remembered in the relatively minor engagement on the Chernaya river on August 16, when a Russian attack against the Sardinian sector was beaten back by the two Sardinian divisions. The total Sardinian losses during the engagement were 25 killed and 200 wounded. The

---
[12] Martinengo-Cesaresco, op. cit., p. 87.

Sardinians did not see any further action. When the news of the battle of Chernaya reached Turin it was hailed as a great triumph and the people ran wild with an enthusiasm not quite commensurate with the military significance of the action, but, as Cavour put it, it wiped out the memory of the defeat of Novara in 1849 and above all opened the way for a visit to France by the King of Sardinia, thereby starting a friendship with Napoleon which was to have such momentous consequences in paving the way for the ultimate expulsion of Austria from Italy.

IV

The Congress of Paris opened in the building of the Ministry of Foreign Affairs in Paris on February 25th, 1856, with Count Walewski [13] and the Baron de Bourqueney representing France, Lord Clarendon and Lord Cowley, England, Count Buol and Baron Hübner, Austria, the Grand Vizir Aali Pasha and Djemil Bey, Turkey, and Count Cavour and the Marquis of Villamarina, Sardinia. Russia appointed Count Orlov [14] and Baron Brunnow as her delegates and it will be noticed that the Russian delegation alone was not headed by the Foreign Minister or the head of the government as was the case with the other delegations. As may have been expected Count Walewski was elected to preside at the Congress and Mr. Benedetti, the future French Ambassador to Prussia was attached to him as general secretary. It was decided at the very outset that the protocol signed in Vienna in February after the acceptance by Russia of the terms of the Austrian ultimatum should be considered as the preliminary of peace on the basis of which an armistice should be concluded up to March 31; and consequently the Commanders-in-Chief of the belligerent armies in Crimea were notified by telegraph to cease hostilities. This having been achieved, the Congress settled down to meeting rather leisurely in the afternoon of every alternate day. It did not meet at all between March 14 and 18 owing to celebrations on the occasion of the birth of the Prince Imperial to Napoleon, the delegates going on the 16th to present their felicitations to the Emperor. This leisurely pace was due in the main to the fact that all the major issues had been decided upon in Vienna and the Congress had merely to work out the details. Some of these were however

---

[13] Appointed Minister of Foreign Affairs in the place of Drouyn de Lhuys.

[14] The same who negotiated the surrender of Paris in 1814.

sufficiently thorny to offer scope for tense diplomatic duels which revealed the future alignment of the powers.

Walewski proposed discussing first the point which had caused the main dissension at Vienna, namely the question of the neutralization of the Black Sea. Russia having agreed to this, there remained to be decided the fate of the great Russian naval bases and arsenals, particularly the one at Nikolaev-on-the-Bug, which the Russians argued was not on the coast of the Black Sea and hence not subject to demilitarization. The British, who had so thoroughly destroyed the docks at Sebastopol, were determined to see the same thing done at Nikolaev. Lord Clarendon, though admitting that the Russian case was geographically correct, declared that it nevertheless was in contradiction to the principles of the agreement of Vienna in view of the size and importance of the arsenal. A sharp clash between the two delegations ensued which was only settled by a compromise proposal, that the wharves and arsenal would not be dismantled on condition that Count Orlov should give the word of honour of the Czar that Russia would not use them for any other purpose than the construction and equipment of light coastal vessels which Russia was permitted to keep in the Black Sea. Thus the first difficulty was surmounted, but it revealed a bitter hostility between the British and the Russians. Lord Clarendon, who had expressed in London his pleasure in negotiating with Brunnow, whom he had known so well for years, now found however that the experienced and subtle Russian diplomat was a hard headed defender of the interests of his country. Once Clarendon observed cattily to him at an evening party, "You were in England long enough to know what a special pleader is; well if all other trades should fail take that."[15] Clarendon was also hurt that on arriving in Paris he found the Russians already there and who had, as he put it, stolen a march on him. The striking appearance of the tall, handsome, elderly Orlov made him very popular with the Parisians and for reasons discussed later the Russian delegation was singled out by the French in a way which was displeasing to Clarendon. A more pertinent reason for the British attitude was that they had come to Paris prepared to impose harsh terms on Russia and found themselves not supported in this respect by the other delegations. "Palmerston", writes Greville, according to his ancient custom is doing all he could to extort

---

[15] The Greville Memoires. A Journal of the Reign of Queen Victoria from 1852-1860 by Charles C. F. Greville, Esq. London 1887, 3rd part, Vol. II, p. 24.

as much as possible from Russia", [16] and he outlines the British desiderata as mentioned to him by Lord Cowley as being the rasing of Nikolaev and the cutting off of Russia from the Black Sea along the Bug, the Circassian coast and the territories along the Caucasian coast which had been acquired by Russia under the Treaty of Adrianople; Russia was furthermore to recognize the independence of states to be formed there. Accordingly, as the conference progressed along lines very much more moderate, Greville is constantly referring in his diary to how low spirited and disappointed the British were. "I asked Cowley what were the points on which the Russians made most difficulty. He said on all except Bomarsund." [17] "Cowley seemed very low coming home. His dejection is extreme", he notes on March 6, [18] and on March 15, "Cowley is still bemoaning the insufficiency of the terms." [19] It is curious to notice Greville's own reaction to these extreme demands: "The war was founded in delusion and error and carried on by a factitious and ignorant enthusiasm and we richly deserve to reap nothing but mortification and disappointment in return for all the blood and treasure we have spent." [20] In his spite, Clarendon went as far as accusing Walewski of double dealing and of secretly informing the Russians of the issues on which their resistance would meet with success.

The next point under discussion revealed the still sharper hostility between Austria and Russia, turning to real hatred on the part of the Russians. It dealt with the problem of the navigation of the Danube which involved the more acute question of the "rectification of frontiers", in other words the cession of Bessarabia to Moldavia. Though the principle established was that there would be no cession of territory except for exchange of territories occupied by the belligerents, the Congress deemed that the retrocession of Kars would not be a sufficient quid pro quo for the evacuation by the allies of Sebastopol and the other occupied points in Crimea, hence Bessarabia was to be included in the territories to be ceded by Russia. It was Austria who was particularly anxious to achieve this deal for thereby Russia would cease to be a Danubian power and would lose the important fortified cities of Ismail and Kilia Nova on the delta of the Danube. Thus the discussion which lasted two days degenerated into an acrimonious duel of words between the Russian

---

[16] Greville Memoires, p. 19.
[17] Greville Memoires, p. 27.
[18] Greville Memoires, p. 30.
[19] Greville Memoires, p. 32.
[20] Greville Memoires, p. 34.

and Austrian delegations. Already previously Orlov, exasperated at the haughty and arrogant attitude assumed by the Austrian, said with acid sarcasm, "Count Buol talks as if Austria had taken Sebastopol." [21] The Russians made desperate efforts to save the portion of Bessarabia along the Danube and on March 8, Brunnow made the proposal to rase the fortifications of Ismail and Kilia and for Russia to cede the islands in the delta. But supported by the other delegations, the Austrians won their point and the new frontier was to run from the Black Sea to the line of Trajan's Moat, (an ancient Roman fortification running across Bessarabia and Moldavia) thence to Bolgrad, the River Yalpuk and the River Pruth, thus excluding Russia from the Danube. At the conclusion of the debate Orlov turned to his neighbour and said prophetically, "The delegate of Austria does not realize how many tears and how much blood this rectification of the frontier will cost his country." [22]

During this debate a question dear to the heart of Napoleon III was raised, that of unifying Moldavia and Wallachia and forming a new country--Roumania. This not only was in harmony with the Emperor's sponsorship of national movements all over Europe but would have had the advantage of creating in the Balkans a state which would cause trouble to both Austria and Russia. The question had already been discussed in Vienna and now met with the enthusastic support of England, equally interested in causing difficulties to Russia in the Balkans, and of Sardinia, anxious to set a precedent in the application of the principle of nationalities. Rather surprisingly the Russians also voted for this scheme, the decision upon which however, owing to the violent opposition of Austria and Turkey, was relegated to a later date. The Russians were anxious to win the good graces of Napoleon and rather overconfidently expected that the measure would not lessen their hold over the Danubian Principalities; but above all they were anxious to stir up trouble for Austria by encouraging the growth of Roumanian nationalism which would menace the tranquillity of the Roumanian populated provinces of the Hapsburg Empire, Bukovina and Transylvania. This desire to strike at Austria at any cost led the Russian delegation to repeat in a smaller way the manoeuvre of Talleyrand at the Congress of Vienna. Like Talleyrand, who saw his chance of embarrassing Russia and dividing the allies by sponsoring the cause of Saxony-Poland, so the Russians now saw their chance of embarrassing Austria and possibly setting their former

---

[21] Rousset, C., Histoire de la Guerre de Crimée. Paris 1887, Vol. II, p. 452.
[22] Rousset, op. cit., Vol. II, p. 452.

enemies at odds by sponsoring the Italian question. Hence
they cultivated the friendship of Cavour and strongly supported
the attempt of the Sardinian delegation to get a hearing at the
Congress over the question of Austria's mistreatment of the
Italians. Thus the unexpected by-product of these intricate
diplomatic moves was the growing cordiality between Russia
and Sardinia. When, after the recess of the Congress on March
18, the Prussian delegation composed of Baron Manteuffel and
Count Hatzfelt joined it, Russia gained further friendly support
at the Congress. The Prussians not having participated in the
war, had no voice in the earlier deliberations, but as signatories
of the Treaty of 1841 dealing with the Straits, which was coming
up for revision, they were to participate in the deliberations
concerning this issue. If we add to this the rapidly growing
cordiality between France and Russia which was being atten-
tively watched by the whole of Europe, we may say that the
Russian delegation, starting out isolated as representing the
enemy power, had in the second half of the Congress the friendly
support of three of the six remaining delegations to the Congress
Of these the Turkish delegation did not count, hence Austria
and England were becoming more and more isolated. The situation once more resembled the position of Russia and Prussia
after Talleyrand had succeeded in breaking up the alliance of
the four powers.

By March 15, the Congress had progressed to a point where
a committee could be formed to draft the final treaty. This
committee was composed of Bourqueney, Cowley, Brunnow,
Buol, Cavour and Aali Pasha. There remained however to be
debated the problem of Turkey and the Christian minorities in
the Ottoman Empire. The Russians wanted some definite clause
binding on Turkey which would not permit the Turks to molest
the Christians. But the Congress was more concerned with
eliminating Russian influence over Turkey than in securing the
safety of the Balkan Christians. Furthermore a Sultan's decree
had adroitly accorded, prior to these discussions, the free exercise of religious worship to the Christians--that this promise
would remain merely on paper the Congress hypocritically refused to believe. Hence after hot debates, the Turks insisting
on their sovereign rights, the innocuous compromise formula
suggested by Walewski was accepted. In the name of the sovereigns represented at the Congress it was declared that the
Sublime Porte was admitted to participate in the advantages of
public law and of the European concert. "Their Majesties
pledge themselves on their side to respect the independence and
the territorial integrity of the Ottoman Empire, guarantee
jointly the strict observation of this pledge and will consider,

in consequence any act of a nature to menace it, as a question of general interest. His Majesty the Sultan in his constant solicitude for the well being of his subjects, having granted a firman which by ameliorating their fate without distinction of religion and race consecrates his generous intentions toward the Christian populations of his Empire... and desirous of giving a new token of his feelings in this respect has resolved to communicate to the contracting powers the said firman spontaneously emanated from his sovereign will... It is well understood that under no circumstances can the right be granted to the said powers to intervene collectively or singly in the relations of His Majesty the Sultan with his subjects or in the internal administration of his Empire." [23] In these words lay the seeds of the war of 1877/78.

The remaining minor issues were settled without difficulty. The question of the neutralization of the Åland Islands caused no friction. The question of international maritime law concerning the blockade and the cargoes on belligerent ships had only an academic interest for Russia and, lastly, the Italian question which Cavour succeeded in bringing up at the very end of the conference had merely the nuisance value of annoying Austria. On March 30 and prior to the discussion of these last two issues, the Treaty of Paris was signed. As M. de Bourqueney said later to Beust, "When one reads the treaty of March 30 no sign is apparent to establish who is the victor and who was defeated." [24] Napoleon expressed his happiness that the treaty contained nothing to humiliate the Russians. He had been, throughout the conference, gracious with all the delegates but had particularly singled out the Russians with his attentions. What had been in his mind? Was he thinking of an alternate alliance with Russia, as the relations with Britain had visibly cooled during the conference? It is difficult to say, for the Emperor's mind was many tracked often harbouring contradictory schemes.

Whatever the reason was, one influence working powerfully in the direction of closer relations between France and Russia cannot be overlooked, namely that of his half-brother, the Duc de Morny. "Louis Napoleon will be the arbiter and the struggle will be between England and Russia to get possession of him", Greville wrote prophetically before the Congress opened. [25]

---

[23] Rousset, op. cit., Vol. II, p. 454, 455.
[24] de la Gorce, P., Histoire du Second Empire. Paris 1908, Vol. II, p. 162.
[25] Greville Memories, Vol. II, p. 17.

Morny did everything in his power to make the balance tip in favour of Russia. He who had made possible through his energetic action the success of the coup d'etat of December 1, 1851, and who was virtually controlling the all powerful financial circles of Paris, was regarded at the time as the main power behind the throne, a sort of alter ego of the Emperor. Some historians have contended that he was the real power during the reign, Louis Napoleon being merely his shadow. Thus his influence in swaying the Emperor one way or the other may have been the determining factor. Already in January, 1853, Nesselrode wrote to Kisselev in Paris, "In your very confidential letter you give me account of the assistance you found in the good spirit and wisdom of the Count de Morny", which letter was forwarded by the Russian Ambassador to Morny.[26] During the war itself Morny got in touch with Prince Gorchakov through the intermediary of a secret agent who was known as Baron E. and who travelled back and forth between Paris and Vienna. The mysterious Baron E. handed the Russian Ambassador a number of unsigned notes from Morny in which the latter gave the Russians some useful hints. Thus in December, 1855, Morny writes, "I think that after the events which have just occurred the two powers which would profit most by peace would be France first and Russia next. In the war England has not been brilliant and Germany showed herself weak and irresolute. These weaknesses will appear more strongly at the time of peace...and there will remain only between France and Russia a sentiment of mutual esteem based on the remembrance of a formidable attack and a heroic defence..." and again in January 1856, "Today I will counsel still more strongly that Russia accept loyally the proposals (of peace) made to her...I hope that Prince Gorchakoff will acknowledge that I am a loyal and benevolent enemy and that he will continue whatever may happen, to communicate with me in a friendly manner."[27] These extracts speak for themselves as to Morny's views on relations with Russia, and during the Congress of Paris he continued his self-imposed task of creating friendship between the two former enemies, always working with an invisible but very effective hand. That Napoleon responded to his half-brother may be seen not only by his cordiality toward the Russians, but by the fact that when the coronation of Czar Alexander took place a few months after the

---

[26] Une ambassade en Russie, 1856. Extrait des Memoires du Duc de Morny. Paris 1892, p. 1-6.
[27] Morny, op. cit., p. 54-56.

Congress of Paris, Morny was sent as an ambassador extraordinary to the Court of Russia by Emperor Napoleon; this mission of good will being Morny's only entry into official diplomacy. Morny's task was to re-establish official good relations after the war and to settle such technical issues as remained outstanding after the signing of the Treaty of Paris. Before relating the details of this most important mission it is necessary to analyse the treaty first to see how it affected Russia.

After a preamble determining the exact measure of the participation of each power in the re-establishment of peace, the treaty stipulated the basic principle that the belligerent powers were to retrocede to each other all occupied territories (Art. 2-4). This clause somewhat euphemistically covered the cession of Bessarabia by Russia as we have seen, but it maintained a fiction which helped to "save Russia's face". With regard to the new international position of Turkey, Walewski's wording was incorporated into the treaty (Art. 7-9). Article 8 stipulated that should a quarrel arise between one of the signatory powers and Turkey, a recourse to mediation by the other signatories should precede any resort to hostilities. Thus the unilateral action of Russia over Turkey which had covered the period from the Treaty of Adrianople to the Crimean War was replaced by the joint action of the European concert. This applies as well to the fate of the Balkan Christians.

Articles 10-14 stipulate the neutralization of the Black Sea, no naval and no military establishments to remain in existence on or around the coast of that sea, but Turkey and Russia were authorized to maintain a small and equal number of light vessels for coast-guard service. Once more, to avoid hurting Russian feelings, euphemistically the neutralization of the Black Sea was to affect equally all countries having a coast line on that sea, but obviously the measure was directed at Russia alone, and this was the one clause that hurt Russia particularly, both in her pride and in her security. She was to do everything in her power to get rid of it. The succeeding articles dealt with the problem of navigation on the Danube. The principles of the Acts of Vienna of 1815 were to be applied to that river and a special international commission set up to handle the problems concerning the navigation of the delta and estuary of the Danube (Art. 15-19). Bessarabia was to be ceded to Moldavia and the Danubian Principalities remained under the suzerainty of the Porte, though from now on they were placed under the collective guarantee of the Powers. Their ancient rights were confirmed and no single power (i.e. Russia) had the right to interfere in their internal affairs. A special commission set up by the Congress was to proceed to investigate on the spot the desires of the Roumanian people as expressed through their local Divans and report to the Powers. Meanwhile the Porte was to issue a Hatti Sherif collectively guaranteed by the Powers, in which document the decisions of the Powers would be endorsed by Turkey. A national army was to be created for the Principalities and Turkey was to desist from sending troops into their territories (Art. 20-27). Though Russia was not specifically mentioned, these clauses marked the end of Russian influence over the Principalities which in a veiled way were promised both union and independence. As for Serbia (Art. 28-29) her rights were reconfirmed, but the Turkish garrison was maintained in Belgrade and once more Turkey could not send armed forces into that Principality without the assent of the Powers. Separate conventions dealt with the neutralization of the Åland Island, and with the renewing of the Treaty of 1841; a convention between Russia and Turkey reserved the right to both powers to maintain on the Black Sea six steamships of 800 tons each and four vessels of 200 tons for coast-guard service.

Summing up the results of the war and of the Congress the French historian Debidour in his notable diplomatic history of Europe says: "Russia appeared to be defeated; but she had gloriously resisted her enemies. She did not come out of the war humiliated and she remained nearly intact within her borders. After a short period of recuperation she was to reassume her forward march and her exclusion from the Black Sea was only a temporary difficulty. The friendship of Prussia was to give her one day an easy revenge... The real vanquished was not the Cabinet of St. Petersburg but the Cabinet of Vienna which thought it was very clever in bluffing everyone but had entirely alienated the whole of Europe."[28] There was much truth in these words as subsequent events were to prove. Meanwhile Russia was still regarded with fear and suspicion to some extent for two weeks after the signing of the Treaty of Paris, England, Austria and France signed on April 15, a convention between themselves obviously directed against Russia. Article 1 of this convention stipulated that the three powers guaranteed the independence of the Ottoman Empire and that any infraction of the clauses of the Treaty of Paris would be considered as a casus belli (Art. 2). The signatory powers would then consult

---

[28] Debidour, A., Histoire Diplomatique de l'Europe Depuis l'Ouverture du Congrés de Vienne jusqu'à la Cloture du Congrés de Berlin. Paris 1891. Vol. II, p. 157, 158.

with Turkey as to the measures to be taken and would use all their military and naval forces. Whether as a warning or as a sign of the new pro-Russian trends of French policy the contents of this secret convention were confidentially revealed by Walewski to Count Orlov two weeks later.

There remained a few minor technical issues outstanding from the Treaty of Paris to be settled and these were taken up by the Duc de Morny on his mission to Russia which has already been mentioned. Morny arrived at Peterhof, where the Russian Court was, on August 5, 1856. Writing to Walewski he says, "Prince Gorchakoff proclaims openly his tastes and aversions. He declares he was always favourable to the establishment of good relations between France and Russia and he professes a great admiration and a personal inclination for the Emperor of the French."[29] In a further letter he says that the Czar had expressed his sincere desire for good relations with France and then, to impress Napoleon in this sense, Morny wrote a personal letter to his half-brother from Moscow dated September 15 giving impressions on Russia and particularly on the army: "The army is fine, the cavalry superb... If its basis is good it will be formidable for it is fanatical, but individual initiative is lacking. The officers are well brought up, polite, speaking French, German, riding well on horseback."[30] As for the people: "The people in the street, composed only of peasants who have become town folk are gentle and peace loving. There is scarcely any police at all the festivities. The people are to be found right in the Emperor's entrance hall without a cry, a quarrel or a murmur. The Emperor goes out alone morning and evening on foot, on horseback or in a drosky in the middle of the crowd-after that compare the governments and the peoples."[31] He urges Napoleon to make small sacrifices to Russia for the Czar is willing to maintain the present situation and to be "Very well with France, well with England, very bad with Austria."[32]

Morny followed these suggestions up by negotiating a treaty of commerce and navigation with Russia and ironing out the small difficulties remaining from the Congress of Paris. Amongst these was the question of Serpent Island off the

---

[29]Morny, op. cit., p. 66.
[30]Morny, op. cit., p. 91, 92.
[31]Morny, op. cit., p. 93.
[32]Morny, op. cit., p. 96.

Danube estuary in the Black Sea where Russia had maintained a garrison of 1 officer and 7 soldiers. Since this island had not been mentioned in the Treaty of Paris, the Turks occupied the island and the British posted a warship in order not to allow further Russian reinforcements to land. The question dragged on until Morny succeeded in persuading the Russians to cede the island to Turkey. The second issue was concerning the new frontier of Bessarabia which, according to the treaty, was to pass south of Bolgrad, but the commission sent to delineate the border discovered there were two cities of this name. Russia claimed that the Bolgrad in question was the one located on the Lake Yalpuk. England and Austria refused to grant this claim on the ground that the lake connected by a channel with the Danube and that Russia could maintain a flotilla on the lake. After threatening serious complications for a while, the issue was settled with a compromise offered by France whereby Russia gave up Bolgrad but kept the Yalpuk. Indeed, Morny informed Walewski that the Czar had authorized that both the question of Serpent Island and that of Bolgrad should be placed in the hands of Napoleon III for an equitable settlement, and in a conference which met in January the arrangements proposed by France were accepted and ratified. Morny returned to France in 1858 well pleased with the result of his mission. From Paris he kept up a friendly correspondence with Gorchakov. Having married a Russian lady, Princess Trubetskoy, he remained staunchly pro-Russian and when in 1863 the Polish issue brought a final rift between France and Russia, he wrote to Gorchakov deploring the anti-Russian tendencies of Napoleon and said that his life work had been destroyed.

But before we can turn to the post-war policies of Russia, one more issue was settled by the Congress of Paris, and has now to be discussed, that of the Åland Islands; the only important question outside the scope of the Balkan and Near Eastern affairs which was covered by the Treaty of Paris and therefore remained an issue, the development of which had nothing to do with the causes of the Crimean War.

V

Composed of 6,554 islands, the Åland archipelago lies in the very center of the Baltic, halfway between Finland and Sweden. These islands command the entrance to the Gulf of Finland on one side, therefore to St. Petersburg and Cronstadt, and on the other to the Gulf of Bothnia, therefore to the Finnish coastal cities and to the Swedish iron mines at Kiruna. The main island of the group, Fasta Åland, is 30 miles from the coast of Sweden and 45 miles from that of Finland, or 70 miles from Stockholm and 75 miles from Abo. Only one hundred of these islands are inhabited and the population of 28,056 according to the last census is 98 per cent Swedish.[33] The first Russian occupation of the Åland Islands dates from 1714, when Peter the Great held them for three years and established a naval base there. They reverted to Sweden by the Treaty of Nystadt in 1721, but were once more occupied by Russia in 1742, to be restored to Sweden the following year by the Treaty of Abo. During the War of 1808/09 their strategic position was so obvious that in April, 1808, they were occupied by minor Russian detachments proceeding over the ice. But the ice which remained solid on the Swedish side, had broken on the Finnish side in the channel of the Skiftet and the Russian forces found themselves cut off. On May 6 three vessels of the Swedish fleet managed to approach the islands while the Russian fleet was still in port, and the next day, supported by landing forces, the islanders took to arms and captured the Russian posts. On the island of Kumlinge a Russian detachment 600 strong under Colonel Vouich was surrounded and after holding out a week was taken prisoner. In March of the following year a Russian army was marched across the ice to the Åland Islands, on the way to Sweden, and the Swedish forces under General Debeln, garrisoning the islands, fell back to the Swedish mainland leaving their supplies, 30 cannon, a flotilla of vessels and 3,000 prisoners in the hands of the Russians. The armistice which led to the end of the hostilities was signed on the Islands on March 21. During the peace negotiations, which led to the signing of the Treaty of Fredericksham, the Russians demanded the Åland Islands as well as Finland up to the River Kalix. The Swedes fought this point bitterly, but Chancellor Rumiantsev replied that "should Russia content herself with Finland alone it would be like taking a trunk and throwing away the key," a statement which tersely and admirably describes the importance of the archipelago.[34] The Swedes then asked that Russia should not fortify the islands, which request Russia refused, but nothing was mentioned in the Treaty of

---

[33] Pedelford, N. Y. and Anderson, K. G., <u>The Åland Islands Question.</u> The American Journal of International Law, Vol. XXXIII, 1939, p. 465-487.

[34] Waultrin, R., <u>La Neutralité des Isles d'Ålands</u>, Revue Generale de Droit International Publique. Vol. XIV, 1907, p. 517-533.

Fredericksham about their neutralization. When Napoleon was informed by the Swedish Minister in Paris of the terms of the treaty he observed that Sweden had now lost her power and that Stockholm had become merely a border fortress. In 1811 he tried to induce Bernadotte to join him against Russia by promising the Åland Islands to Sweden but, fearing war Sweden took a different course. Pressed by Lowenhielm and his other Swedish advisors, Bernadotte rather timidly asked Alexander at the Conference of Abo in 1812 to return the islands, but without success as may have been expected.

At the death of Charles XIII in 1818, Bernadotte, or as he was known Charles-John, came to the throne as King Charles XIV. His policy was one of co-operation, both with England and with Russia, and the Åland question remained dormant for nearly two decades. It was suddenly revived in 1829 and 1830 by the decision of Czar Nicholas I to fortify the islands. Nicholas had envisioned the transforming of these islands into a Gibraltar of the Baltic. On the main island gigantic fortifications, which would house a garrison of 60,000 men, were to be erected at Kastellholm and Bomarsund. Actually the building of these forts proceeded so slowly that at the time of the Crimean War, a garrison of only some 2,000 men was stationed on the island. But Sweden and England were disturbed and Sweden protested in 1833 that Stockholm was menaced by these fortifications. The protest was emphasized the following year by a visit of a British squadron to the Baltic in the nature of a veiled demonstration. But as Nicholas was not impressed by these moves and proceeded with the Åland fortifications, Sweden began fortifying the coast near Stockholm and also began raising fortifications in the far north in Lapland where she was afraid that Russia, expanding along the Arctic coast of Finland, was aiming at gaining a footing in the Varanger Fiord. Thus this twin issue which Sweden viewed as a double menace made the Russo-Swedish relations strained but also resulted in an interesting move. On April 24, 1834, at the session of a secret commission of the Diet, Bernadotte drew a picture of the international situation of Sweden, hemmed in between two powerful rivals, Russia and England; and said that to maintain the strict and impartial neutrality which he had always advocated for Sweden, he had addressed an important communication both to Russia and to England, which had been favourably received by the two powers. In this declaration dated January 4, 1834, Charles XIV officially confirmed the definite renunciation of Finland by Sweden and, after thanking England for her generous protection, the

King, having thus conciliated both sides, suggested a treaty which would guarantee the perpetual neutrality of the Scandinavian states in the event of a conflict in Europe. But with the situation in the Near East envenoming the relations between England and Russia to the point of a possible war, England in particular lost her enthusiasm for a project which would eliminate Sweden as a base of operations against Russia, and the British press openly suggested the importance of the occupation of the Island of Gottland in the Baltic as a menace against Russia. Thus the scheme fell through. When in 1838 the Czar visited Stockholm, he was met once more with great cordiality by the now elderly King. With the death of Bernadotte in 1844 and the advent of his son Oscar to the throne, relations with Russia became once more strained, Nicholas disliking intensely the very aggressive Scandinavianism of the new King, who advocated the union of Scandinavian countries on a democratic basis.

With the Crimean War and hostilities spreading to the Baltic, the position of Sweden became very dangerous and Sweden withdrew into a cautious neutrality. The attempt made by the British and French to get Sweden on their side by promising the Åland Islands failed and, even after the capture and seizure of Bomarsund by the Anglo-French forces in the Baltic, Sweden refused to take them. The most the allies obtained from Sweden was the signing in 1855 of the so-called "November Tractate" whereby in return for a guarantee of Swedish territory by France and England, Sweden promised not to conclude any secret treaties with Russia. During the peace negotiations, Sweden suggested that the Åland Islands should either be given back to Sweden, or made a free state under joint Anglo-French-Swedish protection and demilitarized. At the Congress of Paris, Walewski asked that "Russia should not be in a position henceforth to rebuild or create any naval or military establishment on the Åland Islands." Count Orlov, the Russian plenipotentiary, declared that Russia would accept this clause if an agreement on the other issues had been reached and provided the Åland Question should be consigned to a separate convention to be concluded between England, France and Russia. This was done by the Convention of March 30, 1856, by which the Åland Islands were given back to Russia on condition that they should not be fortified. This solution was satisfactory to Sweden and nothing more was heard of the question until 1904 when Russia once more raised the issue.

CHAPTER IX

BISMARCK AND GORCHAKOV

I

The attitude adopted by the Russian Government after Russia's defeat in the Crimean War was to let bygones be bygones. This attitude was summarized in the statement made by Nesselrode's successor Prince Gorchakov,--"La Russie se receuille mais elle ne boude pas." There were several reasons for this attitude. Internally, with the advent of Czar Alexander II, the era of great reforms was opening and absorbing the energies of the Russian people. This made even more necessary a period of stabilization, peace and respite following the strain of the war. In external relations, following what becomes virtually a law in Russian history, after a defeat in the West, Russia turns her attention to Asia. She was eager not to be drawn into perilous situations in Europe so as to have her hands free to start the great expansions in Central Asia and along the Amur River, which were now being undertaken. However her "receuillement", her aloofness and self-effacement in Western Europe were of short duration for it was checked by two aggressive motivations in her dealings with the West: her desire to get even with treacherous Austria and an even more insistent desire to abrogate the humiliating and dangerous clause of the Treaty of Paris concerning the demilitarization of the Black Sea. These were to form the basis for her foreign policy in Europe for the next 15 years.

When, therefore, scarcely three years after the end of the Crimean War a new war menaced Europe, it offered too great a temptation for Russia to get even with her enemies for her not to come back actively into European politics. Indeed when at the New Year's reception in Paris Napoleon made the significant and ominous remark to the Austrian Ambassador, Baron Hubner: "I regret that our relations with your government are not so good as formerly", there was a flutter of anxiety in European chancelleries, though they did not yet know that in the preceding summer Napoleon and Cavour, in a secret meeting at Plombières, had decided upon a joint war against Austria to deprive her of her Italian possessions. It was not news for

Gorchakov for he had already been confidentially approached on the subject by Napoleon III. The Czar and the Emperor of the French had met at Stuttgart in September, 1857, with both Gorchakov and Count Walewski present, and there Napoleon had raised the question of Russia's attitude in the event of a war in Italy. Napoleon hoped that Russia, in such a contingency, would undertake to keep the various German states in check and thereby make safe for France her frontier on the Rhine. But Alexander II, though courteous, showed such reserve that the conversations never went beyond the realm of the academic. He carefully avoided any reference to Italy and took leave with merely the vague promise "to concert in future on all European questions."[1] This meeting nevertheless marked the first step in a budding Franco-Russian rapprochement and thereby produced a sensation in Europe. The next step was taken after Cavour's talks with Napoleon at Plombières. On his way home from Plombières Cavour stopped at Baden where he chanced to meet the Grand Duchess Helena of Russia and a Russian diplomat whom Cavour calls "Balan." After talks with these two Cavour wrote elatedly to La Marmora: "If one can rely on what was said to me by the Grand Duchess Helena and Balan we can depend on the armed support of Russia. The Grand Duchess said that 'if France supported us (the people of) Russia would compel the Government to do the same'....." As for Balan, Cavour says the latter told him, "If you have a Chasseur de Vincennes on one side of you, you can count on having a soldier of our Guard on the other."[2] Thus the loose and irresponsible talk of two highly placed Russians on a holiday started a trend of thought in Cavour's mind which ultimately resulted in September, 1858, a year after Stuttgart, in a letter, addressed by Cavour to Napoleon III, urging him to undertake further steps to come to an understanding with Russia and Prussia. Upon receipt of this letter on September 21, Napoleon, who was at Biarritz, sent Prince Napoleon the very same day to Warsaw on a confidential mission to the Czar. Prince Napoleon was to induce Russia to hold Germany in check if Prussia or any other German state showed a desire to go to the aid of Austria in the coming war. As a bait for Russia, Prince Napoleon was to suggest compensations for her in Austrian Galicia. On October 6, Prince Napoleon returned from his mission reporting that Russia was prepared to sign a

---

[1] Paléologue, G. M. Cavour. London 1927, p. 137, 138.
[2] Whyte, A. J., The Political Life and Letters of Cavour. 1848-1861. London 1930, p. 258.

military alliance with France and to declare war on the side of France, if France promised to hold England in check. Napoleon immediately sent Baron Roncière de Noury to St. Petersburg to complete these negotiations and Cavour got so excited that he began preparing a military conference for working out the technical questions. A disappointment, however, was awaiting Roncière who was soon to learn that there was a catch in Prince Napoleon's too optimistic diplomatic triumphs. Indeed, Roncière, upon his arrival, reported that the Czar had put the following conditions for the conclusion of the alliance: a two years delay for military preparations, the revision of the Treaty of Paris of 1856 and a guarantee that there be no disturbances in Poland--which was a hint to Napoleon to desist from his visionary dreams with regard to the unification of Poland. This put an end to the whole matter though it did not impair the growing cordiality between the two governments. England anxiously watched this tendency of Paris and St. Petersburg to work for a rapprochment, and Lord Derby's government, magnifying the issue, was as much concerned over a possible Franco-Russian alliance as over the Italian war menace. In accordance with Napoleon's method of having a secret and personal policy apart from his official policy, Walewski had been kept in ignorance of these proceedings, and when he learned about them he was decidedly hurt. Napoleon's dreamy optimism made him believe that Prince Napoleon's visit was tantamount to the conclusion of an alliance with Russia (just as later in 1870 he believed, without any real foundation of fact, that he would have the military cooperation of Austria in the Franco-Prussian war). Against this, Walewski held the practical view that at best one could expect a friendly neutrality on the part of Russia, and that Gorchakov had played a cat and mouse policy with the inexperienced Prince Napoleon. Russia had gained a signal advantage in raising the issue of the revision of the Treaty of Paris without giving any tangible guarantee to France concerning the Rhine.[3]

The negotiations with France thus came to an end without further developments and Gorchakov once more assumed an attitude of aloofness and reserve in regard to the rapidly aggravating European crisis. He was watching, with a somewhat Machiavellian and ill-concealed satisfaction, the development of a situation in which no Russian interests were involved but which was tending to embroil the former foes of Russia--England, France, Sardinia and Austria. All Russian diplomatic

---

[3] Paléologue, op. cit., p. 204.

agents abroad were ordered to maintain a discreet silence but to remain vigilant and watchful. Thoroughly alarmed, the British Government took the lead in organizing a movement amongst the great neutral powers to stop the approaching war. To this effect Sir John Crampton, British Minister in St. Petersburg, approached Gorchakov who replied with scarcely veiled bitterness that Russia could not weigh France and Austria with the same scale for with France her relations were cordial whereas with Austria they were not. As Russia had found herself duped in the past when giving disinterested counsel, she had no further advice to offer. But he added somewhat ominously: "We do not affirm we will remain foreign to the struggle", and Russia would reserve her liberty of action.[4] Thus rebuffed in St. Petersburg, British diplomacy turned to Berlin where it met with much better success and Prussia henceforth was to follow the lead of Britain in all matters pertaining to this crisis. For the next six weeks Russia remained silent; then by dramatically reversing his previous attitude, Gorchakov, on March 18, suddenly issued an invitation to England, Austria and Prussia to meet in a congress for the settling of the war crisis, this move being seconded by France. The invitation was the result of an audience which the Russian Ambassador had had with Emperor Napoleon on March 15, and some historians insist that it was Napoleon who suggested the idea. Whatever may be its origin it was a shrewd move by Gorchakov. It was a courtesy to France, it took from England the credit of having a monopoly in the movement for peace and it was going to place Austria in the position of a guilty defendent before an Areopagus of European nations, forcing her to air the unsavory details of her administration in Northern Italy. The move was very badly received in London where Napoleon was thought to be wanting war while talking peace; and further the Congress, it was thought, would paralyze Lord Malmesbury's single-handed efforts for peace and hence embroil matters. However, it was difficult to refuse and, after much discussion, the British Government accepted on March 19, followed by Prussia. Austria, as may have been expected, put up all kinds of reservations and on March 25 the Paris "Le Moniteur de l'Empire" announced officially, "The cabinet in Vienna has adhered to the Russian proposal concerning the meeting of a Congress."[5] But on April 19 the sudden move of

---

[4] Quoted from a letter of Crampton to Malmesburg, Jan. 26, 1859. de la Gorce, P., Histoire du Second Empire. Paris, 1908, Vol. II, p. 394.

[5] de la Gorce, op. cit., Vol. II, p. 421.

Austria in sending an ultimatum to Sardinia put an end to all efforts for peace and made war inevitable. During the war of 1859 Russia lapsed once more into indifference except that she made it a condition of her neutrality that the Kingdom of Naples should not be touched, thereby thwarting one more visionary scheme of Napoleon III of making Prince Murat King of Naples after the death of Ferdinand II.[6] The peculiar and traditional interest shown by Russia on behalf of Naples was known to Napoleon and already before the war, on May 15, his confidential agent, Dr. Conneau, had written to Cavour to warn him to keep hands off Naples in order not to offend Russia. So for the time being Naples was safe.

The rapid absorption of Central Italy by the growing Kingdom of Sardinia after the armistice of Villafranca was of little concern to Russia. Indeed, so long as Naples was not touched, it was not for Russia to worry about the position of the Pope or of the rulers of the petty Central Italian States who were tied to the House of Austria by family relations. Russia merely proclaimed the principle of solidarity of crowns and the refusal to acknowledge the principle of non-intervention. This done, to quote de la Gorce, "She (Russia) would not deviate from the haughty impartiality which was her customary attitude in dealing with the affairs of Western Europe."[7] But when Garibaldi's thousand landed in Marsala, menacing Naples, and when this was followed by the invasion of Neapolitan territory by the Sardinian Army, Russia acted by severing diplomatic relations with Sardinia, thereby putting an end to the more friendly relations which were established with that kingdom after the Congress of Paris. Following this step the Emperors of Austria and Russia and the Prince Regent of Prussia met to discuss the situation at Warsaw on October 20. This meeting so ominously reminiscent of the Holy Alliance and the alliance of the Three Northern Courts stirred Europe and particularly France. But Alexander II, anxious to conciliate France, said to the French Ambassador in Russia, the Duke of Montebello, "I am going to Warsaw to propose conciliation and not a coalition"; whereas Gorchakov wrote to Morny, "No coalition against France is possible so long as Russia does not desire it."[8] The Duke of Morny proved a useful channel to

---

[6] Martinengo-Cesaresco, Cavour. Foreign Statesmen Series, p. 151.

[7] de la Gorce, op. cit., Vol. III, p. 164.

[8] Letter of Oct. 22, 1860, quoted de la Gorce, op. cit., Vol. III, p. 438.

Gorchakov for confidential negotiations. The desire to maintain good relations with France was motivated by the fact that the meeting of the three rulers was not entirely peaceful. Francis Joseph before going to Warsaw had already signed the order for the Austrian Army to cross into Italy, but decided first to seek the cooperation of Russia so as to keep France quiet; Alexander refused while the Prince Regent of Prussia declined to guarantee Austria's Venetian possessions in case of a new war. Thus nothing was done and Naples was left to her fate.[9] The importance for Russia of these issues concerning Italy was that she had made the first move back to a full fledged participation in European affairs and had discreetly strengthened her relations with France without committing herself. However, this budding friendship soon withered away over the test of the Polish affairs and in place of a friendship with France, Russia once more turned to Prussia. In this change the hand of Bismarck becomes clearly discernible.

II

In a conversation with Queen Victoria, during a flying visit he had made to Paris in 1855, Bismarck paid a left-handed compliment to St. Petersburg. Replying to the Queen's remark that Paris was beautiful he said it was even more beautiful than St. Petersburg.[10] Four years later, rather unexpectedly, he found himself going to St. Petersburg as Prussian Ambassador to the Russian Court. However the circumstances under which this appointment was made were not of a nature to make him rejoice. Indeed, for 7 years he had been holding the key post of Prussian envoy to the Diet of the Germanic Confederation in Frankfurt from which he was recalled as a result of the reshuffling of the Prussian services following the advent to power of the regent (the future King Wilhelm I), and not unnaturally he took this as a sign of disfavour. His appointment to St. Petersburg he viewed in the same light, and it was only after the Regent assured him that St. Petersburg was the most important diplomatic post in the Prussian service that he finally accepted. But once in Russia he felt happy and at home, though he found himself removed, intentionally it appeared to him, from the happenings in his own country. Owing to the fact that the Dowager Empress (the wife of Nicholas I)

---

[9] Martinengo-Cesaresco, op. cit., p. 193.

[10] Matter, P., Bismarck et son Temps. Paris 1905-1908, Vol. I, p. 392.

was Prussian by birth and sister of Friedrich Wilhelm IV, Bismarck was made to feel that he was in a special position at the court, a member of the family as it were, and he noticed considerable jealousy on the part of his colleagues of the diplomatic corps. This feeling was further intensified when Bismarck learned to speak Russian and mastered the language to a point where he could converse with Russian dignitaries, leaving other foreigners in the dark as to what he was saying. He made lasting friendships and established useful relations with the influential circles at court and in society. Prince Gorchakov was very kind and friendly to him, though he exasperated him by his attitude of benevolent condescension. Prince Orlov and Baron Meyendorf, the former ambassador to Vienna who was married to the sister of Count Buol, the Grand Duchess Helena and many others became his personal friends. Life in Russia was pleasing to him and the nature of the country as well as the character of the people congenial. He was impressed as he wrote "by the elemental vigour and tenacity of Russia, upon which the strength of the Russian temperament, as contrasted with that of the rest of Europe depends."[11] He was impressed by the size of things in the country, his love of violent exercise found an outlet in bear hunting while the open Russian hospitality with its excess of food and drink suited his temperament. Politically, he found the power of the autocracy unmitigated by parliamentary institutions and the strict bureaucratic hierarchy entirely to his taste. He would liked to have seen similar conditions existing in Prussia. His Russian impressions were lasting and formed a favorite topic of conversation in his old age. One experience lingered particularly in his memory and impressed even his mental outlook. As he was hunting one wintry day in the forests near St. Petersburg he lost his way and he was struck by the fatalistic confidence of his Russian attendant who kept on saying, "Nitchevo, we will get out somehow." Subsequently he would startle his colleagues in time of acute crisis by saying, "Nichevo, we will get out somehow."[12] He used to declare that the interbreeding of the feminine, sensitive Slav with the logical, practical, hard-headed Prussian would form an ideal race. He was not in a position while in St. Petersburg to have a great influence on the course of world politics though he advocated strict neutrality for Prussia and friendship with Russia in the war of

---

[11]Ludwig, Emil. Bismarck, Boston 1927, p. 172.

[12]Graham, Stephen. The Czar of Freedom. Newhaven, 1935, p. 136.

1859. It was however in its after effects that his stay of three years in Russia was important for during this period his Russophile feelings definitely crystallized themselves and for 30 years to come his pro-Russian policy remained the single unswerving constant in all the vagaries of his political activities.

III

In September, 1862, Bismarck was appointed Minister-President of Prussia after having been transferred from St. Petersburg as Ambassador to Paris for a few months. With his coming to power an opportunity offered itself for guiding Prussian foreign policy toward closer relations with Russia. He had been carefully watching the situation in Russian Poland where the Polish volcano, relatively dormant since 1831 and 1837, was showing signs of erupting once more; and when the Polish insurrection broke out in 1863 it was not only to plunge Russia into a formidable struggle tantamount to a foreign war but was to become the test case revealing the attitude of the major European powers toward Russia. Bismarck alone did not hesitate to throw the weight of his power on the side of Russia. Acting with his customary rapidity of decision, 10 days after the first fighting broke out on January 22, 1863, he dispatched General von Alvensleben to St. Petersburg on a confidential mission. General von Alvensleben left Berlin on February 1, with a personal letter from King Wilhelm to Alexander II, with instructions to offer the Russian Government a convention of mutual assistance in regard to the Polish rebellion, considering that the fighting was taking place in Poland along the Prussian border and both governments were facing the same peril. According to this convention the armies of either country would be free to cross into the territory of the other if such a necessity arose. High officers of both armies were to be attached to each others' headquarters for transmission of intelligence about the movements of the rebels, and the commanders-in-chief were to be given all information from the political and intelligence organs of Prussia in Posen and Russia in Poland. This Convention which was to be effective so long as the situation warranted its existence, was duly signed in St. Petersburg on February 8, 1863, and took the name in history of the Convention of Alvensleben. To buttress its effect, three Prussian army corps were concentrated in Prussian Poland.

All this was the personal policy of Bismarck. True, he had won over the King to support it, but only after long and painful hesitation. Prussian public opinion was kept in the dark, but expressed its hostility to the little that was known about this military alliance with Russia, for the liberals abhorred Russian autocracy and sympathized with Polish aspirations, whereas the German Party remembered the snubs administered to Prussia by Russia in 1850 and the hostility of Nicholas I toward the unification of Germany. On the other hand there was a widespread fear that the insurrection might spread to Prussian Poland. On February 18, the storm broke out in the Prussian parliament where heated debates lasted for several days and Bismarck's policy was subjected to passionate and violent attacks. Bismarck faced these with the haughty and sarcastic attitude of indifference with which he invariably faced parlimentary opposition. Even greater was to be the storm of indignation abroad when the news of this secret Convention leaked out. But this played into the hands of Bismarck for it singled him out in sharp contrast to the hostile attitude adopted toward Russia by the other great powers. He thus safely anchored the foreign relations of Prussia to a lasting friendship with Russia which brought him so many dividends in the future and at the same time thwarted the menace of a Franco-Russian alliance which he had increasingly feared.

In Russia the arrival of General von Alvensleben produced mixed feelings of surprise, in some quarters indignation but on the whole gratitude. Surprise was expressed at the insistance of Bismarck's offer of aid which appeared not to be warranted by the situation. Russian official circles did not feel that "Russia was so sick as that."[13] The Russian ambassador in Vienna, Balabine, said later to M. de Gramont that the Convention was useless from a military point of view and regrettable from a diplomatic point of view.[14] Indeed, before the month of February was over the Russian Ambassador in Berlin, d'Oubril, notified the Prussian Government that Russia would not avail herself of the right of crossing into Prussian territory in pursuit of the rebels. The Russian military circles in Poland considered this Convention humiliating hence, from Grand Duke Constantine downwards, the army cold-shouldered Alvensleben upon his passage through Warsaw. Bismarck wrote to Bernstorff on March 9, 1863[15] that Gorchakov himself was opposed to signing the Convention and

---

[13]de la Gorce, op. cit., Vol. IV., p. 427.

[14]Duc de Gramont to Drouyn de Lhuys on March 3, 1863, de la Gorce, op. cit., Vol. II, p. 432.

[15]Matter, op. cit., Vol. II, p. 80.

did so only upon express orders of the Czar. But Alexander II had received Alvensleben with signs of real gratitude and there remained the feeling in Russia that Prussia was the single true friend. That is why the importance of this Convention goes far beyond the Polish issue itself. With true perspicacity the Austrian newspaper Ostdeutsche Post stated that this was the beginning of a close alliance between the two countries. Viewed from this angle the Convention was beneficial to both parties. For Russia it meant the making secure of her western border and keeping Austria in check. It is not a mere coincidence, observes the Soviet historian Pokrovsky, that Russia embarked on her conquest of Central Asia shortly after the signing of the Convention. Secure in the West, she could turn her attention toward eastward expansion. Gorchakov himself tried to enlarge the interpretation of the Convention in this sense and to use it against Austria. The Russian Chancellor hated Austria with a purely personal hatred. His witticism: "Austria is not a state, it is a government," made the tour of European chancelleries. Hence during the summer the Prussian Government was approached by Russia with a suggestion to transform the Convention into an offensive alliance against Austria. With 400,000 Russian soldiers concentrated in Poland, the offer was tempting to Bismarck; but, though already preparing for his struggle to evict Austria from Germany, he judged the time premature. He feared that a victory over Austria at this point would be followed by a war with France. After long hesitation, and after having discussed the matter with the King at Gastein, he finally turned it down. This offer was due to irritation in Russian diplomatic circles against Austria because of her stand in the Polish crisis--which in Russian eyes was a further sign of her duplicity.

The Austrian attitude in this crisis was indeed ambiguous. Faced with a dangerous fermentation in Galicia, the Austrian government ordered martial law to be proclaimed there, though at the same time secretly encouraging Napoleon III in his dreams of a united Poland.

The Austrian Chancellor, Rechberg sent notes of protest to Berlin and St. Petersburg, invoking the Treaty of Vienna against Russia. Russia on her side, openly accused Austria of being in connivance with the insurrection because the Austrian Government was permitting the Polish insurgents to use Galicia as their base. The French Emperor, dreaming of a united Poland was, in his vague way, even thinking of a war against Russia and Prussia in which Austria would take part, and be given back Silesia as compensation.

The French stand was somewhat more confused. Public opinion, the press and the parliament were ardently pro-Polish, but Emperor Napoleon was moved, as in more than one instance in his career, by contradictory motives. He was still thinking in terms of a Franco-Russian alliance; and yet the principle of nationalities, which had been one of the cardinal principles of his foreign policy, made him dream of becoming the agent for the liberation of Poland even, as we have seen, at the cost of facing a war with Russia. Again as "Caesar," Napoleon did not like revolutionary movements; and yet he had to listen to the clamour of his own public opinion demanding action in favour of the Poles. Under the influence of these contradictory impulses, French policy had been at first very cautious. During the whole "incubative" period of the crisis, and as early as 1861, M. Drouyn de Lhuys had been very careful to avoid any official show of sympathy for Poland; and even as late as February 5, 1863, in reply to a motion in the Legislative Assembly favouring the Poles, the official spokesman of the government spoke of the "danger of useless words which might give food to rebellious passions."[16] In England no such hesitations were to be found. Hating the Russians and traditionally supporting liberal movements in Europe, the British did not take the trouble to study the rights or wrongs of the case, but came out with an open attack against Russia. Immediately all vacillations in Paris and Vienna disappeared, and Russia was once more faced with the same line-up of powers she had seen in the Crimean War--England, France and Austria acting jointly and drawing in their wake Italy, Spain and the petty states of Europe.

On March 6 the British Government approached France for concerted action in the Polish crisis. The signing of the Convention of Alvensleben had produced a storm of indignation in London, Paris and Vienna. Much perturbed, these chancelleries got busy trying to find out the exact implications of the Convention, which had been intentionally minimized by the co-signers as being merely a commercial treaty. When the truth leaked out a violent scene took place in Berlin. The British Ambassador, Sir Andrew Buchanan, said angrily to Bismarck: "Europe will not tolerate this." "Who is Europe?" asked Bismarck ironically.

The stand taken by Great Britain was that the treaty of 1815 having been violated, it was the right and duty of Europe to intervene in the Polish struggle; therefore the signatories

---

[16] de la Gorce, op. cit., Vol. IV, p. 435.

of the Treaty of Vienna should be persuaded to exert pressure jointly on Russia, calling her attention to the stipulations of the Treaty. The Austrian Chancellor went even further and pointed out to the French Ambassador in Vienna that there was little chance of Russia listening to the exhortations of the powers, single or collective, and that Austria would be ready to take part in more energetic action provided it was carried out jointly and with a definitely stipulated program which the Chancellor hinted might be the recreation of Poland. On March 9, Rechberg made his views clearer: ".....the first step would mean war, possibly not immediate, but a war which would be certain to come eventually....."[17] He asked for a treaty with France which would give Austria definite compensations. But, faced with the hesitations of French policy and the reiterated statements of the British Government, which limited their contemplated action to diplomacy alone, Austria withdrew into a cautious reserve. All these cross currents of intrigue finally materialized into a collective note of protest presented by the powers to St. Petersburg on April 17.

England, France and Austria presented notes jointly, followed by Italy, Spain and the small European powers, all invoking the Treaty of 1815 and inviting Russia to execute her engagements as specified in the Treaty so that a durable condition of peace should exist in Poland. Thus Russia was the object of a grand and solemn remonstrance of a concerted Europe. But as the powers showed no desire to back their demands by force, Gorchakov parried and counter-attacked in his turn. Those were the days when diplomacy meant the art of subtle shading and conveying pointed remarks by inference. In this the Russian Chancellor was a past-master. As de la Gorce puts it: "Up to this time Lord Russell appeared to have no equal in writing disobliging (desobligeantes) notes. This time, he had found his master."[18] Indeed, Gorchakov replied to these notes on April 26: moderate with regard to France, disdainful towards Austria, curt with regard to England. He ironically pointed out to Lord Russell that the latter, by invoking the Treaty of 1815, was evidently not familiar with its contents; that the best way for the powers to see a pacified Poland was to put their own houses in order. Very politely he invited the powers to "labor on their side to appease the moral and material disorder which is being

---

[17] de la Gorce, op. cit., Vol. IV, p. 442.
[18] de la Gorce, op. cit., Vol. IV, p. 451.

propagated and thereby to cure Europe of the principal source of the agitation which was so alarming to them" and pointed out that the real source of trouble was to be found "in the permanent instigations of a cosmopolitan revolution."[19] The French press made an attempt to cover up the snub which the powers had received, "La Patrie" writing that the note showed that "Emperor Alexander's intentions corresponded in all points with those of Emperor Napoleon," whereas the "Moniteur" said, hopefully but vaguely, that the "way was now open for conciliatory plans."[20]

But the Chancelleries could not leave so insulting a note unanswered; hence the reply came, after much mutual consultation, in the form of a new note delivered to Russia on June 17. The "Big Three" now proposed to Russia the adoption of 6 points: (1) complete and general amnesty in Poland, (2) restoration of national representation as stipulated by the Treaty of 1815, (3) appointment of Poles to public offices in Poland, (4) freedom of conscience and suppression of restrictions imposed upon the Catholic Church, (5) use of the Polish language alone in the administration of the country, (6) introduction of a special system of recruiting for the army, and in addition a European congress to discuss the settlement of the Polish question on the basis of these points. Gorchakov let a month pass without giving an answer; then when his reply was delivered to the Western Powers on July 13 they were dumbfounded. Gorchakov flatly rejected a European conference as an interference in the internal affairs of Russia, but in his turn suggested, with Machiavellian irony, the calling of a conference of the three powers which had partitioned Poland. This would have eliminated England and France while bringing Prussia into the picture, thus leaving a weakened Austria at the mercy of Russia and Prussia. "Here is something that nobody would have imagined," said the French Ambassador, the Duke of Montebello, after an interview with Gorchakov, and added that he feared that in France this reply would be taken as an insult. Indeed, the point had been reached where the powers would either have to take action or desist. The answer produced a storm both in Paris and in London. Lord Malmesbury in the House of Lords suggested the rupture of diplomatic relations with Russia; "Le Siècle" in Paris proposed a plebiscite on the

---

[19] de la Gorce, op. cit., Vol. IV, p. 451.

[20] La Patrie, May 6, 1863, Le Moniteur, May 5, 1863, quoted de la Gorce, op. cit., Vol. IV, p. 452.

question of armed intervention. Oddly, France, which had been so slow to move, was now the most warlike; Napoleon III suggested a collective note to Russia even in the face of an eventual war. England, however, was not prepared to go to such lengths for the sake of the Poles, while Austria looked uneasily at the 400,000 Russian soldiers concentrated on the open Galician frontier. As usual, therefore, half measures were adopted.

More to cover up their retreat than to achieve results, the Powers sent another note in August to which Gorchakov curtly replied by a refusal to "carry on the discussion" (prolonger la discussion). Napoleon then suggested calling a European conference for the revision of the whole Treaty of Vienna to include the affairs of Poland and to be acceptable to Russia as well; but neither London, Vienna nor Rome gave him any encouragement so the idea was dropped. In London the Foreign Office drafted a menacing note to Russia, but upon second thought Lord Palmerston did not send it; when asked about it in the House of Commons, he replied that he was no more responsible for his drafts than for his thoughts. Thus the action of the Western Powers had collapsed whereas, meanwhile, the Polish rebellion was being settled by the victory of Russian arms. The net result of the whole incident was to strain further the relations with England, to tighten the friendship of Russia with Prussia--who alone had abstained from any action--and to bring to a definite end the budding Franco-Russian alliance. In November, 1863, Napoleon made an attempt to restore better relations with Russia by referring in a speech at the opening of the Legislative Assembly to his cordial relations with Emperor Alexander II, stressing the fact that he regretted that the "interest in a cause dear to the heart of France had resulted in compromising one of the prime alliances of the continent." (a compromettre l'une des premières alliances du Continent),[22] but it was of no avail. Coldness between Russia and France replaced the former friendship.

IV

Scarcely had the Polish crisis been settled when Bismarck reaped the first fruits of his friendship with Russia. The war over the Danish duchies was looming, the first of the three wars from which Bismarck was to forge the German Empire. This issue was a tangled frontier quarrel in which both sides

---

[21]de la Gorce, op. cit., Vol. IV, p. 461.

had rights and legitimate grievances--the only solution being war. Essentially this most complex question amounted to the following: ever since 1459 and also as a result of the act of the Congress of Vienna, the King of Denmark was also the ruler of the duchies of Schleswig, Holstein, and Lauenburg, all contiguous to Denmark. The populations of Holstein and Lauenburg were German,, which meant that these two duchies were members of the Germanic Confederation. The population of Schleswig was half German and half Danish, and under the medieval Charter of Ribe (1460), Schleswig was to remain united with Holstein forever; but by the settlement of Vienna it was not included in the Germanic Confederation. With the rise of the tide of nationalism after the Napoleonic Wars in both Germany and Denmark the issue became inflamed. The Danish Nationalists dreamt of the total incorporation of the duchies into Denmark, whereas the German population of the duchies was looking for a closer union with the Germanic Confederation. When, under the influence of the so-called "Eider Dansk" party, King Frederick VII of Denmark issued a draft for a common constitution which by uniting them with Denmark would have destroyed the individuality of Schleswig-Holstein and would have detached Holstein from the Germanic Confederation, the inevitable result was a war between Denmark and the various German States who answered the call of the Diet of Frankfurt for a "federal execution." Most prominent in this war were the Prussians under General Wrangel. They not only invaded Holstein but crossed into Denmark proper by entering Jutland, and on May 18, 1849, imposed a military contribution of 4 million Rigsdaler, to be paid not later than May 28. At this juncture Russia stepped in and curbed Prussian ambitions even more sharply than at Olmütz. Nicholas I, in reply to an appeal made by the Danish Court to Russia, England and Sweden, informed the Court of Berlin that if Prussian troops did not evacuate the duchies and conform to the Treaty of Vienna, Prussia would face a war with Russia. To buttress this threat several Russian warships appeared before Kiel. Prussia meekly obeyed, sent a hasty order to Wrangel to evacuate Jutland and did not collect the indemnity.[22] The peace which was concluded at Berlin on July 2, 1850, under British mediation, though stipulating the evacuation of Schleswig-Holstein and Lauenburg by the Prussian forces, did not settle the matter, and the situation remained acute.

---

[22] Allen, C. F., <u>Histoire de Danemark.</u> Copenhagen 1878. Vol. II, p. 330.

An additional complication was added to the situation with the impending question of the succession to the throne of Denmark. Fredrick VII was without male issue and the various collateral branches of the reigning house of Oldenburg claimed their rights--some to the throne of Denmark, others (like the branch of Augustenburg) merely to Schleswig-Holstein. Not to be overlooked was also the claim of the Romanovs. They were descended from the Holstein-Gottorp branch of the house of Oldenburg, Peter Ulrich of Holstein-Gottorp having become Czar Peter III; and the Treaty of Tsarskoye Selo between Denmark and Russia in 1773 recognized the Romanov dynasty as having special claims to the Danish throne in the event of the absence of a direct heir. To help settle these thorny and dangerous claims, Nicholas I, by an act dated from Warsaw June 5, 1851, officially renounced his rights to the Danish throne in favor of Prince Christian of Schleswig-Holstein-Sonderburg-Glücksburg; the next year by a treaty signed on May 8, 1852, by Austria, France, Great Britain, Prussia, Russia and Sweden, Prince Christian was acknowledged as successor" to the whole of the Dominions now united under the sceptre of His Majesty the King of Denmark."[23] The renunciation by Russia of her rights to the Danish succession as reserved by the treaty of Tsarskoye Selo, in favor of Christian of Sondenburg-Glücksburg was the decisive factor in eliminating the other candidates and in the choice of Christian as king-elect by the co-signers of the treaty of 1852.

Towards the end of the reign of Fredrick VII the question of the Duchies had become more and more acute. On September 24, 1862, Lord John Russell proposed a settlement whereby Denmark was to be divided into four parts, Holstein to be bound closely with Germany, and Schleswig to enjoy complete autonomy. Russia acquiesced to this proposal, thereby disappointing those Danes who had been hoping for Russia's support. They could not know that from now on in the Danish question Russia was going to take a stand with Prussia. However, in England Lord Russell's mediation was bitterly criticized, public opinion being violently pro-Danish. On March 30, 1863, the Danish Government hastened to issue, as a reply to Lord Russell's suggestion of partition, a constitution separating Holstein from Schleswig; and on July 23, Lord Palmerston made a violent speech stating that if any attempt were made to interfere with the rights and independence of Denmark "those who made

---

[23]Mowat, R. B., History of European Diplomacy 1815-1914. London, 1927, p. 173.

the attempt would find in the result that it would not be Denmark alone with which they would have to contend."[24] Encouraged by such a warlike declaration in their favour, the Danes disregarded a six months ultimatum issued by the Germanic Diet demanding the repeal of the constitution of March 30. They now felt safe to take the next step, that of incorporating Schleswig, after its separation from Holstein, into Denmark. This was done by the promulgation of a common constitution for Schleswig and Denmark on September 28, which was followed on October 1 by a vote of the Frankfurt Diet to initiate a "federal execution on Denmark."

It was under these circumstances that Frederick VII died in November 1863, and Christian of Sonderburg-Glücksburg ascended the throne under the name of Christian IX. The new king was told by his Prime Minister, Hall, that any retracting on the question of the Duchies would mean revolution; hence he endorsed the next step forced upon him by the Eider Dansk ministry, namely, the proclamation on November 18 of a "fundamental law" which would result in a common constitution for all parts of the realm and, thereby the incorporation of the Duchies into Denmark. With the Frankfurt Diet voting that the "federal execution" should be put into effect immediately, and an insurrection breaking out in Holstein, where the Duke of Augustenburg, supported by the German states, was going to proclaim himself reigning duke, the issue had come to a head. Indeed, on December 26, the Saxon and Hanoverian troops in fulfilment of the orders of the Diet crossed into Holstein, and on December 30 the Duke of Augustenburg made a triumphant entry into Kiel where he established an independent German government for Holstein.

The great powers were making desperate efforts to avert war. On the pretence of congratulating the new King upon his accession, Great Britain sent Lord Wodehouse, France General Fleury, and Russia Ewert to Copenhagen. These diplomats made representations to the Danish Government to have the law of November 18 repealed. For once the British and Russian Governments saw eye to eye, and on December 21 Lord Wodehouse reported to Lord Russell that he was very grateful for the friendly and cordial support given him by his Russian colleague, whose views coincided with his own.[25] But these efforts were of no avail. The law came into effect on January 1, 1864, and the issue was brutally settled by Bismarck,

---

[24]Mowat, op. cit., p. 175.

[25]de la Gorce, op. cit., Vol. IV, p. 486, 487.

who, overriding the action of the Federal Diet, issued a joint Austro-Prussian ultimatum to Denmark on January 18 which led to the War of the Duchies.

Now that the war was on, Gorchakov had no further interest in the matter beyond the desire to be agreeable to Bismarck and to repay to Prussia the debt contracted at the time of the Polish rebellion. But when the Duke of Augustenburg, through his confidential envoy, approached the Russian Minister in Frankfurt with a view to obtaining permission to send an official message to the Czar announcing his accession to the throne of Schleswig-Holstein, he received a complete snub. The Russian Minister observed caustically that in such an eventuality Russia would once more raise her dynastic claim to the succession of the Duchies. The Duke, nevertheless, sent the message, but Alexander II left it without an answer. This was not displeasing to Bismarck who, wishing to annex the Duchies to Prussia, was opposed to the Augustenburg venture. Subsequently Russia proposed her own candidate, the Grand Duke Peter of Oldenburg, close relative of the Czar and a member of the branch of the Oldenburg family which had been established in Russia for some time. This candidature was again not displeasing to Bismarck for in due time he could use it to get rid of Augustenburg. The situation was now so completely dominated by the Iron Chancellor that the other powers were forced to become mere onlookers. After a temporary reverse sustained by the Prussians before Duppel, England once more made an attempt to intervene, and called a conference in London to discuss foreign intervention. This conference met on April 20, and Lord Russell suggested a scheme of partitioning the Duchies between the belligerents along a line following the river Slie and the Dannewirke, the Russian delegate once more acceding to this suggestion. However, the conference failed to obtain any results owing to the opposition of Prussia and Austria.

Having eliminated this unwelcome interference of foreign powers by letting the conference waste away in futile talk, Bismarck was now in a position to settle the Schleswig-Holstein matter to suit himself. On June 1 he had an interview with the Duke of Augustenburg in which he read the Duke a telegram from St. Petersburg expressing the Czar's hostility to the Augustenburg candidature and favouring the Duke of Oldenburg. Having thus placed an insurmountable obstacle before Augustenburg, Bismarck notified the Russian Government that he was not going to support the Duke of Augustenburg. On June 2, the Russian Ambassador in London, Baron Brunnow, officially

informed the London conference that the Czar, to facilitate the
conclusion of peace between Germany and Denmark, had transferred to the Grand Duke of Oldenburg whatever rights of succession to the duchies the Russian dynasty had reserved in the
protocol of Warsaw. On June 10, Czar Alexander, passing
through Berlin on his way to Kissingen, had a very cordial interview with the King, in which the Czar supported the necessity
of having the Duchies formed into a state which would not be of
revolutionary origin and therefore would have a ruler appointed
by the powers, i.e., the Duke of Oldenburg. The hostilities
were resumed with energy after the termination of an armistice
on June 26. The Prussians pushed hard, and three weeks later
everything was over, the Danish Government wiring to Berlin
and Vienna on July 12 a request for the suspension of hostilities.
Now Bismarck was in a position to dictate his terms and place
before the world a fait accompli. The Duchies were detached
from Denmark and placed under the joint ownership of Prussia
and Austria. As for the two candidates, Augustenburg and
Oldenburg, they quietly faded out of the picture, nor was it in
Russia's interest to raise any objections to this.

V

Europe had just settled down after the Danish War when it
was faced with a new war crisis. Purposely envenoming the
inevitable frictions resulting from the Austro-Prussian condominium over the duchies, Bismarck was pursuing the goal of
ejecting Austria out of Germany by a second war. The attempt
made at Gastein to settle the difficulties by partitioning the
spheres of influence--Prussia taking Schleswig and Austria Hol-
stein--failed before the obstinacy of Bismarck, and when in the
spring of 1866 the latter had concluded an aggressive alliance
with Italy against Austria, war became inevitable. In this
crisis Gorchakov's policy was once more motivated by gratitude
toward Prussia, coolness toward France and fierce resentment
against Austria. Hence, when in an effort to avert hostilities
Napoleon approached the European courts in March, 1866, with
a suggestion to exchange Venetia for the Roumanian Principalities
which would be given in compensation to Austria for the loss of
her Italian possessions, this merely made Russia more suspicious
of France and she flatly rejected the idea. In May Napoleon
made a last minute effort to call an European congress. Gorchakov coldly stated to the French Ambassador, Prince Talleyrand, who had broached the idea, that he was multiplying his
efforts both in Florence and Vienna to bring about a simultaneou
disarmament and that he would be ready to support (appuyer)

the suggestion of a congress merely as a post-scriptum. [26] To
the annoyance of Bismarck, both Russia and England having
acceded to the idea of a congress, France suggested the sending
of joint official invitations to other governments for the opening
of the congress on June 12. Bismarck was manoeuvring to
place the responsibility for the coming war upon Austria but
now he had to hasten; hence on June 10 he transmitted to the
Federal Diet of Frankfurt a scheme for the revision of the Germanic Constitution excluding Austria, which was to serve as the
immediate cause of the war. On June 12, the very day of the
opening of the congress, diplomatic relations between Austria
and Prussia were broken off and 4 days later the advance of
the Prussian armies began. The defeat of the Austrian armies
followed so rapidly that Europe had no time to evolve a common
policy before it was faced with the smashing Prussian victory
of Königgraetz which opened the way to Vienna. The news was
not entirely welcome to Russia--Prussia's success had been
too complete and rapid and spelled not only the final defeat of
Austria but the destruction of the Germanic Diet at Frankfurt
and as de la Gorce puts it: "How many relatives, how many
clients had she (Russia) in the Germanic Confederation?" [27]
Hence, heeding the desperate appeal of the smaller German
princes about to lose their thrones, Russia's sympathies became
divided: Czar Alexander made the statement that "the dynasties
which are about to be deposed, are reigning by the grace of
God just as the Prussian dynasty was", whereas Gorchakov
said: "I hope that Mr. von Bismarck will not be a meteor, but
a stable star, hence I am recommending to him moderation." [28]
After the preliminaries of peace at Nickolsburg had made their
fate clear, the Kings of Hanover and Württemberg, (the latter
a brother-in-law of the Czar) both sent urgent appeals for aid;
The Emperor dismissed the case of Hanover by merely sending
to the King of Prussia a letter of recommendation "like in the
case of a discharged civil servant." [29] But he regarded Württemberg and the South German States as a different matter.
On their behalf Russia, on July 27, raised the suggestion,
highly unwelcome to Bismarck, of a conference of German
states, and three days later Bismarck received intelligence from
his military attaché in St. Petersburg that Russia and France
had agreed upon this issue.

---

[26] de la Gorce, op. cit., Vol. IV, p. 586 and 620.

[27] de la Gorce, op. cit., Vol. V, p. 28.

[28] de la Gorce, op. cit., Vol. V, p. 58.

[29] Matter, Bismarck, op. cit., Vol. II, p. 508.

So perturbed was Bismarck over this suggestion that he immediately dispatched General Edwin von Manteuffel (August 7) on a secret mission to St. Petersburg. The latter disclosed to the Russian Government Napoleon's insistence upon single-handed mediation in the Austro-Prussian War and his exorbitant demand for the price of French neutrality--the left bank of the Rhine. The result was magic--Russia dropped her demand for a conference; and the friendly coming together, during the course of the war, of d'Oubril and Benedetti, the Russian and French Ambassadors in Berlin, was replaced by a marked coolness and reserve on the part of d'Oubril. Russia tightened her friendship with Prussia and Bismarck was very anxious to maintain and develop this friendship. As a result of the strain of the war and the tremendous burden of responsibility, he suffered a nervous breakdown and was forced to take a complete rest on a country estate in Pomerania. It is significant that though he was not in a position to carry on the management of state business and was forced to cancel his whole political correspondence with regard to foreign affairs, he nevertheless, on November 11, 1866, wrote a long and affectionate letter to Gorchakov.

VI

Following the war of 1866 Europe was perturbed by the menace of a new war, this time between France and Prussia over the question of the Grand Duchy of Luxemburg. Napoleon had been bitterly disappointed at not receiving from Prussia the compensation he had demanded for France's neutrality in the Austro-Prussian War. His prestige had been badly shattered by the snub Bismarck had given him in this respect; as a last resort and a face-saving device he now wanted to acquire the Grand Duchy of Luxemburg in place of his earlier demand for the whole left bank of the Rhine in pursuance of his "policy of tips". But, as under the treaty of Vienna, Luxemburg had been given to the King of Holland, he offered the latter a pecuniary indemnity in exchange for this territory. The sole interest Prussia had in this question was that Luxemburg had been declared by the Congress of Vienna to be a member of the Germanic Confederation, whereas the city of Luxemburg itself had become a federal fortress garrisoned by Prussian troops. The issue was not a vital one for Prussia, the more so that Luxemburg had not been included in the North German Confederation established by Bismarck, but it was in the interest of Bismarck to make an international issue of this question. Hence he bullied Holland into withdrawing from the bargain with France and fanned the crisis to a point where in the spring of 1867, another war appeared unavoidable. His object was two-fold--first, he had repeatedly stated that he considered a war with France inevitable, hence he wanted to test the military machinery of the North German Confederation and, second, he wanted to strengthen the somewhat doubtful allegiance of his South German allies.

In this crisis Russia had no interest except her sympathy toward Prussia, her antagonism toward France and her desire not to see Europe plunged into a dangerous new war in which she really had no direct concern. Hence, with the other great neutral powers, she assumed rather tardily the role of peacemaker. At first Gorchakov remained silent with prudent reserve. When Beust, the former Saxon statesman and now Chancellor of Austria, came out with a workable suggestion for the solution of the crisis, Gorchakov said to the Austrian Ambassador in St. Petersburg, de Revertera, "I wish all the success it deserves to Mr. Beust's attempt (tentative) but I am resolved not to involve (engager) prematurely the policy of Russia."[30] But as the crisis became more and more dangerous Gorchakov's attitude began changing. He declared that the rights of Prussia to Luxemburg were contestable and he came out with the proposal of calling an European conference to settle the question. France did not want war. The French Minister of Foreign Affairs, the Marquis de Moustier, who had been called to office during the crisis, sincerely wanted to find a peaceful solution, the more so that General Niel, the Minister of War, had given a discouraging picture of the condition of the French Army, the strength of which had been dissipated in wild colonial adventures including the Mexican affair. Hence on April 15, de Moustier officially solicited the governments of England, Austria, Russia and Italy for mediation in the crisis. Bismarck on his side was satisfied with the results obtained in Germany, though he decided that some further finishing touches were necessary for the army before it could face a war with France. Yielding to the opposition of the King of Prussia to the idea of a war, and the unanimous stand of the powers, he agreed to the Russian proposal. The conference, to which the signatories of the Treaty of 1839 and Italy were convoked, met in London on May 7. The compromise solution of Beust, to make Luxemburg neutral with the resulting retirement of the Prussian garrison was accepted and the crisis was over.

Despite the war scare over the Luxemburg affair, the great International Exposition in Paris opened in a blaze of glory which made it the last great pageant of the Second Empire.

---

[30] de la Gorce, op. cit., Vol. V, p. 187.

These exibitions were still a sufficiently sensational novelty to attract visitors the world over. To enhance the opening, invitations had been sent to all foreign sovereigns to attend. Some minor rulers responded immediately, but the more important rulers, and particularly the King of Prussia and the King of Italy, showed some hesitancy in accepting, Victor Emmanuel excusing himself on account of ill health which however did not keep him from going hunting in the mountains. But as soon as word was received in European capitals that the Czar had accepted the invitation various sovereigns hastened to follow suit, with the result that the Kings of Prussia, Bavaria, Belgium, Württemberg and the Sultan of Turkey arrived in Paris simultaneously with the Czar or shortly after him. Emperor Alexander II arrived in Paris on June 1, and was received with more pomp than cordiality, pro-Polish sympathies still being very strong amongst the Parisians. The crowds which lined the streets were mostly silent as the Emperor drove from the Gare du Nord to the Palace of the Elysée which had been assigned to him. Only in passing through the shopping district of the Rue de la Paix, Rue de Castiglione and the Rue de Rivoli, did the Czar hear cheers and see Russian colours and emblems decorating the buildings. For here were located the luxury shops which catered mostly to wealthy Russians--the Americans of those days in the eyes of Parisian shop-keepers and hotel keepers. To stress the informality of his visit and the holiday mood, Alexander went the very same evening to see the musical hit of the season, the famous Offenbach operetta, The Grand Duchess of Geroldstein. But the Czar's holiday was marred by the hostility of the Parisians. Indeed, a few days later as he was visiting the Palais de Justice shouts were heard from a group of lawyers present-- "Long live Poland" and "Get out". It was afterwards officially explained that the cries "Get out" were intended for those who had made the noise but not unnaturally Alexander applied them to himself and left the building profoundly irritated. But more was to follow. On June 6, a great military review was held in honour of the Czar and the King of Prussia. While returning from the review the imperial carriage in which Napoleon and Alexander were sitting could not proceed through the Avenue Longchamps because of the crowds which were watching the procession, and was finally forced into side streets. Here, as the carriage halted at a narrow intersection, a young Pole, Berezovski, approached the carriage with a pistol and fired point blank at the Czar. Alexander's life was saved by the presence of mind of an escorting officer who seeing the gun raised, pushed his horse between the assassin and the carriage.

The horse was wounded. The same evening a ball was to be held at the Russian Embassy. At the news of the attempted assassination there was consternation and the ball was to be cancelled, but Alexander insisted it should take place in order not to offend French susceptibilities, and was himself present as if nothing had occurred.

Berezovski was arrested and confessed his intention of wanting to murder the Czar to avenge Poland. On July 15, after the Czar was already back in Russia, Berezovski was brought to trial in Paris where he was defended by one of the most famous French lawyers, Arago, who played so well on the Polish sympathies of the court that the assassin got away with a relatively light jail sentence. When the news of this sentence was received in St. Petersburg it was regarded as a personal insult to the Czar and a storm of indignation broke out in official circles. It was intimated that the French Government had been unofficially asked to pass a death penalty on Berezovski, so as to enable the Czar to make a gesture of magnanimity by asking the repeal of the sentence. Thus the result of the Czar's visit to Paris, instead of cementing the friendship between the two governments, was to produce increased irritation and coldness.[31]

Both Gorchakov and Bismarck had accompanied their respective sovereigns to Paris with the intention of combining business with pleasure and talking political matters over with the French statesmen. Napoleon had here an unique opportunity for ironing out the past difficulties with Russia and for paving the way for a better understanding between the two countries. However in the continuous succession of brilliant festivities no political conversations were held. When, two years later, Napoleon suddenly became aware of the danger of Russia's hostility toward France and her increasing friendship with Prussia he sent his ambassador, General Fleury with instructions to win the friendship of Russia, but it was too late. Bismarck, meanwhile, was leaving no stone unturned to cement further the Russo-Prussian amity. Owing to these efforts of Bismarck the years preceding the Franco-Prussian War reached the high water mark in the cordial relations between Russia and Prussia. Indeed, Bismarck lost no opportunity to write friendly, even cajoling letters to Gorchakov. In December, 1869, General Nostitz was sent to Berlin with the insignia of the Grand Cross of St. George conferred upon King Wilhelm by the Czar. In return the King of Prussia invested Alexander with the Prussian

---

[31]de la Gorce, op. cit., Vol. V, p. 231.

Order of Merit. And Napoleon warned his ambassador in St. Petersburg, General Fleury, "do not forget, everything you say to the Emperor or to Prince Gorchakov will be repeated in Berlin." The French Government's efforts to frighten Russia with the rising tide of Germanism which might engulf Livonia and Courland, or to point out that Roumania under Charles Hohenzollern was the wedge of Germanism in the Balkans, fell upon deaf ears. The French ambassador was treated courteously but coldly at the Russian court, all cordiality being reserved for the Prussian envoy.

CHAPTER X

THE GERMAN EMPIRE AND THE RISE OF PANSLAVISM

I

In the war crisis of July 1870 which suddenly swept over Europe and led to the outbreak of hostilities between France and Prussia, Russia's stand was dominated by the memories of the Crimean War. Hence Russia had no reason to wish for a French victory and she was anxious to checkmate Austria by blocking any aspirations of that power to seek revenge for Koniggraetz by coming into the war on the side of France. But above all Gorchakov was anxious to profit by these events to get rid of the humiliating clause of the Treaty of Paris concerning the de-militarization of the Black Sea. These three motives could be achieved through standing by her Prussian alliance.

In June already, before the crisis over the Hohenzollern candidature to the Spanish throne had come to a head, Czar Alexander, taking a cure at Ems, received a visit from his uncle, King Wilhelm of Prussia, accompanied by Bismarck. The political questions of the day were examined, and Bismarck had the satisfaction of seeing how completely in agreement were the views of the two allies; this gave him the necessary security to deal more energetically with the impending Spanish crisis.

Gorchakov on his way from Russia to Wilbad for a cure, happened to be in Berlin on July 12, and by chance met Bismarck who had been recalled from his estate at Varsin by an urgent message from the King. They arranged to have a meeting the next day, July 13--the fateful day of the Ems telegram. In this interview, Bismarck, it is presumed, made sure of the neutrality of Russia. As Russia had acquitted herself of her debt contracted in 1863 by the stand she took in the war of 1866, Gorchakov could demand a price for the renewal of the benevolent neutrality of Russia in the coming war, and this price would certainly be the cancellation of the de-militarization clause of the Treaty of Paris. It is possible that Russia also promised to keep Austria from intervening in the war. This may be merely presumed, as the conversation between the two statesmen on that day has not been disclosed.[1] One thing is certain: Bismarck was entirely satisfied with this conversation. Had he not been, he probably would not have re-drafted the famous Ems telegram the very same afternoon in a sense to make war inevitable.

Whether or not Gorchakov had pledged himself in that interview to hold back Austria, it was precisely that important service which Russia rendered to Prussia. Indeed, it is now known that Emperor Francis Joseph was very definitely considering recovering his supreme authority in Germany through some action in the coming war. Francis Joseph considered himself still a German sovereign and he felt the alliance of the South German states as a personal defeat. After consultation with Archduke Albert and chancellor Beust, who as a former Saxon was bitterly opposed to Prussia, the Austrian Emperor had made up his mind to join actively in the struggle against Prussia, should Prussia sustain a defeat. What held him back was the fact that he knew Russia had promised to intervene on the side of Prussia should Austria enter the war. Count Andrassy, the future chancellor, essentially Hungarian in his views, and fearing Russia, clashed with Beust on this issue, and at the crucial meeting of the Crown Council which met in Vienna on July 18th to decide Austria's attitude in the war, he won a complete victory by insisting on a decision of absolute neutrality in the struggle.[2]

Beust had been forewarned as early as 1869 by Gorchakov telling him bluntly, "We have no alliance with Prussia, but we are not forbidden to contract one in the future. Should, for instance, a war break out between France and Prussia and should Prussia see you amongst her enemies, we would reserve our freedom of action and vice versa."[3]

Hence Beust wrote a confidential letter to the Austrian Ambassador in Paris, Prince Metternich, on July 20, 1870, explaining Austria's position in the conflict and stating definitely that Austria's entry into the war would be followed by a declaration of war upon Austria by Russia. Hence it was necessary to gain time by keeping the Russians busy ("amuser les

---

[1] Matter, P., <u>Bismarck et son Temps</u>. Paris 1905-1908. Vol. III, p. 56.

[2] Redlich, J., <u>Emperor Francis Joseph of Austria, a biography</u>, New York, 1929, p. 384, 385.

[3] de la Gorce P. <u>Histoire du Second Empire</u>, Paris 1908. Vol. VI, p. 152, 153.

Russes") until the advanced season and the bad weather would make Russian troop concentrations impossible. Thus Napoleon's hope of Austria's active support in the war was shattered.[4] In another direction Russia's action, this time in cooperation with England, proved to be equally efficacious. The French General Staff conceived the idea of paralyzing a part of Prussia's forces by the landing of a French expeditionary corps some 30,000 strong on the coast of Denmark. It was hoped, not unreasonably, that the Danes, seeking to avenge the loss of Schleswig-Holstein, would then join the French with an army of equal size. The high excitement and the manifestation of pro-French sympathies in Danish public opinion seemed to justify these hopes. Accordingly, on July 24 Admiral Bouet-Willaumez with a large squadron sailed to Denmark, reaching the Baltic on August 2. Transports were to follow. But the swift diplomatic action of England and Russia imposed a strict neutrality upon Denmark and these French hopes were also shattered. Thus Russia, though not participating in the actual fighting, had very definitely taken sides with Prussia.

The feeble attempts of Napoleon's diplomacy in the months preceding the war to win Russia away from her friendship with Prussia had failed completely. The reason was that Russia held a grudge against France on three counts during the last 15 years--first, the Crimean War, second, the attitude of France in the Polish rebellion of 1863 and third, the encouragement given by France to Prince Charles of Roumania upon his accession to the throne. To counteract these Napoleon sent General Fleury to St. Petersburg with definite instructions to win over the Russian court circles to France. It was hoped that as a military man, he would appeal to the Czar, while his affable manners would ingratiate him in St. Petersburg society. But the efforts of Fleury were nullified in advance by the strict instructions given him, not under any circumstances to touch upon the Eastern question--the only question which vitally interested Russia. Hence when Fleury, as the Spanish crisis was becoming acute, attempted to win the sympathy of Gorchakov, the latter adroitly shifted the matter by stating that it would first be necessary for the French Government to give Russia a proof of its spirit of conciliation in the East, adding that Russia was painfully aware of the Treaty of Paris.[5] The

---

[4] de la Gorce, op. cit., Vol. VI, p. 344, 345.

[5] Fleury to Gramont, July 7, 9, 11, 1870. de la Gorce, op. cit. Vol. VI, p. 235.

only result Fleury obtained was the promise of a letter from the Czar to the King of Prussia counselling moderation, a gesture of politeness of no political import.

As the news from the battle front increasingly indicated that France was losing, Austria began veering cautiously towards Russia. Indeed, the very next day after the battle of Froeschwiller, Beust sent a dispatch to Count Chotek, Austrian Ambassador in St. Petersburg, instructing him to approach the Russian Government in a very friendly manner with regard to a continued exchange of views on the situation.

Feeling Austria slipping away, Napoleon's government turned, as a last resort, to the only remaining potential ally-- the new Kingdom of Italy. But here again, without being the sole determining factor, the shadow of St. Petersburg weighed upon the decisions of the Florence government. Indeed the King, Victor Emmanuel, the Foreign Minister Visconti-Venosta and a powerful group of army officers formed a war party in favour of France, but when Cavaliere Nigra, the Italian Ambassador in Paris, reported his conversation with the Russian Chargé d'Affaires, Okunev, in which the latter stated: "If Austria ceases to be neutral we will do the same"[6] and the next day (August 6) wired to Visconti-Venosta stating that similar information had been received from the Italian Embassy in St. Petersburg--the Italian Government decided to follow Austria in a prudent neutrality.

Meanwhile England, coming forward with a proposal for a league of neutrals, closed the last channels to France, now desperately searching for active allies. Russia immediately assented enthusiastically to this proposal. At the time of the outbreak of hostilities, Russia had made an official declaration of neutrality, but this neutrality was very benevolent to Prussia. As King Wilhelm wrote to his wife on July 19, 1870, "Russia did not only express her benevolent neutrality but lets us hope for more." (mais encore laisse entrevoir d'avantage).[7] The Grand Duke of Saxe-Weimar, related to both the Czar and the King of Prussia, became the go-between for the two rulers and on August 29 a Russian courier brought him and the King of Prussia letters from the Czar in which the latter expressed his desire to be useful to the cause of Germany, but nevertheless recommended moderation with regard to France. However

---

[6]Letter from M. Jacini de Lanza, Aug. 5, 1870. de la Gorce, op. cit. Vol. VI, p. 212.

[7]Matter, op. cit., Vol. III, p. 88.

after Sedan when the triumph of Prussia became complete and Paris was on the point of being besieged, Gorchakov began raising some opposition to the contemplated annexations of French territory. The result was that King Wilhelm wrote to the Queen asking her to write to the Grand Duchess Helena of Russia (formerly of Wurttemberg, now married to Grand Duke Michael, brother of the Czar) "to stop the intrigues of Gorchakov, who opposes his veto to any annexations."[8]

Meanwhile in October, Thiers, who now was taking upon himself the role of negotiator for France, made a journey around the European capitals in the hope of winning public opinion of the neutrals in favour of the lost cause of his country. In St. Petersburg Gorchakov advised him to negotiate directly with Bismarck and arranged for a pass to the German headquarters.[9] Thus very discreetly Gorchakov was beginning to take a hand in the negotiations in a sense which was not entirely pleasing to Bismarck. He also began talking of calling an European congress to settle the war, a move which would interfere with all Bismarck's plans. The Grand Duke of Weimar began suggesting the necessity of compensating Russia by concessions on the Black Sea. A letter received from Czar Alexander endorsing Gorchakov's scheme of a congress worried Bismarck considerably. He was still pondering his next move when Gorchakov, with dramatic suddenness, demanded payment for Russia's services rendered to Prussia in the past and in the present. On October 31, 1870, Gorchakov sent a circular letter to the great powers of Europe denouncing the clause of the de-militarization of the Black Sea in the Treaty of Paris. Having then sent General Annenkov on a special mission to the Prussian Headquarters at Versailles, to explain his move, Gorchakov quietly awaited the results of his manoeuvre.

II

Gorchakov had never once abandoned the idea of ridding himself of this clause of the Treaty of Paris at the first opportune time, and in this he was supported by the Czar. As far back as 1863 Alexander had said to Gorchakov, "At this table seven years ago I committed an act which I can qualify, for it is I who did it. I signed the Treaty of Paris and it was a cowardly act."[10] Gorchakov, inspired by this attitude of his

---

[8] Matter op. cit., Vol. III, p. 142.

[9] Gorchakov to Bismarck, Oct. 22, 1870.

[10] Goriainow, B., Le Bosphore et les Dardanelles, Paris 1910, p. 147.

master had instructed all the Russian diplomats abroad to work constantly for the abrogation of the onerous treaty. In 1866 Brunnow had reported from London that England might consent to the eventual restitution of Bessarabia to Russia but would under no circumstances accept any change concerning the de-militarization of the Black Sea. Austria too had showed signs of hesitancy in 1859 and 1867, both the Chancellors Rechberg and Beust raising the issue in the hope of getting Russia's support during the Italian and later the Prussian wars, but it was England once more who forced upon Austria a more determined attitude in resisting this change. Prussia had been favourable all along and in England the increasingly powerful voice of Gladstone spoke for the fairness of Russia's demand. Even Beust acknowledged in 1867 that the clause was humiliating and unjust to Russia. Matters stood there except for a conversation which General Ignatiev had in August 1870 with Aali Pasha in Constantinople, a conversation which produced an outbreak of nervousness in London. Aali declared that Turkey would raise less objections to the cession of Bessarabia than to the change of the status of the Black Sea and insisted that whatever might happen the Straits must remain closed. Reporting on this conversation Ignatiev expressed the view that the solution of the problem lay in Europe and not in Constantinople.

The Franco-Prussian War offered a unique chance in this respect, the more so that the Italian Government by its occupation of Rome had set a precedent for breaking international agreements. Gorchakov staked his whole career on the success of the undertaking. Speaking to his assistant, Jomini, in the course of a walk at Tsarskoye-Selo he said, "Well my dear Jomini, if my calculations have deceived me, and if I have raised a storm which will prove to be too dangerous to Russia, the Emperor can always disavow me if he deems it necessary for the good of the country. I will gladly sacrifice myself....."[11] Accordingly in the circular letter he sent to the signatories of the Treaty of Paris he declared that fifteen years of experience had shown that the de-militarization clause which should have made for the avoidance of conflicts and given Russia security had proven to be illusory since, whereas Russia was disarmed in the Black Sea, Turkey could maintain unlimited forces in the Straits and England and France could concentrate great naval forces in the Eastern Mediterranean. Furthermore, the treaty of 1856 had been violated already when

---

[11]Goriainow, op. cit., p. 156.

Roumania was proclaimed a principality without the assent of the great powers and in disregard of Russia's protest. Lastly, under various pretences, foreign naval forces amounting at times to whole squadrons had penetrated into the Black Sea, and with the introduction of the ironclad ships the situation was even more dangerous for Russia. Considering these factors Russia therefore declared that: 1) she does not consider herself any longer bound by the clauses of the treaty of 1856 which restrict her sovereignty over the Black Sea, 2) she denounces the special convention concluded with Turkey concerning the maintenance of forces for coast-guard service in that sea, 3) loyally informs the signatory powers of these steps and 4) gives the Sultan of Turkey full freedom of action and rights in the Black Sea as she assumes them herself. This note was delivered to the Russian Ambassadors in Berlin, Vienna, Constantinople, Paris, London and Florence for transmission to the respective governments. Brunnow in London was further instructed to declare to Lord Stanley, that Russia would consider the acceptance of only such modifications to the treaty as would be participated in by all the contracting parties, and as a special compensation, he was to offer to England secretly the principle of the freedom of the Black Sea to be applied to the vessels of all powers. Having thrown this diplomatic bombshell Gorchakov awaited the reaction of the powers. He was not worried about the possibility of involving Russia in a war: "one does not fight over a declaration," said Jomini.[12]

In London and in Vienna as may have been expected, a storm of indignation greeted Gorchakov's circular. Beust fumed speaking of the consequences of a move which violated an international agreement signed by all the great powers. Lord Loftus was equally vocal in his protestations against an infringement of existing treaties. On October 28, Sir Andrew Buchanan, the British Ambassador in St. Petersburg, declared that if the news was confirmed he might expect to be instructed to demand his passports. But the official reply of the British Government to Gorchakov's note delivered on November 12, though cold was not bellicose, merely stressing it would have been easier to reach an agreement had the other governments been consulted before this move by Russia. In a further note delivered through Sir Andrew Buchanan, the British Government, while declaring England's attachment to the principle of the inviolability of treaties, objected to the form of Gorchakov's

---

[12] Goriainow, op. cit., p. 161.

declaration and not to its substance--a sort of "dissertation on public law" declared Gorchakov sarcastically. As for Bismarck, the Iron Chancellor had been vexed at the suddenness of this move. In writing to his wife on November 15, he said, "the silly fools have started this move four weeks too early." But Gorchakov knew what he was doing: if Russia had waited until Prussia had acquired everything she desired, Bismarck might not have been so amenable. At present, with the war still in progress, it was of paramount importance for Bismarck to have Russia on his side. However, the British Government made a bold effort to win the Prussian Chancellor over in an attempt to form a diplomatic coalition of the three remaining great powers, England, Austria and Prussia against Russia. For this purpose Sir Odo Russell, under-secretary of Foreign Affairs, was sent to the Prussian headquarters at Versailles. Bluntly Bismarck told Russell that the only way to avoid a European war, threatening as a result of Gorchakov's action, was to convoke an European conference. With the assent of the British delegate a wire to that effect was sent to St. Petersburg. The rapidity with which a favourable reply was received (nine hours after the message had been sent) makes it probable that Russia and Prussia had already agreed upon this issue earlier, possibly in conversations between Bismarck and General Annenkov. However, Bismarck dragged out the calling of this conference until January in order to have time to push on the hostilities with France. He also discouraged a Roumanian move to solicit the intervention of all the signatories of the Treaty of Paris which would have included France. The conference was finally convoked in London on January 17, 1871, with France absent. The Russian announcement concerning the abrogation of the de-militarization clause was accepted by the delegates without recriminations. England proposed that the signatories of the Treaty of Paris should have the right of using the Turkish ports on the Black Sea to counter-balance the naval power of Russia. Facing the opposition of the Russian delegation to this proposal, at the second meeting on January 24, the suggestion was made that the Straits should be open to the naval forces of all the powers except Russia, in the event that the security of Turkey was menaced. But Russia demanded equality of treatment and bitter discussions ensued. Finally at the fourth meeting on February 7, a compromise solution proposed by Italy was accepted, whereby Turkey would open the Straits to foreign navies only in the event of necessity of safeguarding the special convention concluded between England, Austria and France on

April 15, 1856, guaranteeing the integrity of the Ottoman Empire. On this basis a convention was signed dated March 13, 1871, declaring that the articles XI, XIII and XIV of the Treaty of Paris had been abrogated and replaced by the following clause: "the principle of the closing of the Straits of Bosphorus and Dardanelles, as established by the separate treaty of March 30, 1856, is maintained with the right granted to the Sultan of opening the said Straits in time of peace to the navies of the allied and friendly powers in the event that the execution of the stipulation of the Treaty of Paris of March 30, 1856, should make it necessary."[13] The other articles, not abrogated of the Treaty of Paris were reconfirmed. Thus the demilitarization clause was excluded from the said Treaty of Paris and Gorchakov had won his point.

III

We have seen that Bismarck was vexed by the suddenness of Gorchakov's denunciation of the Treaty of Paris. Though still very slight, this was the first crack in the structure of the Russo-Prussian friendship. Now that Bismarck had achieved his aim, defeated France and created the German Empire, his foreign policy was to become conservative and dominated by the desire that the new German Empire should not be in danger of an attack from any combination of two or more neighbouring powers, hence as he confessed later, he had from then on "le cauchemar des coalitions--" the nightmare of coalitions. To thwart such a possibility, he still thought in terms of good relations with Russia as being the axis of his foreign policy, to which he would now endeavour to attach Austria. His new idea was therefore to recreate the equivalent of the alliance of the Three Northern Courts which would thereby insure him against the persistent and bitter enmity of France and the cold aloofness of Great Britain. Perhaps this system of alliances eventually might be enlarged to include the newly created Kingdom of Italy. Shortly after Sedan, whilst Bismarck was still at Meaux on his way to Versailles, he had discreetly approached both the courts of St. Petersburg and Vienna with an offer to establish "an alliance of the three Emperors with the ultimate idea that monarchical Italy would eventually join it,"[14] for the purpose of "protecting (soustraire) as far as possible the present generations and

---

[13] Goriainow, op. cit., p. 282.
[14] Matter, op. cit., Vol. III, p. 286.

their children from international and revolutionary socialism," isolating revolutionary France and maintaining the principle of authority in the powerful and vigorous monarchies.[15] Both Vienna and St. Petersburg were reluctant to commit themselves and Bismarck became more insistent, his ambassador in Vienna approaching the Austrian Government once more on December 14. Throughout the winter 1870-71 Austria and Prussia, as a result of German victories in the war, had showed an increasing tendency to come together and both sides reiterated their readiness to forget the past. With Russia, no new developments occurred until the summer of 1871 when, on June 2, Gorchakov passed through Berlin on the way to his annual cure, followed on the 9th by Emperor Alexander; both had interviews with Bismarck which were extremely cordial, agreeing to Bismarck's plan in principle. Beust, the Austrian Chancellor, seeing the trend, made a statement at a meeting of the Austro-Hungarian "delagations" to the effect that Germany was now a friend, that Russia was a friend of a friend and Italy a good neighbour. Thus the ground had been prepared.

The meeting of Emperors Wilhelm and Francis Joseph at Ischl on July 11, 1871, and later at Gastein, followed by Bismarck's visit to Gastein where he met Beust, sealed the Austro-Prussian friendship. Now Germany was virtually allied in fact if not in name to Russia and to Austria, but Bismarck had not yet succeeded in bringing his two allies together. The next year Francis Joseph announced his return visit to Berlin, the date being set for the 6th of September. Suddenly came the news that Czar Alexander would be in Berlin on September 5 following an invitation extended to him in July by Emperor Wilhelm. Alexander was pleased at the opportunity to be present at the meeting of his two powerful neighbours and to see what was going on. The presence of the two Emperors in Berlin was the occasion for a splendid reception on a scale unprecedented in the German capital; while the presence of so many eminent statesmen, Gorchakov, Prince Orlov, Russian Ambassador in Paris, M. d'Oubril, Ambassador in Berlin and Baron Jomini, Assistant Minister of Foreign Affairs of Russia, the new Chancellor of Austria, Count Andrassy and a large delegation gave a prominence to this meeting which attracted the anxious curiosity of other powers. Though no definite treaty was signed the first League of the Three Emperors was born. Bismarck was not pleased, however. By the arrival of the Russians the meeting had slipped out of his hands and he

---

[15]Matter, ibidem, Vol. III, p. 286.

showed his ill humor to Gorchakov on several occasions. He began developing an increasing dislike for Gorchakov personally and never could forgive the patronizing attitude the latter had adopted toward him. His ill humour showed itself shortly afterwards in his refusal to sign a definite military convention with Russia in furtherance of the newly constituted league. The Russians on the other hand were anxious throughout to conciliate the French and Alexander observed significantly to Vicomte de Gontaut-Biron, the French Ambassador at Berlin, "Please tell M. Thiers that he has nothing to fear in what has been taking place here..... France can be certain that I would not have taken part in anything which might have been directed against her....."[16] Thus at the very moment when a great show of solidarity was being made by the Three Emperors, the crack in the structure of the Russo-Prussian alliance had widened slightly. The relations between Russia and Austria, though now officially friendly, remained one of suspicion and mutual distrust. Very little of real value had been achieved in Berlin.

However resplendent had been the meeting of the three Emperors at Berlin in 1872, the practical results of the pact amounted to little, for veiled underneath official speeches of goodwill were the Austro-Russian rivalry on one hand and an increasing irritation of Bismarck against Russia on the other. Further developments tended to increase this irritation. Bismarck viewed any signs of a possible rapprochement between Russia and France with open exasperation, and perhaps the only important result of the meeting in Berlin had been that it gave the opportunity for Czar Alexander II to show courtesy to France, in the statement to Gontaut-Biron that Russia would not participate in anything hostile to that country. This was the first sign of a turn in Franco-Russian relations, so consistently hostile for well nigh two decades. Others were to follow. In 1874 Alexander II went to London to visit his daughter, the Duchess of Edinburgh. At the news of this journey the government of Marechal MacMahon very insistently tried to get Alexander to visit Paris or at least to stop somewhere in French territory on his way to London. Alexander refused, politely explaining to the Duc de La Rochefoucauld, French Ambassador in Russia, that he was going on a private holiday and did not want to discuss any political questions. But once Alexander was in London he received the unexpected visit of the Count of Paris, the Orleanist pretender to the French

---

[16]Matter, op. cit., Vol. III, p. 361,362.

throne, who was now heading the whole Royalist cause in France, since Henry V, the Count of Chambord, the legitimist candidate, had withdrawn. The Count of Paris was eager to win the support of the Czar both for the Royalist cause and the Orleanist branch to which Russia had been so consistently hostile ever since Louis Philippe. Therefore he made a special trip to London to call upon the Czar and had a cordial interview of about half an hour with Alexander, after which the latter returned his call at Claridge's. Though entirely unofficial, these interviews irritated Bismarck.[17]

Meanwhile developments in Spain, where a civil war had broken out, found Russia and France supporting the Carlist cause whereas Bismarck issued a recognition to the government of Marshal Serrano. A circular of Prince Gorchakov giving the reasons why Russia could not recognize the Serrano government gave a sudden prominence to the whole issue in Spain and glaringly revealed the divergence of views on this issue between Prussia and Russia. Bismarck had backed the wrong horse and the restoration of King Alphonse XII to power on December 30 of the same year was a definite setback for the Spanish policy of the Iron Chancellor. Thus the breach was gradually widening. Presently there occurred the war scare of 1875 which produced the first open quarrel between Bismarck and Gorchakov.

IV

In the eyes of Bismarck France had been recuperating dangerously fast. Not only had she paid off her enormous war debt to Germany but, in February, 1875, she had acquired stability by establishing a republican constitution. Shortly afterward an army law was passed by the National Assembly which increased the effectives of the French Army by 140,000 men. Bismarck was watching this comeback of France with an uneasiness which made him plot a Machiavellian design to weaken France once more. In the spring of 1875 he was thinking either in terms of a new war with France or of a move to cajole France by a threat of war. We will never know what was in the mind of Bismarck for he seldom showed his cards openly and, working through others, he was able to put the blame on them when his manoeuvre failed. Whatever

---

[17]Hippeau, Edmond, Histoire Diplomatique de la Troisième Republique, Paris 1889, p. 113.

his intentions may have been, Europe became aware of a war atmosphere being created in Berlin, Bismarck envenoming and magnifying small incidents as he had done in the case of his Austrian war. Some French bishops had endorsed the encyclical of the Pope protesting the arrest of Bishop Ledochowski during Bismarck's drive against the Catholic Church known as the Kulturkampf. Bismarck took a menacing attitude and made an incident out of the issue. In April he asked M. de Gontaut-Biron to explain the armaments of France. Then on April 8, the "Post" published an obviously inspired article headlined "Krieg im Sicht", (War in Sight). The tenseness created by these little incidents spread over Europe and a new Franco-Prussian war seemed to be in sight. But Bismarck was checkmated from an unexpected side. The London "Times" wrote that peace or war depended on an interview between the German and Russian Emperors. To make sure of the goodwill of Russia, Bismarck already in February had sent Radowitz on a special mission to St. Petersburg offering Russia freedom of action in the East in return for a similar freedom of action in the West for Germany. But Radowitz returned empty-handed to Berlin and Russia began showing signs of friendliness to France. The article in the "Post" was construed by Russia as a ballon d'essai to test European public opinion and Russia was not going to be duped. Gorchakov advised the French ambassador, General le Flo, that "France should become strong, very strong." Meanwhile an exchange of views was taking place between London and St. Petersburg, with Rome joining in but Vienna abstaining. Count Shuvalov, Russian ambassador in London, when passing through Berlin had an audience with Emperor Wilhelm who reiterated his pacific intentions, while to Bismarck he had given the advice "to be very careful as to what he was going to do."[18] Lord Odo Russell was active on his side and thus an Anglo-Russian collaboration was insured in the crisis. But Bismarck persevered, and on May 5, the question of French armaments was raised during an interview which his ambassador, Prince Hohenlohe, had with the French Minister of Foreign Affairs.

Meanwhile, thoroughly alarmed, the Duc Decazes, French Foreign Minister, wired on April 29, to Czar Alexander II imploring him to intercede for peace. "Alexander" he wrote, "could secure the peace of the world in stating openly to Germany that, should she attack France, he would not allow such an injustice to be done."[19] This amounted to a virtual

---

[18] Matter, op. cit., Vol. III, p. 386.
[19] Hippeau, op. cit., p. 126.

request for military action on the part of Russia in defence of France. On the eve of his departure for Berlin, Alexander, in reply to this telegram, promised General le Flo to intercede with Emperor Wilhelm whereas Gorchakov said: "We will not draw our sword, and we will not need to; we will achieve our ends without it."[20] Alexander and Gorchakov arrived in Berlin on May 10. The two Emperors discussed the crisis, while Bismarck and Gorchakov had a stormy meeting. According to Paléologue, who may have dramatized the scene,[21] Alexander, receiving Bismarck the next day said: "Without my neutrality Germany would be impotent. Now understand this: I should not remain neutral." Whether said or not, this was the import of the message delivered by the Czar during his visit and there was nothing else for Bismarck to do but climb down. The Iron Chancellor put the whole blame on Field Marshal Moltke and declared once more he had no intentions of going to war. Exultant, Gorchakov sent a circular telegram stating that peace was assured, while Alexander II wired to his sister, the Queen of Württemberg, an open telegram, nonciphered, in French, stating that,"j'emporte de Berlin des assurances formelles de paix," ("I bring from Berlin formal assurances of peace."), which by an amusing error of transmission read on receipt "L'Emporté de Berlin donne des assurances formelles de paix" ("The hot-headed one of Berlin gives his formal assurances of peace"), in which form it became known to the public, to the exasperation of Bismarck.[22] Bismarck had been snubbed for the first time in his career and such was his anger that he offered his resignation, which was, of course, refused. He then left for his estate of Varzin, where in the calm of the Pomeranian forests he nursed his ill humour against Gorchakov, whom he accused of vanity and senility, and indulged in heavy sarcasm at the expense of the Russian Chancellor. Several years later Bismarck expressed his own views on this incident to Mr. Saburov, the new Russian Ambassador in Berlin, and in his words the grudge against Gorchakov still remained. Said Bismarck: "We have a Staff which is perpetually at war with our three neighbours, not even excepting Austria..... In 1875 our tacticians went too far, and I had to intervene. They thought that France was recovering too quickly from her defeat..... That is why

---

[20]Hippeau, op. cit., p. 127.

[21]Graham, Stephen, Tzar of Freedom, Newhaven 1935, p. 182.

[22]Matter, op. cit., Vol. III, p. 388.

I provoked an explanation with the French Government. I knew at least where I would stop; but the military never know. Unfortunately, Prince Gorchakov did not wish to understand this and preferred to score a diplomatic success at my expense."[23]

Bismarck took his revenge at the Congress of Berlin.

V

It is now necessary to note one important change in Russia which was to modify to a certain degree the foreign policy of that country. Up to this time there had been no vocal public opinion in Russia, and the Czar and his ministers were completely free from any outside pressure when laying out their schemes and plans of foreign policy. Occasionally Russian statesmen and diplomats did refer to public opinion but this was usually merely to impress the foreign cabinets. Now, however, a current was rising in the organized circles of Russian public opinion diametrically opposed to the official policy and eventually becoming sufficiently powerful to force a deviation from that policy. This current arose from the blending of the Slavophilism of the 1830's with the idea of Panslavism imported from abroad. Panslavism has always loomed very large in the eyes of Western statesmen and journalists as a Machiavellian imperialistic scheme of Russia to dominate the Balkans and a part of central Europe, and particularly in England the word Panslavist was regarded as synonymous with Russian agent. In actual fact Panslavism neither originated in Russia nor was ever very strong there. It was an importation from Austria-Hungary where the Slav population, following the nationalist trend so fashionable at the time, was fostering its national and cultural claims as opposed to the centralizing and Germanizing policies of the Hapsburgs.

As Bohemia was the region most geographically exposed to Germanization, and its inhabitants, ever since the loss of their nationality in the disaster of the Thirty Years War, had suffered most from this forcible Germanization, it was natural that the doctrine of Panslavism should not only ripen but find a special response amongst the Czechs. Indeed it was at the Slav Congress in Prague in 1848 that Panslavism shaped itself into a doctrine. No such problem existed for the Russians, hence the echoing in Russia to these acute feelings had necessarily to be vague. The nearest equivalent to Panslavism

---

[23] The Saburov Mémoires edited by T. Y. Simpson, Cambridge, 1929, pp. 40, 41.

which existed in Russia at the time was Slavophilism, a school of thought which originated in the thirties and forties as a violent reaction against the trend of excessive westernization of Russia as inaugurated by Peter the Great. The Slavophils advocated a return to the fundamentals of Russian life which were based on Orthodoxy, autocracy and the national roots going back to Byzantium and early Slav traditions, in opposition to the rationalism and individualism of the decadent civilizations of the west. Proclaiming that Peter the Great, in his efforts to westernize Russia, had led the country astray, they opposed the bureaucratic system he had set up, in which German influence subsequently had become so strong. In their intense dislike of what they termed the German domination of Russia, they partially echoed the Panslavist feelings of the Western Slavs. But Slavophilism remained an intellectual, cultural and philosophical movement with no political aspirations and, prior to the Crimean War, had taken little interest in the Slav world outside of Russia. The fact that the western Slavs were Roman Catholic and not Greek Orthodox was in itself a sufficient factor to alienate them from Slavophil sympathies since Catholicism was regarded by Slavophils as one of the essential and worst elements of the Germano-Roman civilization which they despised.

Only very few Slavophils really showed any interest in the Balkan Slavs who were little known to Russia notwithstanding the role played by official Russian diplomacy in moulding their destinies. Amongst the earliest to show any real interest in their fate as Slavs and not as a factor in the Turkish problem was Professor Pogodin who started a crusade for the liberation of the Southern Slavs from the Turkish yoke and, as Professor of History in the University of Moscow, devoted himself to showing the common historical traditions and ties between Russia and Southern Slavdom. He was one of the founders and second president of the Moscow Slavonic Benevolent Committee which was established in 1850 for the purpose of developing a national, cultural and religious consciousness amongst the Balkan Slavs by bringing assistance to their local institutions and founding schools as well as bringing young Slavs to Russian schools. It was supported both by the Church and the Ministry of Foreign Affairs. The main Moscow committee, concentrated principally on Bulgaria and subsidiary committees set up in 1869 and 1870 in Kiev and Odessa, worked through the fairly large local Bulgarian colonies in those cities. The St. Petersburg committee devoted its main attention to the Czechs. In 1867 this Slavonic Benevolent Committee organized a Slavonic Ethnographic Exhibition in Moscow which attracted widespread attention abroad and was interpreted as a counterpart of the Slavonic Congress of Prague. Actually, though representatives of various Slav races were present (except the Poles), and the Czechs put forward a proposal for creating a permanent inter-Slav organization which would meet in regular bi-annual congresses, nothing more than platonic expressions of goodwill were voiced at this meeting. Nevertheless Russia had been awakened to the importance of the Slav question and a kind of skeleton organization had been created. But the absence of the Poles, who were still smarting under the repression of their rebellion of 1863, showed that this was to be one of the major stumbling blocks to the dream of Slavonic brotherhood, since the Poles were oppressed by the Russians themselves. The Russians, on the other hand, considered that the Poles, with their ardent allegiance to Roman Catholicism and their proud claim that they represented the eastern outpost of Western civilization, were traitors to Slavdom.

If cultural contacts had thus been established between the Slavophil circles and Slavdom at large by the Moscow meeting of 1867, and if this event marks the grafting of Panslavism onto Slavophilism, by the very nature of the situation, the Russian Panslavists were more prone to look with sympathy upon the Greek Orthodox Balkan Slavs crushed by Turkey than on the Roman Catholic Western Slavs better treated by the Austrians, and of which one branch at least, the Poles, were bitter enemies of Russia. Thus starting out in Prague as a cultural rebellion against Germanism, in Moscow, Panslavism takes the shape of a struggle against Turkey. Panslavism however never shaped itself into any definite theory or doctrine; it remained the expression of a mood and a dream,--that of the liberation of all Slav nations from foreign domination and the formation of some kind of a federation between them. As far as Russia was concerned, it only gained consistency by its emphasis on the Turkish problem because this harmonized with a fundamental principle of Russia's policy. Its weakness lay in the fact that owing to the vagueness of its aspirations it could not found a school and have a great following. A perusal of the ideas of the leading Russian Panslavists shows how contradictory and mutually incompatible these ideas sometimes were.

According to Ivan Aksakov, Panslavism is identified with Orthodoxy. The historical mission of Russia is to restore pure Christianity as represented by the Orthodox doctrines in opposition to Catholicism, which is leading Western civilization to decay. Thus the Catholic Slavs not only remain outside this scheme but are to be treated as traitors. The Slavs have the choice between the way of Rome, wherein lies decadence, or the way of Moscow, wherein lies salvation--for their strength is in Russia and Russia's strength is in her adherence to Slavonic and non-Western ideals. Aksakov's friends, Prince Cherkassky and Yuri Samarin came to the inevitable conclusion that Russia must become entirely Russian and liberate herself not only from foreign influence but from foreign minorities on her territory as well. Samarin wrote in a private letter in 1864 that Russia must not be "a reproduction very much in large of the Hotel Ragatz (in Brussels) where Russians, Americans and French sit down without knowing each other at the same table,"[24] in other words he advocated the Russification of alien minorities particularly along the western fringe of the Empire. Samarin wrote a book to this effect, "the Borderlands of Russia", and these ideas were to influence government policies under Pobiedonostsev a decade later. The Poles were to undergo the same process of Russification as the non-Slav alien minorities.

With Fadeiev we come to a more militant conception of Panslavism and it widens to include Austria-Hungary. When a general in the army he wrote a work "Russia's Armed Forces" which was translated into foreign languages and caused a sensation, particularly in Germany. He was finally forced to resign his commission by the Minister of War, General D. A. Miliyutin, after which he devoted himself to journalism. In discussing Russia's military problems in this book he advocated the doctrine that force alone solves international problems and therefore Russia must be strong, particularly in view of the mission she has to fulfil. It is curious to notice how German public opinion was aroused at the statement of what amounted to Bismarckian doctrines. In his second book "Opinion on the Eastern Question", published in 1869, he discusses more fully Russia's historical mission. With the conquest of Poland "Russia now stands in the midst of the enemy's lines--such a condition is only temporary: she must either drive back the enemy or abandon the position."[25] Therefore Russia must either expand to the Adriatic by absorbing the Slavs or retire behind the Dnieper. The Slavs were to be guaranteed an independent political and social life but were to be merged with Russia in a

---

[24]Sumner, H. B., Russia and Panslavism in the Eighteen Seventies. Transactions of the Royal Historical Society, 1935, p. 36.

[25]Sumner, op. cit., p. 43.

federation in which each Slav nation would have a sovereign for its own affairs but would recognize the Great Slav Czar as overlord--once more a Bismarckian conception. Such an advance of Russia over the Balkan peninsula would have Austria on her flank, therefore the key to the solution of the Eastern question is to be found not in Constantinople but in Vienna, and a war with Austria must be considered inevitable. "Russia's chief enemy is by no means Western Europe but the German race in its enormous pretensions."[26] As all Panslavists, he stresses the antagonism of Europe to Russia, a theme lucidly analysed by Danilevsky in his book "Russia and Europe" published the same year (1869).

Danilevsky, a natural scientist, attempted to explain history in terms of laws governing the natural sciences. He discusses the rise and decline of civilizations in terms of the law of evolution and growth and death of species; he foreshadows Spengler in many of his ideas and he foresees the death of the Romano-German civilization, to be replaced in the future by a glorious Slav civilization. Russia must prepare for this day by emancipating the Slavs and welding them into a federation under her leadership. It is because Europe feels her inevitable decline and senses the destiny of Russia that Russia is so much hated in the West. "Cannot Western Europe's hatred of Russia be explained by the instinctive feeling of the West that its own culture is dying and that Russia will be its cultural successor?"[27]

A war for hegemony between Russia and the Western powers is inevitable but this war should lead to the establishment of a great Slav federation into which the non-Slav Greeks, Roumanians and Magyars would have to be brought by virtue of their geographic position. The capital of such a federation should be Constantinople. Approaching the problem from a somewhat more mystical angle, Dostoievsky in his "Diaries of a Writer" preached the necessity for the annexation of Constantinople by Russia, which city would then become the Rome of Orthodoxy. Striking a somewhat different note on the same theme came Konstantin Leontiev who had an intimate knowledge of the East through ten years of consular service in the Balkans and Crete. He advocated Byzantinism as opposed to pure Panslav nationalism. He was much impressed by Danilevsky's

---

[26] Sumner, op. cit., p. 43.

[27] Danilevsky, N., Russland und Europa, Stuttgart und Berlin, 1920, p. 175.

work and particularly with his idea that civilizations are complete organisms which pass through phases of growth and decay. He developed the idea by dividing this growth into three periods; the first being elemental and therefore primitively simple; the second that of maturity and exuberance of creative work through complexity, variety of forms and inequality; and the third that of decay and death, of which the manifestations are a tendency to uniformity and oneness. Europe had passed through the first two stages and the modern democratic tendencies, developing since the eighteenth century, with their levelling processes and stress on equality and sameness, were a sign that she was passing through the third stage. Russia had to be segregated from this contagion of death. "We must freeze Russia to prevent her from rotting." Thus Russia has to be frozen in a state of conservatism, inequality and richness of forms, with its mystical religious traditions and its creed of absolute authority inherited from Byzantium.

As for the Slavs outside of Russia, he denied to them any independent cultural entity. The Slavs were merely a part of the European cycle of growth and decline and by their democratic tendencies condemned to be merged with the West. Leontiev hated the West for its lack of individualism, its cult of herd psychology and its rationalism and atheism. He advocated an aristocratic ideal, a state, ruthless and powerful with a free, active, dominating church. His contempt for mass psychology and democracy as well as for common morality link him with Nietzsche, whereas he is also the forerunner of Spengler, whose theory of Vorkultur, Kultur, and Zivilisation closely parallels the three stages mentioned by Leontiev. The major writings of Leontiev were published in his "Vostok, Rossia i Slavianstvo" (The East, Russia and Slavdom) in 1885-86 but two early essays belong to the period under consideration-- "Panslavism and the Greeks", and "Byzantinism and Slavdom", published respectively in 1873 and 1875.

This rapid survey of the ideas of the leading Panslavist writers permits us to draw some conclusions as to the actual strength and weakness of the movement. It will be seen that there was no unity of concept in the ideas expressed and the sole common denominator was a kind of Pan-Russian nationalism based on a devotion to the Orthodox Church. This led to the negation of Roman Catholicism and the denial of any rights to Polish and to some extent Ukrainian national aspirations within the borders of Russia proper, limiting the ambitions of Panslavists to the Orthodox Balkan Slavs--thus Panslavism was a house divided against itself. Even a greater divergence existed in the fact that democracy and nationalism were becoming more and more synonymous and could hardly be reconciled with Russian autocracy. True, Russian Panslavists made strenuous efforts to bridge the gap by stressing the liberal reforms which had just been passed in Russia and particularly the liberation of the serfs. However Gorchakov in a private letter to Novikov, May 9, 1872, very pertinently expressed his doubts on the subject. "I do not hide from you that it is difficult for me to believe in a sincere sympathy of the Slav races for autocratic Russia."[28]

Lastly, Panslavism was in direct opposition to the official foreign policy of the government based on friendship with Germany and Austria. Furthermore the opposition to Germanism on the part of Panslavists extended to the German influence at the Russian Court and in the St. Petersburg bureaucracy. Though veiled, this criticism could not remain unnoticed and both the Czar and influential government circles were highly displeased and showed no liking for Panslavism. To speak therefore as the foreign press did of Panslavism as being a Machiavellian policy conceived and officially supported by the government, was sheer nonsense. However, the Panslavists did have sympathizers and supporters in influential circles and if small they were nevertheless a powerful minority. The Cesarevitch Alexander (the future Alexander III) and his wife, with their circle, were believed to be openly sympathetic to Panslavism; amongst other outstanding Panslavists were the famous generals Cherniaev, Skobelev and Dragomirov and a host of minor officers; the leading journalist of the day Katkov; and the outstanding diplomat Count Ignatiev. Furthermore, like all such movements, it had the power of emotional appeal which, given a set of favourable circumstances, could set the masses aflame. Such a set of circumstances was produced by a new crisis in the Balkans.

VI

The Balkans, from the standpoint of Russian politics had been extraordinarily quiescent since the Crimean War. Neither the Turko-Montenegrin war, nor the Cretan insurrection, nor even the proclamation of independence by Roumania had sufficiently affected Russian diplomacy to deter it from the main objectives set by Gorchakov. But this was accomplished in the summer of 1875 by the 164 inhabitants of the obscure

---

[28]Sumner, op. cit., p. 35.

village of Nevesinje in Herzegovina. Unable to find redress
against exorbitant taxes in a year of bad harvests, they took
up arms and presently the insurrection spread to the whole of
Herzegovina and neighbouring Bosnia. For a whole year the
rebels successfully fought off the Turkish Army, which was attempting to force the pass of Muratovitza, and finally obtained
from the Sultan a promise of administrative reforms which, as
usual, remained on paper. But this insurrection stirred up
the two neighbouring Serb states, Serbia and Montenegro, and
by its example started a revolutionary movement in Bulgaria.
In Serbia the idea of a greater Serbia was gaining ground under
the sponsorship of the Prime Minister Ristitch, who was one
of its leading and most aggressive advocates. Furthermore
Prince Peter Karageorgievch, pretender to the Serbian throne
and bitter opponent of the Obrenovich dynasty, was winning a
dangerous popularity by placing himself at the head of the Bosnian rebellion, while Prince Nicholas of Montenegro allowed
his subjects to cross the border and join the insurrection.
While Prince Milan of Serbia was hesitating as to what course
to take, the rebellion reached Bulgaria, where national feeling
was fostered by a revolutionary committee organized in Bucharest under the leadership of a certain Benkovski, and a revolt
broke out on May 2 which lasted only ten days and was crushed
by the Turks with utmost severity. The Turks retaliated by a
series of massacres, the worst of these at Batak (May 9, 1876)
taking a toll of 5,000 out of a population of 7,000. During the
month of May it was estimated that some 12,000 men, women
and children had been murdered. These events stirred the
public opinion of Europe, and while Gladstone in England wrote
his famous pamphlet on Bulgarian atrocities, in Russia, owing
to the rise of Panslavist trends, a regular crusade on behalf
of the oppressed Slav brethren was gaining ground. Committees were formed for the collection of funds which received
lavish donations and volunteers were enrolled to go to the aid
of the rebels. All the more striking under these circumstances was the question put by the British High Commissioner,
Baring, to the Turkish authorities--How much Russia had paid
for a massacre which would be the beginning of the end of the
Ottoman Empire?--a monstruous insinuation typical of the
trend of British political thought at the time.

  Under the stress of these events, and partly encouraged by
the response they felt coming from the public opinion, if not
from the government of Russia, Serbia and Montenegro finally
decided upon war with Turkey. The Serbian Government, meanwhile, got into touch with the Russian General Cherniaev and

offered him the command of the Serbian Army. Cherniaev had become famous as one of the heroes of the conquest of Turkestan. In 1864 he had made a celebrated march with 1,000 men across a sandy desert to Chimkent and captured the main city in Turkestan, Tashkent, against the orders of his superiors. This act of heroic insubordination was typical of the man. Later he became the editor of the newspaper "Russky Mir" to which he gave a strong Panslavist character. When the government in St. Petersburg learned of Cherniaev's appointment in Serbia, the Russian Minister of Foreign Affairs, anxious to avoid entanglements, insisted that a foreign visa be refused him and a telegram was sent to the authorities to detain him at the Russian border. However, Cherniaev succeeded in getting out of Russia and in June reached Belgrade. A few days later (June 29) Serbia and Montenegro declared war upon Turkey.

The lure of Cherniaev's name acted as a powerful stimulus to stir up further the sympathies of the Russian public in favour of the Southern Slavs. Several thousand Russian officers and privates left the army to enroll as volunteers in the Serbian Army. The Moscow Zemstvo (provincial council) voted 20,000 roubles for relief in Serbia. The newspapers attacked the government violently for showing indifference toward the oppressed brethren. Church sermons, resolutions of townspeople and industrial organizations all advocated a crusade against the Turk. Hospital units were organized and sent to the front. The death of one of the most notable Panslavists, Nicholas Kireiev, brother of the famous Olga Novikov, further stirred public excitement. He had gone to Serbia at the head of a hospital unit but took command of a volunteer brigade which he led into action on July 18 at the battle of Zaitchar. Whilst advancing against a Turkish battery, dressed in a spectacular white uniform which made him an easy target, he was wounded three times but kept on advancing until he was struck by a fourth bullet and fell shouting "Forward". His body was captured by the Turks and dreadfully mutilated.

The Serbs put 100,000 men in the field and Montenegro 28,000 as against 100,000 Turks. But Cherniaev was soon to discover that these were raw levies, inferior to the enemy in armament, discipline and fighting qualities. He had his doubts about starting an offensive, but was overriden and ordered to cross the Turkish frontier early in July at Kniajevatz and to march on Pirot. A week later he was falling back pursued by the energetic Osman Pasha (later the hero of Plevna) who cut his communications by capturing Kniajevatz. Cherniaev attempted to outwit his opponent by a second offensive and the war dragged on with alternating success until August. The Serbs turned down all offers of the Great Powers to mediate. They were encouraged by the flow of Russian volunteers which made them believe Russia would come to their aid, and by Cherniaev's clever move of having the army operating on the Timok front proclaim Prince Milan king. But when Cherniaev in September started a second major offensive, a counter offensive of the Turkish Army led to the smashing defeat of the Serbian Army at Alexinatz (October 12-16) and the road to Belgrade was open. In despair Prince Milan wired for help to the Czar and, though unwilling to get entangled, Alexander II ordered the Russian Ambassador in Constantinople, Count Ignatiev, to issue a 48 hour ultimatum (October 19), demanding the cession of hostilities under a threat of the break of diplomatic relations with Russia. The Turks complied by granting an armistice for two months and Russia came one step nearer being involved in the war. Meanwhile the Montenegrins had won some signal successes over the Turkish Army advancing into their mountains.

Certainly neither Alexander II nor Gorchakov wanted war. War would mean interference with internal reforms and the crumbling of the structure of financial stability erected by Count Reitern, the Minister of Finance. Russia moreover was just engaged in a program of railway construction which, in the decade preceding 1875, had added 12,000 versts to the existing 5,000 of the Russian system and this had heavily taxed the country's resources. As for Gorchakov, a war in the Balkans would endanger his whole scheme of foreign policy in Europe. Moreover neither the Emperor nor the Chancellor had any liking for Panslavism. But under pressure of the rising excitement of public opinion Alexander gave in to the point of shifting his view from absolutely vetoing a war to that of declaring that there was a limit to national patience under the provocative policy of the Turks. Thus the drift toward war had begun. In the subsequent development of events two men and one woman were to play especially important rôles. These were the Russian Ambassadors in the key diplomatic positions of Constantinople and London, Count Ignatiev and Count Shuvalov, and Madam Olga Novikov. Few men have borne a greater brunt of hatred with hostile and caluminous insinuations on the part of the British press and later of British historians than Ignatiev. His portrait in history can only be made real if one first pierces this fog of vehement and hostile propaganda built around him. Some British historians have lost their balance to the point of calling him "the father of lies" and it is difficult to find the expression of an impartial judgement.

Count Paul Ignatiev had had a remarkable career. In his early twenties he was sent on a dangerous mission to Khiva and Bokhara, preceding the Russian conquest of these two Central Asian states. The Khan of Khiva had laid plans to detain him as a hostage, but he managed to escape and brought back as well a valuable treaty signed with Bokhara. In 1860 at the age of 28 he acted as mediator between the Chinese Government and the Franco-British forces, which had occupied Peking, and secured for Russia the possession of the Amur region. Appointed Ambassador to Constantinople four years later, he showed the same restless energy and very soon made himself the dominating figure in the diplomatic corps of the Turkish capital. This and the fact that he had ardently espoused the creed of Panslavism caused him to be regarded by the British as their chief enemy. In 1870 he secured from the Turks a beginning of national independence for the Bulgarian Church, previously under the rule of the Greek Patriarchate. He then conciliated the Greeks by supporting the cause of the Cretan revolutionaries. In 1875 when the Khedive of Egypt, Ismail, was seeking to reorganize his army for the purpose of a campaign in Abyssinia, Ignatiev succeeded in having General Fadeiev (the Panslavist) appointed to this important mission. Fadeiev went to Egypt but, in the spring of 1876 with the Balkan crisis becoming acute, was recalled to Russia.

Quite opposite to Ignatiev in character and policy was Count Peter Shuvalov. Of an aristocratic Russian family, he had entered the army and for 20 years led the leisurely life of a Guards officer. Then as Governor of the Baltic Provinces he had showed administrative ability. Later he became head of the dreaded Third Section of the Imperial Chancellery (the political police).

In 1873 he was sent on a secret mission to London with the delicate double task of ironing out the rivalry over Central Asia and paving the way for the marriage of the daughter of Alexander II, Grand Duchess Maria Alexandrovna, with the Duke of Edinburgh. The success of this mission resulted in his appointment as Ambassador to England, the Czar being anxious to remain friendly with that country and Shuvalov having become persona grata in London. Moreover he was known not to have Panslavist sympathies and his political views were in accord with those of Gorchakov. He believed that both Russia and England had a civilizing mission in Asia and that the co-operating of the two great Empires would produce the best mutual results. During the Balkan crisis he found himself equally embarrassed by the friends and the foes of Russia in English political circles, and he steered a cautious middle course working all the while for the prevention of war. On one side he had to face the stand taken by Disraeli and his government, who advocated that "The Turk is a gentleman" and that the whole Balkan crisis was a plot of Russia against British imperial interests. On the other hand there was Gladstone's passionate crusading for the Balkan Slavs and the anti-Turkish agitation of those who might be termed British Slavophils, including such outstanding figures as Thomas Carlyle. Olga Novikov, the sister of Kireiev who was killed in Serbia, herself an ardent Panslavist, became the soul of this movement and her energy and activities made her known as the "M. P." for Russia, to the great embarrassment of the cautious Ambassador.

Following the ultimatum which Russia sent to Turkey to stop the Serbian war, Russian diplomacy began gradually taking a more determined stand. Of the intricate, half-hearted and insincere efforts of the great powers during the following months to prevent war and to do something to help the Slavs, we need not concern ourselves over much, limiting it simply to the study of the main developments.

At the outset of the trouble the position of Austria was made clear in a conversation between Andrassy and the Russian Chargé d'Affaires Novikov (October 13, 1875) in which Andrassy declared that Austria would not oppose some form of autonomy for the Slavs of Bosnia-Herzegovina provided this did not lead to the formation of a great Slav state on her southern border. Austria did not desire to annex Bosnia-Herzegovina for she would only lose thereby, as these provinces, poor and wild, would be a drain on her treasury. Hence Andrassy remitted a memorandum of the same date proposing the maintenance of the authority of the Sultan over these provinces, provided the Christian populations would be guaranteed religious freedom, legal equality with the Turks and definite fiscal and administrative reforms. Russia, notwithstanding Ignatiev's warning that the Turks could not be trusted, adhered to this proposal, but Bismarck characteristically asked the Russian Ambassador, d'Oubril, if Russia could trust Andrassy. On the other hand, though Bismarck himself had declared that Germany had no interests in the Balkans, he seemed to be anxious to play the role of mediator and offered the suggestion (January 5, 1876) that Russia should permit Austria to take Bosnia-Herzegovina in return for the cession to Russia of

Bessarabia, with a guarantee offered to England concerning the security of the Suez Canal. To D'Oubril's question whether, in case of a conflict with England, Germany would follow England, Bismarck replied categorically "No". Gorchakov was struck by this insistence of Bismarck on mediating either between Russia and Austria or between Russia and England, and he saw a trap in Bismarck's suggestion with regard to Bessarabia. Thus a profound mutual distrust seemed to exist between the allies.

Nevertheless in May a meeting was arranged in Berlin between the three Chancellors with Gorchakov presiding and the so-called "Memorandum of Berlin" was drawn up in which a demand was made upon Turkey for reforms and cessation of hostilities, coupled with the warning that should no results be obtained within two months, certain measures would be taken jointly by the Great Powers. On May 13, the Ambassadors of France, England and Italy were notified of this step and their governments were requested to adhere. France and Italy agreed but England refused categorically; this made war inevitable. England's refusal made Russian diplomacy anxious to come to terms with Austria. After an interview with the Emperor of Germany at Ems, Alexander II proceeded to Reichstadt in July to talk matters over with Francis Joseph and by protracted negotiations the basis was laid for an Austro-Russian agreement. These negotiations dragged on till March 1877, that is to say until a month before the opening of hostilities. The main difficulty lay in the insistence of Austria that Serbia, Montenegro and Herzegovina should be neutralized and closed to Russian and Austrian armies alike. Finally the Austrians agreed to allow the Serbian and Montenegrin forces to co-operate with the Russian armies provided the Russians did not occupy Serbia. Novikov was then instructed by his government to conclude a military convention which was duly signed on January 15, 1877, followed by a second convention which was negotiated in March but antedated to January 15, concerning the partition of the spoils of the war. Under these conventions, based on the agreements reached at Reichstadt, Russia and Austria pledged themselves not to allow the formation of a great Slav state along the borders of Austria (Art. III). Regarding the results of the coming war, Bulgaria, Albania and Rumelia were to become independent from Turkey and be provided with constitutions. Greece was to receive Thessaly and Epirus, Constantinople was to become a free city, Russia was to receive Bessarabia and Austria was to occupy Bosnia-Herzegovina but not the Sanjak of Novi-Bazar.

Possible Russian gains in Asia were left outside the convention at the insistence of Gorchakov who declared that Asia was of no concern to Austria (Art. I). The convention was to be operative only in case the war resulted in the dismemberment of Turkey or in the transfer of Turkish territory to other states. The two powers pledged mutual diplomatic support if such contingencies should result in a collective deliberation of the great powers of Europe (Art. II). This article foreshadowed the convocation of the Congress of Berlin. Thus a satisfactory agreement was reached with Austria which fulfilled most of Andrassy's desires. Russia now turned to ascertain the position of Germany. In a letter to Kaiser Wilhelm, dated November 2, 1876, Alexander II said it was impossible to carry on the sterile work of diplomacy and since Europe did not wish to accomplish what Russia deemed just, human and necessary, he (Alexander II) had decided to do it single-handed. Gorchakov wrote to Bismarck in the same vein and the replies from both the Emperor and the Chancellor were deemed to be entirely satisfactory, Bismarck stating that the friendship of Germany for Russia would not be affected by a question entirely outside of Germany's interests.

The events in Turkey seemed to foreshadow the early disintegration of that country. Sultan Abdul Aziz had been deposed on May 30, 1876; and was found dead five days later. He was succeeded by the imbecile Murad V, deposed in turn on August 31. During his short reign, in July, the Turkish Government was forced into bankruptcy and had to declare itself insolvent as to its foreign debts. The successor and brother of Murad, Abdul Hamid II, whose later record was to be so sinister, started out with an attempt to placate European public opinion by promulgating a constitutional decree even more liberal than the previous ones of Gulhane and Hatti Humayoun. But as usual these reforms remained merely on paper and, encouraged by the stand of England, the Turks adopted a policy of procrastination with regard to all real reforms suggested to them by the Powers. Under these circumstances the Conference of Ambassadors at Constantinople, in December, with its hesitant suggestions of reforms, was a useless gesture doomed to failure. Lord Derby in his Guildhall speech (November 10) had menacingly declared England's readiness to fight for the preservation of her Empire. British naval and army officers were arriving in Constantinople to take command of the Turkish forces. Russia began mobilizing and on January 19, 1877 Gorchakov sent a circular note asking the Powers what they intended to do. Turkey had declared that she refused to execute any reforms so long as they were the result of interference in her internal affairs by the Powers, an answer obviously inspired by England. In February, General Ignatiev was sent on a special mission to Paris, Berlin, London and Vienna to determine under what conditions Russia would demobilize. The result of this mission was the Protocol of London on March 19 in which the six Powers issued a last appeal for immediate reforms in return for which Russia would demobilize. On April 12 Turkey answered by a refusal and war was declared.

CHAPTER XI

THE WAR OF 1877 AND THE CONGRESS OF BERLIN

I

From the military standpoint the Turks had certain very important advantages over the Russians which however were nullified by the purely oriental inertia they exhibited. The first advantage the Turks had was in numbers. On the European theater of war they put into the field 225,000 men and maintained that strength throughout the war; whereas the Russian Army, composed of seven army corps and two brigades, numbered 200,000 men when it crossed the frontier, but by the time it reached the Danube, where it first got into touch with the enemy, it had been reduced by detachments, sickness and other causes to 180,000 men. "From this great defect of insufficiency of numbers more than from any other cause came the checks and reverses which Russia met with after crossing the Danube."[1]

Not only was the Turkish Army larger by 45,000 men but, according to the American military observer of the campaign, their armament in some respects was superior to the Russian. Indeed, their artillery was entirely composed of German Krupp steel breech-loaders while their infantry was supplied with American Peabody Martini or British Snyder rifles, which Lieutenant Green considered superior to the Russian models. But the most effective advantage the Turks possessed was on the Black Sea where the Russians had no navy and had not yet had the time to build up any appreciable force since their denunciation of the Treaty of Paris. The Turkish Navy was composed of 132 vessels manned by 18,292 officers, seamen and marines, and was under the command of a British admiral, Hobart Pasha. This force was composed of 15 ironclads of English construction, 5 steam frigates, 11 corvettes, 7 armoured river gunboats and auxiliary craft. Considering that the coastal fortifications of Russia had been dismantled, the Turkish Navy could have inflicted a heavy punishment on the

---

[1] Greene, Lieutenant, F.V., Report on the Russian Army and its Campaigns in Turkey in 1877-1878. New York 1879. p. 40.

THE WAR OF 1877

Russian cities along the Black Sea in addition to blocking the transportation of Russian troops and supplies by sea. For this reason the Russian plan of campaign did not follow the lines of the war of 1828, when the army advanced along the coast through Dobrudja to get control of the easier and lower eastern passes of the Balkans and was supplied and supported by the navy. Instead it was decided that the army was to proceed from Bessarabia into Moldavia and, pivoting toward the Danube, to attempt to cross the river in its middle course between Nikopolis and Rustchuk, then invade Bulgaria proper and force its way over the main range of the Balkans.

Under the command of Grand Duke Nicholas, brother of the Emperor, the army, in April, concentrated along the Russian border on the river Pruth with headquarters at Kishinev. Within a month, on May 24, the army reached the line of the Danube, the main force halting around Bucharest, the right flank at Slatina and an observation corps on the lower Danube around Galatz. The date for the crossing of the Danube had been set for June 6, but the river, very wide in this section, had reached near flood proportions, being 15 feet above its level at Galatz on June 1. Hence additional pontoon equipment had to be brought up and a further delay occurred. It was during this period that the only naval engagement of the war took place. The Turks had on the lower Danube, below Braila, a fleet of 8 ironclads and, in the middle course of the river between Hirsovo and Vidin, 7 iron-plated gun boats and 18 other vessels carrying in all 60 guns and 1,000 men.[2] These forces could very effectively hinder the crossing of the Danube. To oppose them the Russians had merely ordinary steam launches which were rigged with spars for torpedoes. With this improvised craft the Russians succeeded in gaining control of the river. They were successful first in placing a line of mines across the river at Reni and at Braila, thus cutting off the Turkish ironclads operating in the delta of the river from their gunboat flotilla. On May 6 a direct hit from a Russian coastal battery at Braila sank one of the largest gunboats, the "Lufti Djelil", with a loss of 17 officers and 200 men. Two weeks later Lieutenant Dubassov accomplished a daring exploit which has been compared to Cushing's sinking of the Albermarle. One rainy night a party of 6 officers and 40 men in steam launches managed to approach two Turkish ironclads and a wooden ship. Dubassov launched a torpedo which sank the Turkish warship "Seife" and escaped in the

---

[2]Greene, op. cit., p. 152.

general confusion under heavy Turkish fire. Following this the Russians succeeded in establishing another barrage of mines five miles above Nikopolis. The Turks became so demoralized that their vessels remained inactive under shelter of their coastal batteries, thus permitting the crossing of the Danube to be undertaken in safety.

On June 22 the observation corps crossed without difficulty at Galatz, forcing the Turks to abandon their line on the lower Danube and to fall back to the Dobrudja. The point selected for the crossing of the main body was at Nikopolis and here the Turks put up a stiff resistance. However the Russians succeeded in ferrying the 14th Division (General Dragomirov) across, and after a sharp fight they gained a foothold on the right bank at Sistovo at a cost of 31 officers and 700 men (June 27). The rest of the army followed over pontoon bridges and the first major operation of the war was successfully accomplished. Ahead, however, lay a second formidable obstacle--the range of the Balkans. Between the Danube and the Balkans were two short railway lines and a network of 8 good macadamized highways, still in the possession of the Turks. These had to be secured next.

The second phase of the campaign, which opened up after the crossing of the Danube, was marked by the invasion of Bulgaria by the main forces while an advance guard under General Gurko was thrust ahead for the purpose of securing control of the passes of the Balkans. Gurko's spectacular raid must be dealt with in some detail. His detachment was composed of 8,000 infantry (10-1/2 battalions including 6 battalions of the Bulgarian Legion), 4,000 cavalry (31-1/2 squadrons of which 2 regiments of Don Cossacks) and 32 guns (18 field and 14 mountain). With this force totalling 16,000 men in all (including transports, etc.) Gurko left his base at Sistova and began moving southwards, his first objective being the ancient Bulgarian capital of Tirnovo. This city was captured without much difficulty on July 7 notwithstanding the fact that it lies in a narrow gorge of the Yantra river with perpendicular bluffs 500 feet high on each side. The Turks retreated in disorder leaving much war material and ordnance. From Tirnovo Gurko's plan was to cross the Balkans by a blind trail between the Elena and Travna passes, then to turn the range and attack the main Shipka pass from the south, while a regiment of Cossacks, left at Tirnovo for the purpose, would make a demonstration at the main north entrance of the pass which was still held by the enemy. The crossing of the Balkans meant hastily converting the trail, which was merely a footpath, into a road passable for artillery. This was done by the engineers in two days. The road ascended to an elevation of 3,700 feet and was so steep that the guns had to be dragged by the infantry. The Turks offered resistance and counter-attacked at the outlet of the Elena pass, but Gurko drove them in front of him and started his march toward the Shipka pass. The double attack from both sides of the pass was to have taken place on July 17 but Gurko was delayed by the stiff resistance of the enemy, with the result that he lost a day, and the attack from the northern side, carried out according to schedule but alone, was beaten off. Indeed the task which befell the detachment remaining at Tirnovo was to attack with some 2,400 men and 6 guns a high mountain pass held by 5,000 infantry, 12 guns and strong entrenchments; it was sheer folly. Nevertheless, on the 18th Gurko started his attack, and the two attacks thus being disjoined, Gurko in his turn was repulsed. Meanwhile, General Skobelev with nine companies succeeded in getting to the summit of St. Nicholas hill and forced the Turks to withdraw from the pass. Thus, with this help Gurko gained possession of the Shipka pass, the main highway over the Balkans, as well as two other passes (Hankioi and Travna) capturing 11 guns and much ordnance and ammunition in addition. Panic reigned in Constantinople when the news reached the Turkish capital and the government considered removing its seat to Brusa in Asia Minor. It was finally decided to bring up a new army 30,000 strong by sea from Montenegro and Albania to Enos and thence by rail to Tirnovo. Together with the forces already in the field, Gurko now had to face 50,000 men. On July 23 he resumed his offensive toward Eski Zagra and beyond, but here he clashed with this new army which was placed under the command of the able Suleiman Pasha.

For two days Gurko's small force held this army and then began retreating slowly to the passes in the mountains (August 5). Here he posted strong rear-guard forces, thereby securing the hold on these vital strategic passes for the duration of the war. The total losses during the whole raid amounted to 34 officers and 947 men.[3] To quote Lieutenant Greene: "This expedition of Gurko's was more than a mere cavalry raid; it was an admirably conducted movement of an advance guard composed of all arms. With 8,000 infantry, 4,000 cavalry and 32 guns, it had in less than a month gained possession of one of the principal passes of the Balkans, from which the Russians, though terribly attacked, never let go and which

---

[3] Greene, op. cit., p. 183.

they finally used in January for the passage of a large portion of their army; it had carried panic throughout the whole of Turkey between the Balkans and Constantinople; and its scouting parties had penetrated to within 70 miles of Adrianople, the second city of the Empire, and had destroyed the railroad and telegraph on the two principal lines; finally it had gathered accurate information concerning the strength and positions of the large Turkish force advancing toward the Balkans."[4]

The main body of the Russian Army had in the meantime hit a serious snag. In accordance with the plan of campaign, after Gurko's capture of Tirnovo, two army corps were detached to form a separate left wing force under the command of the Cesarevich Alexander (the future Alexander III), and took up a position on the Yantra river. From there, moving slowly and cautiously, by August 1 they reached the line of the Lom where they remained on observation occupying a purely defensive position. The rest of the army captured Nikopolis (July 16) but four days later found its advance blocked at Plevna. The task of capturing Nikopolis was assigned to the 9th Corps under General Krüdener and though it achieved a brilliant success there--for with the fortress the Russians captured 7,000 prisoners, 6 flags, 110 guns and two of the river monitors on the Danube--the losses had been the heaviest thus far incurred, namely 31 officers and 1,278 men. Meanwhile the cream of the Turkish Army, some 50,000 strong under Osman Pasha, was advancing towards Plevna. Though informed by his cavalry pickets of the approach of the enemy, Krüdener seems to have attached little importance to it and allowed the Turkish Army to come up on the Russian flank without doing anything about it.

It was only on July 18 that General Krüdener received orders to occupy Plevna. Seemingly ignorant of the size of the Turkish Army there and without any preliminary reconnoitring he sent a force of 6,500 men and 46 guns to attack an enemy which was found to be more than four times their number entrenched behind very strong positions. The result was the repulsing of the Russian attack with a loss of 74 officers, 2,771 men and a considerable part of the baggage. This defeat made it necessary to bring up additional forces (the whole 9th Corps strengthened by a division and a brigade of infantry). The delay caused by these troop movements permitted the Turks, with the aid of Italian engineers, to strengthen the defences of Plevna so as to transform it into a real fortress. The second attack on Plevna carried out on July 30 by a corps

---

[4] Greene, op. cit., p. 183.

30,000 strong resulted in a still graver defeat. The Russians attacked in two separate columns which could not support each other and their numbers were too inferior in view of the strength of the positions. The regiments spent themselves in trying to reach within 100 paces of the Grivitza redoubt, on the main Turkish defence line, and held on there till nightfall. After one regiment (126th Infantry) lost 757 of its effectives, the attacking columns were withdrawn during the night to their initial position. They had lost 169 officers and 7,136 men; the only redeeming feature of the day was the brilliant cavalry action of General Skobelev who, with a small force, saved the Russian left wing by vigorously attacking an enemy ten times stronger than himself.

Though "the trait which more than any other distinguishes the Russian soldier is his steadiness and solidity, he never has taken a panic and there was none now",[5] the defeat of Plevna meant a great deal more than merely the repulsing of an attack. It placed the whole Russian army in a dangerous position. Indeed the Russian front stretched in a wide triangle of ninety by ninety miles from the Danube at Nikopolis, to the Balkan passes, then to the line of the Lom and back to the Danube at Rustchuk. This front, after deducting the losses incurred, was held by 132,000 men and 648 guns (exclusive of 25,000 men under General Zimmerman detached to the Dobrudja to cover the communications along the seaboard and completely out of touch with the army proper). Against this army were now operating three Turkish armies, 195,000 in all. The disparity in numbers was so great that all plans for an advance had to be abandoned and new forces had to be brought up. Hence the Guards Corps and 6 divisions of infantry plus one cavalry division (total 120,000 men, 460 guns) were ordered to the front from Russia. But before they could reach the Danube there was a delay of about two months in which the situation was dangerous and similar to the one experienced in the war of 1828. The Russian command accordingly asked for the immediate assistance of the Roumanian Army (32,000 infantry, 5,000 cavalry and 84 guns) which crossed the Danube and moved up to Plevna.

While the Russian war machine had thus been stalled waiting for reinforcements, the temptation for the Turks to counterattack was too great not to be acted upon, and all three armies were set in motion. The army of Suleiman attacked the Shipka

---

[5] Greene, op. cit., p. 200.

pass on August 21, while Mehemet Ali[6] on August 30 threw his 65,000 men against the corps of the Cesarevich holding the Lom, and the next day Osman Pasha brought his 50,000 men into action at Plevna. Of these three independent battles the most spectacular one was the attack on the all-important Shipka pass. "For impetuous assaults and tenacious dogged defense, for long-continued fighting and physical endurance this five days battle in the mountains is extremely remarkable...."[7] Indeed a force of 5,000 Russians and Bulgarians held out against the vicious and continuous attacks of 25,000 to 30,000 Turks who completely surrounded the Russian positions located on the three spurs and ridges of the pass. The Russians were thus completely cut off with one day's ration of biscuits while the only water to be found was in a spring 3 or 4 miles back, and which had to be brought up in canteens by the men who carried the wounded to the rear. The heat was terrific, the ammunition gave out and the Turks, from the surrounding heights (at this point about 5,000 feet), commanded every point of the Russian positions with their fire. All attacks were successfully repulsed. When the hastily summoned Russian reinforcements arrived and attacked the Turks from the flank and the rear, the Turks abandoned the assault and Shipka remained in Russian hands, the Russian losses being 100 officers and 3,500 men, whereas the Turks lost 8,350 men. Shipka thus became a Plevna in reverse and, whereas during the next few months the Russians kept on hammering at Plevna, the Turks on their side concentrated on trying to secure the Shipka pass but failed.

The advance against the Russian Army on the Lom began even more encouragingly for the Turks. Mehemet Ali opened his attack on the 45,000 Russians, spread over a 50 mile front, with a force of around 65,000 men.[8] In a series of sharp engagements the corps under the Cesarevich were forced to abandon the line of the Lom and fall back within a period of 15 days to the line of the Yantra, but here the Russians had the advantage of getting their forces into closer and more compact

---

[6]Not to be confused with the famous Pasha of Egypt who died in 1849.

[7]Greene, op. cit., p. 214.

[8]German Sources place the figure as high as 85,000. See Rüstow, F.W., Der Orientalischer Krieg. Zurich 1877, 1878, pp. 332, 333.

positions. Hence they stopped the Turkish onslaught and counter-attacked, regaining the line of the Lom by the end of September. The Turks retreated in such haste as to leave a large amount of war material in Russian hands. The main front nevertheless during this period remained at Plevna and here Osman made his attempt at an offensive on August 31. During a day of close hand-to-hand fighting the Turks succeeded in gaining possession of some Russian trenches, which changed hands several times, but were ultimately driven back to Plevna with a loss of about 3,000 men as against 1,000 Russians. Osman had brought into action only 25,000 of the 50,000 he had under his orders and these forces proved insufficient to break through the Russian lines. With the failure of these three offensives, the aggressive spirit of the Turks seemed to vanish and the Russians regained the initiative of the operations which for a while had slipped out of their hands. The Russian plan now was to gradually invest Plevna from the north, the east and the south. But for this it was necessary first to gain possession of Lovcha, a village 20 miles from Plevna at the cross roads of the three highways leading to the Balkans.

Already as early as August 6 General Skobelev with a mixed force of 5 battalions of infantry, 105 squadrons of cavalry and two mounted batteries made a reconnaissance against Lovcha and forced the Turks to show their strength, revealing that they had 15,000 men there. Skobelev was showing such boldness and tactical skill in handling the operations assigned to him that, though still in his early thirties, this young general was rapidly assuming the rôle of a national hero. A larger Russian force, (20,000 men) under Prince Imeretinsky was sent to capture Lovcha. Skobelev in command of the left flank not only drove the Turks out of their advanced positions, but during the night consolidated his position by building trenches and preparing positions for the artillery, so that when the bulk of Imeretinsky's troops arrived, they were able to dominate the ridge overlooking the city. On September 3 the Turks attacked the Russian right flank (General Dobrovolsky), but the Russian artillery by a well-directed fire, silenced the Turkish batteries and inflicted such damage on the Turkish lines that when, in support of Dobrovolsky, Skobelev attacked he not only carried the city but virtually cut the whole Turkish force to pieces. This victory enabled the Russians to start their major operation against Plevna.

Here the command of the Russo-Roumanian forces was given to Prince Charles of Roumania, and Czar Alexander II joined him at his headquarters at Poradim. When the concentration of troops had been completed, it was decided to make a general assault on Plevna upon which the fate of the war depended. An army of 90,000 men (74,000 infantry, 10,000 cavalry, 10,500 artillery and engineers, 442 guns), of which 30,000 were Roumanians, had been assembled. Osman's strength was estimated at 60,000 men. Plevna by this time was formidably fortified with a system of several lines of trenches and 18 redoubts, the key to the position on the north side being the Grivitza redoubt already mentioned, and to the south, the Krishin group of redoubts. Orders for the assault were issued on September 6, and during the night the troops marched to their respective positions. The battle opened on September 7 at 6 A.M. and lasted nearly a week. During the first 4 days the Russians merely kept up a continuous artillery preparation which silenced the Turkish guns in the Grivitza redoubt. Skobelev, in command of the advance guard, was alone engaged, and at a loss of 900 men, secured some approaches to the Turkish lines. The general assault took place on September 11, the Roumanians and the 9th Corps attacking the Grivitza redoubt, the 4th Corps the redoubt No. 10 and Skobelev attacking from his advanced position. But owing to a fog Skobelev's units lost contact with each other and, advancing too far, got under a terrible flanking fire as they occupied the first line of enemy trenches. When the fog lifted their position became critical but, instead of retreating, Skobelev ordered to continue the attack. His men advanced to within 200 yards of the Turkish line where they found themselves in the open exposed to both artillery and rifle fire from the redoubts on both sides. Having used up his reserves and seeing his men wavering, he rode down the knoll from where he was directing the battle, on his white horse and in his white uniform which was known to the entire army, and led the attackers himself. His presence encouraged the troops, they made a final effort and captured the redoubt at a loss of 3,000 men. Skobelev's horse was killed under him. Every member of his staff, except Colonel Kuropatkin (later Commander-in-Chief in the Russo-Japanese War), was either killed or wounded. But owing to the failure of the supporting Russian attack on redoubt No. 10, Skobelev's position once more became critical, for he was wedged in between Turkish redoubts, which kept him under constant cross-fire. Notwithstanding five Turkish counter-attacks and the order given him to retreat, he held on to his position for 36 hours until his men were exhausted and ammunition ran out, and only then did he retreat to the knolls from which he had started his attack--his total losses being 160 officers and 8,000 men out of 18,000 engaged. "Skobeleff's extremely reckless courage, while it compels that personal admiration which such qualities always command, is of course open to serious criticism when it is remembered that he was the commanding general on all that part of the line. On the other hand, there is no doubt that without the aid which this display of daring gave to his men, the position would not have been carried or held as it was."[9]

Meanwhile the Roumanians advanced toward the key position of Grivitza. Their first attack was repulsed but, supported by a Russian brigade, they attacked a second time, finally capturing this all important redoubt after bloody hand to hand fighting. The Roumanians lost in this attack 2,576 men and the Russians 1,327. But the Russians sustained a bloody reverse in their central attack on redoubt No. 10, where they were thrown back with a loss of 5,310 men or nearly half the force engaged. It was this failure which put Skobelev in a critical position. Thus came to an end the third battle of Plevna. At a loss of 18,000 Russians and 3,000 Roumanians the allies had merely succeeded in indenting the Turkish line of defence without breaking it. Hence after this repulse it was decided at the council of war of the 13th and 14th of September to abandon all further attacks on Plevna and invest the place instead: the cavalry was assigned the task of cutting the Turkish communications to prevent the bringing up of supplies and reinforcements. But, as the infantry stood only on one side of Plevna and the cavalry cordon covered the three other sides, the investment of the city was merely nominal, since, owing to the inefficient handling of his task, General Krilov, commander of the cavalry forces, let important Turkish reinforcements and transports slip by.

On October 19 the Roumanians made an effort to gain the second Grivitza redoubt in the rear of the one they had captured. This attack was repulsed and was the last frontal attack on Plevna. Meanwhile important Russian reinforcements had come up including the crack Guards and Grenadier Corps. The hero of the siege of Sebastopol, General Todleben, was appointed in charge of the siege, and the inefficient Krilov was replaced by the energetic Gurko. The plan now was to extend the Russian lines and make them converge pincer-like until the city was completely cut off. This led to the battle of Gorni Dubniak. On the Russian left wing, the Turks had established

---

[9]Greene, op. cit., p. 261.

along the Sofia-Plevna road four fortified places which had to be taken first. About 45,000 men were assigned to this task. On October 24 the Guards in a terribly bloody frontal attack carried Gorni Dubniak which the Turks defended with the utmost stubbornness. The Russian trophies were one Pasha, 53 officers and 2,235 men taken prisoner, one standard, 4 guns and sundry supplies. But their losses had been 116 officers and 3,195 men including two commanders of regiments killed. With the capture of Gorni Dubniak, Gurko had gained a foothold in the center of the Turkish fortified line along the Sofia road. When Gurko resumed his attacks on the next fortifications at Telis, the Pasha surrendered with 100 officers, 3,000 men, 4 guns, after which the Turks, demoralized, abandoned their whole line of fortifications. Thus a whole Turkish army recently brought up from Adrianople and Sofia to come to the aid of Plevna, fell back to the foothills of the Balkans.

This permitted the complete encircling of the fortress. On November 8 Skobelev once more attacked the positions he had taken previously and this time held them, thereby shortening the Russian line. The Roumanians at the same time occupied some heights on their right flank. A demand to surrender Plevna made to Osman Pasha by the Grand Duke Nicholas on November 13 was turned down. However by December 10 Osman's position had become critical--his provisions were running low and a third of his army was disabled by sickness. He therefore decided to attempt to break through to Sofia. He concentrated his forces along the Vid and about 7:30 on the morning of December 10 made a desperate sortie, attacking with fury the first line of Russian trenches held by the 3rd Division of Grenadiers. The Turks succeeded in penetrating these trenches and killing most of the defenders. The survivors fell back. But Russian reinforcements came up and counter-attacked with vigour, not only capturing the lost trenches but driving the Turks back to their own line. By noon the Turks, who had been retreating slowly keeping up a steady fire, broke and their retreat turned to a rout. A general counter-attack along the whole line was ordered and as the Russo-Roumanian forces were breaking into Plevna, Osman Pasha sent his Chief of Staff to announce his surrender. Ten Pashas, 2,130 officers and 41,200 men were taken prisoner with 77 guns.

II

The siege of Plevna, if we count from the time of the first attack July 20, had lasted 142 days and had cost the

Russians about 35,000 men and the Roumanians about 5,000. It was only after the fall of Plevna that the Russians could resume their original plan of campaign.

The attention of the belligerents having been concentrated for so long on Plevna, the operations on the other fronts had temporarily lost their importance though they did not cease. At Shipka on September 17 the Turks made another general assault, directing their main efforts against St. Nicholas Hill. Their successive attacks were repulsed at a loss of 3,000 men. The Russians on their side lost over 1,000 men which, considering that no reinforcements were available as all were being diverted to Plevna, weakened the little defending force considerably. Happily winter set in early and the heavy snowfall in these high altitudes, while it brought suffering to the soldiers, made all further fighting come to a standstill. Suleiman Pasha, who had been transferred from Shipka to the command of the army on the Lom, was determined to break through the line held by the Cesarevich and come to the aid of his colleague besieged in Plevna, hence the end of November saw considerable Turkish activity along the Lom. On the 4th of December 30,000 Turks fell upon two Russian regiments of the 8th Corps and drove them back to Elena with a loss of 1,850 men and 11 guns. This is the only time during the whole war that the Turks took Russian prisoners and the 500 captured men were paraded through Constantinople. But Russian reserves drove the Turks back and the old line was resumed. They repeated their attack on the day Plevna surrendered but were again heavily defeated. After the fall of Plevna, Suleiman abandoned his line and retreated to the south of the Balkans, merely leaving some troops in the forts of Rustchuk and Shumla. While Suleiman was operating along the Lom, Mehemet Ali, also transferred to a new command, was ordered to assemble an army around Sofia to march to the relief of Plevna. To meet this danger the Russians detached a corps of 35,000 men from the army of investment and placed it under the orders of Gurko, who had completed his task of surrounding Plevna. Gurko was ordered to start a counter-offensive in the direction of Sofia and the Balkans. He began his march toward Sofia on November 15. The Turks had three fortified lines along the Sophia-Vidin highway at the point where it reached the Balkans. These lines were held by a total of 25,000 men. Gurko's plan, upon reaching the foothills on November 21, was to make an attack on Pravetz while two strong demonstrations on Lulikova and Etropol were to divert the enemy to the flanks. Participating in the attack were the

crack Guards regiments. This manoeuvre was carried out on
schedule except for the delay caused to the left flank column
(Major General Rauch) owing to the impassability of the mountain trails it had to follow. However, no definite results were
achieved by the frontal attack until Rauch's column, climbing
the steep slope of a mountain in the Turkish rear, forced the
enemy to abandon its positions. General Rauch made his way
over the mountain range so speedily that the Turks were
obliged to abandon their second line as well and concentrate on
the Araba-Konak pass. Here they had well constructed and
virtually impregnable fortifications rising on the slope of the
mountain.

This position was in turn evacuated when the Russians repeated their turning manoeuvre by once more climbing steep
slopes. Several men died of exhaustion while pulling the heavy
guns up by hand. There was nothing for the Turks to do but
hold on to the main Shandarnik ridge on the very crest of the
Balkan range. Gurko occupied a parallel ridge 4,000 feet above
sea level (Mount Greote) and, as there were no roads, 60 guns
were hauled up the slope by drag ropes. As the Turkish fortifications on Shandarnik were too powerful for an assault, Gurko
remained on the ridge, thus immobilizing the enemy. However,
the Turks still had 150,000 men remaining with which to oppose this advance, plus reserves in Asia and Constantinople.
On the other hand the Russian line of communications had become dangerously extended, particularly since the ice on the
Danube had carried away all the bridges. Furthermore, ahead
of the Russians was the formidable Balkan range and, with
winter having set in, the Russian armies could use only two
highways (Sistova-Shipka and Plevna-Sofia). Snow, sleet and
mud had rendered all other roads impassable. Thus the position of the Turks was by no means hopeless.

They withdrew nearly all their forces to the Balkan range
where they were placed under the orders of Suleiman Pasha,
now Commander-in-Chief. Only fortress garrisons were left
on the northern side of the range and the Roumanians during
November had cleaned up a few of these along the Danube by
taking Rahovo and advancing to Lom Palanka. On the Russian
side the fall of Plevna had released 110,000 men. The Roumanian Army, now 25,000 strong, was to remain along the
Danube while Serbia, having once more come into the war at
the time of the fall of Plevna, brought in about an equal number of fresh troops. General Todleben, more cautious, recommended putting the troops in winter quarters at the foot of the
Balkans, limiting the operations to the siege of the important

Turkish fortress of Rustchuk on the Danube, and to await the spring before attempting the forcing of the Balkan range. However Grand Duke Nicholas, enthusiastically supported by his most daring generals, Gurko and Skobelev, decided upon the more adventurous course of attempting to force the range during the winter in spite of the snow, the lack of roads and the exhaustion of supplies, so as not to give the Turks time to recuperate or receive more aid from England. Therefore the Plevna army was broken up and sent to reinforce the corps holding the Balkan passes and the range. Gurko's force was thus increased to a total of 65,000 men while General Radetsky, on the Shipka, brought his forces up to 56,000 and the Cesarevich maintained his at 55,000 men. The rest remained in reserve or were assigned to special minor tasks. Gurko and Radetsky were to attempt to force the range and join their forces in front of Adrianople. The Cesarevich was to protect the line of communications on the left flank and at the same time proceed with the siege of Rustchuk, assisted by General Todleben.

The success of the operation of crossing the Balkans depended on the endurance of the troops and this was taxed to the utmost. All transports and baggage had to be left behind. "From the time the movement was well under way the men never saw their knapsacks, which remained north of the Balkans, till sometime after the armistice. They marched and fought and slept in snow and ice, and forded rivers with the thermometer at zero. They had no blankets, and the frozen ground precluded idea of tents..... Their clothing at night was the same as in the day and it differed from that of the summer only in the addition of an overcoat, woollen jacket and a 'bashlik' or woollen muffler for the head. Their food was a pound of hard bread and a pound and a half of tough stringy beef driven along the road; they were forced to carry six and even eight days' rations on their backs (in addition to an extra supply of cartridges in their pockets)..... Yet in the face of these unusual privations and hardships there was not a single case of insubordination....."[10] In addition a heavy five-day winter blizzard had set in on December 18, and Gurko reported 2,000 casualties from freezing. Worse still was the situation on the Shipka, where the 24th Division lost from freezing and exposure 6,000 men or 80% of its complement and had to be withdrawn. The troops coming up from Plevna suffered equally, the transport wagons and guns having to be dragged by

---

[10]Greene, op. cit., p. 369.

hand as the horses were not sharp shod and thus useless on roads covered with ice. The Turks, on the advice of their foreign experts, were confident that under these circumstances the crossing of the mountains was totally impossible. But the energy of Gurko, Radetsky and Skobelev, who was appointed second in command on the Shipka, were to disprove this assurance. Radetsky ordered his advance on the Shipka to start on January 5, his forces divided into three columns, one of which remained at the summit for a frontal attack whereas the other two were to cross the mountain and attack the pass from the rear to synchronize with this frontal attack. These columns had to make their way through snow ten feet deep and presently were engaged by the Turks. For two days the columns, commanded respectively by Prince Sviatopolk-Mirsky and Skobelev, fought their way to their assigned goals. On the third day in a snowstorm which made visibility nil, Radetsky ordered his frontal attack to start, judging what was happening to the columns in the valley by the sound of gunfire. It was however the attack of Skobelev's troops, "the most brilliant assault of the whole war",[11] that decided the day and the whole Turkish Army surrendered to Skobelev, 36,000 men, 96 guns and 10 colours. The Russian losses were 5,484 men. Both Skobelev and Mirsky carried on their operations without any artillery, which had to be left behind.

Gurko's plan of action against the 35,000 Turks opposing him on and near the Shandarnik range was somewhat similar to the operation concluded on the Shipka. Leaving forces in front of each sector, he sent flying columns over the mountains to turn the Turkish positions. The main column composed of 31 battalions, 16 squadrons and 44 guns was to make its way over the mountain range on a road built by the sappers. But this road was so steep, having curves with a radius of 10 yards and a slope of one in three, and so slippery that the horses had to be unharnessed and the guns and caissons pulled by men hauling drag ropes. In coming down the slope after crossing the summit the drag ropes were fastened around stumps or trees while two other ropes holding the guns were slacked so as to allow it to slide down to the end of the ropes and then the whole procedure was repeated. The slope was so slippery the men could not stand on their feet without the use of sticks. No carriages or guns were lost and only one man was killed. This labour took four days (December 26-30) but Gurko's column reached the valley safely on the left of the

---

[11] Greene, op. cit., p. 353.

Turkish position of Araba Konak. Less fortunate was the left flank column under General Dandeville which during its descent was hit by a snowstorm. The drifts of snow burying its artillery, the column lost 53 men frozen to death and 810 men permanently disabled from frostbite. But the main range had been negotiated and though the Turks offered some resistance in the valley, they abandoned their positions and fell back to Sofia. After some further resistance Sofia was captured on January 4 and the troops were given a few days rest. Gurko's losses during the eleven day operation amounted to 1,035 men, including three generals. "..... And among the wars of this century, since those of the Great Napoleon, we will seek in vain an instance of a movement more bold in conception, more energetic in execution, more overwhelmingly successful in its results, than the passage of the Balkans....."[12] The Turks had fallen back to a new line of defence along the so-called Trajan's gate--a position of great natural strength at the opening of a narrow gorge. Suleiman had just received 20,000 reinforcements but upon the news of the capitulation of Shipka he decided upon a further withdrawal. Gurko, having given his troops a rest, resumed his advance and after fighting a series of hot engagements with the Turkish rear-guards, captured Philippopolis. By now the Turkish armies were completely disorganized and Suleiman escaped from Philippopolis with some 15,000 men leaving in the hands of the Russians all the baggage, 114 guns and a great number of prisoners. The remnants of the Turkish Army trickled through the mountains in disorganized bands to the Aegean Sea, where a fleet of transports under the command of a former British officer brought them to Constantinople and Gallipoli. Suleiman was demoted and sentenced to imprisonment for 15 years by a Turkish court martial.

Now the two wings of the Russian Army re-established communication with each other and proceeded to advance on Adrianople. The advance guard under Skobelev moved rapidly toward the fortress which the Turks had strengthened during the war to make it impregnable. But the wildest panic broke out in the city and on January 22, 1878, Skobelev entered Andrianople without any resistance. On the 25th Gurko brought up his forces and the next day the General Headquarters of Grand Duke Nicholas moved in. When negotiations for an armistice started the Turks showed signs of resisting Russian demands. Orders were forthwith issued for a march on

---

[12]Greene, op. cit., p. 366.

Constantinople; the advance guard under Skobelev to move along the railway, the right wing under Gurko to march to Rodosto on the Aegean Sea from where it could menace either Gallipoli or Constantinople; one division to go to Enos to prevent any possible landing from the sea and the left wing under Ganetsky to move on Constantinople over the northern road via Kirkilisse. This decided the war. A last cavalry skirmish occurred on January 29 at Tchorlu and two days later an armistice was signed. The Russians had won the war from the military standpoint. There now remained to win it in the field of diplomacy.

III

At the very outset of hostilities Germany and Austria had shown their true attitude toward Russia by appointing full fledged ambassadors to Constantinople in place of the Chargé d'Affaires who had been there during the Bosnian crisis. Bismarck was embarrassed in explaining this move to the Russian Ambassador in Berlin and the unfriendly import of this act did not escape the Russian Government. As for England, already on May 6, that is to say two weeks after the beginning of hostilities, she declared in a note from Lord Derby to the Russian Ambassador in London, Count Shuvalov, that she would abandon her neutrality in the event of any attempt on the part of the belligerents to endanger the security of navigation in the Suez Canal, or should Russia attack Egypt, or even temporarily occupy Constantinople. To this note the Russian Government replied that Russia would not menace Egypt or Suez. As for Constantinople, without committing herself as to what might become necessary with regard to the development of the military situation, Russia declared that she had no intention of occupying Constantinople and in any case the question of the future status of that city was a matter to be solved by common agreement and Constantinople should not belong to any one single power. As for the Straits, it would be desirable to solve that question by common agreement in an equitable way. Gorchakov however, on May 18, instructed his Ambassador in London to avoid committing himself with regard to a possible temporary occupation of Constantinople, should the obstinacy of the Turks force the Russians to dictate peace in the Turkish capital. With regard to the Straits "their political status should be revised in a spirit of fairness. The arrangement by virtue of which the Black Sea, closed in time of peace, is open in time of war to all enemy fleets of Russia has been conceived in a spirit of defiance and hostility."[13] Further, Russia would be prepared to promise that her armies would not advance beyond the line of the Balkans if the powers remained neutral. Should Turkey ask for peace before this line had been reached, such a peace would be concluded on the basis of autonomy for Bulgaria, reforms for Bosnia-Herzegovina, some territorial compensations for Serbia and Montenegro, restitution of Bessarabia to Russia as well as the cession of the port of Batum and adjoining territory. Russia would not oppose Austria demanding as compensation the cession of Bosnia and a part of Herzegovina.[14]

In this important secret document Russia revealed therefore the true objectives she had in view at the beginning of the war. Lord Derby, on receiving the official Russian note (not the secret one), declared that it was "not reassuring". Accordingly when the Russian armies crossed the Danube, England concentrated her fleet at Besica Bay in the Aegean Sea under the pretence of offering protection to British nationals in Constantinople in the event of troubles. She further assembled troops at Malta and approached Austria with a proposal for common action, which Andrassy refused. With British officers openly aiding the Turks both in their army and in their navy, the position occupied by England was therefore one of open hostility. British apprehensions seemed to be heightened by Gurko's first raid across the Balkans for in July Lord Derby declared that the British Fleet would proceed to Constantinople in defence of British nationals, should the Russian Army approach Constantinople, and that this measure would not be a violation of neutrality; to which Shuvalov retorted that the protection of Christians in that city was a matter pertaining to all the powers and not to Great Britain alone.

The Russian reverses at Plevna allayed British fears for a while. Austria on her side showed signs of uneasiness and proposed to Germany a common mediation in the war, which Bismarck declined. To quiet Austrian apprehensions Russia announced (July 4) that she would respect her engagements made at Reichstadt. A few weeks later the Emperors of Austria and Germany were informed of the conditions of peace which Russia would accept, viz., autonomy of Bulgaria, reorganization of Bosnia and Herzegovina under Austrian

---

[13] Goriainow, B, Le Bosphore et Les Dardanelles, Paris 1910, pp. 346, 347.

[14] Goriainow, op. cit., p. 346, 347.

administration, cession of Bessarabia, Kars and Batum to Russia and the closing of the Straits to foreign men-of-war, the powers with a coastline on the Black Sea reserving the right to request the Sultan to allow the passage of one single warship.

The second phase of diplomatic activity opens with the crossing of the Balkans. Already in December Lord Derby handed a memorandum to Count Shuvalov offering Britain's mediation and declaring that England would consider herself free to adopt whatever measures she deemed necessary in defence of her interests, should the Russians occupy Constantinople, even temporarily. At the same time, under the instigation of Sir Charles Layard, Turkey asked the powers to mediate. Germany declined, followed by Austria, but England accepted with alacrity and asked Russia whether she was prepared to make peace. Gorchakov replied that the question must be handled by direct negotiations between the Commanders-in-Chief of the contending armies, a reply which irritated Lord Derby to the point where he said to Shuvalov: "It is therefore a peace over the head of Europe which you are seeking to conclude."[15] Furthermore, Great Britain declared that she would only recognize peace terms which had received the approbation of the signatories of the treaties of 1856 and 1871. A question was also put whether the Russian troops intended to march on Gallipoli, to which Gorchakov replied in the negative provided the Turks did not concentrate there and on the understanding that the peninsula should not be occupied by the British.

In the meantime, as we have seen, the temporary breakdown in the negotiations for an armistice led to a march of the Russian armies toward both Constantinople and Rodosto. The signing of the armistice on January 31 resulted in the halting of the troops a few miles away from Adrianople, but on January 29 Grand Duke Nicholas was informed by the Turkish authorities that the British Fleet had made an attempt to enter the Dardanelles and, halted by the Turks, had returned to Besica Bay. The Russian Commander-in-Chief immediately informed the Turks that such a move would result in the occupation of the heights around Constantinople by the Russian army. Shuvalov on his side in London informed Lord Derby that the entrance of the British fleet into the Straits would absolve Russia from all pledges given not to occupy Constantinople and Gallipoli, and that furthermore the Russians as well as

---

[15] Goriainow, op. cit., p. 359.

THE WAR OF 1877

the British would feel obliged to extend the protection of their arms to all Christians in Constantinople. But notwithstanding this declaration the British Fleet in February received orders to override any protests the Turks might make and to anchor at the Princes Islands off Constantinople. The Czar then ordered Grand Duke Nicholas to immediately resume his march on Constantinople. As for Gallipoli, on the margin of a telegram from Shuvalov stating that Lord Derby had declared that the occupation of Gallipoli by the Russians would endanger the British Fleet, the Czar wrote: "That is the very reason why we must do it." Thus an armed clash between Russia and England seemed to have become inevitable.

Under the terms of the armistice the Turks were to surrender the Danube fortresses of Vidin, Rustchuk and Silistria and evacuate the Balkan fortresses of Belgradjik, Razgrad and Bazardjik. They were further to retire beyond the last line of defence of Constantinople, that of Buyuk Tchekmedje, and the Russians were permitted to advance to the line of Tchadalja, leaving a neutral space of ten miles between the two armies. Thus the Russians were to reach the peninsula twenty miles wide which connects the Black Sea with the Sea of Marmara in the hinterland of Constantinople, and the Turks were to fall back to a point about 10 miles from the capital. Accordingly Skobelev reached the line of Tchadalja and Gurko that of Tchorlu and Rodosto. Having received orders to march on Constantinople, Grand Duke Nicholas opened negotiations with the Sultan to arrange for the Russian occupation of the suburbs of the capital in view of over-crowded conditions existing in the city. The Sultan had to yield and the Russians occupied San Stefano, 6 miles from Constantinople, extending their line over the heights overlooking the city to Kuyuk-Tchekmedje. The General Headquarters of the Grand Duke moved into San Stefano on February 23 and additional troops were brought up from Rodosto and Adrianople. These military movements brought the Anglo-Russian tension to a climax and England threatened to break off diplomatic relations to which Gorchakov cabled to Shuvalov:[16] "The British Squadron has passed through the Dardanelles notwithstanding the protests of Turkey. If our troops enter Constantinople without consent of the Sultan to protect the Christians, the British Government declare they will be obliged to recall their Ambassador from St. Petersburg. They will do as they please." But a compromise solution was found by the Sultan granting permission, as we have

---

[16] February 22, Goriainow, op. cit., p. 367.

seen, to occupy the suburbs including San Stefano in return for which Grand Duke Nicholas declared he would not enter the city proper (Stambul) provided the British did not enter the Bosphorus. Otherwise he reserved his freedom of action. A week later on March 3 the treaty of peace of San Stefano was signed and Turkey immediately appointed Reouf Pasha as Ambassador to Russia, thus resuming normal diplomatic relations.

The Treaty of San Stefano in its essence embodied the clauses of the armistice. It provided for the recognition of complete independence for Montenegro, Serbia and Roumania. Montenegro and Roumania were to receive territorial aggrandizements, in the case of Montenegro according to the military status quo, in the case of Roumania to be determined later. A new Balkan state, Bulgaria, came into existence as an autonomous but tributary state with a ruling prince to be elected by the people but to be confirmed by the Sultan with the assent of the powers. The territory of this new state was generously drawn along ethnographic lines taking in even Bulgarian minorities. Thus it included the whole of present day Bulgaria, the greater part of Macedonia and a portion of Albania. It was thus given the coast lines of the Black Sea and the Aegean, the courses of the Vardar and the Struma, and to the west stretched as far as the lakes Ochrida and Presba and the Albanian city of Koritsa. In size it would have been equal to that of the medieval Bulgarian Empire of Czar Simeon. Its administration was to be organized by a committee of notables under the supervision of a Russian commission and a Russian army 50,000 strong was to remain in occupation of the country pending the formation of a Bulgarian national militia. Turkey was further to pay an indemnity of 1,410,000,000 roubles to Russia but, in view of the bankrupt condition of Turkish finances, a part of this payment was to be made in cession of territories to Russia, including the province of Dobrudja in the Balkans, and in Asiatic Turkey the cities of Batum, Ardahan, Kars and Bayazid. Russia reserved the right to retrocede Dobrudja to Roumania in return for Bessarabia. As for Bosnia-Herzegovina, their status was to be settled jointly by Turkey, Russia and Austria along the lines decided upon by the Conference of Constantinople of 1876, and finally the Straits Question was to be settled by a new agreement in conformity with Russia's interests.[17] There was an immediate outcry against these terms both in England and in Austria. Austria protested

---

[17]See Peace Handbook issued by the Historical Section of the British Foreign Office, London, 1920, Vol. XXIV.

the treaty and on March 27 confidentially approached England for a loan to cover the expense of mobilization of her armies. A further acute and unsolved question heightened the tension-- the question of the evacuation of the Russian armies. Grand Duke Nicholas wanted the Russian troops to embark at Buyukdere on the Bosphorus but the Turks replied that this would give the British an excuse to enter Constantinople. The Sultan requested Queen Victoria to recall the British warships to which the British retorted by demanding a simultaneous withdrawal of Russian armies and British naval forces to an equal distance on both sides of the Bosphorus (March 27) and, notwithstanding the intervention of Bismarck, no satisfactory solution to the problem was found. In distant Russian Turkestan, three columns of Russian troops began their march toward the Afghan frontier with India as their objective. A Russo-British and possibly an Austro-Russian war loomed in the offing.

But Russia, exhausted by the campaign of 1877, certainly did not want a new major war, while England and Austria were anxious to achieve their aims without fighting if possible. Under these circumstances a peaceful solution depended on how much Russia was prepared to yield. Shuvalov in London reported on March 29 that Lord Derby had said to him: "I know my colleagues well; they do not want war, but are seeking to satisfy their party by a demonstration. Find a compensation for us, not in Egypt, but some naval base, even outside the sea of Marmara and the Dardanelles, and an agreement could be speedily reached."[18] Lord Salisbury, in succeeding Lord Derby, informed Gorchakov through Colonel Wellesley, the British Military Agent in St. Petersburg, that England desired to call an European congress and would welcome peace with Russia provided the Russians would be willing to submit all pending matters to the discussion of the congress. Upon Gorchakov's reserved attitude Bismarck suggested a compromise by which the Treaty of San Stefano alone should be submitted for discussion; upon which Shuvalov on May 8 left his post in London for a confidential mission to Russia, and returned to London on May 23 with concrete proposals based on a statement that Russia had no intentions of going beyond the Treaty of San Stefano in extending her conquests either in Europe or in Asia. The result of the subsequent negotiations led to the signing of three memoranda in London on May 30 and 31 by Salisbury and Shuvalov in which Russia met British desires with regard to the reduction of the territory of

---

[18] Goriainow, op. cit., p. 372.

Bulgaria. According to the first memorandum containing 11 clauses, Bulgaria was to be partitioned into two sections, the northern, which was to become an autonomous principality extending to the Balkan range, the southern to be returned to Turkey as a province with a name to be specified, under a Christian governor but with administrative autonomy. Turkish troops were not to cross the frontier into Bulgaria proper. Furthermore the powers were to have a voice in organizing the Epirus, Thessaly and Macedonia. England would not oppose the retrocession of Bessarabia to Russia and would recognize the acquisition by Russia of Batum and other points in Asiatic Turkey.

In the second memorandum Great Britain reserved the right of discussing at the coming congress the organization of the two Bulgarias and the name to be given to the southern portion. The question of the Straits was to be settled by the maintenance of the status quo and similarly the question of the navigation of the Danube was to be opened for discussion. The third memorandum dealt in detail with Russia's acquisitions in Asiatic Turkey. Thus the main points of disagreement were ironed out and it was left to the coming congress to register these decisions. On June 4 England signed with Turkey the Cyprus Convention by which she obtained the possession of that valuable island but this Convention was kept secret from Russia. Thus the stage was definitely set for the Congress of Berlin.

IV

Much has been written on the Congress of Berlin but its importance should not be over emphasized. We must remember that three previous treaties had determined and circumscribed its labours--the Treaty of San Stefano, the Austro-Russian Convention of January 1877 and the Anglo-Russian agreement of May 30, 1878. These had already settled the major issues. However, psychologically, the Congress was to leave a very important imprint not only on the policies of Russia but on the fate of Europe itself. It was at the Congress that the definite estrangement, so momentous in its consequences, between Bismarck and Russia was to shape itself. Smarting under the snub he had received from Gorchakov during the French war scare of 1875, Bismarck was gradually re-orientating Germany's policy from Russia to Austria. Hence his dubious attitude in the War of 1877-1878 as already noticed by Gorchakov. Writing to King Louis II of Bavaria in June,

1876, Bismarck said, "Nothing would be more dangerous for us than a conflict between Austria and Russia."[19] But he had made up his mind that should such a conflict arise he would side with Austria. Subsequent events only strengthened his resolve and at the same time gave him an opportunity to conciliate Austria by diverting her ambitions toward the Balkans and helping her to forget the humiliation of the Austro-Prussian War of 1866. Indeed Austria, expanding in the Balkans, would be grateful to Bismarck for regaining her lost prestige and at the same time would neutralize and hold Russia in check--a clever and doubly profitable policy for Germany. But it made the role of "honest broker" which he assumed at the Congress appear insincere and the Russians saw through it; all his subsequent attempts to prove to Russia that he had been her friend during the Congress failed to appear convincing. This brings us to the important point of just how far did the course of events, as shaped at the Congress, depend on Bismarck. In his secret report to the Sublime Porte on the Congress of Berlin, the Turkish envoy Karatheodory Pasha gives us a graphic picture of Bismarck's power.[20] "The Congress of Berlin has been completely dominated by Prince Bismarck", he writes. "The protocols and treaties which resulted from it are in a great measure the expression of his ideas, of his desires and sometimes of his impatiences." And again....."Prince Bismarck has been able so completely to concentrate the Congress around himself, that one could not say today what would have happened to that high political assembly and what would have resulted, if it had not had the great German Chancellor in the chair."[21]

The selection of Berlin was an obvious compromise between St. Petersburg, unacceptable to the British, and London, unsuitable to the Russians. Vienna was suggested but quickly discarded for the days were gone when Vienna could become the center of European negotiations. Thus it was that, through the selection of Berlin, Bismarck found himself occupying the same position that Metternich had occupied at the Congress of Vienna. Furthermore the circumstances were somewhat the

---

[19] Matter, P., <u>Bismarck et Son Temps</u>. Paris 1905-1908, Vol. III, p. 427.

[20] Karatheodory Pacha, <u>Le Rapport Secret sur le Congrés de Berlin addressé à la Sublime Porte</u>. Paris 1919, pp. 5, 67.

[21] Le Prince de Bismarck a su si complètement concentrér en lui le Congrés dans son ensemble, Karatheodory, <u>op. cit.</u>, p. 67.

same inasmuch as both Congresses acted as a kind of European high tribunal; not against the defeated nations, France at Vienna, Turkey here, but in both cases against victorious Russia. As at Vienna, a grouping of powers against Russia took place in Berlin; Bismarck, though claiming to be the impartial mediator, nevertheless threw the weight of his influence on the side of Russia's foes, more discreetly and more cautiously than Metternich had done but however just as effectively. Lastly, if at Vienna the settlement of the whole status of Europe brought about the assembling of the most important Europeans sovereigns--here, the occasion was deemed sufficiently grave to bring together the four leading Chancellors and Prime Ministers: Prince Bismarck, Gorchakov, Lord Beaconsfield and Count Andrassy. Lord Beaconsfield was deaf and walked laboriously with a cane, Gorchakov in his eightieth year had to be carried into the council room in an armchair. Thus the junior members of both the British and Russian delegations, Lord Salisbury and Count Shuvalov, carried the weight of the negotiations on their shoulders, Beaconsfield and Gorchakov merely giving the general directions as well as the prestige of their names. Nevertheless, the presence of the four leading statesmen resulted in most of the deliberations being conducted in confidential and direct private discussions between them, which have remained unrecorded; hence it is that the available records do not give the correct picture of what went on and there is perhaps no congress so shrouded in mystery as this one. For this very reason the delegates of the other attending powers found themselves playing a somewhat subsidiary role. France sent her recently appointed Foreign Minister, M. Waddington, accompanied by her ambassadors to London and Berlin but, significantly, not by the one to St. Petersburg. Italy appointed Count Corti, her former Ambassador to Constantinople and a specialist on Balkan affairs. The Turkish delegation was particularly self-effacing, with Karatheodory Pasha, a cultured Greek phanariot, and Mehemet Ali, a German from Magdebourg who had embraced both the Turkish nationality and the Moslem faith, thus making himself in the eyes of Bismarck twice a renegade. The representatives of the Balkan nations, Bratianu, Kogalniceanu, Delyanis, Rhangabé and Ristich were admitted only on special occasions and treated more than cavalierly by the Iron Chancellor.

Bismarck, in the first session of the Congress, defined its object as, "to submit the work of San Stefano to the free dis-

cussion of the signatories of the treaties of 1856 and 1871."[22]
In reality the Congress became a duel between Russia and England. Beaconsfield took the offensive at the very outset by declaring that the presence of the Russian armies at the gates of Constantinople was "abnormal and perilous". Bismarck immediately side-tracked the issue by declaring it outside the competence of the Congress and suggested direct negotiations between the Russians and the British to settle it. The suggestion of settling thorny questions by direct negotiations was to be Bismarck's method of keeping the Congress rolling smoothly and accounts to a great extent for the dearth of material about its work. Four days therefore elapsed before the Congress could meet again. After this first skirmish the main British attack came on the issue of Bulgaria. Beaconsfield, having declared that the frontier suggested by Russia was "outrageous and a gross insult to England", suggested at the second sitting that the line of the Balkan range should serve as the new frontier. As for the portion of Bulgaria south of it, that was to revert to Turkish domination in such a way that the authority the Sultan exercised over it should be not nominal but real. Shuvalov accepted the Balkan frontier line, but balked on the status of Southern Bulgaria declaring that he could not give an answer without the authorization of the Czar.

On the other hand the Turks were battling to retain Varna as the key defence position north of the Balkan range and Salisbury was insisting on the inclusion of Sofia into the portion to be retroceded to Turkey, thereby depriving the new state of its capital. Bismarck once more took the matter out of the plenary meetings and suggested the formation of an Austro-British-Russian committee to settle it. These three powers were selected as being the ones directly interested in Balkan affairs; but it will be noted that by the inclusion of Austria, a country friendly to Britain, a two to one majority against Russia was assured. The committee was soon deadlocked, the Russians maintaining that without Imperial consent they could not accept any proposal. Thus the issue dragged on until June 20 and 21 when a crisis was reached which endangered the very existence of the Congress. What happened then is well known. Beaconsfield let it be known privately that the British proposals regarding the Balkan line and the status of the territory south of it were to be considered an ultimatum. At a dinner given at the Italian Embassy he took a most pessimistic view of the progress of the negotiations and spoke of

---

[22] Seton Watson, R.W. Disraeli, <u>Gladstone and the Eastern Question</u>. London, 1935, p. 446.

breaking up the Congress. The next morning he ordered a special train to carry the British delegation home. Bismarck, alarmed, visited Disraeli to find out just how much the British were in earnest and, according to Beaconsfield's report to Queen Victoria, left convinced that it was not a sham. Accordingly Bismarck went to see Gorchakov who, meanwhile, had received the reply from the Czar telling him to go the limit to avoid war. Therefore, on June 22, the Russians yielded, accepting the British conditions and Beaconsfield scored a first class diplomatic victory.

The question as to what would have happened if the Russians had stood firm has now merely an academic interest, but still it may be asked whether England would have gone to war over the question of Bulgaria. Had the Russians called the bluff, if bluff it was, it would have made a different history of Europe in the years to come. The Russian capitulation assured the survival of the Congress and the details were subsequently ironed out by the three power commission. The British insisted upon the territory retroceded to Turkey being named Eastern Rumelia, a name artificially coined to avoid any connection with Bulgaria. Shuvalov proposed the splitting up of Rumelia into Eastern and Western Rumelia in an effort to weaken the administrative hold of Turkey over the territory, but this proposal was voted down. As for the Turkish claim on Varna, Bismarck browbeat the Turkish delegation into submission by declaring that after having signed the Treaty of San Stefano they had nothing more to say in the matter. Many technical details, such as the status of the new Prince of Bulgaria and the duration of occupation by the Russian army of the territory north of the Balkans, remained to be settled, giving the Russians an opportunity to fight a "rear guard action." By the fourth plenary session of the Congress a full agreement on the Bulgarian question could be officially announced.

The Austrians had helped the British effectively by their support both in plenary meetings and in committee. They were now to be repaid in cash. On June 28, in a written statement, Salisbury proposed that the powers should give Austria a mandate to occupy Bosnia-Herzegovina. Bismarck promptly endorsed the proposal, also in a written speech; the assent of the French delegation followed; When the Turks attempted to protest, Lord Beaconsfield, with delightful irony, stated that the amputation of two Turkish provinces was a friendly act of the powers for it would prevent any further partition of Turkey. The Russians, bound by their agreement with Austria, remained silent but made reservations concerning the extension of Austrian domination over the Sanjak of Novi-Bazar; however, acting upon special instructions from St. Petersburg, they later withdrew this reservation should circumstances make it necessary for Austria to extend her occupation (July 13). Thus, in a few minutes, a carefully prearranged diplomatic comedy disposed of the fate of two provinces.

There remained the Turkish territories on the Caucasian frontier which Russia claimed as her reward for the war and which, together with Bessarabia, were the only actual territories she claimed for herself. Once more the British fought tooth and nail to thwart Russia and a French observer commented ironically upon how Salisbury's "eagerness to save remote Asiatic tribes from Russian rule fitted with his readiness to replace Macedonia and half of Bulgaria under the discredited yoke of Turkey."[23] The struggle here centered around the port of Batum and the districts of Kars, Ardahan and Bayazid. Salisbury declared emphatically that it was England's moral duty "to defend a gallant Moslem nation which objects to Russian rule," whereupon Shuvalov asked him to name the people in question. Salisbury could not recall their name and declared that having mislaid his notes he could not remember of whom he was speaking. Finally, after much searching, Sir Odo Russell produced the notes and Salisbury said he was speaking of the Lazes of Lazistan, whereupon a dispute started with regard to their numbers, Gorchakov declaring they did not exceed 50,000 and Mehemet Ali stating they numbered 150,000. Bismarck bitingly suggested that the Russian and British delegations should be left to discuss alone "this interesting tribe". Whereupon Gorchakov and Beaconsfield came together and at the next session were able to announce their complete agreement. But when they were invited to show on the map the new frontier about which they had reached an agreement, Beaconsfield and Gorchakov produced maps upon which different frontiers had been traced, the Russian map showing more and the British map less territory to be ceded to Russia. In great excitement Gorchakov shouted, "I have been betrayed; they have the map of our staff." What actually happened has never been clarified. One thing is known and that is that Gorchakov had been supplied by the Russian General Staff with maps bearing two suggested frontier lines, the one being the frontier that Russia desired to obtain and the second being the limit of the concessions Russia was prepared to grant should the first line be unobtainable. It was the second line which was on Beaconsfield's map. The Russian

---

[23] Seton Watson, op. cit., p. 439.

version of the incident is that the British had secretly obtained knowledge of this minimum line or that Gorchakov had inadvertently shown the map to them. The British claim--that Gorchakov had actually lent this map to Beaconsfield--does not seem very plausible. More plausible is Salisbury's explanation that he and Shuvalov had already agreed upon the retrocession to Turkey of a territory inhabited by some 80,000 Moslems and had drawn the corresponding line on the map. But he continues to say that Gorchakov had attempted to deceive Beaconsfield, profiting by the latter's nearsightedness, and deliberately submitted the wrong map. Both sides accused the other of double dealing and, which ever version is correct, an element of high comedy enlivened the pompousness of the Congress. The final result was a compromise. The British, not being able to get Batum for Turkey, fell back upon a claim that it should be made a neutral free port, and the Russians yielded on this point. Russia also obtained the territory desired except for Bayazid which went back to Turkey. Thus came to an end the duel between England and Russia so bitterly fought at the Congress.

The other questions dealt with were of no direct concern to Russia except for the question of Bessarabia and the status of the Danube, which was linked up with the Roumanian problem. The Roumanian delegates, Bratianu and Kagolniceanu, who were admitted to the Congress while the status of Bessarabia was being debated, insisted that no Roumanian territory should be ceded and bitterly protested the prospective cession of Bessarabia. They further insisted that the Russian troops in Bulgaria and Turkey should not be allowed to pass over Roumanian soil. As positive claims they demanded independence for Roumania and the payment of an indemnity. But their chances of success were slim. England showed no interest in the fate of Bessarabia but showed a vital concern in keeping Russia away from the Danube, while Austria was trying to get control over that all-important waterway. Andrassy therefore proposed that the river should be neutralized from the Iron Gates down, and Russia immediately welcomed the exclusion of all war vessels from the Danube, as well as the razing of all Turkish fortresses. Furthermore, Andrassy demanded the right for Austria to control the navigation and deal with the technical problems arising at the treacherous narrows of the Iron Gates and, lastly, suggested the indefinite prolongation of the powers of the International Commission of the Danube with its seat at Galatz and jurisdiction over the Delta. These points were finally conceded and in the heat of the discussions Russia not only obtained Bessarabia, but the mouth of Kilia in the Danube delta as well. The Roumanians had to be content with the proclamation of their independence, the strip of Dobrudja, the mouth of the Danube and Serpent Island in the Black Sea. Serbia was also granted independence and given a few districts, those of Vranja, Trn and Pirot on the Bulgarian frontier and Mali Zvornik on the Bosnian border. As most of these acquisitions were at the expense of Bulgaria, Russia was the only power to protest them and thereby incurred the ill will of the Serbs. Austria on the other hand supported the Serbs, and thus subsequently obtained a separate convention whereby Serbia granted her the right of building railways on her territory and also a very favourable commercial treaty.

Thus was laid the cornerstone of the Austro-Serbian alliance which was to play such an important part in subsequent developments in the Balkans. Finally the Greek delegates, Delyanis and Rizo Rhangabé, were admitted to present their desiderata and lay claim to Crete, and to Epirus and Thessaly on the northern border of Greece. Though privately the delegates of the powers extended their sympathy to the Greeks, nobody was prepared to face a new crisis over this issue, hence the Congress merely invited Turkey, upon the proposal of Waddington supported by Corti, to negotiate directly with Greece for a rectification of the northern frontier along a line running from the valley of Salamirias on the Aegean Sea to the valley of Kalamas on the Ionian Sea.[24]

The question of the cession of Cyprus to England, not being within the provisions of the Treaty of San Stefano, was outside the scope of Russia, but through an indiscretion the Russians gleefully learned about the secret Cyprus Convention. Similarly the implied promise of Tunis to France did not concern Russia directly. Thus on July 13, a month after its opening, the Congress concluded its labours with the signing of the Treaty of Berlin and closed its doors amidst much mutual expression of goodwill which did not ring sincere. The Treaty of Berlin did not cancel the agreements of 1856 and 1871, it merely invalidated those clauses of these preceding treaties which had been replaced by new ones. In this respect it did not provide for revolutionary changes but formed merely one more link in the chain of international agreements on the Eastern Question. Its most important proviso, and the one in which it differed most from the Treaty of San Stefano, was of course

---

[24] See Medlicott, W. N., *The Congress of Berlin and After*. London, 1938. Chapter on the Congress.

in the Bulgarian question. The Great Bulgaria of the Russian scheme was mutilated and replaced by three separate portions. 1) The autonomous Principality of Bulgaria north of the Balkans remained a vassal state of the Sultan, with a Christian Prince to be elected, a national army and a constitution, a "Réglement Organique," to be worked out by the National Assembly. This new state was to be administered and garrisoned by the Russians for a period of nine months with the aid of a Turkish delegate and foreign consuls, during which time the election of the Prince and the organization of its administration was to be completed. Following the precedent adopted in the Belgian issue half a century earlier, no member of the ruling houses of the great powers could be elected to the Bulgarian throne (Art. I, IV, VI, VII) and no Turkish troops or fortresses were to remain on Bulgarian soil. 2) Eastern Rumelia was given back to Turkey, but with the intermediate status of an autonomous province to be governed by a Christian governor appointed by the Sultan for a term of five years. Its administration remained Turkish and it was to be garrisoned by Turkish regulars, to the exclusion of irregulars (Circassians, Bashi Buzuks). 3) Macedonia and Thrace were simply reinstated under full Turkish rule though a pledge was to be given by Turkey to carry out reforms for the betterment of their administration, which applied as well to Albania, Epirus and Thessaly. Needless to say this pledge was never carried out and had been inserted hypocritically by the Congress which was fully aware of what had happened to a similar clause in the Treaty of Paris (Art. XXII).

Bosnia-Herzegovina was to be occupied by Austro-Hungary which reserved the right to occupy similarly the Sanjak of Novi Bazar (Art. XXVI-XXIX). The acquisitions and the new status of Roumania and Serbia have already been mentioned (Art. XXXIV, XXXVI, and XLIII) as well as the international status of the Danube (Art. LIII). In the Caucasus, Russia obtained Batum which became a free port, Kars, Ardahan, but not Bayazid. Finally Turkey pledged for her Christian subjects full religious liberty and equality with the Moslem citizens within her Empire. Other clauses dealt with the status of the monks on Mount Athos and the status quo in the Holy Land.

Gladstone summed up the Treaty in a speech in November 1879: "Everything that will make the treaty of Berlin an epoch in the history of Europe was due to the sword of Russia and to that sword alone".[25] The truth of that assertion stands out

---

[25] Seton Watson, op. cit., p. 431.

more glaringly if one compares the settlement of Berlin and the settlement of San Stefano. For good or for evil the Russians imposed peace. The Treaty of San Stefano was a complete and thorough solution of the Eastern problem where it was most acute--in the Balkans--and, though not perfect, it did offer a basis for a stable system of equilibrium in that turbulent peninsula and above all it eliminated the most troublesome factor--Turkish misrule. The truncated Treaty of Berlin, with its contradictions and timidities, sacrificed this solution in the name of the balance of power and left half solutions which worked themselves out in new wars. For the time being Beaconsfield had scored a resounding diplomatic triumph and brought home "peace with honour" but at the cost, for future generations, of Austro-Russian rivalry and unrest in the Balkans, the break up of the solid front of German-Russian cooperation to be replaced by the splitting of Europe into two rival camps. Had he foreseen the Balkan Wars, the first and second World Wars and their results, perhaps he would have shuddered at the chain of events to which the Congress of Berlin was a powerful contributing factor.

BIBLIOGRAPHY

Allen, C. F., Histoire de Danemark. Copenhagen 1878. 2 Vols.

Bapst, E., Les Origines de la Guerre de Crimée. Paris 1912.

Bell, F. C. F., Lord Palmerston. New York 1936, 2 Vols.

Blanc, Louis, History of Ten Years, 1830-1840. London, 1844, 2 Vols.

Bogdanovich, M. I., Vostochnaîa Voina, 1853-1856. St. Petersburg 1877, 4 Vols.

Chateaubriand, Vicomte F. R. de. Congrés de Vérone. Oeuvres Complètes. Paris without date. XII Vols.

Corti, Egon, Elizabeth Empress of Austria. New Haven 1936.

Creasy, Sir Edward S., History of the Ottoman Turks. New York 1877.

Danilevsky, N., Russland und Europa. Stuttgart und Berlin 1920.

Debidour, A., Histoire Diplomatique de l'Europe Depuis l'Ouverture du Congrés de Vienne jusqu'a la Cloture du Congrés de Berlin. Paris 1891. 3 Vols.

Driault, Edouard et L'héritier M., Histoire Diplomatique de la Grèce de 1821 à nos Jours. Paris 1925-1926. V Vols.

Dubrovin, Colonel, N. F. Istoria Krimskoi Voiny i Oborony Sevastopolia. St. Petersburg 1900. III Vols.

Finlay, George, History of the Greek Revolution. London 1861.

Gorce, de la P., Histoire du Second Empire. Paris 1908. VII Vols.

Goriainow, S. M. Le Bosphore et les Dardanelles. Paris 1910.

Graham, Stephen, The Tzar of Freedom. New Haven 1935.

Greene, Lieutenant F. V., Report on the Russian Army and Its Campaigns in Turkey in 1877-1878. New York 1879.

The Greville Mémoires. A Journal of the Reign of Queen Victoria from 1852-1860 by Charles C. F. Greville, Esq. London 1887. III Vols.

Guedalla, P., Palmerston. London 1926.

Guichen, Vicomte de, La Guerre de Crimée et l'Attitude des Puissances Europeennes. Paris 1936.

Guizot, F., Memoires to Illustrate the History of My Time. London 1861. VIII Vols.

Hamley, General Sir Edward, War in the Crimea. London 1910.

Hertslet, E., The Map of Europe by Treaty Showing the Various Political and Territorial Changes which Have Taken Place Since the General Peace of Vienna. London 1875-1891. IV Vols.

Hippeau, Edmond, Histoire Diplomatique de la Troisième Republique. Paris 1887.

Iorga, N., Histoire des relations russo-roumaines. Jassy 1917.

Jomini, A. G., Etude Diplomatique sur la Guerre de Crimée (1852-1856). St. Petersburg 1877. IV Vols.

Karatheodory, Pacha. Le Rapport Secret sur le Congrés de Berlin addressé à la Sublime Porte. Paris 1919.

Lafuente y Zamalloa, M., Historia general de Espana desde los tiempos, más remotos hasta nuestras dias. Madrid 1840-1867. XXX Vols.

Lazarovich-Hrebelianovich, Prince S., The Servian People, Their Past Glory and Their Destiny. New York 1910. II Vols.

Leger, L., A History of Austria Hungary. London 1889.

Lutostanski, K., Les Partages de la Pologne et la Lutte pour l'Independance. Paris 1918.

Lytton, H. Bulver, Life of Henry John Temple, Viscount Palmerston. London 1871-1874. II Vols.

Maggiolo, Vicomte A de, Corse, France et Russie. Pozzo di Borgo, 1764-1842. Paris 1890.

Martens, F. F., Recueil des traités et conventions conclus par la Russie avec les puissances étrangerès. St. Petersburg, 1874-1909. XV Vols.

Martens, K., Causes Célébrès du droit des gens. Leipzig 1861.

Martinengo-Cesaresco, Countess, Cavour. Foreign Statesman Series.

Matter, P., Bismarck et son temps. Paris 1905-1908. III Vols.

Medlicott, W. N., The Congress of Berlin and After. London 1938.

Metternich, Mémoires, documents et ecrits divers laissés par le prince de Metternich, chancelier de court et d'Etat. Paris 1880-1884. VIII Vols.

Miller, William, The Balkans, Roumania, Bulgaria, Servia, Montenegro. London 1923.

Moltke, Baron von, The Russians in Bulgaria and Rumelia in 1828 and 1829. London 1854.

Morfill, W., A History of Russia from the Birth of Peter the Great Till the Death of Alexander III. London 1902.

Morny, Une ambassade en Russie 1856. Extrait des Mémoires du Duc de Morny. Paris 1892.

Moseley, Philip E., Russian Diplomacy and the Opening of the Eastern Question in 1838 and 1839. Cambridge 1934.

Mowat, R. B., History of European Diplomacy 1815-1914. London 1927.

Napier, Sir Charles, The History of the Baltic Campaign of 1854. London 1857.

Nesselrode, Count C. R., Lettres et papiers du chancelier Cte de Nesselrode, 1760-1850 [-1856], extraits de ses archives. Paris 1908-1912. XI Vols.

Paléologue, G. M., Cavour. London 1927.

Peace Handbook issued by the Historical Section of the British Foreign Office. London 1920. Vol. XXIV.

Pirenne, H., Histoire de Belgique. Brussels 1928. V Vols.

Polievktov, M., Imperator Nikolai I. Moscow 1918.

Puryear, V. J., England, Russia and the Straits Question, 1844-1856. Berkeley 1931.

Potemkin, V. P., Histoire de la Diplomatic. Paris 1946.

Rambaud, A., History of Russia. New York 1882. III Vols.

Redlich, J., Emperor Francis Joseph of Austria, a Biography. New York 1929.

Révue d'Histoire Diplomatique. Paris 1923.

Rousset, C., Histoire de la Guerre de Crimée. Paris 1887. II Vols.

Rüstow, F. W., Der Orientalischen Krieg. Zurich 1877, 1878.

Sabry, M., L'Empire Egyptien sous Mohamed Ali et la Question d'Orient. Paris 1930.

Saburov, The Saburov Mémoires, edited by J. Y. Simpson. Cambridge 1929.

Sbornik, Imperatorskogo Russkogo Istoricheskogo Obshchestva. St. Petersburg, 1864-1916. CILVIII Vols.

Schiemann, T. Geshichte Russlands unter Kaiser Nikolaus I,
  Berlin 1904-1919. IV Vols.

Seton Watson, R. W., Disraeli, Gladstone and the Eastern
  Question. London 1935.

Sorokin, P., Social and Cultural Dynamics. New York 1937.
  III Vols.

Stockmar, F., Denkwürdigkeiten aus den Papieren des
  Freiherrn Christian Friedrich von Stockmar. Braunschweig 1872. III Vols.

Tatishchev, S. S., Imperator Aleksandr II, Ego Zhizn i
  Tsarstvovanie. St. Petersburg 1903. II Vols.

Tatishchev, S. S., Imperator Nikolai i Inostrannye Dvory.
  St. Petersburg 1889.

Thureau-Dangin, P., Histoire de la Monarchie de Juillet.
  Paris 1897.

Transactions of the Royal Historical Society, 1935.

Victoria, Letters of Queen Victoria. First Series. New
  York 1907. III Vols.

Webster, Sir Charles, The Foreign Policy of Palmerston,
  1830-1841. London 1951.

Whyte, A. J., The Political Life and Letters of Cavour, 1848-
  1861. London 1930.

INDEX

A

Aali Pasha 204, 208, 248

Abdul Aziz, Sultan, 270

Abdul Hamid II, Sultan 270

Abdul Medjid, Sultan 75, 139

'Aberdeen, Lord 48, 50, 82, 83, 146, 150, 153, 157, 163, 179

Achmet Pasha 44

Acre 79

Adrianople 42, 43, 44, 92, 159, 276, 282, 285, 287, 291

Adrianople, Treaty of (see Treaties)

Aegean Sea 77, 287, 288, 289, 292, 301

Ahmed Fewzi Pasha 75

Aidos 40, 41, 42

Aix la Chapelle, Congress of (see Congresses)

Akkerman, Convention of 17, 18, 20, 23, 24, 56, 59

Aksakov 259, 260

Aland Islands 164, 165, 166, 167, 209, 212, 214, 215, 216, 217

Albania 269, 275, 292, 302

Albert, Prince Consort 156, 157

Algeria 45

Alexandria 21, 23, 69, 72, 74, 75, 77

Alexander I, Czar 4, 5, 6, 7, 8, 9, 10, 11, 12, 13, 14, 15, 46, 86, 91, 96, 136

Alexander II, Czar 90, 190, 210, 218, 219, 222, 223, 225, 227, 230, 231, 235, 236, 240, 241, 242, 247, 252, 253, 254, 255, 256, 266, 269, 270, 279

Alexander III, Czar 263, 276

Alfonso XII, King 254

Alliances
  Anglo-French-Russian 19, 24
  Anglo-Turkish 74
  Austro-Russian 1726 2
  Austro-Serbian 301
  Four Power Alliance of Chaumont 11, 136
  Franco-Russian Alliances 6, 12, 26, 226, 231
  Holy Alliance 12, 18, 19, 52, 94, 103, 104, 105, 122, 123, 128
  League of the Three Emperors 252
  Russo-Turkish 66, 72
  Three Northern Courts 19, 62, 87, 99, 102, 103, 105, 106, 107, 108, 114, 136, 222, 251

Alma, Battle of 173, 174

Alopeus 91

Alvensleben, General von 225, 226, 227

American Revolution, (see Wars)

Anapa 32

Ancillon 111

311

Ancona 102

Andrassy, Count Julius 125, 252, 268, 270, 289, 296, 300

Antwerp 101

Apponyi, Count 97

Arad 125

Armenia 68

Athens 20, 134

Austria 2, 3, 4, 5, 6, 7, 10, 11, 12, 36, 52, 59, 60, 61, 62, 66, 67, 69, 70, 76, 77, 78, 79, 82, 84, 91, 92, 94, 95, 97, 101, 102, 103, 105, 107, 108, 109, 111, 112, 114, 117, 118, 121, 122, 125, 126, 128, 129, 130, 131, 132, 133, 136, 145, 149, 151, 153, 154, 158, 159, 169, 170, 177, 193, 194, 195, 198, 199, 200, 202, 203, 204, 208, 212, 213, 214, 219, 220, 221, 222, 227, 228, 229, 230, 235, 236, 239, 243, 244, 245, 246, 248, 252, 256, 257, 260, 261, 263, 268, 269, 270, 288, 289, 292, 293, 294, 295, 297, 298, 299, 300, 301

Austrian Army 2, 3, 7, 12, 18, 71, 95, 102, 120, 123, 129, 132, 161, 223

Austrian Navy 18

Austrian Succession, War of (see Wars)

Augustenburg, Duke of 234, 235

Aupick 135, 139

Austerlitz, Battle of 5, 25

B

Baden 11, 219

Balkan Countries 13, 28, 45, 50, 53, 60, 92, 131, 132, 135, 207, 242, 257, 268, 273, 283, 284, 289, 292, 295, 298, 301, 303

Balkan Range 25, 30, 32, 35, 36, 37, 40, 41, 42, 43, 46, 49, 153, 154, 201, 263, 266, 274, 276, 279, 282, 285, 287, 290, 294, 297, 302

Balaclava, battle of 176, 177, 179, 180, 181, 186

Baltic Provinces 267

Baltic Sea 1, 2, 6, 163, 164, 167, 168, 169, 170, 190, 214, 216, 217

Batthyany, Count 125

Batum 154, 289, 290, 292, 294, 299, 300, 302

Baudin, Admiral 119

Bautzen, battle of 7, 100

Bavaria 55, 69, 100, 129, 240

Bayazid 299, 300, 302

Bazaine 191

Beaconsfield (see Disraeli)

Beauharnais, Eugene Prince 100

Belgrade 2, 60, 61, 62, 212, 265, Treaty of (see Treaties)

Belgium 73, 82, 93, 94, 96, 99, 100, 101, 104, 136, 240

Bem, General 120, 122, 124

Benedetti 204, 238

Berlin 7, 18, 70, 90, 91, 94, 97, 98, 105, 107, 109, 112, 116, 126, 127, 128, 129, 226, 232, 236, 241, 242, 249, 252, 256, 271, 288

Bernadotte 216, 217

INDEX

Berg, General, Count 114

Berezina 7

Besika Bay 148, 149, 151, 289, 290

Bessarabia 2, 28, 35, 58, 59, 170, 196, 197, 206, 207, 211, 214, 218, 248, 269, 273, 289, 290, 292

Bibescu, Hospodar 58

Bismarck-Schonhausen, Otto von 130, 197, 199, 200, 223, 224, 225, 226, 227, 228, 231, 234, 235, 235, 237, 238, 239, 241, 243, 244, 247, 250, 252, 253, 254, 256, 268, 269, 270, 288, 289, 293, 294, 295, 296, 297, 298

Bohemia 5, 104, 121, 127, 257

Black Sea 2, 3, 23, 25, 30, 36, 44, 45, 45, 63, 76, 68, 79, 81, 84; Black Sea Fleet 32, 65, 68; 144, 153, 154, 157, 158, 167, 169, 191, 194, 195, 196, 201, 202; Neutralization of 205, 206, 212, 214; demilitarization of 243, 247, 248, 249, 250, 273, 288, 290, 291, 292

Blanc, Louis 96

Bolgrad 28, 207, 214

Bomarsund 167, 206, 216, 217

Borodino, battle of 6

Bosnia 264, 268, 269, 289, 298, 302

Bosphorus, Straits of 24, 25, 26, 37, 45, 63, 65, 67, 69, 73

Bothnia, Gulf of 166, 214

Bourqueney, Baron 76, 208, 209

Braila 29, 30, 35, 57, 160, 273

Brandenburg-Prussia (see Prussia)

Brandenburg, Count 127, 128, 129

Bratianu 296, 300

Broglie, Duc de 67, 93

Breslau 113

Britain (see Great Britain)

Brussels 99, 101, 110

Brunnow, Baron 78, 79, 118, 135, 147, 158, 196, 205, 207, 208, 235, 248, 249

Buchanan, Sir Andrew 163, 228, 249

Bucharest 28, 57, 58, 59, 145, 264

Budberg, Baron 193

Bug 169, 170

Bukovina 58, 207

Bulgaria 30, 37, 38, 42, 44, 61, 98, 157, 170, 258, 264, 269, 273, 289, 292, 294, 297, 298, 299, 300, 301, 302

Bulgarian Exarchate 267

Bulgary, Count 46, 48, 51

Buol, Count 131, 132, 149, 150, 159, 193, 194, 195, 197, 200, 204, 207, 208, 224

Burgas 37, 40, 41, 42, 44, 154

Buteeniev 61, 65, 72, 73, 74, 76

Byzantine Empire 138, 258, 262

C

Canada 84

Canning, George 14, 16, 18, 19, 131

Canning, Stratford 15, 47, 64, 125, 142, 143, 148, 150, 153

Canrobert, General 172, 184, 185

Capo d'Istria 14, 46, 47, 48, 49, 51, 52, 53, 54, 55,

Cardigan, Lord 178, 179

Carlsbad 103, 104

Castlereagh, Lord 8, 10

Castelbajac, General de 133, 134, 135, 158

Catherine II 2, 3, 4, 9, 13, 29, 45 109, 201, 204

Caucasus 144, 154, 169, 302

Cavalla 64

Cavaignac, General 119

Cavour 200, 202, 203, 204, 208, 209, 218, 219, 220, 222

Champagne 9

Chambord, Count of 254

Charles X, King of France 15, 86, 88, 89, 93

Charles, Archduke of Austria 98

Charles Albert, King of Sardinia, 102, 121

Charles Felix, King of Sardinia 102

Charles I, Prince of Roumania 242, 245, 279

Charles XIV of Sweden (see Bernadotte)

Charlotte, Princess of Prussia 90

Chernaya 186, 187, 191; battle of 201, 202, 203, 204

Chernyshev, Count 69, 94, 116

Cherniaev, General 263, 264, 265, 266

Chotek, Count 246

Clarendon, Lord 148, 191, 204, 205, 206

Coburg, Prince Ferdinand 61, 98

Codrington, Admiral 21, 22, 24, 46

Collin, General 113

Congress Poland, (see Poland)

Congresses of:
Aix-la-Chapelle 9
Berlin 257, 270, 294, 295-303
Chatillon 8
Constantinople, Conference of 150, 292
London Conference 1871 250
Paris 62, 204, 205, 206, 207, 208, 209, 213
Prague, Slav Congress 257, 259
Troppau-Laibach 12, 104
Verona 12
Versailles 1
Vienna 1, 10, 104, 110, 207, 232, 238, 295
Westphalia 1

Constantine, Grand Duke 10, 12

Constantine, Grand Duke 94, 100, 106, 197

Constantinople 14, 15, 16, 20, 21, 22, 23, 25, 26, 27, 43, 44, 46, 47, 48, 50, 55, 56, 59, 60, 61, 63, 64, 65, 66, 68, 69, 72, 74, 76, 82, 84, 89, 139, 140, 141, 142, 143, 145, 146, 147, 148, 152, 154, 156, 157, 203, 248, 249, 261, 266, 270, 275, 276, 287, 288, 290, 291, 293, 297

INDEX

Copenhagen 234

Corfu 21, 26, 47

Corti, Count 296, 301

Coundouriottis 53

Courland 242

Couza, Alexander 59

Cowley, Lord 148, 204, 206, 208

Cracow, Republic of 84, 91, 107, 109, 110, 111, 112, 113, 114, 154

Crampton, Sir John 221

Crimea 2, 59, 161, 169, 170, 171, 177, 179, 184, 190, 192, 194, 202, 203

Crimean War (see Wars)

Crete 47, 48, 49, 52, 53, 55, 64, 261, 263, 267, 301

Croatia 118, 121

Custozza, battle of 118

Cyclades 48, 50, 51

Cyprus 47, 301

Czartoryski, Prince 9

D

Danilevski 261

Dannenberg, General 59, 159, 160, 181

Dantes, M. G. 136

Danton 22

Danube 5, 25, 28, 29, 30, 34, 35, 38, 44, 47, 56, 59, 65, 124, 131, 132, 144, 152, 154, 159, 160, 161, 162, 169, 194, 196, 206, 211, 214, 272, 274, 277, 284, 285, 289, 291, 300, 301, 302

Danubian Principalities 120, 144, 148, 149, 153, 159, 161, 162, 170, 193, 194, 196, 199, 206, 211, 236, 273

Danzig 2, 106, 164

Dardanelles 3, 4, 22, 25, 36, 37, 47, 48, 63, 66, 72, 73, 76, 77, 85, 125, 140, 148, 151, 152, 154, 251, 290, 291, 293

Dashkov 63

Decazes Duc 255

Decembrist Revolution 12

Delyanis 296, 301

Dembinsky, General 122

Denmark 1, 136, 163, 232, 233, 234, 235, 245

Derby, Lord 220, 270, 288, 289, 290, 291, 293

Diebitch, Field Marshal 36, 37, 38, 40, 42, 43, 44, 50, 63, 94, 95

Disraeli 268, 296, 297, 298, 299, 300, 303

Dnieper River 2, 29, 191

Dniestr 25

Dobrudja 161, 273, 277, 292, 301

Dolgoruky, Prince 260

Dombrowski 112

Don Carlos 103, 107

Don Pacifico 134

Dostoievsky 261

Dragomirov, General 263, 274

Drouyn de Lhuys 133, 135, 137, 141, 148, 152, 157, 228

Dundas, Admiral 190

Dvina 2

E

Edinburg, Duke of 266

Egypt 47, 63, 64, 70, 73, 74, 75, 77, 78, 79, 267, 288, 293

Elba 8, 10

Elizabeth, Empress of Austria 131

Ems 243, 244, 269

England, (see Great Britain)

Engelhardt, General 120

Epidaurus 14

Epirus 14, 47, 49, 269, 294, 301, 302

Erfurt Union 126, 127, 129

Esterhazy, Count 18, 196, 197

Eubea 47, 48, 51

Eugene, Prince of Württemberg 31

Eupatoria 171, 173, 177, 182, 186, 191

Eylau, Battle of 5

F

Ferdinand I, Emperor of Austria 105, 114

Ferdinand I, King of Naples 12

Ferdinand II, King of Naples 102, 119, 222

Fenwick Williams 190

Ficquelmont, Count 105

Finland 2, 3, 5, 6

Finland, Gulf of 163, 215, 216

Fleury, General 234, 241, 242, 245, 246

Florence 202, 236, 249

Fokshani, battle of 3

France 2, 3, 4, 5, 6, 8, 9, 10, 15, 22, 25, 26, 46, 47, 48, 50, 51, 52, 53, 54, 56, 58, 64, 67, 68, 69, 70, 71, 72, 76, 78, 79, 80, 82, 86, 87, 88, 89, 94, 98, 99, 102, 105, 107, 111, 113, 114, 116, 117, 119, 120, 125, 133, 134, 135, 136, 138, 140, 141, 143, 145, 146, 149, 153, 158, 193, 194, 196, 208, 209, 210, 212, 213, 214, 217, 219, 220, 221, 222, 228, 229, 230, 231, 238, 239, 241, 243, 245, 246, 248, 251, 254, 255, 256, 269, 296, 301

Frankfurt 120, 129, 130

Frankfurt Diet 126, 127, 128, 129, 200, 223, 232, 234, 235, 237

Francis, Duke of Modena 102

Francis I, King of France 138

Francis I, Emperor of Austria 8, 22, 103, 105

Francis Joseph, Emperor of Austria 121, 122, 123, 124, 126, 127, 128, 131, 132, 145, 151, 153, 154, 193, 194, 223, 244, 252, 269

Franz, Karl, Archduke 106, 107

Frederick the Great, King of Prussia 3, 8

INDEX

Frederick William III, King of Prussia 90, 91, 94, 101, 104, 107, 198

Frederick William IV, King of Prussia 104, 109, 130, 193

Frederick William I, Elector of Hesse-Cassel 127

Frederick VII, King of Denmark 232, 233, 234

Franco-Russian Alliance (see Alliances)

French Army 4, 6, 49, 101, 176, 177, 178, 188

French Fleet 77, 141, 142, 148, 149, 152, 157, 165, 166, 171, 180

French Revolution 1, 3, 4, 13

Friedrichshafen 69

Friedland, Battle of 5

Frimont, General 12

G

Galicia 6, 112, 118, 121, 122, 123, 194, 198, 219, 227

Galatz 28, 160, 273, 274, 300

Galipoli 287, 290, 291

Garashanin, Elia 62

Garibaldi 222

Gastein 227, 236, 252

Geismar, General 34

Gerlach, General von 198, 200

Germanic Confederation 130, 200, 232, 238

German Legion

Germany 11, 69, 81, 90, 97, 116, 117, 120, 121, 126, 130, 226, 227, 236, 254, 263, 268, 288, 289, 290, 294, 295

Ghica, Prince Gregory 59

Gibraltar 81

Gladstone 248, 264, 268, 302

Gorchakov, Prince (Chancellor) 59, 107, 129, 130, 172, 195, 196, 197, 210, 213, 214, 218, 219, 220, 221, 222, 223, 226, 229, 230, 235, 236, 238, 239, 241, 242, 243, 245, 247, 248, 250, 252, 253, 254, 256, 263, 266, 270, 290, 291, 294, 296, 298, 299, 300

Gorchakov, Prince M., General 145, 152, 159, 160, 172, 181, 182, 187, 188, 190

Gordon, Sir Robert 50

Görgey, General 121, 122, 123, 124, 131

Gottland, Island of 215, 216, 217

Gramont, Duc de 226

Grand Duchy of Warsaw (see Poland)

Granville, Lord 70, 84, 136

Great Britain 4, 5, 7, 10, 11, 15, 16, 17, 19, 22, 23, 24, 25, 36, 45, 46, 47, 50, 51, 54, 56, 58, 60, 61, 62, 67, 68, 69, 70, 71, 72, 74, 76, 77, 78, 79, 80, 81, 82, 83, 84, 85, 86, 88, 93, 94, 97, 102, 105, 107, 109, 111, 112, 113, 114, 120, 126, 136, 141, 145, 146, 149, 151, 157; declaration of war 1853 158; 179, 193, 194, 205, 206, 212, 213, 214, 216, 217, 219, 220, 221, 228, 229, 230, 231, 232, 234, 245, 246, 248, 251, 257, 267, 269, 270, 288, 289, 290, 292, 293, 297, 298, 300, 301

Great Britain
  British Army 4, 171, 173, 174, 176, 178, 181
  British Fleet 21, 48, 67, 72, 77, 85, 141, 148, 149, 152, 163, 164, 180, 289, 290, 291

Great Northern War (see Wars)

Greville 205, 206, 209

Greco-Turkish War (see War)

Greece 4, 13, 15, 16, 17, 18, 19, 20, 22, 23, 36, 44, 45, 46, 47, 48, 49, 51, 52, 53, 55, 60, 64, 73, 87, 88, 99, 134, 135, 136, 269

Greek Revolution 27, 46, 64

Gregory XVI, Pope 102

Grünne, Count 132

Guizot 78, 79

Gurko, General 274, 275, 276, 281, 282, 283, 284, 286, 287, 288

H

Hafiz Pasha 74

Hague, the 101

Hamburg 7

Hamley, General, Sir Edward 170, 171, 189

Hangö 165, 166

Hanover 89, 127; King of 237

Haynau, General 123, 124, 125

Hermannstadt 123, 124

Herzegovina 144, 145, 264, 268, 269, 289, 298, 302

Hesse-Darmstadt, Grand Duke of 106

Hesse-Cassel 127, 128, 129

Hetairia 13

Heyden, Count Admiral 20, 21, 22, 36, 37, 44, 47

Holland 4, 44, 99, 101, 136, 238

Holy Roman Empire (see Austria)

Holy Places 143, 148

Holy Alliance (see Alliances)

Hübner, Baron, 204, 218

Hungary 14, 121, 122, 123, 124, 125, 131, 194

Hunyadi 40

Hussein Pasha 31, 38, 39, 40

Hydra 53, 54, 55

I

Ibrahim Pasha 14, 15, 16, 21, 23, 47, 64, 66, 77, 79

Ignatiev, Count 248, 263, 266, 267

India 4

Inkerman, battle of 181, 182

Ionian Islands 4, 25

Ischl 127, 252

Ismail 3, 29, 160, 162, 206, 207,

Italinsky 25, 26

Italy 4, 10, 11, 93, 102, 114, 121, 200, 223, 228, 239, 246, 251, 269, 296

INDEX

J

Jaffa

Janissaries 13, 27

Jannina 14

Jassy, Treaty of (see Treaties)

Jassy 28, 35, 56, 57

Jellachich, Baron 118

Jena 5

Jerusalem 138, 139, 142, 143

Jesuits 86

Jomini, Baron 248, 249, 252

Joseph II, Holy Roman Emperor 3

Jutland 232

K

Kalish 106, 108; Treaty of (see Treaties)

Kankrin, Count 94

Karageorg 13

Karageorgievich, Prince, later King Peter 264

Karageorgievitch, Prince Alexander 61, 62

Karatheodory Pasha 295, 296

Kars 190, 206, 290, 292, 299

Katkov 263

Kauffmann, General 111

Kerch 186

Kherson 68

Khosrew Pasha 75, 79

Kiel 167, 232, 234

Kiev 258

Kilia 29, 207, 301

Kinburn 191

Kisselev, Count Nicholas 117, 133, 135, 136, 147, 158, 210

Kisselev, Count Paul 57, 58, 116, 117, 197

Kissingen 236

Kagolniceanu 58, 296, 300

Kolettes 55

Kolokotrones 55

Komorn 122, battle of 124

Königstein 113

Konieh 65, 74

Königgraetz, battle of 237, 243

Kornilov, Admiral 154, 155, 172, 180

Kossuth 122, 125

Kosludja 30

Krassovsky, General 38, 40

Kuban 44

Kuchuk-Kainardji, Treaty of (see Treaties)

Kulm, battle of 100

Kulturkampf 255

Kunersdorf, battle of 3

Kurland 2

Kustendji 29, 30

Kutuzov 5, 7

L

La Ferronays, Count 18, 24, 87, 88

Lafayette 95, 96

Lafitte 97

Laibach 13

Lamartime 117

La Marmora, General 202, 219

La Rochefoucauld, Duc de 253

Lauenburg 232

Lavalette 139, 140

Lazarev, Admiral 46, 65

Lazistan 299

League of Neutrals 3

Lebzeltern 119

Le Flo, General 119, 121, 255, 256

Lemberg 122

Leopold, King of Belgium 52, 83, 84, 100, 156

Leontiev, K. 261, 262

Leuchtenberg, Dukes of 100

Libau 164

Lieven, Princess 93

Lieven, Prince 16, 17, 18, 19, 24, 48

Limburg 100

Liprandi, General 161, 178, 187

Lithuania 1, 2, 112

Livonia 242

London 16, 18, 20, 24, 47, 48, 50, 51, 53, 55, 69, 70, 71, 72, 73, 74, 76, 77, 78, 79, 81, 82, 87, 98, 107, 109, 110, 114, 135, 147, 157, 228, 230, 231, 235, 248, 249, 253, 266, 267, 271, 288, 293, 296

London, Conference of 23, 92, 99, 100, 107

Lombardy 118

Louis XIV, King of France 1, 8, 9, 15, 86

Louis Philippe, King of France 82, 93, 95, 96, 98, 100, 116, 254

Lubeck, 164, 165

Lüders, General 124, 161

Lutzen, battle of 7, 100

Luxemburg, Fortress of 94

Luxemburg, Duchy of 100, 101, 238, 239

M

Macedonia 292, 294, 299, 302

MacMahon, Marshal

Maina 53

Mahmoud II 14, 21, 27, 28, 45, 64, 72, 75

Maison, Marshal 93

INDEX

Malta 4, 22, 26, 141, 289

Malcolm, Admiral 36

Malmesbury, Lord 221, 230

Manchester 85

Manteuffel, General 129, 208, 238

Maria Fedorovna, Empress of Russia 91

Marmora, Sea of 63, 152, 291, 293

Massena, Marshal 4

Matussewich, Count 48, 98

Mavromichalis 53, 54, 55

Mavrocordatos 53

Mazzini 102

Mecklenburg 2, 127

Mecklenburg-Schwerin 106

Mediterranean, Sea 4, 18, 22, 24, 25, 36, 44, 48, 51, 67, 70, 79, 81, 82, 163, 169

Mehemet Ali 14, 18, 21, 36, 53, 64, 65, 66, 68, 69, 70, 71, 72, 73, 74, 75, 77, 78, 79, 80, 107

Melbourne, Lord 82

Memel 98, 164, 165

Menshikov, Prince 140, 141, 142, 143, 145, 147, 148, 153, 171, 172, 173, 174, 177, 178, 181, 182

Metternich, Prince 7, 8, 10, 11, 14, 15, 17, 18, 19, 22, 67, 69, 71, 75, 76, 77, 79, 93, 97, 98, 103, 104, 107, 108, 111, 112, 113, 115, 117, 121, 295, 296

Metternich, Prince Richard 244

Metternich, Princess 104

Metz 192

Meyendorf, Baron 112, 126, 128, 129, 132, 145, 149, 197, 224

Miaoulis 53, 54

Michael, Grand Duke 90, 124, 125

Mieroslavski, L. 112

Milan IV, Prince of Serbia 62, 264, 266

Milos 21, 47

Milosh Obrenovich, Prince of Serbia 13, 59, 60, 61

Minciaky 17, 56

Missolonghi 18

Modena 102

Moldavia (see Danubian Principalities)

Molé de, Count 70, 71

Moltke 29, 30, 32, 34, 35, 43, 68, 256

Montebello, Duc de 222, 230

Montenegro 146, 264, 265, 269, 275, 289, 292

Morea 17, 23, 47, 49, 50

Moricière, de la, General 133, 134

Morny, Duc de 196, 209, 210, 211, 213, 214, 222

Mortemart, Duc de 88, 89, 96, 97

Moscow 4, 6, 10, 213, 258, 259, 260, 265

Moustier, Marquis de 239

Muffling, Baron, General 44

Munchengraetz, battle of 67, 101, 104, 105, 107, 111

Muraviev, General 65

Muruzi 26

N

Nakhimov, Admiral 154, 155, 172, 187

Napier, Sir Charles 163, 164, 166, 167, 168, 169, 170, 190

Naples 4, 5, 12, 48, 119, 136, 142, 200, 233

Napoleon I 1, 4, 5, 6, 7, 8, 13, 25, 59, 90, 287

Napoleon III 120, 123, 134, 135, 136, 137, 139, 140, 141, 147, 149, 151, 153, 157, 185, 186, 190, 194, 195, 196, 197, 204, 209, 210, 211, 213, 214, 217, 218, 219, 220, 221, 222, 228, 230, 231, 236, 238, 241, 242, 245

Napoleon, Prince 218, 220

Napoleonic Wars (see Wars)

Nauplia 46, 54, 55

Navarino, battle of 20, 21, 36, 64

Neidgart, General 95

Nemours, Duc de 99, 100

Nesib 74

Nesselrode, Count 14, 17, 22, 23, 24, 63, 64, 65, 69, 71, 72, 73, 75, 77, 81, 82, 83, 88, 89, 91, 93, 94, 95, 97, 99, 103, 105, 107, 108, 111, 112, 114, 117, 118, 120, 126, 128, 133, 135, 142, 143, 145, 146, 147, 150, 152, 158, 159, 195, 196, 197, 210

Netherlands 99

Newcastle, Duke of 170

New York 164

Nicholas I, Emperor 12, 13, 15, 16, 18, 19, 22, 29, 45, 46, 48, 56, 67, 68, 69, 70, 71, 77, 81, 87, 88, 89, 90, 92, 93, 95, 96, 98, 104, 105, 106, 107, 109, 111, 112, 113, 114, 116, 117, 118, 120, 121, 122, 123, 124, 125, 126, 128, 129, 130, 131, 133, 134, 135, 136, 139, 140, 144, 146, 148, 151, 152, 156, 158, 193, 197, 198, 200, 216, 217, 226, 232, 233

Nicholas II, Emperor 124

Nicholas, Grand Duke 273, 282, 287, 290, 291, 292, 293

Nicholas, Prince of Montenegro 264

Nicopolis 35, 44, 160, 273, 274, 276, 277

Niemen 5

Nigra Cavaliere 246

Nikolaev-on-the Bug 205

Nikolsburg 237

North German Confederation 238, 239

Novi-Bazar 269, 298, 302

Novikov, Olga 265, 266, 268

Nouri Effendi 78, 79

O

Odessa 65, 66, 143, 152, 167, 168, 177, 181, 258

Oldenburg 233

INDEX 323

Olga, Grand Duchess 106

Olmütz 121, 122, 129, 130, 133, 151, 152, 154, 198, 199, 232

Olympus, Mount 47

Omar, Caliph 138

Omer Pasha 152, 159, 160

Orëbro, Peace of 7

Orleans, Duke of 98

Orlov, Count 65, 66, 94, 101, 116, 117, 193, 194, 197, 204, 207, 213, 217, 224, 252

Osman Pasha 265, 276, 278, 280, 282

Osman Pasha, Admiral 155, 156

Ostroshenko, General 40

Otto, King of Greece 55, 56, 134

d'Oubril 226, 238, 252, 268, 269

P

Pahlen, Count 28, 44, 56, 57, 98

Palermo 109

Palmerston, Lord 64, 67, 70, 71, 73, 74, 76, 78, 79, 81, 82, 84, 97, 99, 105, 111, 114, 118, 125, 126, 134, 135, 157, 179, 202, 205, 231, 233

Panslavism 257, 259, 260, 262, 263, 266, 267

Panutin, General 153

Papal States 102

Paris 4, 8, 9, 10, 18, 69, 70, 71, 77, 78, 79, 90, 95, 96, 98, 99, 107, 110, 112, 114, 116, 117, 119, 125, 153, 137, 147, 152, 157, 184, 192, 196, 197, 205, 210, 223, 228, 230, 239, 240, 246, 249, 253, 271

Paris, Count of 253

Paris, Peace of 9

Parker, Admiral 134

Palma 102, 118

Paskevich, Field Marshal 69, 98, 110, 112, 123, 161, 162, 170, 177, 195

Patras 134

Paul I, Emperor 4

Paul, Prince of Württemberg 91

Peel, Sir Robert 82, 84

Pelissier, Marshal 172, 185, 186, 188, 190, 191

Perier, Casimir 97

Persiani, Admiral 134

Persia 44, 82, 85

Pertew Effendi 21

Peter the Great 2, 27, 215

Peter III, Emperor 3, 258

Peter of Oldenburg, Grand Duke 235

Petöfi 124

Piacenza 119

Piedmont (see Sardinia)

Pisani 56

Pitt, William 11

Plèisswitz, Armistice of 7

Plevna 192, 265, 276, 278, 279, 280, 281, 282, 283, 284

Plombières, Meeting of 218, 219

Podgorce 110, 111

Poland 1, 2, 3, 4, 5, 6, 7, 9, 10, 68, 82, 91, 94, 96, 97, 99, 105, 106, 107, 110, 111, 112, 113, 116, 117, 118, 120, 169, 170, 196, 220, 225, 226, 227, 228, 229, 230, 231, 241, 260

Polish Succession, War of (see Wars)

Polish-Saxon Question 10

Polignac, Prince 87, 88, 89

Pomerania 2, 238

Ponsonby, Lord 67, 72, 73, 74, 75, 125

Porros 47, 48, 54

Portsmouth 20, 21

Portugal 87, 105

Poti 44

Pozzo di Borgo, Count 9, 70, 71, 72, 86, 87, 88, 89, 95, 96, 98

Pressburg 123

Protocol of St. Petersburg 17, 18, 20, 61, 87

Protocol of March 1829 48, 49, 50, 51, 52

Prussia 1, 2, 3, 4, 5, 6, 7, 8, 10, 12, 44, 67, 69, 78, 79, 80, 89, 90, 92, 94, 96, 97, 98, 101, 102, 103, 104, 109, 110, 113, 114, 117, 126, 127, 129, 136, 137, 151, 152, 158, 193, 194, 196, 198, 200, 208, 212, 219, 221, 223, 224, 226, 227, 230, 232, 235, 237, 238, 240, 241, 243, 244, 246, 248, 252

Prussian Army 5, 7, 90, 95, 101, 128, 225

Pruth 13, 28, 44, 57, 144, 145, 170, 207, 273

Pushkin 58, 136

Pyrénees 103

R

Radetzky, Field Marshal 108, 118, 123, 132

Radowitz, General 127, 128, 129

Raglan, Lord 170, 172, 176, 178, 179, 182, 186, 187, 203

Rakoczy 124

Rasgrad 31, 39

Rayneval 89

Read, General 187

Rechberg, Chancellor 227, 229, 248

Reform Bill 183

Reichstadt 269, 289

Reitern, Count 266

Reshid Mohammed Pasha 36, 38, 42, 49

Reshid Pasha 72, 74, 79, 149

Reval 164, 165, 166

Revolution of 1830 93, 99, 102, 103

Revolution of 1848 8, 58, 112, 126, 133, 140, 198

Rhangabé 296, 301

INDEX

Rhine 2, 7, 80, 94, 219, 220, 238

Rhodes 47

Ribe, Charter of 232

Ribeaupierre 20, 23, 47

Richelieu, Duc de 9

Ricord, Admiral 47, 54, 55, 56

Riga 165

Rifaat Pasha 141, 142

Rigny, Admiral 21, 22

Rimsky-Korsakov, General 41

Ristitch, Prime Minister 264, 296

Roman Catholic Church 58, 138, 140, 258, 259, 262

Rome 231, 248, 255

Roncière de Noury, Baron 220

Roth, General 38, 39, 41

Roumania 2, 3, 14, 15, 17, 23, 28, 35, 42, 44, 56, 58, 59, 68, 69, 108, 120, 127, 132, 169, 207, 242, 249, 263, 292, 300

Roumanian Army 277, 279, 281, 284, 289

Roussin, Admiral 65, 66

Rückman, Baron 56, 60

Rudiger, General 42, 124

Russel, Lord John 146, 147, 229, 233, 235

Russel, Odo, Lord 250, 255, 299

Russian Army 2, 3, 4, 6, 7, 9, 12, 13, 23, 28, 29, 31, 32, 33, 34, 35, 36, 40, 43, 49, 57, 59, 65, 90, 92, 95, 96, 99, 106, 108, 118, 120, 123, 173, 174, 194, 272, 276, 278-288, 291, 293

Russian Fleet 3, 4, 22, 24, 25, 26, 36, 67, 106, 158, 163, 164, 165, 175

Rustchuk 38, 39, 44, 159, 160, 273, 274, 277, 283, 285, 291

S

Saarbrucken 98

Sacken, General 9

Saida Pasha 120

Salamin, Bay of 134

Saladin, Sultan 138

Salisbury, Lord 293, 296, 297, 298, 299, 300

Samos 49, 52, 53, 55

San Stefano 291, 292

San Stefano, Treaty of (see Treaties)

Sardinia 102, 118, 119, 136, 200, 207, 208, 220, 222

Sardinian Army 187, 188, 191, 201, 203

Sass, General 123

Saxony 1, 7, 10, 89, 127

Schleswig-Holstein 106, 120, 127, 198, 232, 233, 235, 245

Schwarzenberg, Prince, Chancellor 121, 122, 126, 127, 128, 129, 131, 132, 136, 181

Schwarzenberg, Prince, Field Marshal 7, 8

Sebastopol 68, 141, 148, 154, 155,
   158, 170, 171, 172, 173, 174, 175,
   179, 180, 181, 182, 183, 184, 185,
   186, 187, 188, 189, 190, 191, 195,
   205, 281

Sebastiani, General 79, 139

Sedan, battle of 247, 251

Selim III, Sultan 27

Seniavin, Admiral 20

Serbia 13, 17, 44, 45, 59, 60, 61, 62,
   108, 144, 145, 212, 264, 265, 284,
   292, 301

Serrano, Marshal 254

Seven Years War (see Wars)

Shipka Pass 274, 275, 277, 278,
   283, 285, 286, 287

Shumla 30, 31, 32, 24, 35, 39, 40, 42,
   43, 152, 159, 161

Shuvalov, Count 255, 266, 288,
   289, 290, 291, 293, 296, 298, 299,
   300

Silesia 7, 111, 112, 227

Silistria 30, 34, 35, 37, 39, 40, 159,
   160, 161, 162, 164, 166, 169, 172,
   291

Sistova 44

Simpheropol 191

Sinope, battle of 157, 187

Skobelev, General 263, 275, 277,
   279, 280, 282, 285, 286, 287, 288,
   291

Slavophilism 257, 258, 259

Smolensk 6

Smyrna 73

Spezzia 53

Sobieski, John, King 187

Sofia 282, 283, 287, 297

Solovetski Monastery 168

Sophia, Archduchess 98, 131, 132

Soult, Marshal 76, 78

St. Arnaud, Marshal 172

St. Dizier 8

St. George, Chanel of 44

St. Petersburg 15, 16, 18, 24, 31, 46,
   56, 57, 60, 63, 64, 69, 71, 75, 81, 88,
   89, 90, 91, 97, 99, 101, 103, 104, 105,
   108, 116, 119, 121, 124, 125, 133, 134,
   136, 137, 147, 149, 150, 157, 158, 212,
   219, 221, 223, 224, 225, 229, 238, 241,
   242, 245, 250, 252, 255, 258, 263, 293,
   296, 299

Stadion, Count 122

Stambulov 61

Stewart, Lord 95

Stirbeiu 59

Stockholm 69, 215, 216

Stockmar 84, 109

Stopford, Admiral 77

Stratford de Redcliffe (see Canning,
   Stratford)

Stuttgart 79, 219

Sturdza, Hospodar 58

Suleiman the Magnificent, Sultan 138

Suleiman Pasha 275, 283

Suvorov, Field Marshal 3, 4

Sweaborg 163, 164, 165, 166, 167, 190

Sweden 1, 2, 3, 5, 6, 7, 163, 164, 165, 166, 199, 215, 216, 217, 232

Switzerland 4, 14, 46, 136

Syria 53, 54, 64, 70, 74, 77, 78, 79, 147

T

Tabriz 85

Tahir Pasha 21, 22

Talleyrand 9, 207, 208, 236

Tarnopol 110

Taurus Mountains 64, 66, 75

Tchesme, battle of 3

Tchorgun 186, 187

Tenedos, 63, 67

Teschen, Treaty of (see Treaties)

Theiss 123

Thessaly 47, 269, 294, 301, 302

Thiers 79, 247, 253

Thirty Years War (see Wars)

Thouvenel 134

Thrace 302

Tilsit, Treaty of (see Treaties)

Titov 195

Tocqueville de 126

Todleben, General 171, 172, 175, 183, 184, 185, 186, 187, 281, 284, 285

Toeplitz 69, 104, 105, 106, 107, 111

Tokay 123

Tombazis 53

Traktir, battle of 187, 188

Transcaucasia 169, 190

Treaties of
  Abo 215
  Adrianople 45, 50, 56, 63, 65, 84, 88, 103, 120, 157, 206, 211
  Akkerman, Convention of 20
  Alvensleben, Convention of 225, 226, 227, 228
  Anglo-Russian Agreement of 1844 82, 83, 147
  Balta-Liman, Convention of 59
  Belgrade 2
  Berlin 301, 302, 303
  Bucharest 17
  Cyprus, Convention of 294, 301
  Firman of 1740 135, 139
  Fredericksham 215, 216
  Jassy 2
  Kalisch 7
  Kuchuk-Kainardji 2, 3
  London 1827 20, 21, 23, 24, 36, 45, 49
  London 1829 49
  London 1831 100, 134
  London 1832 55
  London, Convention of 1871 251
  Nystadt 215
  Paris 1815 9, 136
  Paris 1856 59, 209, 211, 212, 214, 218, 220, 243, 245, 247, 248, 250, 251, 272, 302
  Reichstadt, Agreement 269, 294
  San Stefano 292, 293, 294, 298, 301, 303
  Teschen 3
  Tilsit 5, 9, 26

Treaties of
  Treaty of 1839   101, 239
  Treaty of 1840   80
  Treaty of 1841   140, 194, 208, 212
  Treaty of Eighteen Articles 100
  Tsarskoye Selo 223
  Unkiar-Skelessi 56, 67, 68, 70, 71, 74, 75, 78, 80, 84, 104, 105, 169
  Vienna 1, 10, 91, 93, 97, 99, 110, 114, 119, 137, 211, 227, 229, 230, 231, 232, 238
  Westphalia 1

Tricoupis 53

Troppau-Laibach (see Congresses)

Tuchkov, General 29

Tunis 146, 301

Turkey 2, 3, 5, 9, 11, 13, 14, 15, 16, 17, 19, 20, 22, 23, 24, 25, 29, 43, 44, 45, 47, 49, 50, 52, 53, 56, 59, 60, 61, 63, 65, 67, 68, 69, 71, 73, 76, 77, 79, 80, 82, 83, 85, 88, 92, 103, 104, 107, 108, 125, 126, 130, 135, 137, 139, 142, 145, 146, 148, 150, 152, 154, 157, 169, 194, 208, 240, 249, 251, 259, 264, 268, 270, 276, 289, 291, 296, 298, 300, 302

Turkish Army 23, 28, 29, 30, 32, 33, 34, 36, 37, 40, 42, 43, 46, 59, 60, 68, 74, 154, 161, 182, 186, 201, 264, 266, 272, 276, 282, 286, 287

Turkish Fleet 21, 22, 25, 36, 37, 72, 73, 75, 77, 154, 155, 158, 272

Turkish Legion 191

Turin 201, 203, 204

Turtukai 28, 29, 159, 160

Tuscany 102

Tyssowski 113

U

Ukraine 3, 7, 169

Uleaborg 166

Uniat Church 108

United States 68

Unkiar Skelessi 66, Treaty of (see Treaties)

Utrecht 1

V

Vaillant, Marshal 191

Varna 30, 31, 32, 33, 34, 35, 37, 38, 40, 41, 154, 157, 161, 168, 170, 297, 298

Venetia 118, 223, 236

Verona 12, 104, Congress of (see Congresses)

Versailles 250, 251

Victoria, Queen 81, 82, 83, 84, 114, 135, 156, 164, 223, 293, 298

Victor Emmanuel I, King 102

Victor Emmanuel II, King 202, 246

Viddin 44

Vienna 8, 18, 76, 89, 97, 103, 104, 105, 107, 115, 118, 121, 124, 125, 131, 136, 145, 149, 152, 185, 193, 195, 197, 205, 207, 226, 228, 229, 231, 236, 244, 249, 251, 252, 261, 271, 295, 296

Vienna, Congress of (see Congresses)
  Treaty of (see Treaties)

Villafranca, Armistice of 222

Villagos, Capitulation of 124

Villèle 86, 87, 88

Visconti-Venosta 246

Vistula 114, 164

Vladimirescu 14

Volo 48, 55

Volkonsky, Prince 86, 116

Vorontsov, Count 197

Voutchich 61

Vrione Omar 33, 35

W

Waddington 296, 301

Wagram, battle of 6

Wallachia (see Roumania)

Walewski, Count 79, 148, 196, 204, 205, 206, 208, 211, 213, 217, 219, 220

Warsaw 2, 10, 124, 127, 128, 129, 130, 151, 152, 154, 164, 198, 222, 223, 233

Wars
American Revolution
Austrian Succession 3
Austro-Prussian 238, 295
Balkan 303
Bavarian Succession 3
Carlist 103, 107
Crimean 45, 59, 61, 64, 68, 125, 126, 132, 133, 136, 137, 154, 158, 193, 198, 200, 201, 211, 214, 216, 217, 218, 228, 243, 245, 258, 263
Danish 236
Franco-Prussian 220, 241, 248
Great Northern 1, 2
Hungarian 84, 130, 131

Wars
Napoleonic Wars 1, 2, 5, 7, 8, 13, 26
Polish Succession 2
Polish Insurrections 101, 111, 120, 225, 226, 227, 228, 229, 231, 245, 259
Russo-Turkish 1736-1739 2
Russo-Turkish 1769-1774 3
Russo-Turkish 1787-1792 3
Russo-Turkish 1828-1829 20, 28, 29, 30, 31, 32, 33, 34, 35, 36, 37, 38, 39, 40, 41, 42, 43, 44, 88, 92
Russo-Turkish 1877-1878 209, 272-288
Russo-Swedish 1808-1809 215
Serbian Independence 27
Serbo-Turkish 264, 265, 266, 268
Seven Years 2, 3
Thirty Years 1, 257
Turko-Montenegrin 263
World War I 1, 2, 203, 303
World War II 303

Waterloo, battle of 8

Wellington, Duke of 9, 16, 17, 18, 24, 48, 82, 106, 131

White Russia 1, 2

White Sea 170

William I, King of Holland 99, 100

Wilhelm I, Emperor 90, 92, 223, 225, 241, 243, 246, 252, 270

Windishgraetz, Prince 121, 131

Witzleben, General 94

Wittgenstein, Count 36

Wodehouse, Lord 234

Württemberg 11, 69, 237, 240

Wrangel, General 232

Y

Ypsilanti, Alexander 13, 14

Ypsilanti, Demetrios 14

Ypsilanti, Hospodar 126

Yussuf Pasha 33

Z

Zaporog Cossacks 29

Zante 21

Zholtukhin, General 57

Zurich 4

- - - - -